AMERICAN MAELSTROM

PIVOTAL MOMENTS IN AMERICAN HISTORY
Series Editors
David Hackett Fischer
James M. McPherson
David Greenberg

MICHAEL A. COHEN

AMERICAN
MAELSTROM

The 1968 Election and the
Politics of Division

OXFORD
UNIVERSITY PRESS

OXFORD
UNIVERSITY PRESS

Oxford University Press is a department of the University of Oxford.
It furthers the University's objective of excellence in research, scholarship,
and education by publishing worldwide. Oxford is a registered trade mark of
Oxford University Press in the UK and certain other countries.

Published in the United States of America by Oxford University Press
198 Madison Avenue, New York, NY 10016, United States of America

Library of Congress Cataloging-in-Publication Data
Cohen, Michael A., 1971– author.
American Maelstrom : The 1968 Election and
the Politics of Division / Michael A. Cohen.
pages   cm.—(Pivotal moments in American history)
Includes bibliographical references and index.
ISBN 978-0-19-977756-3
1. Presidents—United States—Election—1968.
2. United States—Politics and government—1963–1969.
3. Nixon, Richard M. (Richard Milhous), 1913–1994.
4. Humphrey, Hubert H. (Hubert Horatio), 1911–1978.   I. Title.
E851.C65   2016
324.973'0924—dc23   2015032225

1 3 5 7 9 8 6 4 2
Printed by Sheridan, USA

For Sarah, Isadora, and Scarlett

"Men want to be a part of a common enterprise—a cause greater than themselves. Each of us must find a way to advance the purpose of the Nation, thus finding new purpose for ourselves. Without this, we shall become a nation of strangers."

—President Lyndon Johnson, Inaugural Address, January 20, 1965

"It's never stopped being 1968."

—An unnamed White House aide in the George W. Bush administration, April 7, 2004

CONTENTS

EDITOR'S NOTE

David Greenberg

When President Bill Clinton spoke at the 2000 Democratic National Convention—taking a victory lap before passing the baton of a revitalized liberalism to Vice President Al Gore—he reminisced about the glory days of the 1960s, when he had just graduated from high school. Clinton recalled the progress America had made toward racial equality and the prosperity that allowed Lyndon Johnson to enact sweeping liberal legislation. But then came 1968, the year when his heroes Robert Kennedy and Martin Luther King were killed and the nation came apart. "The next election," he cautioned, "took America on a far different, more divisive course." The liberalism of the 1960s came screeching to a halt.

Many books make strained claims that this year or that year marked the turning point of the century's most turbulent decade. But no one denies that 1968 upended American politics in a dramatic and lasting way. Michael Cohen's *American Maelstrom: The 1968 Election and the Politics of Division* approaches the pivotal presidential race of that annus horribilis with a keen appreciation of how it unleashed a host of profound changes in our public life. The wild campaign was full of strong-willed, larger-than-life men with sharply divergent visions of their country's future, and in battling one another for the presidency, they exposed the fissures that were forming. Using each contender's story to spotlight a different aspect of the times, *American Maelstrom* presents the momentous drama of 1968 as both a scholarly analysis of political culture and a distinctively personal tale.

The years before 1968 had testified to what a capacious liberal vision of government could achieve. But as the year's election contest opened, there were signs that the "New Deal order"—the skein of political attitudes and patterns of partisan loyalty that had sustained this vision since FDR's day—was crumbling. An angry backlash was mounting—a bitterness, pronounced among working-class voters, about overreaching government, shifting cultural mores, and the liberals' indulgence of chic radicalisms that preached violence or anti-Americanism.

The backlash came from many quarters. In California, Ronald Reagan honed a John Wayne conservatism that assailed the coddling of lawless protesters and the erosion of America's global standing. From Alabama, George Wallace found followers far beyond Dixie with a hate-filled populism that reviled racial integrationists, Washington bureaucrats, the national news media, and "pointy-headed intellectuals who can't park their bicycles straight." Most cannily, Richard Nixon, recovering from a string of supposedly career-ending failures, grabbed the issue of "law and order" to combine anxieties about rising crime, urban protests, and antiwar activists into one potent brew.

Equally consequential was the outcry against the Vietnam War. The intolerable body count and LBJ's refusal to change course fed a simple demand that the United States get out of Southeast Asia, the sooner the better. The budding antiwar movement shattered the old Cold War consensus and birthed a critique of all American intervention abroad as counterproductive at best and imperialistic at worst. When no politician of high standing volunteered to challenge Johnson, the antiwar mantle fell to the shambling, headstrong Eugene McCarthy—a largely undistinguished junior senator from Minnesota who preferred writing poetry to reading policy papers. McCarthy's shocking second-place finish in the New

Hampshire primary forced President Johnson to quit the race and invited the more beguiling RFK to enter it.

Kennedy captured the country's imagination. For a spell his candidacy promised to revive the hope and purpose of his late brother's unfinished presidency. But RFK's assassination in June, along with McCarthy's increasingly evident inability to act like a leader, left the Democrats fractured and directionless. Handed the party's nomination by default, Vice President Hubert Humphrey entered the fall campaign with the confused mandate of defending LBJ's record while pledging a new course.

The fall race had almost as much drama as the spring and summer. Late in the game, Humphrey—who, ironically, had privately warned Johnson to avoid the Vietnam quagmire—broke with the president and promised voters a withdrawal. The race narrowed. But with southern Democrats flocking to Wallace's third-party bid and Humphrey unable to rebuild the New Deal coalition, Nixon held on, just barely, to claim the victory that had eluded him eight years before.

Each of these titanic figures left a mark. Democrats clung atavistically to Humphrey's labor liberalism, even as blue-collar voters abandoned them; not until the 1980s would a new wave of politicians offer fresh analyses to meet the challenges of a transformed economy. Eugene McCarthy's candidacy, on the other hand, fueled a neo-isolationism that became something close to Democratic Party orthodoxy—diminishing the wider public's faith in the party of Roosevelt and Truman to run foreign affairs. Robert Kennedy ascended alongside his brother to the realm of mythology, embodying yet another lost hope that the country might yet bridge its political, racial, generational, and class divides.

If the Democrats moved left after 1968, the Republicans moved right. The liberal and moderate Republicanism espoused by Nelson Rockefeller and George Romney that year would grow steadily more irrelevant. Nixon, for his part, having styled himself a golden mean between Reagan and Rockefeller, would draw upon both Reagan and Wallace in fashioning his own conservative populism. Though Nixon was later turned out of office and disgraced, his campaign and his presidency would provide the themes and vocabulary for Republican politicians up through and including George W. Bush.

It's widely observed that we live in a time of polarization, populist anger, impatience with political solutions, and fierce disagreement over America's role in the world. To understand how we got here, there is no better place to start than the presidential election of 1968 that *American Maelstrom* vividly recounts.

AMERICAN MAELSTROM

Johnson delivers the Inaugural Address, January 20, 1965. Courtesy of the LBJ Presidential Library, Austin, Texas. Photo by Cecil Stoughton.

Introduction

On January 20, 1965, more than a million people came together on the grounds of the US Capitol and the National Mall to witness the most celebratory of American political traditions—a presidential inauguration. Tens of millions of others gathered around their televisions and radios in family rooms and offices. While the 38° weather may have chilled the spirits of some, an unmistakable feeling of optimism, excitement, and hope for the future defined the day. Fourteen months after the unimaginable assassination of President John F. Kennedy, America appeared to be turning the corner.[1]

Spurred by seemingly limitless economic prosperity and apparent political consensus in Washington, a Gallup poll, with the title "America's Mood in the Mid-Sixties," found a population remarkably content with nearly every aspect of their lives—and confident that the good times would continue. For African Americans, inauguration day was particularly special. The re-election of the man who had signed into law the most far-reaching civil rights legislation in the nation's history offered an implicit validation of their struggle for equal rights.[2]

For Lyndon Johnson this day represented the pinnacle of his political career. He felt "carefree" and "zestful," according to the *New York Times*. He "had a smile, a wave, a handshake or a kiss for everyone," wrote the *Washington Post*. That night he would become the first president to dance at his own inaugural ball. His festive mood reflected the historic political and personal achievement that was his overwhelming victory in the 1964 presidential election. "Millions and millions of people, each marking my name on their ballot. Each wanted me as their president. For the first time in all my life, I truly felt loved by the American people," Johnson later said, in a quote that unintentionally but pointedly illuminates Johnson's constant need for affirmation.[3]

His win had been no ordinary triumph. The Democratic Party's New Deal coalition of urban ethnics, farmers, blacks, and (some, though not all) white southerners united behind him—just as they had done for six of the eight previous presidential elections. This time, however, it produced the most resounding electoral victory in American history. Johnson didn't just defeat his opponent, Republican nominee Barry Goldwater; he crushed him. LBJ won 61 percent of the popular vote, a margin so outsized that it helped Democrats pick up thirty-six seats in the House of Representatives and two in the Senate, for an imposing 66–34 advantage. Johnson had won more votes than his predecessor, John Kennedy; more votes than his hero, Franklin Roosevelt—more votes than any president in the nation's history. Johnson was—by his own definition—the most loved man in American history.

Still, for all the gaiety of inauguration day, signs of trouble—though perhaps only visible to the most far-sighted of observers—had peeked above the surface. Earlier that spring in Wisconsin, Indiana, and Maryland, Alabama governor George Wallace, running on a platform of strident opposition to civil rights legislation and boosted by growing white anxiety over integration and rising crime rates, scored impressive results in Democratic presidential primary elections. Major riots broke out in Harlem, Philadelphia, and a host of other East Coast cities. On Election Day in California, a state Johnson won handily, voters by a two-to-one margin backed Proposition 14, a ballot measure to overturn the Rumford Fair Housing Act, one of the nation's first legislative remedies for housing discrimination against blacks. While trounced practically everywhere else, Goldwater, who had opposed the Civil Rights Act, won five southern states—and by wide margins. Indeed, a deeper look at public opinion polling shows that the president's victory had not been quite as overwhelming as it appeared. More Americans self-identified as conservative than liberal; more feared "big government" than they did big business; more wanted Johnson to stick to the political center than wanted him to move to the left; and more than half hadn't even heard of his ambitious Great Society agenda.[4]

None of these facts, however, would dampen Lyndon Johnson's spirits, and they certainly weren't going to stop his plans for the nation. In early 1964—only months after taking office—he'd declared a far-reaching War on Poverty. Later that year he broke the southern filibuster in the Senate to pass the seminal Civil Rights Act. And in May 1964, at the commencement ceremony of the University of Michigan, Johnson laid out a vision of American society that went beyond anything modern liberalism had previously contemplated. "We have the opportunity," Johnson told the graduating seniors, "to move not only toward the rich society and the powerful society, but upward to the Great Society."[5]

Achieving this goal would involve "an end to poverty and racial injustice," but Johnson refused to limit himself even to such lofty ambitions. "The Great Society," said Johnson, would be a place that would not only enrich the lives of all Americans but a place "where men are more concerned with the quality of their goals than the quantity of their goods." It would be, said the president, "a challenge constantly renewed, beckoning us toward a destiny where the meaning of our lives matches the marvelous products of our labor."[6]

Johnson's efforts would be informed by the belief that his Great Society plans reflected the desires of a majority of his fellow citizens. After all, the *New York Times* wrote in a postelection editorial, Johnson's victory had reconfirmed the nation's "popular attachment to the policies of moderate liberalism that have prevailed through more than three decades of Democrats and Republican rule." *Newsweek* went a step further, noting that LBJ had embedded "the foundation blocks of his Great Society...safely and securely, into the American consensus."[7]

These sentiments reflected the nation's abiding political narrative in the mid-1960s—namely, the so-called liberal consensus. This broad, elite agreement—shared by Democrats and Republicans alike—took largely for granted the idea that the federal government had a responsibility to ensure that economic growth stayed robust, employment remained "full," and support for the working man—through generous benefits for his family, but also protection from the vicissitudes of the free market—remained in place. "Ideology, which once was a road to action, has come to a dead end," wrote Daniel Bell in his 1960 book, *The End of Ideology*. Acceptance of the "welfare state" and the need for "decentralized power," a "mixed economy," and "political pluralism" formed the outer boundaries of the consensus, ensuring that politicians no longer argued about weighty policy issues but debated instead the technocratic means to implement them.[8]

Enabling this consensus was one of the most extraordinary periods of economic growth and transformation in the nation's history. More women had joined the work force; more Americans attended college; and more families owned their own homes filling them with affordable and cutting-edge consumer goods. They even took annual two-week vacations as they enjoyed the full benefits of membership in the American middle class. The economic anxiety that had defined America in the 1930s and 1940s felt increasingly like a relic of the past. Holding this new era of startling growth and broad social opportunity together was the federal government and its involvement in a wide array of public initiatives, from building new highways and mass transit systems and supporting the growth of suburbs with subsidized housing, to bolstering and protecting American industry, and above all to maintaining and even strengthening the social welfare programs created during FDR's New Deal. While acceptance of such immense authority in the hands of the federal government ran counter to the nation's historic suspicion of centralized power, the liberal consensus held firm, under both Democratic and Republican presidents.

In the realm of foreign affairs, the consensus stood on similarly solid ground. Few dissented from the view that the United States had a sacred responsibility and obligation to uphold liberty and contain Communism wherever it reared its head. When Johnson said in his inaugural address, "If

American lives must end, and American treasure be spilled, in countries we barely know, that is the price that change has demanded of conviction and of our enduring covenant," few Americans questioned it. Whether the liberal consensus truly existed—and whether it was as powerful as it may have seemed—is a matter for historical debate. What did matter, is the shared assumption among the nation's political leaders that it did exist.[9]

So as Lyndon Johnson prepared to take the oath of office again, this time on the Capitol's east front, the notion of consensus dominated official Washington. Given the nation's broad economic prosperity, disarray among Republicans, and (seemingly) strong popular support for reform, Johnson found himself in an unparalleled position to move the country in a fundamentally liberal direction. His inaugural address spoke directly to this possibility. In tones alternately inspirational and solemn, and in language plain-spoken, Johnson told his countrymen, "Men want to be a part of a common enterprise—a cause greater than themselves. Each of us must find a way to advance the purpose of the Nation, thus finding new purpose for ourselves. Without this, we shall become a nation of strangers."[10]

For all of Johnson's soaring rhetoric and the heady tone of harmony that resounded in the nation's capital, America's path looked very different than the one described by its president. That inauguration day would be a high-water mark for liberalism, never again to be matched in the lifetimes of those who gathered to hear Johnson speak. In reality, the tectonic plates of American politics had already begun to shift, almost imperceptibly, toward head-on collision. The United States was, in fact, very much on the path to becoming a "nation of strangers."

Over the next three years, Los Angeles, Detroit, Newark, and countless other American cities would be rocked by violence, looting, and mayhem. Hundreds of thousands of young men would be sent to Vietnam, and tens of thousands would come home in caskets. The social upheaval and dissent from the youth counterculture became increasingly pronounced as more and more Americans came to believe that the nation was coming apart at the seams. In January 1968, a report from the liberal interest group the National Committee for an Effective Congress captured the feelings of many: "At all levels of American life, people share similar fears, insecurities and gnawing doubts to such an intense degree that the country may in fact be suffering from a kind of national nervous breakdown...a depression of the national spirit."[11]

Three years after his presidential victory, rather than being venerated, Johnson was barely able to show his face at public events. Conservatives attacked his big-spending ways, his expansion of federal power, and his inability to keep Americans safe from seemingly out-of-control crime. Liberals lacerated him for his fixation on victory in Vietnam at any cost. Blacks demanded that he fulfill the promises he'd made to them. Meanwhile, most Americans simply pleaded for a respite from the growing and palpable feeling of national dislocation. By the fall of 1967, on the eve of his likely decision to run for re-election, Johnson was quite far from being the most loved man in America.

These feelings would become even more pronounced in the year to come as the nation was buffeted by violence, disorder, and political unrest rarely before seen in the nation's history. If the election of 1964 had been defined by optimism about the future, the election of 1968 would be defined by the national trauma that preceded it. By Election Day, Richard Nixon, Hubert Humphrey, and George Wallace competed to lead a nation sharply divided by race, culture, age, and class. In a year marked by a political backlash, 57 percent of the electorate supported candidates decidedly opposed, at least in rhetorical terms, to the revamped and rejuvenated liberal consensus that Lyndon Johnson had offered to the American people four years earlier.

This book is about the before, during, and after of the 1968 presidential election. While others have examined this period—and this election—from social, racial, and economic perspectives, this book is focused primarily on the political. It will show how the dynamics and images of the two parties—many of which had deep roots in American political culture—emerged more fully formed out of 1968 and fundamentally changed the way Americans think and talk about politics, up to today. *American Maelstrom* does not provide a traditional retelling or comprehensive recounting of the 1968 election. Readers will notice that some of the year's key political events go unmentioned, including some that may seem directly relevant. To cover everything would mean a book double the size of the one you hold in your hands, but it would also mean focusing on elements of the campaign that tell us little about the politics of today. Rather, *American Maelstrom* considers the election from the perspective of what happened then, but also what happened after.

The 1968 election marked a turning point in the nation's politics and in the relationship between the American people and their elected leaders. It began the move away from New Deal–style liberalism to the rhetorical embrace of antigovernment conservative populism—though it did not represent a full embrace of conservative economic and social policies. In foreign policy, the Cold War bipartisan consensus was shattered, as liberals began to voice the first comprehensive critique of American foreign policy since the dawn of the nuclear age. It was the year in which the Democratic Party's New Deal coalition of labor, blacks, southerners, and white ethnics began its slow multi-year decline. The influence of traditional powerbrokers, like big city mayors and union leaders, also began to wane as Democratic politics took a decided turn to the left. For Republicans, the 1968 election confirmed the party's shift to the right and the ascendancy of the conservative movement within the GOP. For both parties, 1968 represented a crucial turning point, one in which the ideologically committed wings of each side began to more forcibly assert themselves.

These developments in of themselves were historic and transformative, but their impact would be felt far beyond Election Day. Out of 1968 a defining political narrative would emerge. The political stereotypes that have characterized American politics over the past forty years—the "strong and resolute," "tough on crime," "defender of cultural values," "small government" Republican, as opposed to the "weak," "unpatriotic," "tax and spend," "big government," "liberal elite" "beholden to special interest" Democrat—emerged or were reinforced. Since 1968 they have become the prism through which Americans view both political parties—and in turn their own government. Many of these stereotypes had, of course, existed for years. But after 1968 they took on far greater importance and political resonance.

So today, every time a Democratic politician thinks first of the politics of national security rather than national security policy; every time a Republican unleashes an attack on wasteful government spending or on out-of-touch liberal elites, they are echoing the newly dominant political narrative that emerged that year. Welfare queens driving Cadillacs, "law and order," Willie Horton, "white hands," and "Sister Souljah"—all would become the catchwords of racial politics, post-1968. Fears of social change would be reduced to static debates between "traditional family values" on one side and permissiveness, the "homosexual agenda," "abortion on demand," and "radical feminism" (among other alleged ills) on the other. On economic policy, the liberal consensus would be replaced by calls for lower taxes, reduced regulation, and less government spending. The politics of growth had been supplanted by the politics of austerity. Government no longer would be seen as a necessary evil, but instead as "the problem." After 1968, Democrats were condemned to be perpetually on the defensive. The "era of big government" would be declared over and replaced by one leaner and less focused on economic justice. On foreign policy, image trumped reality: the blame-America-first stereotype would be affixed to Democrats and become a permanent feature of the nation's politics. Americans have become so inured to these shorthand depictions that current political debates are still largely focused on either perpetuating or inoculating against them.

While the immediate impact of 1968 may not have been evident at the time (Democrats continued to wield political power in Congress, and it wasn't until the 1980s that conservatism reached its political apex with the election of Ronald Reagan), the events of that year serve as an inflection point in the language and the tenor of American politics. So much of how we talk about politics today—the stereotypes we hold about our nation's political parties and the shorthand political messaging and efforts at image-making that we take for granted today—can trace its lineage, in some manner, to the 1968 election.

These seismic political changes, however, did not herald a dramatic shift in governance. Post-1968 did not see a major shift away from the basic tenets of postwar liberalism. A Republican sat in the White House in 1969, but activist government kept chugging along. The welfare state didn't shrink—it expanded, and Republican presidents often did the enlarging. Nor did the 1968 election turn America into a more conservative society. If anything, in the decades that followed, America would become a fundamentally more liberal country, more accepting of civil rights for all Americans and more tolerant of social progress and of ideas and values that in the 1960s seemed alien and threatening.

What would change, however, was the attitude of Americans toward their government. If runaway economic growth and an apparent liberal consensus that saw government as essential shaped pre-1968 America, post-1968 America would be defined by economic, cultural, even spiritual anxiety, informed by a fundamental and seemingly unwavering mistrust of those in positions of authority. Conservatism had found its narrative for convincing Americans that freedom from want and freedom from despair meant freedom from the federal government. So while Richard Nixon continued the process of social provision begun under Roosevelt, he cloaked it in the language of populist antigovernment and anti-elitist rhetoric. Eventually a crop of real conservatives would replace him, with ideas and plans for dramatically limiting the role of government. While they found an electorate suddenly receptive to their message, their efforts enjoyed limited success—because while Americans applauded the idea of constraining the federal government, they were never quite as happy about the specifics. So, for example, Americans would repeatedly endorse the position that federal spending should be cut, but not if it meant cutting Social Security, Medicare, defense spending, student loans, money for police, roads, schools, even programs that helped poor people heat their homes. Indeed, the only area where a majority of Americans generally support spending cuts is foreign aid—and largely because they tend to overestimate how much of the budget is directed to it. This would become the fundamental divergence in American politics: between the electorate's ideological views about the role of government and their operational interest—reinforced at the ballot box—in maintaining a robust welfare state that served *their* interests.

The election of 1968 did not dramatically move the country either to the right or to the left, but rather trapped it in the middle—enfeebled by the pull of politics and the parochialism bred by the middle-class prosperity of

the postwar years. The energy and the activism that Lyndon Johnson artic-
ulated from the east wing of the Capitol on that January morning in 1965
would not be repeated. Instead, an acceptance, even embrace, of the nation's self-imposed limits replaced it. Nearly fifty years later the United
States is still caught in the maelstrom of 1968.

There is no better word to describe the powerful forces that converged in
the presidential campaign trail in 1968 than maelstrom. This one election
year drew in an extraordinary array of economic, racial, social, and cultural
forces. Middle-class Americans began to narrow their aspirations to the
protection and maintenance of the profound economic gains they'd made.
White privilege was under attack, not just in the Jim Crow South but also in
the schools, workplaces, and neighborhoods of the North. Escalating crime
rates sowed fears about walking city streets safely at night. The Black Power
movement, aggressive, confrontational and demanding immediate social
change, began to overtake the more temperate civil rights movement of an
earlier era. Old-school urban bosses found themselves pushed aside by a
new generation of political reformers. Conservatism became ascendant,
and an emboldened—and long-ignored—group of liberals flexed its muscles on the left. An emerging counterculture and an increasingly vocal fem-
inist movement declared war on traditional values. Drugs, sex, pornography, divorce, and rock 'n' roll seemed to threaten what was once sacrosanct.
America's Cold War consensus collapsed over rising anger and disillusionment about the war in Vietnam. Above all, the postwar liberal consensus
that had defined twenty years of American politics began to crumble.

Still, these forces provide only a partial explanation for 1968. They cannot
tell us why, in a country in which half the population identified themselves
as Democrats, the Democratic Party went from getting 61 percent of the
popular vote in 1964 to 43 percent in 1968. Nor do they explain why low
unemployment coupled with steady and strong economic growth provided
such little benefit to the incumbent party. Above all, they don't tell us why
the Republican Party, so discredited four years earlier, reasserted its position as the country's presidential party—one that it would hold for all but
four of the next twenty-four years.

Indeed, in a presidential election like 1968, decided by so few votes—and in which a different outcome is easily imaginable—contingency and personality loom large. This one election cycle featured a remarkable assemblage of political talent: Lyndon Johnson, Richard Nixon, Hubert Humphrey, Robert Kennedy, Eugene McCarthy, Nelson Rockefeller, George Romney, Ronald Reagan, and George Wallace. They were presidents, vice presidents, senators, governors, and congressmen. These men shaped and defined American politics during the postwar period, and their legacy is still felt today. Each would leave an indelible stamp on 1968 and the years that followed.

So while the election of 1968 can be retold in many ways, the stories of these nine men offer the most compelling approach. This book will thus focus on the campaigns they ran, the decisions they made (and did not make), and their ultimate effect on the final outcome. Eugene McCarthy is today seen as a political gadfly, a second fiddle in 1968 to the much more prominent Robert Kennedy. But his decision to challenge Lyndon Johnson, which would contribute directly to LBJ's eventual withdrawal from the '68 race, ended up being the most important decision of the entire campaign—and the one most responsible for the drama that unfolded that year. Had he not run, American politics today would be very different. George Wallace would only receive 13 percent of the vote as an independent candidate—and mostly from the Deep South—but his campaign rhetoric depicting an out-of-control federal government and his outreach to alienated white working-class Americans would within four years became the idiom of Republican politics. Even though he lost in 1968, he may have done more to reshape American politics than any politician of the postwar era.

Robert Kennedy's legend from 1968 is perhaps the best remembered from that year, but there is more hagiography to his story than significant political impact. Ultimately, his campaign rival, McCarthy, would play a far greater role in shifting the direction of the Democratic Party than Kennedy, whose legacy is tragically one of "what might have been." Hubert Humphrey would become the Democratic nominee that year, but in his tortured effort to separate himself from an unpopular war (and unpopular president) while trying to pacify the antiwar wing of his party, his campaign offers a glimpse of the forces roiling the Democratic Party in 1968. A respected, genial man and committed liberal, Humphrey, perhaps more than any other political figure that year, found himself caught helplessly in the maelstrom of 1968.

On the Republican side, three candidates challenged Richard Nixon for the nomination that year—Ronald Reagan, George Romney, and Nelson Rockefeller. All three would fall short, in part, because they alienated too many of those in their own party. But in their campaigns—and the political philosophies they represented—we get a clearer sense of the ideological battles in the Republican Party of the late 1960s. In Rockefeller's and Romney's demise we see the fall of the moderate wing of the party; and in Reagan's rise, along with Nixon's embrace of conservative rhetoric on law and order and race—as well as his courting of southern Republicans—we see the future direction of the GOP. Finally, there is the president who these men sought to replace and whose political decisions at home—and his choice to fight an American war in Vietnam—laid the groundwork for the tumult of 1968 and the fundamental transformation in American politics that emerged out of the wreckage.

How each of these nine men engaged with and reflected the maelstrom of 1968 offers the best prism for understanding what happened that year. The story of 1968 is theirs.

Part I

Before

"A Lotta People...Ain't Gonna Put Up with It Much Longer"

n January 1965, Lyndon Johnson strode into the White House's Roosevelt Room and declared to the congressional liaisons from all the executive departments under his purview who were gathered there, "I was just elected President by the biggest popular margin in the history of the country—16 million votes." But according to Johnson, "Just by the way people naturally think and because Barry Goldwater had simply scared the hell out of them, I've already lost about three of those sixteen." Once he engaged Congress over his domestic agenda, he said, "I'll lose another couple of million." Within a "couple of months," he warned, he could be down to eight million.[1]

Johnson's understanding of the national mood was not far off. To liberals, a vote for LBJ in 1964 would complete the unfinished business of the New Deal. For the majority of Americans, a ballot for Johnson meant something else: an endorsement of the status quo, particularly since his opponent, Goldwater, risked moving the country in a very different direction. So the White House's political strategy would not be oriented toward ensuring that the American people remained supportive of the president's agenda, but rather toward accomplishing as much as possible before they lost interest. For Johnson, the electorate was a fickle beast that he would be forced to work around in order to realize his goals.

Johnson was, according to one of his more prominent biographers, Robert Caro, "master of the senate"—a brilliant student of not only legislative minutiae but the very particular needs, wants, and political constraints of his fellow senators. Less sturdy was his grasp of the nation that he governed. "He could make a deal with another man," wrote the journalist Hugh Sidey in his assessment of Johnson's presidency, "but he could rarely inspire an audience." He could easily reel off the list of his accomplishments—the money spent, the bills passed, and the people affected by them (a "box-score mentality" in Sidey's words)—because he viewed politics in transactional terms in which loyalty and ideology could be bartered away for some parochial benefit. How else can one explain his apparent belief that the North Vietnamese leader Ho Chi Minh could be convinced to give up his dream of a unified Vietnam with the promise of a Tennessee Valley Authority for the Mekong Delta? As president, Johnson acted as though the more programs he could shower on the American people the more popular he would be. But, as he would soon discover, politics rarely works in such a linear manner.[2]

In the immediate wake of his landslide victory, however, Johnson's "masterful" legislative skills would prove decisive. LBJ utilized his intimate knowledge of Congress to fulfill the aspirations of his hero Franklin Roosevelt and remake America. "He had one goal," presidential aide Jack Valenti later wrote of Johnson, "to be the greatest president doing the greatest good in the history of the nation." Over the next two years, with the political wind at his back and an unshakable congressional majority in his pocket, he would steamroll through Congress the single most ambitious set of domestic initiatives since the New Deal. National challenges were identified, political obstacles overcome, and legislation drafted. Out of the congressional meat grinder emerged Lyndon Johnson's vision for a Great Society. "Get those coonskins up on the wall," Johnson told his aides.[3]

Practically every American received some benefit. There was expanded public education, from elementary and secondary to college and university;

Medicare for the aged, Medicaid for the needy; more money for medical research and a host of new initiatives on mental health and children's health care; voting rights and urban development for blacks; immigration reform for Asians and Hispanics; legal services and job training for the poor; restrictions on air and water pollution and highway beautification for the emerging environmental movement; a new Department of Transportation, tougher highway and traffic safety laws for the nation's drivers, and mass transit moneys for city-dwellers; and new agencies promoting the humanities and arts for cultural edification. Bills that had been bottled up in Congress for years, even decades, suddenly became the law of the land.

From January 4, 1965, to October 23, 1965, the White House sent eighty-seven bills to Congress; eighty-four of them were signed into law. If Johnson didn't surpass Roosevelt's achievements, he came close. "Lyndon believed anything can be solved, and quickly," Lady Bird Johnson said of her husband. Fearful that any flagging momentum would undermine the cause of reform, Johnson believed that he had to act without delay. There would be little time to worry over the details of how legislation would be implemented—not with still more mountains to climb.[4]

This lack of attention to execution would come to haunt Democrats. Neither the federal government nor the states were adequately prepared to carry out such a wide array of initiatives. Establishing hundreds of antipoverty programs—and having them run by often inexperienced practitioners with minimal oversight—ensured there would be a share of high-profile failures that would be used by Johnson's opponents to delegitimize the entire undertaking. Johnson had failed to build and cultivate the powerful constituencies that would be needed to sustain the programs created. So when the attacks came, blame was affixed to the White House. The president also promised more than he could possibly deliver, as his claims about his Great Society programs frequently exceeded the funds actually earmarked for them.[5]

Those problems, however, would emerge later. Johnson's efforts would initially be met with great fanfare. In 1965, according to public opinion polls, support for his legislative program was sky high—82 percent of voters approved Johnson's Medicare polices; 90 percent supported aid for higher education; 95 percent backed the voting rights bill; and 69 percent gave him high marks on his handling of the economy. Even antipoverty legislation was endorsed by nearly three-quarters of Americans. And why not? Except for the ideologically orthodox who opposed expanded government on principle, few Americans had reason to be against better schools, a helping hand for the poor, and improved access to medical care. It wasn't as if they were being asked to sacrifice themselves. So for the first year of Johnson's presidency the liberal consensus that had supported the three-decade expansion and maintenance of the welfare state not only remained intact but from all appearances had been strengthened.[6]

On June 4, 1965, Johnson delivered the commencement speech at Howard University, the elite, predominately black college in Washington, DC. There he previewed what he described as the "next and the more profound stage of the battle for civil rights...not just freedom but opportunity." A year earlier, Johnson had pushed through Congress a landmark civil rights bill, which remains his seminal legislative accomplishment, but also the one for which public support had been the most tenuous. As he noted at the time, the bill's passage risked ending the Democratic Party's electoral domination of the Deep South. The political peril, however, was not restricted to the former Confederacy. While an end to Jim Crow had broad support among white northerners, they were decidedly cooler on the idea of integration in their own neighborhoods, workplaces, and schools. Yet, with the same fervor with which he had passed his domestic policy agenda, Johnson charged ahead on civil rights. At Howard, Johnson offered a corrective to those who saw the passage of civil rights legislation as the end of the black struggle in America. Rather, it represented the end of the beginning. The task of this generation, Johnson said, was to "give 20 million Negroes the same chance as every other American to learn and grow, to work and share in society, to develop their abilities—physical, mental and spiritual, and to pursue their individual happiness." It was not enough "to open the gates of opportunity. All our citizens must have the ability to walk through those gates."[7]

Johnson was now staking the future of his Great Society, his presidency, and his party on improving the lives of black Americans. While a noble and long overdue undertaking, it also represented a risky political shift. Roosevelt's New Deal had been a historic effort to use the powers of the federal government to expand economic opportunity and create a strong safety net for elderly, poor, and working Americans. But these policy initiatives also disproportionately benefited whites—and, in some cases, purposely excluded blacks. Now Johnson was pushing an agenda that took direct aim at the interests and privileges of the white voters who formed the bedrock of the Democratic Party's base. On August 11, only six days after Johnson signed the Voting Rights Act, which represented the final nail in the coffin of Jim Crow, a traffic stop gone awry in the poor, black Los Angeles neighborhood of Watts would deliver the first major blow to Johnson's plans.

Throughout the summer of 1964, America's restive African American ghettoes had experienced a steady stream of disturbances. By 1965 the signs of growing tensions—highlighted by Martin Luther King's initial forays into the poorer, urban neighborhoods of the North and the increasing prominence of uncompromising Black Power advocates—became even more pronounced. Watts, however, represented something else altogether. Six days of violence left thirty-four people dead, just under a thousand injured, more than four thousand under arrest, and millions of dollars in property damage. LBJ eventually sent more than twelve thousand National Guardsmen into the streets of Los Angeles to subdue the rioters.[8]

Whites responded with panic. Gun sales doubled the weekend after the riots; traffic on the city's freeways halted; whites fired their black housekeepers; movie theaters closed. A young lawyer, quoted in the *New York Times*, summed up the views of many, "All it proves is what I've known for a long time. The Negroes hate me and I hate the Negroes." Los Angeles Chief of Police William Parker blamed the riots not on unemployment or poor living conditions but rather on "young hoodlums who have no respect for the law." Nationwide polls showed that whites largely shared Parker's view.[9]

Johnson initially refused to even acknowledge what was happening. "How is this possible after all we've accomplished?" he exclaimed. That such violence occurred in the immediate aftermath of the greatest allocation of resources and national commitment to assist poor black Americans would have a sizable impact on his political agenda. Looking back in 1970 on the decade that had passed, *Life* magazine would editorialize that Watts—not the assassination of President Kennedy—represented the decade's true "dividing line," one that "set the tone of confrontation and open revolt so typical of our present condition." It also provided a political opening for Republicans, and left Democrats skittish. Not long after Watts, Congress finally began to resist Johnson's legislative demands, defeating a bill in September 1965 that provided home rule for the predominately African American District of Columbia.[10]

Like at other points in the Johnson presidency, these signs of trouble were pushed to the side. In fact, at virtually the same moment that the reaction to Watts exposed the fragility of the liberal consensus, Johnson ramped up direct American involvement in Southeast Asia, with the announcement that he would be sending 125,000 combat troops to Vietnam. Johnson was playing with political fire both at home and abroad. Still he plunged ahead. In his 1966 State of the Union address Johnson demanded that Congress "bring the most urgent decencies of life to all of your fellow Americans." He wanted more money for health, education, and antipoverty programs, and more resources for the slums, open housing legislation, political reform, a Department of Transportation, and new environmental regulations. The list of priorities was matched by a continued commitment to the war in Vietnam. "Whatever the cost or whatever the challenge," Johnson pledged, "we will stay as long as aggression commands us to battle."[11]

Privately, Johnson felt increasing skepticism that he could successfully pursue such a policy of guns and butter, and he told cabinet officials and staffers to prepare to operate with fewer resources. Yet his public statements indicated little such concern. The president "believes what he reads in the papers," a White House aide told the *Baltimore Sun*, and "he thinks the way to change things is to change what's printed in the papers.... You can't trust people with the facts, but you can create facts that people will believe."[12]

As time went on, however, he could no longer ignore the mounting political pressures. LBJ's spending priorities, the 1964 tax cut that he'd pushed through Congress after Kennedy's death, and the increase in military appropriations for Vietnam kept the economy growing at a rapid pace. In

1966 alone it expanded by 6.5 percent, which brought with it rising inflation. Counseled by his economic advisors to raise taxes in order to cool the e- conomy down, Johnson balked, fearing that it would lead to congressional demands for spending cuts.[13]

Maintaining his governing coalition, however, presented a more serious challenge. Johnson found himself stuck between a liberal constituency with high expectations for his presidency and a broader swath of voters increas- ingly alarmed about the larger impact of his Great Society plans. In the early years of the New Deal, the federal government became a lifeline for mil- lions of Americans living in poverty. But by the mid-1960s those same ben- eficiaries no longer experienced such want—and they believed that racial integration put their hard-earned gains in peril. Local Democratic bosses and union leaders found themselves directly at odds with black activists. In the South, there was even less middle ground.

No matter how well-intentioned, Johnson's legislative agenda took direct aim at the mainstays of the Democratic Party: the rural South and the urban North. With Johnson forced to navigate a narrow political channel, while guiding a governing coalition that was fragile at best and unwieldy at worst, it seemed almost inevitable that some Americans, particularly those most affected by black advancement, would begin to feel angry and abandoned. "America's real majority is suffering a minority complex of neglect," warned Johnson's speechwriter Horace Busby. "They have become the real foes of Negro rights, foreign aid, etc., because as much as anything, they feel for- gotten, at the second table behind the tightly organized, smaller groups at either end of the U.S. spectrum." That those at the poor end of the spectrum were overwhelmingly black—and those in the middle overwhelmingly white—further heightened tension and suspicion. These strains contrib- uted to an emerging political movement of white anger and frustration, which after Watts threatened not only Johnson's presidency but the very aspirations of American liberalism.[14]

The white backlash of the late 1960s represented one of the most powerful and enduring political forces of the era. It would in time, transform not only American politics, but also how the nation was governed. Yet the backlash, characterized by an incoherent mass of resentments, frustrations, and misperceptions, defies easy description. In his 1969 treatise, *The Emerging Republican Majority*, Kevin Phillips argues that the key force fueling it was the "Negro socioeconomic revolution and liberal Democratic ideological inability to cope with it." This would become a dominant view. But such monocausal explanations are incomplete and insufficient, particularly since public polling throughout the 1960s consistently showed that a majority of whites believed Negro political and economic grievances were real and had to be addressed. Rather, the backlash would be shaped by a confluence of factors. Two political analysts, Richard Scammon and Ben Wattenberg, would call it the "social issue," because it embodied a broad set of social, economic, and even generational conflicts. It wasn't just the perception that muggers, burglars, and rapists were proliferating on city streets or the growing dread in every major American city that what happened in Watts would happen there, or even white fears about the impact of black advancement on their communities and their workplaces. All of that played a role.[15]

But so too did the long-haired hippies—smoking pot, protesting the war in Vietnam, defying authority, and thumbing their collective noses at long-standing national tenets on sex, marriage, religion, and even language. In April 1968, journalist Bil Gilbert traveled to Millersburg, Pennsylvania, a small town north of Harrisburg, where the residents were largely white and middle and working class. Places like Millersburg, said Gilbert, represented the most "benign environments our species has ever found or created for itself." Residents there had no direct connection to the traumas of urban America and little interaction with antiwar demonstrators or black militants. Yet they deeply feared them all the same. "Crime, the street being unsafe, strikes, the trouble with the colored, all this dope-taking, people leaving the churches. It is sort of a breakdown of our standards, the American way of life," said one woman. There was seemingly no escape—even in Millersburg—from these worrying national trends. "Everything seems so prosperous and secure now," said another woman, "but I have never felt more insecure in my life."[16]

The anger and apprehension in Millersburg could be felt across America. Among black Americans resentment about promises unfulfilled was strong.

The stifling constraints of 1950s and early 1960s American culture bred rebellion, which drove the beats, then the hippies, and later the larger counterculture. The Vietnam War further fueled the backlash, among both those who supported it and those who opposed it. All of this national anger and frustration coursing through America in the late 1960s would coalesce around one specific target: Washington and the increasingly popular notion that the federal government and powerful elites were at the root of the nation's problems.

Everyone was angry. Those on the right were frustrated by the liberal bureaucrats with their ambitious plans for "social engineering"; the outrage on the left would be directed at the warmongers in the White House, squandering the Great Society on an immoral war in Southeast Asia. The lower middle class was enraged by the erosion of traditional values—and the politicians and judges deemed responsible. The focus of popular anger was no longer directed at big business and the wealthy—those William Jennings Bryan once called the "idle holders of idle capital" or the ones labeled "economic royalists" by FDR in the midst of the Great Depression. The once-revered protections provided by liberal governance were now seen as contributing to the national feeling of dislocation. Polling showed Americans increasingly embracing the view that "Washington is getting too powerful for the good of the country" and that the government could not be trusted "to do what is right" most of the time. From 1966 to 1968, trust in government fell sixteen points, from 61 to 45 percent. Over time, these numbers would decline further.[17]

While the various factors that drove the tumult of the late 1960s would fade from national consciousness, the amorphous anger that many Americans began to feel toward their government hardened. Suspicion of the government became the default position in American politics, leading to the observation years later by the political reporter E. J. Dionne that the real winners in the 1960s cultural and political wars had been libertarians and their ideological distrust of centralized authority. By 1974, at the height of the Watergate scandal, a majority of Americans reported that they trusted the government only "some of the time"—a number that would remain above 50 percent to the present day, with the exception of the period after

September 11, 2001. This would become the backlash's most enduring legacy, even if there was a massive disconnect between Americans mistrust of government and their support for a broad swath of government programs.[18]

In 1967, two public opinion researchers, Lloyd A. Free and Hadley Cantril, published a small tract entitled *The Political Beliefs of Americans*, which looked closely at these fundamental contradictions that lay at the heart of American politics. Voters, they argued, could best be defined as ideologically conservative and operationally liberal. They embraced rugged individualism and decried big government even as they expressed overwhelming support for Great Society programs and a large majority wanted to maintain or increase spending on a host of federal antipoverty initiatives. From this perspective, Johnson's observation in 1964 that the "old argument over the 'welfare state' has been resolved in favor of Federal action" appeared to be correct. But polls also showed that a sizeable segment of the population believed the federal government was out of control, that the nation was trending dangerously toward socialism, and that there was growing "Communist and left-wing influence in government." Two-thirds agreed that the "relief rolls are loaded with chiselers and people who just don't want to work." Three-quarters held the view that any able-bodied person who really wanted to find a job could do so. According to Free and Cantril, Americans continued to pay "ideological...lip service to an amazing degree of stereotypes and shibboleths inherited from the past," most of which stemmed from a conservative, "laissez-faire philosophy" rather "than from the operating assumptions of the New Deal, the Fair Deal, the New Frontier, or the Great Society." They argued, "The generally conservative stance [of Americans] at the ideological level indicates that the liberal trend of policies and programs" that had come to define American politics since the New Deal "has little secure foundation in any ideological consensus." In the postwar period—at a time of broad-based economic prosperity—the operational liberalism of the American political identity mattered most at the ballot box. By the end of the 1960s the ideological conservative side began to more forcefully exert itself.[19]

This process would widen the sharp divisions so evident in American politics today. After 1968, voters would continue to value government

programs, particularly Medicare, Medicaid, and expanded public education, all of which came out of Johnson's Great Society. Yet their mistrust of
"government," in all its abstraction, would only grow stronger, fostering an
almost reflexive resistance to any new government initiative. Rather than
being seen as a continuation of the New Deal programs that had built and
sustained the American middle class, new programs invariably were perceived as risks to those same benefits. After 1968, the size of government
didn't shrink. In fact, it grew in size and responsibility—but never with the
same vitality and focus as it had in the mid-1960s. Meanwhile, conservative
complaints about the ineffectiveness of public spending, the importance of
reducing business regulation and lowering taxes, and the need for smaller
government became the lingua franca of American politics.[20]

No one element drove the backlash quite like its racial component. But
even here, Americans were of two minds. On the one hand, they strongly
endorsed civil rights measures such as equal employment opportunity and
equal access to public accommodations. After the passage of the Civil Rights
Bill in 1964 this support continued to rise. The instrumentals, on the other
hand—open housing, integrated schools, and black entry into white-
dominated workplaces—created enormous friction. As African Americans
pushed for greater economic and social opportunities, whites who felt
threatened by their advances pushed back. White support for government
activism was largely predicated on the notion that government would provide protections for them. By flinging open the doors of opportunity to black
Americans the Great Society put these privileges at risk.[21]

In June 1965, 51 percent of all Americans said that Johnson was pursuing the cause of racial equality either "not fast enough" or "about right." In
the fall of 1966 this figure had fallen to 39 percent. By the summer of 1967,
it dropped to 24 percent. In the fall of 1966, 85 percent of white Americans
agreed that blacks were "trying to move too fast." Two years earlier only 34
percent had felt that way.[22]

These numbers represented both explicit racial hatred and implicit racial
fear. "Please can you explain to us why the black people want to be near us
when we don't want them deep from our hearts & never will," asked one

white constituent in a letter to Richard Hatcher, the first black mayor of Gary, Indiana. "We have nothing against them or ever to do them any harm. We just don't want them to mingle with us." Many white Americans took for granted the idea that more blacks in their community meant increases in crime and the introduction of social pathologies, such as drug and alcohol abuse and out-of-wedlock births. The poverty and deterioration of black inner-city neighborhoods came to be viewed less as a phenomenon of economic and social inequality than as a failure of morality and personal lassitude.[23]

Millions of whites believed that an influx of blacks threatened not just their communities, but their homes—and their self-identification as members of the middle class. A neighborhood transformed most animated white fears. Gallup regularly asked whites how they would feel about "great numbers" of "colored people" moving into their neighborhood. In 1963, 78 percent said they would either definitely or might move in such a situation. Over the next four years that number remained largely unchanged, even as whites continued to back other key elements of the civil rights agenda.[24]

Johnson's reaction to these attitudes did not help matters. "I know that as President I couldn't make people want to integrate their schools or open their doors to blacks," he told his speechwriter Richard Goodwin, "but I could make them feel guilty for not doing it.... The guilt was the only chance we had for holding the backlash in check." This approach effectively ignored the growing sense among white working-class voters that those pushing the hardest for racial integration cared little about the impact of these policies on their lives. "Everyone, deep down, wants something a little better for his children," Johnson said in justifying his ambitions. But not every American defined "a little better" the same way.[25]

The fight for control of predominately white urban neighborhoods increasingly became a zero-sum game. Across American cities a vicious cycle would be repeated—a black family would move in and demonstrations would ensue; occasionally even violence would break out. In the end, someone would flee, either the black family or the whites who didn't want to live with them. For those who stayed, the imperative to stop further integration became even more encompassing. "Go...into any home, any bar, any barber shop and you will find people are not talking about Vietnam or rising prices or prosperity," noted Illinois congressman Roman Pucinski. "They are talking about Martin Luther King and how they are moving in on us and what's going to happen to our neighborhoods."[26]

For decades, white voters had relied on local political leaders—and often Democratic Party institutions—to look out for their interests and, above all, to keep the races apart. Many whites would cast a split ballot, for local, conservative quasi-segregationists like Sam Yorty in Los Angeles, Richard Daley in Chicago, or Albert Cobo in Detroit and pro–civil rights senators and congressman at the national level. But when these same white voters began to see that the national party's fight for racial integration and poverty reduction was directly undermining their interests, attitudes changed. Suddenly, voting Democratic became a potential liability.[27]

Whites, after all, hardly found themselves in positions of stability. "Even the Well-Off Americans Feel Poor" blared a headline in *US News and World Report* in early 1968. Many who had come of age in the Great Depression were inclined to view their gains as ephemeral. Squeezed between economic uncertainty on one side and political leaders they perceived as being more interested in assisting minorities than helping them on the other, many began to feel a potent mix of resentment and fear. Nixon would call them the "forgotten Americans," and later the "silent majority." Their anger, and even more their anxiety, would fundamentally transform the politics of the era to come.[28]

That this ire would be directed at the public institutions actually helping white Americans would create a tragic irony. Liberalism's advance in the Johnson years lifted millions of blacks out of poverty. It also helped many more whites, particularly in strengthening the social safety net (the 1965 passage of Medicaid being a prime example). The lack of public support for an expansive and activist government role in maintaining these protections played directly into the hands of conservatives who had little actual interest in using the levers of government to improve the economic prospects of America's working and middle class. Much of the next four decades of public policy would be defined by a steady erosion of focus on the working class and greater attention to the wealthiest and most well-connected Americans.

Embracing the mantra of small-government conservatism would end up a massive miscalculation for whites on the bottom rungs of the economic ladder. None of this, of course, was obvious in the late 1960s. Instead, a different set of emotions and concerns dominated.[29]

Writing in *New York* magazine, Pete Hamill viscerally captured these attitudes. In a 1969 article entitled "The Revolt of the White Lower Middle Class," Hamill quoted a white ironworker named Eddie Cush about his economic challenges: "I'm going out of my mind. I average about $8,500 a year, pretty good money. I work my ass off. But I can't make it. I come home at the end of the week, I start paying bills, I give my wife some money for food. And there's nothing left." The difficulty in making ends meet was bad enough, but that others were benefiting from government largesse bred real resentment. "Look in the papers. Look on TV," another blue-collar worker told Hamill. "None of them politicians gives a good goddam. All they worry about is the niggers. And everything is for the niggers.... And they get it all without workin'.... I'll tell ya somethin'. There's a lotta people who just ain't gonna put up with it much longer."[30]

While a fight over resources became central to the backlash of the 1960s, it would be matched if not surpassed by growing fears about personal security. The focus on crime, or "law and order," as it was often described, has frequently been framed as a blatant political appeal for white voters. In part, this is true. But the fears were also quite real. The period between 1963 and 1968 saw an extraordinary and unprecedented growth in national crime rates. The number of violent crimes in America more than doubled; robberies jumped by close to 150 percent. Rape, murder, auto theft, and burglary all rose dramatically.[31]

Then there were the riots. They started with Watts, but more and more American cities would be added to the list, reaching a crescendo in the "long, hot summer" of 1967, as major disturbances occurred in 159 cities, with Newark and Detroit hit the hardest. The pictures of black urban dwellers—young and old, male and female—engaging in carefree looting, whole city blocks being burned to the ground, and tales of gunfire being exchanged between police officers and armed hoodlums all had a major impact on white consciousness.[32]

Beyond the statistics, crime is one of those issues in which anecdote, perception, and emotion play a dominant role. Constant media portrayals of the rising tide of disorder heightened public unease. Magazines like *US News and World Report* showed a city-by-city breakdown of the crime rates and the frequency of various acts of violence, "a murder every hour," "a rape every 23 minutes," and so on. *Esquire* featured actress Ursula Andress on its cover with a Band-Aid over her eye and a caption reading "Our Growing Obsession with Violence." Writing for the same magazine, Garry Wills traveled the country, talking to police officers in departments gearing up for racial disorders as if preparing to face off against the Soviets. He turned the reporting into a book ominously titled *The Second Civil War: Arming for Armageddon.*[33]

A lengthy March 1967 essay in *Time* said crime had become "a national disgrace" and that "by any standard of measurement, the statistics are staggering, and their impact can be felt at every level of American life." Worst of all, "There is a growing tendency to believe that the Government cannot or will not protect the average citizen." The article, entitled "Crime and the Great Society," made an explicit connection between the policies of the Johnson administration and growing national disorder.[34]

Richard Nixon, in a charge echoed by fellow Republicans, argued that "permissiveness toward violation of the law and public order" and "decline in respect for authority and the rule of law in America" was the cause. According to Ronald Reagan, who successfully ran for governor of California in 1966, Johnson and his fellow liberals had made the problems of the ghettoes worse by promising too much and failing to deliver. For others, such as Alabama governor George Wallace, who had challenged Johnson in the 1964 Democratic primaries, the blame lay with the Supreme Court, which he claimed had steadily made it harder for the police to punish criminals.[35]

Democrats, fearful of alienating black voters, frequently sought to minimize the issue. Attorney General Nicholas Katzenbach compared the chances of being "raped by a stranger" to being "hit by lightning," which, while perhaps statistically accurate, missed the point, particularly since half of female urban residents said they were afraid to walk in their neighborhoods at night. Democrats found themselves caught between two seemingly incompatible and implacable forces—the desire for social justice and the desire for social order and safety. But Johnson in his formulation of the Great Society had conflated these two aspirations into one overarching program. "The war on poverty…is a war against crime and war against disorder," Johnson had argued in 1965. So it hardly should have come as a surprise that when the latter showed little progress, the estimation of the former declined precipitously.[36]

On a question of visceral importance to many Americans, liberals had ceded ground to Republicans, who suddenly had found an issue that matched, or even trumped, Democrats' three-decade-long advantage on economic matters. Ultimately, the crime problem became to many voters a symbol of liberalism's failures and, in the hands of Republican politicians, a tool for attacking the left and its conceits of social transformation. It all fit within an increasingly persuasive conservative narrative—namely, that liberalism was at odds with the interests and values of ordinary Americans. Liberalism, and the left in general, had come to represent leniency and laxness; a funnel through which the tax dollars of the middle class went to the poor; forced integration of workplaces, schools, and communities that put white economic security at risk; a failure to protect citizens from criminal predators; and a cause of the country's deteriorating values. This final tenet would prove to be the backlash's most durable legacy. Long after crime rates went down, the disorder of the 1960s and the rhetorical focus on "values" would continue to play a dominant role in the country's political discourse.[37]

In popular lore, the 1960s are portrayed as an era of protest and social change. Hair got longer, skirts got shorter, and sex, drugs, and rock 'n' roll became the new watchwords of American youth. These depictions offer more than just a shorthand history of the 1960s; they are reflective of a generational divide that emerged at the time—and one that saw its most ostentatious displays on the left.

In calling the under-twenty-five generation the Man of the Year in 1967, *Time* described these baby boomers as "cushioned by unprecedented affluence and the welfare state" and possessing "a sense of economic security unmatched in history." Far more young people attended college, and few could relate to the economic apprehension that had defined their parents' upbringing during the Great Depression. With greater freedom emerged a yearning for more than a forty-hour work-week, a steady union job, and a house with a white picket fence. Out of this tumult came the so-called New Left and the counterculture, which began to openly question the basic constructs and values of American society. The counterculture had gained momentum with the free speech movement in Berkeley in 1964, but it took off with the growing anger and demonstrations against the war in Vietnam. Among blacks, the lack of immediate and tangible results from civil rights and antipoverty legislation—as well as continued and pervasive discrimination—became the impetus for that community's own radicalization.[38]

By the fall of 1967, the far left was practically in full revolt. The hippies were annoyed at the "squares"; the blacks were pissed at the "honkies" and the "Uncle Toms"; the antiwar activists at the "war-mongers"; the feminists at the patriarchy; the Yippies at pretty much everything. Virulent critiques of Democrats came not just from the right but also from those in their own camp who assailed the party for no longer being responsive to the larger goals of racial equality, a more equitable society, and an end to American militarism. Indeed, as civil rights legislation became the law of the land and the edifice of southern apartheid was torn down, the left's attention would be drawn to other issues. The young activists who served as the foot soldiers for liberalism's most significant accomplishments had become some of its loudest opponents.

Ultimately, however, the political impact of liberal activism came not from the power of its critiques but rather from the negative image of protest and dissent that its leaders cultivated. Protest in the 1960s took many forms—antiwar marches, flagrant drug use, free love, long hair, and radical ideas. Yet all of it seemed to inflame. For many Americans the protesters came to be seen as emblematic of the country's declining moral values. A similar pattern was evident in the evolving reaction to civil rights demonstrations. Public opinion polling of the era consistently showed strong opposition to any public act that fed the creeping national sense of social disorder—even by those who sympathized with the grievances of the protesters. All of this produced a double whammy for Democrats: the left's most ideologically supportive constituency was up in arms, and the way they chose to show their displeasure led to the estrangement of the party's most important political constituency—the socially conservative white working class. Though they sought to expand liberalism's ultimate goals, the left's radicalism had the opposite effect.[39]

The radicals in the streets would not be the only ones riling up Americans; there were also the "social engineers in black robes." Beginning in the early 1960s the Supreme Court, led by Chief Justice Earl Warren, issued a series of rulings that nourished conservative resentment. The Court provided a host of new rights for criminal defendants (at a time when crime was seemingly out of control); it weakened laws banning obscenity (at a time when foul language and open sales of pornography were increasingly prevalent); it legalized the sale of contraceptive devices and led to the widespread use of the pill (at a time when women were doing things they weren't "supposed to do"); and it ended prayer in schools (at a time when *Time* magazine was asking, "Is God Dead?"). "They've put the Negroes in the school, and now they've driven God out," complained one Alabama congressman. By 1968, seven out of ten Americans believed that liberal judges bore some responsibility for the decline in law and order.[40]

Sensing a political opportunity, conservatives placed all these affronts into the law-and-order basket. There may not have been a straight line between rebellious college students and rioting slum dwellers, but this was the connection being made in the minds of many voters—and encouraged by politicians. For all the mythology around the Age of Aquarius and the flowering of the baby boom generation, the majority of the voters in 1968 could best be defined, as Scammon and Wattenberg noted, as "unyoung, unpoor, unblack" and "middle-aged, middle-class and middle-minded."[41]

In 1964, Barry Goldwater's stern conservative ideology doomed his candidacy. But by the fall of 1967—as many felt the country unraveling around them—the nation's political ground shifted in his ideological direction.

The first signs of political trouble for Johnson and the Democrats came in 1966 and the party's trouncing in midterm elections. While this defeat is frequently portrayed as the beginning of the nation's conservative ascendancy (in part because of the election of Reagan as governor of California), GOP moderates like Edward Brooke in Massachusetts, Charles Percy in Illinois, George Romney in Michigan, Mark Hatfield in Oregon, Nelson Rockefeller in New York, and Spiro Agnew in Maryland benefited too. The election offered a repudiation of Johnson rather than an embrace of conservatism. Indeed, the GOP's key critique of the president and Democrats had less to do with full-scale opposition to the Great Society and more with concern that too much was being done too soon. As Reagan said, "The people now have shown they want a pause, a chance to ask: 'Where are we going? How fast? How far?'" Still, the election provided an ominous indication to Democrats that Republicans could challenge the liberal consensus in a way that paid substantial—and immediate—political dividends.[42]

While the backdrop for the Democrats' defeat at the polls in 1966 had been the backlash, something deeper was happening: diminishing confidence in the notion that the government could solve every national problem. This represented more of a backlash against activism than the programmatic elements of American liberalism, which still remained popular. The warning signs for Johnson and Democrats were blinking red. In late 1966, Johnson's poll numbers dipped below 50 percent, where they would remain for virtually the rest of his term. The political momentum resided with Republicans, who, for the first time in decades, saw their conservative worldview become aligned with the mood of the electorate. Johnson could not arrest the undoing of the New Deal coalition. LBJ possessed many skills, but navigating the choppy waters of national turmoil and social division was not one of them. The moment required a politician more inclined to bend decisively in the direction of public opinion, particularly on the war in Vietnam, which had become a near-obsession in the Johnson White House. Johnson's increasingly myopic focus on the war—and his refusal to change course—would make it nearly impossible for him or his party to respond to the nation's larger social and structural changes.[43]

Over the next two years, as the cities exploded in violence, the civil rights movement gave way to Black Power, and protests against the war became more public and vocal, the war continued its inexorable trajectory toward stalemate. In the jungles of Southeast Asia, the Great Society and the liberal consensus, already badly weakened by the assaults on order and the growing white backlash, would be dealt a proverbial kill shot.

Losing the "Middle Ground"

Lyndon Johnson bore a good portion of the responsibility for the backlash against his Great Society. He charged far ahead of the American people with his reform agenda. He failed to take into account the increasing social, economic, and cultural anxiety of the white working class; and he did not do nearly enough to address growing national fears about rising crime rates. Still, one can lay only so much blame at his feet. Informed by a larger set of societal and cultural changes, the backlash represented a political force that no president could be expected to control. Assigning him the major culpability for its many discordant elements is like blaming King Canute for failing to hold back the waves.

The same cannot be said about the war in Vietnam. Johnson alone made the decision to escalate the war in Indochina and to resist all efforts to resolve it politically. He initiated the bombing of targets in North Vietnam and then the gradual entry of half a million US troops into South Vietnam. He consciously chose to mislead the American people about the conflict and the full extent of US involvement. He turned a deaf ear to the growing voices of concern within his own party. He interpreted any criticism of the war effort as a personal attack, and even when presented with evidence of incipient failure in Vietnam, he rejected every call to stray from his chosen course of action—until it was far too late.

Above all, Johnson refused to settle on a clear policy in Vietnam, attempting instead to navigate between two unpalatable political options—a full commitment to the war and de-escalation. In his memoirs, written in 1971, two years after he left office, Johnson would perhaps better than any other historian, analyst, or political scientist note the dilemma in which he had placed himself:

> I stuck to the middle ground, for I realized that my Presidency would require dealing simultaneously with major military crises abroad and urgently needed reforms at home. That course was not comfortable. It would have been easier in the short run to break out the flag for an all-out military effort, and perhaps easier still to abandon our commitment in Asia and concentrate on domestic tasks. But I was convinced that the middle ground was the right course for the United States. That was the fundamental approach of my administration, and I was not going to abandon it. Holding to it, however, eroded my popularity from two directions—with those who wanted to do more in the war and with those who wished to do more at home.[1]

Attempting to maintain this "middle ground" would fatally undermine Johnson's presidency and his dreams of a Great Society.

LBJ was caught in a political bind on Vietnam. The liberal consensus that swept him into office in the fall of 1964 was oriented around two ideas that formed the basis of postwar American politics—activist government at home and muscular anti-Communism abroad. This represented the Faustian deal that liberals made during the early stages of the Cold War. To realize the dreams of a more just and fair society at home, many liberals came to believe that they needed to maintain a hawkish position on containing the Soviet Union and global Communist movements. Doing so would protect liberalism's right flank from GOP charges of insufficient rigor in fighting the "red threat." Tough-minded anti-Communism would also allow the party to maintain political support for their vision of an engaged federal government, in a country traditionally suspicious of such activism.

Johnson believed so sincerely in this political construct that he allowed it to drive his decision-making on Vietnam to a disconcerting degree. At the dawn of the Cold War he witnessed, firsthand, the piercing attacks on well-meaning Democrats not sufficiently and stridently anti-Communist. As president, Johnson convinced himself that only by upholding his commitment to fighting Communism could he maintain support for his governing agenda. "I knew from the start that I was bound to be crucified either way I moved. If I left the woman I really loved—the Great Society—in order to get involved with the bitch of a war on the other side of the world, then I would lose everything at home...but if I left that war and let the Communists take over South Vietnam, then I would be seen as a coward and my nation would soon be seen as an appeaser."[2]

By the summer of 1967 Johnson's decision to try to serve both masters was eating away at his presidency. When Johnson had announced the entry of combat troops into the war in July 1965, he gave Americans the impression that the United States had entered into a limited engagement. Behind the scenes, however, policymakers assumed that the war would entail a far larger military commitment (potentially as many as one million troops)—and even then might not succeed. At the same time, Johnson consistently vetoed calls from his military chiefs to ramp up the fight against North Vietnam.[3]

He also rejected moves that he feared would inflame domestic discontent, such as calling up the military reserves or raising taxes to pay for the war. In his 1966 State of the Union address Johnson said, "We are a rich nation and can afford to make progress at home while meeting obligations abroad—in fact we can afford no other course if we are to remain strong." While he would later be forced to ask Congress for a tax increase to help pay for the costs of the war, he rebuffed demands for cuts in domestic spending programs to make that increase more politically palatable to both Republicans and Democrats in Congress.[4]

Johnson adopted his middle path on Vietnam because he believed it to be the least bad option. But trying to win a war against a resolute foe while only partially committing to it made for an impossible task. Moreover, by depicting the war in existential terms and refusing to actively pursue a political resolution to the conflict, Johnson left himself with little room to find an easy path out of Vietnam. His "middle-ground" policy ensured that the United States would simply continue to muddle through, escalating just enough not to lose, but not enough to win.[5]

LBJ developed his own deeply held rationalizations for the path he'd chosen. "Don't worry about the hippies and the students and the Commies," he told his undersecretary of state and in-house dove, George Ball, even as he publicly derided the war's opponents as "nervous Nellies." "They'll raise a lot of hell but can't do real damage. The terrible beast we have to fear is the right wing; if they ever get the idea I am selling out on Vietnam, they'll do horrible things to the country, and we'll be forced to escalate the war beyond anything you've ever thought about." In Johnson's mind, he wasn't the instigator of the war in Vietnam but the last man standing against a far worse outcome.[6]

The president's fears of the "terrible beast" were emblematic of the outsized influence he ascribed to the right-wing bogeyman that had flayed Democrats during the "Who Lost China" debate and the McCarthyite witch-hunts of the 1950s. It became a ready-made excuse for Johnson to maintain the status quo. "I knew that Harry Truman and Dean Acheson had lost their effectiveness from the day that the communists took over in China," he later claimed. "The loss of China had played a large role in the rise of Joe McCarthy. And I knew that all these problems, taken together, were chickenshit compared to what might happen if we lost Vietnam."[7]

This historical assertion didn't quite stand up to scrutiny. Indeed, the more accurate lesson to be drawn from Korea is that Americans would punish a politician who fought a losing, stalemated war, as they did with Truman and Democrats in 1952. For Johnson, the proposition that tangling with the hawks would not end in disaster but could actually be weathered always went untested. Johnson's belief in a straight line between showing weakness on Communism and a Republican electoral victory and subsequent military escalation became both a self-fulfilling prophecy and a deeply self-affirming one.

Making the situation even more intractable is the fact that Johnson, amid rising crime rates, worsening race relations, urban riots, and a general rupturing of the nation's social fabric, sought to enact the most far-reaching set of domestic reforms in American history. These challenges required the president's full attention and also the sort of commitment—both personal and political—that would be derailed by a major foreign war. By the summer and fall of 1967, with just over a year to go before he faced the voters again, Johnson would clearly have to make a choice on Vietnam—escalation, as one final push for victory, or a face-saving way out.

Johnson chose neither. For two years his administration had sought to convince Americans that progress was being made in Vietnam, that the enemy was on the run, and that US national security depended on continuing the fight. As the credibility of that position came under direct assault, Johnson hunkered down. In time, the failure to make a clear choice about which policy to pursue in Vietnam would reshape the 1968 presidential election, destroy the remnants of his presidency, and deal the Democratic Party a political wound that would not heal for years.

In the fall of 1967, in whichever direction Johnson looked from his increasingly isolated seat within the confines of the White House, the signs of disenchantment about the war in Vietnam—and his leadership—were unmistakably clear.

The latest polls spoke volumes. In June his approval rating stood at 47 percent with a disapproval rate of 39 percent; by early August these numbers had completely flipped. A majority of the country, 54 percent, now viewed his stewardship of Vietnam in negative terms. Two-thirds of the country had lost confidence in his conduct of the war and didn't believe he kept them "fully informed" about its progress. The announcement in early August 1967 that another forty-five thousand troops were headed to Vietnam—pushing the total number over half a million—contributed to the growing belief that Johnson would not accede to any limit on the US commitment to South Vietnam. By the late summer, Gallup reported for the first time since the organization had begun polling Americans on Vietnam that a majority called the decision to get involved in the war a "mistake."[8]

In the first week of September, *Newsweek* splashed the headline "LBJ in Trouble" across its cover. Inside, the magazine offered a devastating snapshot of the national frustration boiling up around Johnson's presidency. "In Pocatello, Idaho, a sixty-ish but sprightly grandmother and good Democrat said: 'I'm beginning to hate that man.' In Portland, Ore., Charles Snowden said: 'I've switched. I'll vote for almost anybody except Johnson.' In a modern office off New York's Fifth Avenue a young executive said: 'Johnson's too clever. He's always got something up his sleeve.' In Los Angeles, Mrs. Aljean Harmetz said: 'I don't think I like Johnson now. I don't think he's an honest man.'" Johnson, said the magazine, had become "his own worst enemy."[9]

Others piled on. "He has attempted the impossible feat of trying to please all of the people all of the time, chiefly by posing as a benign granddaddy and an openhanded Uncle Sugar. In consequence, he has managed to alienate a sizable number of them," wrote Time. The root of the problem, said the *Wall Street Journal*, was the "chasm of mistrust, anger and frustration—mostly over . . . Viet Nam" that Johnson's actions had created.[10]

Americans desperately wanted Johnson to lay out a clear path for ending the conflict. Gallup even found that 55 percent of Americans backed a policy of military escalation in order to get the war over quickly. It was a nineteen-point jump from a year earlier. Only 10 percent supported "complete withdrawal."[11]

At the same time, antiwar voices became increasingly strident in their denunciations of the war. In April, Martin Luther King condemned it as "a blasphemy against all that America stands for." The National Council of Churches called US military action in Vietnam "morally unjustified." The same month saw a massive mobilization in San Francisco as fifty thousand people marched against the war and hundreds of thousands gathered in New York's Central Park. In October, nearly one hundred thousand demonstrators assembled at the Pentagon for what at the time was the largest antiwar protest in American history. Signs at antiwar rallies read "Where Is Oswald When You Need Him?" The cries of "Hey, Hey, LBJ, How Many Kids Did You Kill Today?" from Pennsylvania Avenue could be heard inside the White House, and theater-going liberals began turning out for a new play called *MacBird*, which intimated that Johnson had been responsible for the Kennedy assassination.[12]

Johnson wrote off these public signs of disapproval. The young people stridently opposed to the war "wouldn't know a Communist if they tripped over one," he said. Their criticisms, some argued, actually brought potential benefit. "The more he is denounced by Stokely Carmichael and the 'New Left,'" wrote Stewart Alsop in the *Saturday Evening Post* about Johnson, "the more likely it is that...Mr. Average...will vote for him."[13]

For Johnson, a far more troubling political development was taking place at the other end of Pennsylvania Avenue—the steady erosion of congressional support for the war. The *New York Times* reported that a "notable new fact of life" had emerged in Washington—an "allergic reaction to further United States involvement abroad." The new mantra on Capitol Hill, said the *Times*, became "no more Vietnams"—and both doves and hawks were chanting it. An August survey found that a majority of senators had lost confidence in Johnson's management of the war. Even among traditional Republican backers of the military effort, more than half considered themselves either skeptical of or directly opposed to Johnson's policies. Oregon Republican Mark Hatfield complained that "misleading the American public" had become a "consistent policy of the Administration," and his colleague the Republican senator Thruston Morton from Kentucky expressed the sentiments of many in Washington when he said, "I was all for the bombing; I thought once we started the war would be over in six months. I was wrong."[14]

Johnson's political allies were no kinder. The senate majority leader, Democrat Mike Mansfield, a longtime skeptic of the war, set Washington abuzz with public criticism of the White House's rosy optimism on Vietnam. "Reports of progress are strewn, like burned-out tanks, all along the road which led this nation ever more deeply into Vietnam and Southeast Asia during the past decade and a half," Mansfield said, as he called for the "greatest restraint" in any further use of American military force in Vietnam. Privately, Democrats like South Carolina senator Fritz Hollings signaled to the administration that the war and the public's growing discontent had the potential to do real political damage to the party's chances in 1968—up and down the ticket. In the House, the defection of the prominent Democratic leader (and future Speaker) Tip O'Neill dealt another blow to the White House, one that personally outraged the president.[15]

Yet even while concerns about entanglement in Vietnam grew, few questioned the idea that America must continue to play an outsized role in global affairs—or confront Communist advances. Vietnam came to be seen, in some respects, as a diversion from that goal. For most, the overriding issue was the fear that the war had turned into a quagmire and that the man in the White House had no idea what to do about it.

These doubts would soon be aired publicly. On August 7, the influential Saigon bureau chief for the *New York Times*, R. W. Apple, wrote a blockbuster front-page article that argued the war had become a "stalemate" and little reason for optimism about an immediate American breakthrough could be found. Contrary to the optimistic tales of military success, Apple wrote, "Victory is not close at hand." In fact, "it may be beyond reach. It is clearly unlikely in the next year or even the next two years, and American officers talk somberly about fighting here for decades." Apple offered an unsettling tale of woe. US airpower couldn't stop the flow of weapons into the country; the Communists had a seemingly unending source of fighters; little of the South had actually been secured, and even "if the North Vietnamese and American troops were magically whisked away the South Vietnamese regime would almost certainly crumble." Worst of all, security in the countryside—pacification—remained "as bad as ever." Apple's analysis offered nary a single positive development on which US policymakers could hang their hats.[16]

Johnson and his advisors pushed back vigorously. Privately LBJ described Apple as "a Communist" and a "threat to national security." Inside the military, however, as the *Pentagon Papers* would later establish, the article "merely confirmed what many had been saying officially and unofficially for some time." The *Times*, which had generally been supportive of the war effort, took a cue from Apple's reporting and published a series of editorials harshly criticizing Johnson's conduct of the war. Calling Vietnam a "bottomless pit" and bemoaning the diminished attention to domestic priorities, the paper said that it seemed "increasingly questionable that anyone in

Washington is at all clear on what it is this country is seeking to achieve in Vietnam."[17]

Two months later, *Time*, which had also long been a vocal supporter of the war, joined in the criticisms of the administration. On October 6 the magazine ran a lengthy dispatch from Con Thien, a muddy, isolated military outpost six miles from the Demilitarized Zone separating North and South Vietnam. Buffeted by relentless monsoon rain and constant artillery bombardment from an enemy they couldn't see, the marines spent most of their time in underground bunkers, living off C rations and fending off daily harassing attacks from North Vietnamese foot soldiers or "a horde of bold rats," who were the only other signs of life in a spot one marine said "must be the worst place in the world." In all its misery, Con Thien, the magazine reported, dramatized the "cumulative frustrations of the painful war"—frustrations that were now bubbling to the political surface. While once opposition to the war had been restricted to intellectuals and young people, the ranks of opponents of the war were swelling with politicians and "apolitical businessmen." A week later the magazine noted that the "only audible consensus" in the country was "the one that is building against" Johnson.[18]

The president's dramatic loss of support was not limited to the home front. In the summer of 1967 Johnson sent his friend and outside advisor Clark Clifford along with General Maxwell Taylor to East Asia and Australia to plead for greater troop contributions from allied nations. The two men were met not just with flat refusals of additional forces but with open and pointed questioning of US strategy in Vietnam. In Bangkok, Wellington, Seoul, and Canberra they heard the same message—the political costs of upping troop commitments would be too great for any of these nations to consider. When word leaked out about the purpose of the Clifford-Taylor mission, Philippine strongman Ferdinand Marcos canceled the visit in advance.[19]

According to the domino theory, if South Vietnam fell to the Communists, these countries—and their leaders—would be next. Yet none of them saw the threat in the same terms as the United States or felt that the benefit of maintaining strong ties with Washington on the war justified the political costs of deploying additional forces to Vietnam. If there was any question about America's isolation on the world stage—even among its key allies—the Clifford-Taylor jaunt should have answered them.[20]

Still none of these developments moved Johnson toward a decisive shift in policy. If any moment, however, should have given him pause, it was in early November 1967, when his own secretary of defense, Robert McNamara, called for a significant change in policy. Fairly or unfairly, the Vietnam War had come to be seen as "McNamara's war." Through two administrations he had been the public face of the conflict, with his soothing assurances— backed by reams of statistical data—that America was winning in Vietnam. His reasonableness; his consistently rational, technocratic demeanor; his encyclopedic memory for and recitation of key facts and figures about the war; and his commitment and devotion to America's goals in Southeast Asia enchanted both Presidents Kennedy and Johnson—and made him an effective public advocate for the war.[21]

As time went on, however, McNamara began to see the contours of the conflict with greater clarity, and his doubts about US policy grew stronger. He first raised the idea of a bombing halt in the spring of 1967, with the admonition to Johnson that the "picture of the world's greatest superpower killing or seriously injuring 1,000 non-combatants a week, while trying to pound a tiny backward nation into submission...is not a pretty one." His recommendation, that the United States begin actively pursuing a "political settlement" in Vietnam, sent shock waves through official Washington and enraged the Joint Chiefs, who were convinced that limitations imposed by the White House were the real problem. Undaunted, McNamara told a congressional committee that summer that the US bombing raids simply weren't working. "Short of the virtual annihilation of North Vietnam and its people," said McNamara, the unceasing aerial bombardment could not and would not end the war. "Ho Chi Minh is a tough old S.O.B.," McNamara told his staff. "He won't quit no matter how much bombing we do."[22]

On November 1, 1967, McNamara delivered his own bombshell to the White House—a memo urging Johnson to dramatically shift course in Vietnam. "The American public, frustrated by the slow rate of progress, fearing continued escalation, and doubting that all approaches to peace have been sincerely probed, does not give the appearance of having the will to persist," he wrote to the president. McNamara questioned whether it would still be "possible to maintain our efforts in South Vietnam for the time necessary to accomplish our objectives there."[23]

In antiseptic, bureaucratic language, McNamara urged Johnson to get ahead of the emerging political currents. The president should halt the bombing of the North before year's end to spur political negotiations and stabilize the US military presence. McNamara recommended no further increase in US troop levels, no expansion of the bombing, and a gradual transfer of military responsibilities to the South Vietnamese. In the context of the narrow debates inside the Johnson White House on Vietnam, these proposals were sweeping in scope, but not necessarily that radical. They came on the heels of a secret CIA report sent to Johnson in September that said withdrawal from Vietnam would likely "not be permanently damaging to [America's] capacity to play its part as a world power." Unmoved, Johnson instead railed against McNamara, who he complained had gone "dovish" on him.[24]

The day after McNamara's memo arrived at the White House, the president met with a team of foreign policy "Wise Men" that included, among others, former secretary of state Dean Acheson, retired four-star general Omar Bradley, Clifford, and former national security advisor McGeorge Bundy. Shielded from McNamara's growing concerns about the war's prospects, the Wise Men instead received briefings that reflected the military's chronically upbeat view of the conflict. Unsurprisingly, they told the president precisely what he wanted to hear. "Getting out of Vietnam is as impossible as it is undesirable," said Bundy.[25]

Nonetheless, throughout the fall of 1967 Johnson continued to pursue multiple avenues for negotiation, hoping to find some way out of a conflict that he was unconvinced could be won militarily. In late September he traveled to San Antonio, Texas, and offered a drooping olive branch to the enemy. "The United States is willing to stop all aerial and naval bombardment of North Vietnam when this will lead promptly to productive discussion," said Johnson. "We, of course, assume that while discussions proceed, North Vietnam would not take advantage of the bombing cessation or limitation." The San Antonio formula represented a shift in America's approach to the North in that, as LBJ later put, the United States was no longer "insisting that [Ho Chi Minh] immediately end the military effort, only that he not increase it." But the San Antonio proposal was initially transmitted to the North Vietnamese just as a (temporary) moratorium on bombing around Hanoi was set to begin. So a series of heavy air raids preceded the message, which left the North's leadership convinced that Johnson intended to force them militarily into making concessions. They rejected the offer.[26]

A political breakthrough would require stronger measures, and above all a realization that the White House needed to make a more dramatic move if they truly wanted to end the war. But Johnson would only go so far in the pursuit of peace. Ultimately, he was seeking Hanoi's surrender, rather than a deal that satisfied both sides. Privately he told his closest advisors that he believed that North Vietnamese were, "playing us for suckers. They have no more intention of talking than we have of surrendering." No major concessions to the enemy would be proffered—the middle ground would be maintained.[27]

There is of course no guarantee that had Johnson taken a bold concessionary step toward peace, the North Vietnamese would have accepted—but he barely tested the hypothesis. He vacillated between seeing no military way out of the conflict to believing that continued aerial attacks of the North could finally spark a diplomatic breakthrough. "I know this bombing must be hurting them," said Johnson in an October meeting. "Despite any reports to the contrary, I can feel it in my bones.... We need to pour the steel on."[28]

He convinced himself that taking McNamara's advice and showing any inclination toward compromise with the Communists would spell disaster. In an unusual "memorandum for the file" in response to McNamara's proposal, Johnson wrote, "A unilateral and unrequited bombing stand-down would be read in both Hanoi and the United States as a sign of weakening will. It would encourage the extreme doves; increase the pressure from withdrawal from those who argue 'bomb and get out'; decrease support from our most steady friends; and pick up support from only a small group of moderate doves." McNamara was in a fractured emotional state; his relationship with Bobby Kennedy influenced his judgment, or so Johnson told himself. At the end of the month Johnson offered him the presidency of the World Bank, in a transparent effort to rid himself of his defense secretary and his contrarian views.[29]

Beyond the perceived political costs of a dramatic shift in policy, personal and psychological explanations for Johnson's inaction loom large. By 1967, Vietnam was no longer simply a question of maintaining US credibility. "The war," writes LBJ biographer Robert Dallek, "had become a personal test of his judgment, of his wisdom in expanding the conflict in the first place.... Having invested so much of his presidency in the conflict... he would not acknowledge that his principal foreign policy initiative had largely failed." When Johnson said, "I'm not going to be the first American president to lose a war," he meant it—and that vow played a dangerously outsized role in the president's thought process on Vietnam.[30]

The combination of Johnson's conviction that anything less than a victory in Southeast Asia would be a personal and humiliating defeat and his belief that the politics of Vietnam necessitated staying the course crippled his decision-making. For all of Johnson's many positive attributes—his empathy, his passion for reform, his genuine identification with the poor, the humble, and the downtrodden and his mastery of the legislative process—his insecurity, pride, and stubbornness came to clearly define the later stages of his presidency. The American people (and certainly the people of Vietnam) were decidedly unblessed to have such a man as president in the fall of 1967.

———

Still even as Johnson ignored or compartmentalized the signs of trouble on Vietnam, he refused to give his generals what they wanted to win the war. The Joint Chiefs continued to call for increased bombing of the North, the mining of North Vietnam's harbors, more troops, and even the invasion of North Vietnam and Vietcong sanctuaries in Laos and Cambodia. While Johnson ramped up aerial attacks, he rejected the other measures. To take such steps, he believed, would risk bringing the Soviets or the Chinese more directly into the fight and increase the cries at home to fully "take the wraps off the men in the field" and go for the win. For Johnson, neither escalation nor de-escalation appeared palatable. But staying the course, in the face of such widespread opposition, was not a viable option either, particularly since there appeared to be little reason to believe that the situation in Vietnam would be demonstrably improved a year from then when Johnson would be asking Americans for another term as president.[31]

A choice had to be made, and once again Johnson refused to make it. Instead he tried to convince Americans that the sky was not blue, but in fact green. Johnson complained in October, "We've almost lost the war in the last two months in the court of public opinion." Determined to reverse these losses, he redoubled efforts to, as he put it, "sell our product to the American people." National Security Advisor Walt W. Rostow instructed General Westmoreland, Bunker, and Robert Komer (who was responsible for pacification efforts in Vietnam) to "search urgently for occasions to present sound evidence of progress in Vietnam." Johnson did his part as he launched the so-called Success Offensive with a 5,100-mile tour of eight US military bases. In Fort Benning, Georgia, he read a message that he said he had seen on the side of a box of C rations: "We're going to win this war if it takes our lives to do it." In Johnson's public statements, the path to victory in Vietnam was clear, and his advisors—both military and civilian— became willing accomplices in the telling of this tall tale. "Steady progress" was being made in Vietnam, said Vice President Humphrey, who in a visit to Saigon in October declared, rather embarrassingly, "This is our great adventure—and a wonderful one it is." Privately, however, the vice president told friends that the war increasingly appeared to be a lost cause.[32]

Nothing, Johnson believed, would buck up the American people's flagging enthusiasm for the war in Southeast Asia better than the presence of a ribbon and medal festooned, ramrod-straight general. William Westmoreland, US commander in Vietnam, arrived in the United States in November to make the public case for the administration's policy. Before largely sympathetic audiences, "Westy" offered an upbeat view of the war's progress. The trajectory of US efforts, he maintained, moved in only one direction—forward. "I have never been more encouraged in my four years in Vietnam," he declared.[33]

Westmoreland told a country eager for the war in Vietnam to be over that he could foresee troops coming home within two years. "We have reached an important point when the end begins to come into view," he claimed. For a brief moment the White House's subterfuge worked. A late November item in the political newsletter of the journalistic duo of Rowland Evans and Robert Novak reported that Johnson had become convinced the war had finally "turn[ed] around the corner." No longer did LBJ need to "extract cheerful noises from underlings trained to tell him what he wants to hear." Johnson's public approval began to creep northward, but it wouldn't last. Two months later, when the North Vietnamese launched the surprise Tet Offensive, the false promises of the "success offensive" further widened Johnson's "credibility gap."[34]

A dramatic shift in policy, particularly one opposed by most of the president's civilian and military advisors, would not have been easy for Johnson to embrace. Even so, maintaining political support for the war was Johnson's key responsibility as president, and he failed to appreciate how desperate the political situation regarding Vietnam had become. A decision to de-escalate in 1967 would have strengthened his support within the Democratic Party, neutralized the increasingly vocal antiwar wing of the party, and put him in a far better position for re-election. While Johnson cowered in fear at the prospect of attacks from the right, there existed little consensus among Republicans on the right policy option for Vietnam. Moderate congressional Republicans were beginning to sound more dovish. George Romney, now actively seeking the GOP nomination, had become critical of the war effort, and even Nixon, who had previously never missed an opportunity to push for escalation, began to soften his tone. A close read of often contradictory public opinion polls suggested one overriding impulse—end the war. The "how" mattered far less. Had Johnson made the case in the fall of 1967 for stopping the bombing and opening peace talks as the best way to end the war, it's quite likely this call would have been met not by denunciations but hosannas. But the same president who demonstrated such remarkable political courage on civil rights continued to be driven by crippling fear on foreign policy—and a self-validating dread about the right wing's red-baiting. Johnson could not find it within himself to veer from the path he'd chosen.[35]

When finally forced to change course in March 1968, his dreams of a Great Society lay in tatters, his hopes for a second term had been dashed, and his party was mired in open revolt. In hindsight, the two moments were inextricably linked. Had Johnson shifted course in the fall of 1967, he almost certainly would not have been forced from the presidential race. A decision to de-escalate would have meant that Senator Eugene McCarthy— whose rationale for running was Johnson's refusal to change his policy in Vietnam—would likely not have challenged the president for the Democratic nomination. No McCarthy would have also meant no Robert Kennedy candidacy. Instead, if he'd chosen to run, Johnson would have been the Democratic nominee for president in 1968, if as much by default than by universal acclaim.

Ironically, he also would have been a narrow favorite to win re-election, as he would likely have been able to rely on a relatively united party as well as the traditional advantage that Democrats enjoyed, at the time, in presidential elections. By taking on the mantle of the peace candidate with a plan for ending the war, Johnson had the opportunity to put his likely Republican opponent in the difficult position of either embracing his policy on Vietnam or taking a more hawkish stance that promised more war and more American deaths. Instead, Johnson's willingness to begin his re-election campaign, having done nothing to patch up the rifts in his own party or minimize his most glaring political weakness, left him vulnerable to precisely the more serious problems he would confront in the spring of 1968. What is most striking about Johnson's machinations in the fall of 1967 is that he gave almost no weight to what either his presidential challengers (both Democrats and Republicans) or the American people felt about the war. Johnson's beliefs as to how the politics of national security played out—developed at the height of the nation's anti-Communist hysteria—appeared to be practically immune to new information.

From this perspective, the decision by Johnson in the fall of 1967 to "continue" in Vietnam should not be viewed as simply a missed political opportunity, but rather as the most momentous and fateful decision of the entire political year. From it, the course of the entire 1968 presidential campaign—and the trajectory of four decades of American politics—flowed.

For Lyndon Johnson, not choosing would be the worst choice of all.

Part II

The Democrats

"A Quiet, Witty Man of Gray Presence"

A poet, a writer, and an absorbing orator, well-versed in history, philosophy, and theology, Senator Eugene McCarthy of Minnesota was a man of great intellectual gifts. He was also a talented politician. He could be charming and thoughtful, with a quick wit and a puckish sense of humor. Urbane and handsome, McCarthy had the look of a politician whose ultimate potential went beyond just serving as a backbencher on Capitol Hill.

Still, for all his personal attributes, if one had asked McCarthy's Senate colleagues how best to describe him, they most likely would have said he was a pain in the ass. "Detached. Philosophic. Cynical. Moral. Learned. Lazy." These were the qualities most "commonly attributed" to McCarthy, said the *Wall Street Journal.* "Out of one hundred liberals, McCarthy would be ninety-nine on my list," said one of his Democratic colleagues in the Senate. "He is not worth a damn." The political journalist Nick Thimmesch perhaps described him best, as a "quiet, witty man of gray presence."[1]

McCarthy, who had been elected to the Senate in 1958 after five terms in the House of Representatives, derided the institution that quickly came to

bore him as "the last primitive society in the Western World," and compared his fellow senators to "the savages of New Guinea." Even those who
liked and respected McCarthy found him haughty and thin-skinned. He
never got over being snubbed by Johnson for the 1964 vice presidential
nomination—which went to his colleague from Minnesota, Hubert Humphrey.
In fact, some would speculate that the slight motivated him to try and
unseat Johnson three years later, a charge which spoke volumes about how
McCarthy's peers viewed him.[2]

McCarthy was a jumble of contradictions and conflicting impulses. The
New York Times dubbed him "a political-scholar gypsy," and said he was as
likely to be found reading Yeats as the Congressional Record. Yet while
McCarthy resisted the pull of politics, he also made it his life's work—and
he hardly lacked ambition or self-confidence. "I'm twice as liberal as
Humphrey, twice as Catholic as Kennedy and twice as smart as [Stuart]
Symington [the Democrat senator from Missouri]," a Time reporter once
overhead him say.[3]

Restraint, composure, and a belief in reasoned discourse defined his
core political philosophy. It led him to adhere to a remarkably hidebound
view of the institutions of American democracy. In his book Frontiers in
American Democracy, published in 1960, he wrote, "Change does not necessarily
call for radical revision of philosophy and theology or for total recasting of
social, economic and political organization and procedure. It demands only
attentive re-examination of accepted beliefs, practices and institutions and
adjustment or accommodation where necessary." McCarthy would have been
happy debating his way into the White House, rather than actively campaigning for it (even though he was an unusually good retail politician).
Perhaps unsurprisingly, the news media viewed him as the stolid and conservative Democratic candidate in 1968.[4]

Such perceptions, however, are belied by the substance of his quixotic
presidential campaign, namely a set of policy proposals that would have
dramatically reshaped American foreign policy and involved the federal government more deeply in social transformation than anything even Johnson
contemplated. While McCarthy might have appeared to be philosophically
resistant to the so-called New Politics of the late 1960s, which called for

new voices and new ideas to be integrated into the political process, he would energize a generation of antiwar activists to change the country's political status quo. He seems even today to be the least imaginable person to launch an insurgent intraparty campaign, topple a sitting president, and spark a year of unparalleled political change.

The war in Vietnam would spur McCarthy from senatorial slumber to action. The country, he warned, risked moving toward what he called a "kind of dictatorship on foreign policy" because of Vietnam, and he believed that this risk demanded a political response. McCarthy's decision to take on Johnson in 1968, however, did not reflect a desire to win the White House. If anything, in his criticism of Johnson's personalization of the presidency (Johnson's recurrent references to "his helicopters" and "his boys" fighting in Vietnam), McCarthy ran *against* the office he was seeking and the imperial aura that had developed around it. When McCarthy announced his candidacy in the fall of 1967, he didn't even say that he sought to win the White House—a feat which, at that point, no one would have deemed even slightly plausible—but instead argued that there must be a way for those opposed to the war to have their voices heard within the political process. By taking on Johnson, McCarthy provided that outlet, and his decision to do so, with no real hope of victory, ended up being the most transformative event of the 1968 election.[5]

By refusing to shift from his middle course on Vietnam, Johnson laid the groundwork for the challenge that would upend his presidency. But McCarthy set that process in motion. "We should expect politicians, if the issue is important enough, ... to understand the obligation to take political risks when necessary," he later wrote in a memoir of the '68 campaign. For all his personal and political shortcomings—many of which would become evident over the next year—Gene McCarthy remained true to these words.[6]

From March 12, 1947, when President Harry Truman told a joint session of Congress that it "must be the policy of the United States to support free peoples who are resisting attempted subjugation," until November 30, 1967, when Eugene McCarthy announced his intention to run against Lyndon Johnson in four Democratic presidential primaries, the United

States possessed a basic civic religion when it came to America's role in the world. It was the abiding belief that the United States had a solemn responsibility to serve as the standard-bearer of global freedom and the scourge of global Communism. For the first two decades of his political career McCarthy remained a faithful devotee.[7]

Like virtually all Democrats who came of political age in the 1950s and 1960s, McCarthy largely embraced the bipartisan Cold War consensus of aggressive anti-Communism and confrontation with the Soviet Union. The threat from the Soviets was real, but there was a more essential rationale for vigilance. Quite simply, it was smart politics. Truman's portrayal of Communism as an existential threat to American security—and the need to confront Soviet expansionism—united both Democrats and Republicans and created a clear political narrative for US foreign policy during the Cold War. The Joe McCarthy–led anti-Communist witch-hunts of the early 1950s—and the accompanying charge that Truman and his party cohorts bore responsibility for "losing China" to the Reds—chilled any inclination to challenge the emerging conventional wisdom.

The experience of Helen Gahagan Douglas, a California Democratic congresswoman, offers an instructive case study. Douglas publicly argued that the "irrational fear of Communism" was being used as a political tool to "blind us to our real problems," and she pushed back against the idea that it represented a clear and present danger to the United States. When she ran for Senate in 1950, this questioning of the emerging Cold War consensus became her political downfall. Douglas's opponent, Richard Nixon, a young Republican congressman, branded her the "Pink Lady," accusing her of Communist sympathy all the way down to her "pink underwear." He taunted her for being soft on Communism and intimated that she worked in league with other "fellow travelers." On Election Day she would be humiliated, losing the race by nearly 20 points. Other vicious and scurrilous Republican campaigns branding Democrats as Communist sympathizers and socialists would knock off the Senate majority leader Scott Lucas of Illinois and Democrats in Maryland, Utah, and Washington.[8]

From that point forward few national leaders of either party or even major media figures were willing to question the basic premises of

US-Soviet rivalry and America's responsibility to fight and contain Communism around the world. If anything, politicians consistently sought to outdo one another in depicting the perils of the Red threat, preaching sacrifice in pursuit of national security or blasting their political opponents for insufficient fortitude. Many liberal Democrats, of course, sincerely—and quite legitimately—believed in the evils of Soviet power and the need for America to actively confront Communist expansion. But those who had doubts kept them to themselves.

McCarthy largely traveled with the herd. In August 1964, he joined eighty-seven of his Senate colleagues in voting for the Gulf of Tonkin Resolution, which gave Johnson virtually unfettered power to wage war in Southeast Asia. As US involvement in Vietnam began to escalate, McCarthy stayed on the sidelines. Through the entire year of 1965 he didn't speak once on the Senate floor about the war.[9]

Though McCarthy understood the essential politics of the Cold War, he was always not a true believer. While McCarthy said all the right things about confronting Communism, he showed philosophical resistance to a militarized approach to pursuing American interests. In both the House and the Senate he waged lonely (and unsuccessful) crusades to increase congressional oversight of the Central Intelligence Agency, which he claimed had "taken on the character of an invisible government answering only to itself." A forceful defender of Senate prerogatives, he also believed that Congress's foreign policy role must be strenuously defended. As early as 1960 he expressed fears about what he termed "the cult of the presidency." These concerns became the basis for his first, somewhat tepid, public dissent on Vietnam.[10]

In January 1966, McCarthy joined fourteen other senators in co-signing a letter to Johnson publicly calling on him to prolong a moratorium on the bombing of North Vietnam that had been imposed the previous month. Johnson's reply infuriated McCarthy. In a slight to the more senior legislative body, Johnson responded with a letter he had recently dispatched to the House of Representatives regarding the war. Particularly galling was inclusion in the missive of a reference to the Gulf of Tonkin Resolution, which implied that Johnson had received a congressional permission slip on Vietnam and could do as he pleased. As McCarthy later noted in his memoirs, "Johnson's actions could only be interpreted as a slap at the Senate."[11]

Stung by the incident, McCarthy went to the Senate floor to voice his concerns. His remarks offered a preview of the themes that would define his campaign for the presidency. McCarthy argued that restarting the bombing would do little to further America's military or political goals in Vietnam. But he went a step further, asserting that the country had reached "a proper point for the beginning of a much deeper and more extensive discussion not only of Vietnam, but also of the whole function of America in history during this second half of the twentieth century.... It calls for a national debate, a national discussion and a real searching of the mind and soul of America."[12]

Days later, Johnson phoned McCarthy and offered to send General Maxwell Taylor to brief the senator on the situation in Vietnam. "If you had the information I had," said Johnson, "you might be ... relieved somewhat." Johnson, however, had little interest in hearing McCarthy's concerns. When he tried to reassure the president that he didn't have to worry about fighting with him over the war, Johnson loudly interrupted. "Oh hell, you don't have any idea what it costs us," he said, and then suggested that McCarthy's letter "cost me more than fifty planes shot down." In a more than ten-minute phone call McCarthy barely got more than a few words in amid Johnson's complaints that the constant criticism of the war effort from Congress and the *New York Times* provided assistance to the enemy.[13]

At the same moment that McCarthy first voiced opposition to Johnson's Vietnam policy, the Senate Foreign Relations Committee, of which he was a junior member, began pushing ahead with a broad examination of the administration's policies in Vietnam. The committee's nationally televised hearings featured prominent critics of the war, who also happened to be principled anti-Communists. They included the international relations theorist Hans Morgenthau, former army general James Gavin, and George Kennan, the author of the containment doctrine, who said that the US military presence in Vietnam increased the potential for conflict with China. Kennan argued the United States had few security interests in Southeast

Asia, and that the war had become a distraction from more pressing international concerns and needed to be wound down as quickly as possible. The hearings legitimized criticism of the war. For long-haired protestors to deride US policy in Vietnam was one thing; for members of the foreign policy establishment to make the same critique was something else altogether. Almost overnight, support for Johnson's handling of Vietnam dropped by fourteen points.[14]

The man behind the congressional inquiry, Arkansas senator William Fulbright, had increasingly become one of Washington's most vocal and prominent critics of the war. Like most Democrats, Fulbright had long been a firm supporter of the Cold War consensus. When asked by Johnson in August 1964 to shepherd the Tonkin resolution through the Senate, he embraced the task (an act he would later come to view with shame). Yet Fulbright possessed a more nuanced view on American foreign policy than his commander in chief. He warned in March 1964 against falling prey to the "master myth of the Cold War," namely, that the "Communist bloc is a monolith" made up of countries "all equally resolute and implacable in their determination to destroy the free world." Fulbright argued that victory in the Cold War or a near-term end to ideological competition was unlikely to be achieved.[15]

In April 1965, Fulbright's relationship with the president suffered an irreparable break when he lambasted Johnson for his evasions and misstatements about the invasion of the Dominican Republic. In Johnson's mind, criticisms of the war, or any other administration policy, were not a matter of reasonable differences of opinion; they were examples of treachery and betrayal. Sympathetic senators, lined up by the White House, openly accused Fulbright of being hoodwinked by the Communists. Invitations to White House state dinners were rescinded, requests to fly overseas denied. The reaction to Fulbright's criticism, wrote columnist Joseph Kraft, "was not unlike the stoning reserved by the high priests of primitive communities for those who question the efficacy of blood sacrifice."[16]

Few stood up for Fulbright. But McCarthy did. He took to the Senate floor—in his first real break with the White House—to defend both Fulbright and the role of Congress in setting foreign policy priorities. "Our function in the Senate is not merely to find out what the administration policy is and then say yes or no to it—and often times too late," said McCarthy.[17]

Fulbright followed up his hearings on Vietnam with a series of lectures at Johns Hopkins University that later became a best-selling book, *The Arrogance of Power*. In it Fulbright argued that the war in Vietnam had become a tragic symbol of a larger, flawed assumption of US power and influence on the global stage and a dangerous belief in the unquestioned rightness of American actions.

This line of argument began to inform McCarthy's own foreign policy thinking, which had started off primarily as a defense of congressional prerogatives and evolved into a more thoughtful critique of US Cold War policy. In 1967, he published a slim volume on the subject entitled *The Limits of Power*. In it he argued that American foreign obligations had become practically "unlimited," and he called for a reassessment of burden sharing among allies and a more selective response to global crises. "America's contribution to world civilization," he wrote, "must be more than a continuous performance demonstration that we can police the planet." While the book broke little new ground, its significance lay in McCarthy's willingness to publicly voice such concerns.[18]

The book's publication came at a precipitous moment; McCarthy's growing alienation from conventional foreign policy wisdom—and his disagreements with the White House—had brought him to a breaking point. At a Senate Foreign Relations Committee hearing in August, McCarthy listened in anger as Deputy Secretary of State Nicholas Katzenbach told the assembled members that there were basically no restrictions on the president's actions in pursuit of American objectives in Vietnam. When asked about the lack of a formal declaration of war, Katzenbach replied that the formality had "become outmoded in the international arena" and added that the Tonkin resolution essentially gave the president a free hand to do as he saw fit in Southeast Asia. "What could a declaration of war have done that would have given the President more authority and clearer voice of the Congress of the United States than that Resolution?" Katzenbach asked. McCarthy stepped out of the room and began pacing in the hallway. When reporters caught up to him, he unloaded, "This is the wildest testimony I've ever heard. There is no limit to what he says the President can do. There is only one thing to do—take it to the country."[19]

McCarthy spoke later of the lasting impact that Katzenbach's testimony had on his decision to challenge Johnson. "I concluded that if this was really the judgment of the president, then in a way the engagement in Vietnam was secondary and that more important than that was the conception of the role of the presidency in the field of foreign policy.…I didn't decide then that I should run, but I think I decided that there had to be some kind of showdown challenge to that point of view." For McCarthy, Vietnam did not represent the root of his disagreements with Johnson; instead, the war was symptomatic of a much larger affliction in America's approach to world affairs.[20]

If McCarthy were truly intent on challenging Johnson, a key question remained: How could he take on a sitting president of his own party without a political organization or the campaign infrastructure necessary to back up the effort? At that moment, a charismatic thirty-eight-year-old political activist from New York named Allard Lowenstein sought to answer exactly that question. Beginning in the spring of 1967, Lowenstein made it his mission to bring down Johnson, which seemed at the time like the most "far out" notion imaginable. Nonetheless Lowenstein's effort followed a clear logic: "When a President is both wrong and unpopular, to refuse to oppose him is both a moral abdication and a political stupidity," he said. The sentiment summed up well Lowenstein's cross-cutting traits—a burning sense of purpose combined with the pragmatism of a political organizer.[21]

Lowenstein cultivated a following of like-minded liberals who saw the political process, not demonstrations, as the best path for ending the war. They raised money from liberal antiwar donors, secured endorsements from Democrats fed up with the war, built an infrastructure of activists committed to toppling Johnson, and in short time became a force to be reckoned with inside the party. The next step, however, would be the hardest: finding a candidate willing to take up the mantle against Johnson. Lowenstein's first choice, not surprisingly, was Bobby Kennedy, who quickly turned him down. He approached John Kenneth Galbraith, who expressed interest but noted that as a Canadian-born citizen he would be constitutionally prohibited from running. Next he spoke with Congressman Don Edwards of California and Senator Frank Church from Idaho. Both said no. Then he met with General Gavin, who said he would only run as a Republican. Finally, he reached out to South Dakota senator George McGovern, the first person to show real interest. But with his re-election looming in November 1968, McGovern didn't believe he could take the political risk of challenging Johnson. "Have you talked to Gene yet?" McGovern asked Lowenstein. "I know he's feeling very frustrated about the war."[22]

By this point McCarthy had been speaking publicly about Vietnam for several months. Letters, phone calls, and messages encouraging him to run had been pouring into his Senate office at a regular clip. Throughout the fall of 1967 signs reading "Peace with McCarthy" or "We Want Gene" greeted him at public events. Young activists began wearing buttons from his '64 Senate campaign with the word "President" pasted over "Senator." At home, his daughter Mary, then a student at Radcliffe, became one of the most influential voices calling on him to run. But McCarthy preferred that someone else take on Johnson (like Lowenstein, his first choice was Robert Kennedy). When finally approached by Lowenstein, he reacted coyly. But he also asked a host of technical questions about how the campaign might be assembled and what would be required to get things off the ground. Lowenstein had good answers for the prospective candidate: by the end of November 1967, there would be roughly thirty state chapters, all prepared to take the baton once a candidate entered the race.[23]

In late October McCarthy traveled to Los Angeles to meet with a San Francisco attorney named Gerald Hill, chairman of the liberal California Democratic Council and an early Lowenstein backer. The council wanted to run a slate of anti-Johnson delegates in the June California primary and sought a candidate to lead the effort. While the group reached out to many of the same individuals Lowenstein lobbied, only the Minnesota senator responded. After discussing the details of a potential run with Hill and Lowenstein, McCarthy stood up and told the group, "You guys have been talking about three or four names. I think you can cut the list down to one now."[24]

Whatever finally convinced him—his growing outrage over the war, Johnson's cavalier and dismissive attitude toward Congress, "maybe boredom," as he suggested after the campaign, or perhaps the fact that no one else bothered to take up the torch—on November 30, 1967, McCarthy stood before a row of microphones in the Senate Caucus Room to announce that he would be entering four presidential primaries in 1968. McCarthy described his decision to run against the president as the only appropriate response to Johnson's "evident intention to escalate and to intensify the war in Vietnam" and his apparent refusal to consider a negotiated end to the war. The administration, he asserted, "seems to have set no limit to the price which it is willing to pay for a military victory," even if it meant higher inflation at home, less money for "national needs" like housing and education, and a "deepening moral crisis in America."[25]

McCarthy offered his candidacy as a political outlet for Americans sick of the war and dismayed with Johnson's leadership. His challenge, he hoped, could alleviate the country's "sense of political helplessness" and restore "a belief in the processes of American politics and of American government." Giving opponents of the war a platform and allowing for "a politics of reason" (a favored phrase of McCarthy) remained perhaps the most essential component of his presidential campaign. Weeks earlier, in noting the "deep anxiety and alienation" among young people, clergymen, and intellectuals, he argued, "Someone must give these groups entrance back into the political process." According to McCarthy, he "might lose" but, he said, "By fighting within the political framework, we'll have reduced the alienation."[26]

While Fulbright had bravely questioned the country's foreign policy consensus from the Senate, McCarthy became the first presidential candidate to challenge it in the open forum of national politics. He refused to fall back on the typical campaign trail rhetoric of American exceptionalism. Instead, he openly questioned the notion of American virtue in global affairs. McCarthy's candidacy gave voice to those who questioned the role America played in the world as well as the nation's inflated conception of its national interests—a legacy that would live long past his short-lived presidential campaign, and would in time become a dominant foreign policy view inside the Democratic Party.

Walter Lippmann, whose columns highlighted his growing frustration about the war and with Johnson's leadership in particular, said McCarthy preserved the "deepest and most cherished values of American political life." The Minnesota senator upheld the notion that the American political system "is a valid way by which the mass of our people can redress their grievances, and express their will, and can participate in the government of the nation." Even Barry Goldwater had kind words for McCarthy. "If there had to be a Democratic president in 1969, I would pick McCarthy," said Goldwater, who appeared to believe that his colleague from Minnesota's "calm and reasonable way" masked a conservative heart.[27]

None of this, however, meant that political observers took McCarthy seriously. Reporters openly speculated that his candidacy was a stalking horse for Robert Kennedy. The candidate did himself no favors in that regard. "I would have been glad if he had moved early," said McCarthy at one point in the fall. "If he had, there'd have been no need for me to do anything."[28]

No major Democrat endorsed him. A *New York Times* reporter sent to cover the campaign had difficulty getting his articles published because his editors didn't consider McCarthy a viable candidate. McCarthy offered little help to the effort, as his initially desultory campaign events left even nominal allies in the liberal media deflated. The *New Republic* asked, "How is McCarthy doing? The answer—on which all reporters accompanying him agree—is, not too well." He would step on his applause lines, engage in moral reasoning rather than politicking, and leave his listeners emotionally limp, and he often didn't even bother to bring his speeches to a climax, instead allowing them to "trail off and stop when he thinks he has talked enough." Writing in the left-wing magazine *Ramparts*, the journalist Andrew Kopkind complained, "His campaign for the Democratic presidential nomination has had its occasional moments of exuberance, but mostly it has been flat, tasteless and strangely out of context with the crisis of its time."[29]

LBJ aides confidently boasted to reporters that "McCarthy won't be much tougher than a Dr. Spock–Martin Luther King peacenik candidacy." By the beginning of 1968 the words of McCarthy's fellow Minnesotan Orville Freeman, the secretary of agriculture, seemed prophetic. His campaign, said Freeman, "will be a very small footnote, if a footnote at all, in history."[30]

4

The (Un)happy Warrior

When Hubert Humphrey became vice president of the United States on January 20, 1965, he understood all too well the idiosyncrasies and petty cruelties of the man who had become his boss. For sixteen years Humphrey had served alongside Lyndon Johnson in the United States Senate and had seen firsthand the brutally effective manner in which he corralled his fellow legislators in pursuit of his legislative goals. While Johnson repulsed many of his liberal colleagues, Humphrey found the majority leader's encyclopedic knowledge of the Senate and mastery of legislative politics beguiling. "It was like sitting at the feet of a giant," said Humphrey of the political education he received from Johnson. He "knew how to woo people," who to "push aside," who to threaten, and who to "nourish along." Watching him work, said Humphrey, was like seeing "a cowboy making love."[1]

On the surface Johnson and Humphrey seemed like polar opposites. Intensely persuasive and profane, Johnson possessed a fierce energy that drove his obsessive pursuit of political power. He didn't care for movies, books, sports, or, as his speechwriter Harry McPherson put it, "anything that would connect with the curiosities and pastimes of private citizens." Only the world of American politics gave him sustenance. Humphrey, who could be gregarious to the point of grating, had earned the nickname in the US Senate of "Happy Warrior" for his unshakable optimism, sunny disposition, and dogged pursuit of a host of liberal priorities. Humphrey, wrote one observer, liked people the way an alcoholic likes booze.[2]

Yet despite their many outward differences, these men shared two important similarities—a desire to extend the bounty of the New Deal to all Americans and the ambition to be the president responsible for such an achievement. In pursuit of these goals the Senate majority leader came to see his colleague from Minnesota as a bridge to other northern liberals. For the idealistic Minnesotan, his nominal Senate boss served as a benefactor and mentor in the ways of Washington dealmaking.

Humphrey also viewed Johnson as a friend, someone with whom he shared not just a connection of tactical convenience but also one of personal affinity. Even after leaving the White House, Humphrey maintained a rosy assessment of his rapport with Johnson. "I think it's fair to say that he liked me as an individual, as a human being.... And he always showed a great deal of friendship towards me—a warmth," Humphrey recounted in 1971.[3]

When Humphrey entered the Johnson administration, he believed that while his responsibilities had changed, his relationship with the president would remain as collegial as it had been in the Senate. "My vice presidency is going to be more than just four years of mothballs and doldrums," he told friends. He believed his "honest, reasoned opinion could only help" Johnson and his agenda. After all, LBJ had told Humphrey upon selecting him as his running mate, "I want you to feel that you can confide in me and I want to be able to confide in you." In the first week of February 1965 Humphrey would put these words to the test. The experience would teach him a painful lesson about the limitations of the position to which he had ascended, and a deeper understanding of the true nature of the man who held the nation's highest office.[4]

The issue on which the Johnson-Humphrey team (as Humphrey was prone to call their administration, though Johnson less so) would split would be the same one that would fatally divide the Democratic Party over the next four years—Vietnam.

Since the 1950s the United States had been supporting the government in South Vietnam with both political and military assistance in its war against Vietcong insurgents supported by Communist North Vietnam. The issue of direct US military involvement, however, remained an open question—and one that Johnson, since taking office in November 1963, had consistently downplayed to the public. On January 27, 1965—only a week after his second inauguration—a moment of decision arrived. National Security Advisor McGeorge Bundy told Johnson (in a view shared by McNamara) that current US policy in Vietnam "can lead only to disastrous defeat." The president had to choose, Bundy wrote, between two alternatives: "To use our military power in the Far East and to force a change in Communist policy" or "deploy all our resources along a track of negotiation, aimed at salvaging what little can be preserved with no major addition to our present military risks."[5]

Both Bundy and McNamara clearly favored the former course—as did Johnson. He responded to what became known as the "Fork in the Y" memo with the declaration that "stable government or no stable government, we'll do what we ought to do. We will move strongly." Johnson's quick decision to ramp up the US role would have come as a surprise to the millions of Americans who had voted that past November for a presidential candidate who pledged at the tail end of the campaign that he would not "send American boys nine to ten thousand miles away...to do what Asian boys ought to be doing for themselves." For those inside the government Johnson's decision came as much less of a shock. Direct American involvement in the war in Vietnam represented the logical culmination of more than fourteen months of internal White House deliberations that, Johnson's public statements notwithstanding, had pointed unswervingly in one direction: toward the Americanization of the war and the dispatching of combat troops to Southeast Asia.[6]

With the wheels set in motion for escalation, the dependents of US personnel already stationed in South Vietnam were quickly ordered home. Naval operations began off the coast of North Vietnam with the objective of baiting Hanoi into an attack. On February 7, 1965, the Communists obliged. A company of Vietcong guerrillas bearing small arms and mortars assaulted an American helicopter base near the town of Pleiku in Vietnam's central highlands. Nine Americans were killed and more than 140 were wounded. This constituted the worst attack against a US target in the war up to that point, but also fit a regular pattern of Communist raids on US and South Vietnamese targets in the winter of 1965. The difference this time was that the administration now had the "opportunity to put into a motion a policy which they had already decided upon," wrote Chester Cooper, a close aide to Bundy and member of the National Security Council. Within fourteen hours of the attack, American planes were over the skies of North Vietnam hitting suspected guerrilla targets.[7]

Back in Washington, Johnson found little opposition within his inner circle to a military response. Several days later, however, when the Vietcong raided a US base in the Vietnamese city of Qui Nhon, Humphrey sounded a discordant note. He warned against what he called a "dangerous escalation" in Vietnam, particularly since Soviet Premier Alexei Kosygin happened to be visiting North Vietnam just then. Johnson ignored the advice, but Humphrey persisted. He reached out to Rusk and McNamara to enlist their support. Both men shared Humphrey's concerns about Kosygin's presence in Hanoi but held their tongues in an Oval Office meeting with Johnson, leaving the vice president abandoned. (Humphrey would privately complain two years later, "If only a few of those men would have stood with me that day—especially McNamara—this war wouldn't be the disaster it is.")[8]

For those familiar with Humphrey's public statements about the war, his lack of ardor for a sustained military response should not have come as a major surprise. Humphrey was a hawkish anti-Communist. But on Vietnam—and in particular major US military involvement—he, like many Democratic senators at the time, drew a line. In a memo to Johnson in June 1964, then-Senator Humphrey told the president that while he hoped "for an independent and free Southeast Asia" and believed that the United States had a role to play in guiding the South Vietnamese effort, "it is they (not we) who must win their war."[9]

In a speech in Los Angeles in August 1964, only two weeks after the Gulf of Tonkin Resolution, Humphrey called for staying in Vietnam "until the security of the South Vietnamese people has been established," while at the same time arguing against any "attempt to take over the war from the Vietnamese." Humphrey demonstrated a notable willingness, at least initially, to take a less than vigilant approach to stopping Communism in Southeast Asia. Then again, having not been privy to White House discussions that predated his becoming vice president, Humphrey took a position on the war that appeared to be very much in line with the president's own publicly stated views.[10]

In adopting such a contrarian stance after becoming vice president Humphrey misjudged his standing with Johnson. But his refusal to leave well enough alone did far greater damage. Humphrey's initial dissension had left him out of the direct decision-making over Vietnam, but his long-time aide Thomas Hughes, then serving as the director of the Bureau of Intelligence and Research at the State Department, kept him in the loop. On February 13, Hughes called Humphrey and told him that "the die was cast," and that if he wanted to dissuade the president from escalating in Vietnam, he would need to weigh in immediately. The two men huddled together over the latest intelligence reporting and composed a nearly 1,700-word memo to Johnson arguing against Americanizing the conflict in the only terms Humphrey believed he could use to communicate with LBJ—the politics of Vietnam.[11]

The Humphrey memo is a remarkable historical document. It offers a window into the vice president's keen grasp of national politics, but also a glimpse of the path that could have been taken on Vietnam. The president had just won in a massive landslide, Humphrey wrote, and on a policy of "firmness in the face of Communist pressure but restraint in the use of military force." This stood in stark opposition to the position of Goldwater and the Republicans who "favored a quick, total military solution in Vietnam, to be achieved through military escalation of the war." This contrast resonated with voters, because Democrats had traditionally been seen as the party able to "obtain the best possible settlement without provoking a nuclear World War III." So why throw that political advantage away by beginning a bombing campaign and, in effect, adopting the Goldwater position on Vietnam once safely ensconced in office?[12]

According to Humphrey, foreign wars had to be "politically understandable" to the American public. This had been the case in the first two world wars and to a lesser extent Korea (although as Humphrey pointed out, even public support for that conflict had been difficult to sustain). With Vietnam the case would be much more difficult to make, because it relied on "the simple argument of our 'national interest,'" a notion that Humphrey said would not be "interesting enough at home or abroad to generate support." Making matters worse, the United States risked allying itself with a government in South Vietnam that seemed "totally unable to put its own house in order." In Humphrey's view, the tactics likely to be utilized by American forces, "sustained, large-scale U.S. air bombardments across a border as a response to camouflaged, often non-sensational, elusive, small-scale terror," would be "hard to justify over a long period of time."[13]

Beyond what Humphrey called the limited chances of success in Vietnam lay the broader potential fallout from escalation. It would undermine US relations with key European allies and "progress toward détente with the Soviet bloc," while encouraging Moscow and Beijing to end their political disagreements and come together in opposition to US policy. Worst of all, Humphrey said, "It would tend to shift the Administration's emphasis from its Great Society oriented programs to further military outlays" and risk damaging both "the image of the President ... and that of the United States."[14]

Humphrey even noted that the administration's political problems would be more likely to come from "new and different sources" (including "Democratic liberals," "Church groups," "independents," and labor) rather than hawkish Republicans. While it was politically difficult "to cut losses," Humphrey wrote that the Johnson administration was "in a stronger position to do so than any Administration in this century." Humphrey described 1965 as "the year of minimum political risk"—the first and probably last time Johnson could face the "Vietnam problem without being preoccupied with the political repercussions from the Republican right." Continuing down the road for full-scale military intervention would, Humphrey said, make the White House look like a "prisoner of events in Vietnam."[15]

Decades later, the memo is prophetic. Johnson is today generally considered to be a political wizard, but Humphrey's analysis suggests he possessed the sharper political antenna. While Johnson liked to say that Humphrey had "all heart and no balls," in his call to cut bait on South Vietnam, abandon the US commitment to Saigon, and risk provoking the wrath of hawkish Republicans, Humphrey showed himself to be the far more unsentimental of the two men.[16]

The vice president's apostasy, not surprisingly, incensed LBJ. "We don't need all these memos," he derisively told the vice president. Humphrey had violated the cardinal code that governed the Johnson White House. "The President's rule," Marvin Watson, Johnson's chief of staff, later wrote, "was that although any of us were free to disagree with him, there were two caveats: our difference of opinion must remain private, and once the President reached a final decision, it was our obligation to support it and him—or resign." For Johnson, few personal attributes mattered more than loyalty and discretion, and already Humphrey violated both by showing initiative and gumption in ways that little interested the president.[17]

Johnson quickly and unceremoniously dispatched Humphrey to the presidential doghouse. He stripped him of the responsibilities he'd been granted to coordinate the administration's efforts on civil rights; his political allies were denied presidential appointments; and word quickly spread in the White House that Johnson had lost confidence in him. On Vietnam, Humphrey found himself frozen out completely. According to his top foreign policy aide, John Rielly, Humphrey was "kept out of all the important meetings to an unimaginable extent." "He just didn't appear anymore," said George Ball.[18]

In May 1965, while Johnson debated with his advisors on a naval blockade along the coast of Vietnam, Humphrey traveled to New York to be inducted into the Girl Scouts. "Just wait until I tell the President about this," Humphrey told his audience of now fellow scouts. In July, when Johnson's National Security Council met to discuss General William Westmoreland's request to more than double the number of troops in Vietnam, neither Humphrey nor an opposing point of view could be found.[19]

Chastened by the reaction to his February memo (he later wrote of it in his memoirs, with striking understatement, "I don't think it was very helpful"), Humphrey quickly came to understand that the man who had plucked him from the Senate and put him on a fast track to the presidency held him captive. No longer did Johnson need Humphrey to serve as his conduit to Senate liberals; now he just needed him to sit down, salute, and keep his mouth shut. There would be no room for independent thought for the four years—and maybe more—that he served under Johnson.

The Johnson White House, like all White Houses, expected the president's number two to demonstrate complete loyalty. But for Humphrey a more visceral motivation drove his deference to Johnson. Fourteen months before he had written his fateful Vietnam memo, and on the very day President Kennedy was laid to rest in Arlington National Cemetery, Humphrey deputized his close aide Max Kampelman to begin laying the groundwork for him to join LBJ on the presidential ticket in 1964. "I want to become president, and the only way I can is to become vice president," he told his staff. Humphrey quickly became the president's indispensable ally in the Senate, shepherding the civil rights bill across the legislative finish line while crisscrossing the country gathering political chits that would strengthen his ties to influential party figures. It helped smooth the path to Humphrey being selected as Johnson's running mate at the 1964 Democratic Convention in Atlantic City.[20]

After starting off his vice presidential tenure on such a sour note, Humphrey understood that he had to do everything in his power to quickly repair the damage and move past his disagreement over Vietnam. He soon became the president's point man on the Great Society, giving innumerable speeches and building public support for the ambitious project. Backing Johnson's domestic agenda could hardly be considered a difficult chore; after all, Humphrey was as much a liberal as Johnson. Still, he took to the task with an almost disquieting sense of devotion. A vice president, Humphrey said at one point, "must have a quality of fidelity, a willingness literally to give himself, to be what the President wants him to be, a loyal, faithful friend and servant." A mischievous letter writer to *Time* noted that this amounted to "a very good description of a dog." On Vietnam, Humphrey kept his lingering doubts tightly locked away. When asked by British prime minister Harold

Wilson for advice on how to get on Johnson's good side, Humphrey told him the best strategy would be to offer "unquestioned support" for the war.[21]

His newfound hawkishness on Vietnam emerged fully formed when, in February 1966, Johnson finally released Humphrey from his foreign policy exile. Johnson sent the vice president on a fourteen-day trip to Asia, including a stopover in Vietnam. In typical LBJ-style, where crude demonstrations of presidential control were considered effective management techniques, the president got word to Humphrey (who was traveling in the Midwest) that he would be needed the next day in Los Angeles. Johnson had just returned from meetings in Honolulu with South Vietnamese officials where an agreement had been reached to launch a Great Society for South Vietnam. He dispatched Humphrey to be the messenger.

Humphrey took to the job with his usual enthusiasm. "Bouncing kindergarten toddlers on his knee at Tanphu in Vietnam, exchanging the two-handed Thai greeting sign with a naked 2-year old in the rice paddy at Nong Khai, solemnly returning the Boy Scout salute to a grave-faced Wolf Patrol member in Saigon, lighting up the sad brown faces of the six little girls at the Bienhoa Provincial Hospital in Vietnam—in all these scenes Mr. Humphrey was the big, warm-hearted, smiling American of legend," wrote the *New York Times*.[22]

No issue animated Humphrey more than the nefariousness of the enemy. The Vietcong are not "the forces of freedom" he told reporters; "we are." For Humphrey the war offered a lesson in the "dramatized, concentrated example of what the Communists intend to do elsewhere.... [T]here is a master plan, a designed conspiracy." But his most indelible—and personally damaging—words came at the tail end of the trip, in New Zealand. Back in Washington, Robert Kennedy had taken to the Senate floor to call for a new coalition government in Saigon that would, if necessary, include the National Liberation Front, the political wing of the Vietcong. Humphrey ridiculed the idea. He said it would be like putting a "fox in the chicken coop." For many of his former liberal allies Humphrey's comments provided the most telling indication the vice president had been taken in by LBJ's dark side and now fully embraced the idea that there could be no solution to Vietnam other than a military one. Humphrey's old liberal ally Alfred Kazin put it best; the vice president had been afflicted by the "Hemingway syndrome: you can never be tough enough and you have to prove your masculinity."[23]

Not everyone, however, felt so dismayed. Upon returning home, Johnson gave Humphrey a public bear hug—an unmistakable sign that his star was no longer in descent inside the administration. Humphrey, said *Time*, had become the White House's "most articulate and indefatigable exponent of U.S. Asian policy." He had bent almost completely backward to return to Johnson's good graces. "Instead of supporting the President 100 percent, he did it 200 percent," said Rielly. "He was now more for Johnson's policies than Johnson."[24]

At a Jefferson-Jackson dinner in Minnesota, Humphrey accused those who opposed US war aims of saying that "we are able to keep our commitments to white people, not to brown people and yellow people." He evoked the specter of "Hitler in the Rhineland," warning that in Vietnam "you do not satisfy the appetites of an aggressor by handing him pieces of territory." In April 1966 reporter Eric Sevareid asked him if the relationship between the United States and Asia could be seen as "fundamental" and "as long-lasting, intimate and possibly expensive" as America's historic alliance with Europe. "I think so," replied Humphrey, in a comment that left political observers (and Sevareid) stunned and White House officials "surprised." Even Johnson supporters increasingly saw Humphrey's over-the-top rhetoric as an embarrassment. An *Esquire* profile in the fall of 1966, which pictured Humphrey as a ventriloquist's dummy on Johnson's knee, criticized him for making the war "and the problems in Asia sound no more morally complex than whether or not we should ship surplus grain to India."[25]

How could Humphrey have argued that the United States should "cut losses" in Vietnam, as he did in his 1965 memo, and just a year later compare Ho Chi Minh to Hitler? Perhaps in the interim the vice president had become a true believer on Vietnam. The more logical explanation, however, is that he came to believe that being a strong public supporter of the war—and an unfaltering endorser of the president's policies—was a better political position than contrarianism.[26]

Humphrey's abrupt conversion on Vietnam did not come as a surprise to those who had long followed his career. It would not have been the first time he had embraced an aggressive and hawkish policy position—and one that also happened to bring with it significant political and personal benefit. Humphrey, like many liberal Democrats, embraced the mantle of anti-Communism. He helped to found the ADA (Americans for Democratic Action) in 1947, which became one of the loudest voices on the left warning that Communism was inimical to progressive values. Still, Humphrey approached the issue with particular intensity. As mayor of Minneapolis, he ruthlessly purged the state's Farmer-Labor Party of Communist influence with tactics that verged on McCarthyism, including blacklisting and even police intimidation. While unsavory, these efforts helped pave the way for his political rise. In 1952, as a US senator, he conducted a shallow and largely ineffective investigation into Communist involvement in American labor. While publicly critical of the bullying tactics of Joe McCarthy, Humphrey rarely spoke up in the Senate or defended those whom the Wisconsin senator targeted with charges of disloyalty and Communist sympathy. An early biographer of Humphrey claimed that he was "probably torn more by the conflicting forces of the McCarthy era than most politicians." Still, he kept quiet.[27]

If anything, his public actions continued to move in a very different direction. Only months before the 1954 midterm elections, Humphrey introduced legislation in the Senate declaring the Communist Party of the United States an "instrument of a conspiracy to overthrow the government," thus making membership in its ranks illegal. Humphrey's move represented a political gambit to protect vulnerable liberal Democrats from charges of insufficient anti-Communism. The final bill would be so watered down that when it was signed into law by President Eisenhower, its effectiveness as an anti-Communist tool was in serious doubt. Still, the move paid major dividends in protecting vulnerable Democrats up for re-election and insulating Humphrey against charges in his home state of Minnesota that he was a Communist "stooge." Yet while the legislation may have been politically motivated, Humphrey made no effort to disavow the harshness of the measure or its actual intent. "These rats will not get out of the trap," he said of Communist Party members in the United States. Humphrey even dismissed the criticisms of civil libertarian groups. "I anticipated some of the rather emotional reaction from the liberal community because I was hitting somewhat of a sacred cow," he privately told a friend at the time.[28]

Humphrey's hometown paper, the *Minneapolis Star*, bemoaned the "strange political season...when 'liberal' politicians who have heretofore vociferously denounced McCarthyism now attempt to out-McCarthy McCarthy." A friend of Humphrey would say of the bill that it "was the only time I was ever ashamed of Hubert." Years later, Humphrey admitted the measure was "not one of the things I'm proudest of." At the time, however, Humphrey's actions reflected a dominant view among Democrats that tough anti-Communism was an essential bulwark against the worst excesses of McCarthyism—and the path of least political resistance. It would prove to be a difficult lesson for Humphrey to unlearn.[29]

"As could be said of most politicians, it would be hard to argue that Humphrey ever staked out a position that wasn't motivated in part by his political ambitions," says his close confidante Thomas Hughes, who had known Humphrey since the 1940s. At the 1948 Democratic National Convention Humphrey delivered a historic address urging Democrats to walk in the "bright sunshine of human rights" when it came to civil rights and reject the southern segregationists in their midst. The moment turned Humphrey into a national figure. Yet, in the spring of 1967, he literally put his arm around the shoulder of the state's Democratic governor, Lester Maddox, who had wielded a pickaxe handle to prevent blacks from being seated in his restaurant. Maddox, said Humphrey, remained "a good Democrat" who had shown a "constructive and reasonable attitude on many problems."[30]

In January 1968 Robert Sherrill and Harry W. Ernst, two writers for the left-wing magazine *The Nation*, published a polemic on Humphrey entitled *The Drugstore Liberal*, which argued that Humphrey was nothing more than a political opportunist whose beliefs were at best "casual." At the same time, there is no questioning the fact that a fervent desire to do good drove Humphrey's political career. In an unpublished interview in the summer of 1968, he said of his passion for public service, "My father felt that if you cared about people you must be prepared to involve yourself in political action.... It sounds corny, and it's been said many times before, but the truth is that I went into politics because I like people and because I thought society could be altered so that people could get a good deal instead of a bad deal." Here lies the source of Humphrey's ardent support for organized labor, civil rights, foreign assistance, and even global nonproliferation. "When I see things that need to be done, I want to get at them. It bothers me when something isn't being done about a problem or need."[31]

With that drive to do good came a style of politics that led Humphrey to make compromise after compromise, both personally and professionally. Upon his arrival on Capitol Hill in 1949 Humphrey played the role of the young rabble-rouser, introducing numerous reform measures and refusing to abide by the Senate's sclerotic traditions. But ostracization—in part from southern senators angered by his impassioned defense of civil rights—and failure to make much headway legislatively convinced him, in his words, to "stop kicking my foot against the wall." Thereafter, supplication rather than determined opposition became his response to political resistance. It bred his chronic earnestness and abiding, almost debilitating, belief that every person—and every audience—could be won over by the force of his words. "He wanted to please everyone," says Hughes, who adds, "As was once said of Theodore Roosevelt, 'He was not insincere. He believed it at the time he said it.'" When he spoke to a labor crowd, he was the best friend a union man could ever hope to have. If he spoke to a business crowd, well, no one stood up for entrepreneurs like Hubert Humphrey. If he talked to those suspicious of and uncomfortable about US policy in Vietnam, then, by gosh, Humphrey would convince them of the rightness of the war.[32]

This persistent congeniality also shaped Humphrey's relationship with the president. As someone so eager and anxious to please, Humphrey became easy pickings for a bully like Johnson, who preyed on such outward signs of weakness. While he served as vice president, there seemed to be no limits to what Humphrey would accept with a smile firmly fixed on his face—whether donning cowboy garb to go hunting with LBJ at his Texas ranch or being forced to humiliatingly recite his speeches in the middle of his living room when the president and his wife came over for dinner.[33]

Humphrey's desire to make a difference by becoming president led him to take an end-justifying-means approach to national politics—and on no issue more so than Vietnam. If "one wanted to do a study of what the war in Vietnam had done to a generation of older American liberals," wrote David Halberstam, "Humphrey would have been exhibit A." Humphrey's twenty-year struggle between doing what he believed to be right and doing what he believed to be politically advantageous was about to catch up to him.[34]

"The Most Misunderstood Man in American Public Life"

On January 31, 1968, as tens of thousands of Vietcong and North Vietnamese foot soldiers launched the surprise Tet offensive that would transform the war in Vietnam, Senator Robert Kennedy sat down in the private President's Room at the National Press Club with fifteen of the nation's most prominent political writers. The event, organized by Godfrey Sperling, of the *Christian Science Monitor*, represented a grand tradition in the clubby world of Washington politics: an opportunity for policymakers to unburden themselves, off-the-record, to members of the media.

The Kennedy breakfast quickly became one of the hottest tickets in town. There might finally be an answer to the question that had become the number one topic of practically every dinner party in Washington, DC, and the subject of miles of news copy: Would he take on Lyndon Johnson for the Democratic presidential nomination? Kennedy wasted little time in ending the suspense. He would not "under any conceivable circumstances" challenge Johnson, he told the reporters. (Hours afterward Kennedy's press secretary softened the statement to "under any foreseeable circumstances" to leave the door at least slightly ajar.)[1]

Still, Kennedy could not hide his deep dissatisfaction with Johnson, his frustration with the "unhappiness in the country," and his fatalistic belief that he was powerless to do anything about it. Said one of the reporters, "It was like seeing a man do battle with himself right there before your eyes." Sensing Kennedy's despair, the assembled journalists pushed him: "If you feel so strongly about some of these issues, why don't you take a stand and run despite the possibility of defeat?" Kennedy returned to the same explanation he had been privately offering for months to those urging him to take on LBJ: his entry into the race would divide the party and guarantee that a Republican would win the White House. "If I thought there was anything I could do about it, I would try to do something," said Kennedy.[2]

These are ironic words, coming from a man fond of echoing his brother's dictum that the hottest places in hell were reserved for those who in times of great moral crisis maintain their neutrality. Around the same time, Kennedy published a book of his speeches and writings entitled *To Seek a Newer World,* in which he wrote, "Moral courage is a rarer commodity than bravery in battle or great intelligence. Yet it is the one essential, vital quality for those who seek to change a world that yields most painfully to change." Clearly Kennedy could do *something* about the inevitability of Lyndon Johnson's renomination.[3]

Kennedy's growing anger over the war in Vietnam had led him, in early 1968, to the edge of a presidential run. Allard Lowenstein and his passionate young Senate staffers vigorously lobbied him, telling him that for the good of the country he must challenge Johnson. But he also heard from his seasoned advisors who in 1960 had supported his older brother when he leapfrogged ahead of the old Democratic guard, Humphrey, Johnson, Symington, and Adlai Stevenson, for the presidential nomination. By 1968, these men, battered by the traumatic events of the previous half-decade, soberly urged restraint. An unsuccessful run would doom his chances in 1972, they counseled. Kennedy heeded their advice, with the full knowledge that his refusal to get in the race would leave Johnson as the almost certain Democratic nominee.[4]

However, in a year when the political "no" repeatedly evolved into a political "yes," Kennedy, six weeks later, finally identified the "foreseeable circumstances" that would allow him to throw his hat in the ring. In his tortured decision to sit out '68 and his ensuing reversal, the two sides of Kennedy—the pragmatic politician and the true believer—would be brightly illuminated.

In the decades that followed, Robert Kennedy's 1968 presidential bid has taken on a mythical aura in American politics. Had Kennedy won the presidency, family confidante and Kennedy speechwriter Ted Sorensen claimed, "He would have brought black and white together," and America would have become a "different country." In an admiring 2008 book on Kennedy's '68 campaign Thurston Clarke called it "a template for how a candidate should run for the White House in a time of moral crisis." A closer look, however, reveals a wide gulf between the imagined Kennedy campaign and the one actually waged. Kennedy jumped in the race only after the political terrain in the Democratic Party had clearly shifted in a direction that favored his candidacy. Moreover, at a time when the more democratic and participatory "New Politics" of the era entranced liberals, Kennedy sought his party's nod by relying on tactics more reminiscent of "old politics."[5]

Equally broad was the gap in public attitudes toward Kennedy. He inspired both feverish adulation and profound loathing. In May 1967, a Gallup poll found that twice as many Americans felt an "intense dislike" of Kennedy than they did of Johnson. The more time he spent on the campaign trail in 1968, the more his public standing fell. His critics called him "cold, cynical, arrogant," and above all "ruthless," the one word that became predominant in his public persona. According to the novelist William Styron, "Unless you include the fact that he could put people off horribly…you're not going to get an honest picture." Yet at the same time Kennedy was also one of the most popular politicians in the country. Many of his colleagues and supporters described him as "warm," "witty," "shy," and "reflective." "Some saw him as a compassionate savior, some as ruthless opportunist, some as [an] irresponsible demagogue plucking at the exposed nerves of the American polity," wrote Arthur Schlesinger. Kennedy, said journalist Penn Kimball at the time, was perhaps "the most misunderstood man in American public life."[6]

Yet the affirming myths around Kennedy's candidacy in 1968 have endured—few more pervasive than the notion that his campaign devised a new liberal political coalition by melding together blacks and working-class whites. "We have to write off the unions and the South now, and to replace them with Negroes, blue-collar whites, and the kids....We have to convince the Negroes and the poor whites that they have common interests," he told newspaperman and close confidante Jack Newfield. But as would be evident in the campaign to come, Kennedy's focus on social justice and racial reconciliation held little appeal for traditional blue-collar Democrats. Rather than create an esprit de corps between the races, his close relationship to the black community turned many whites off. If anything, the 1968 campaign exacerbated the growing divide between working-class whites and blacks. In the years to follow, benefit would accrue not to those politicians who sought a Kennedy-style middle ground but rather to those most effective at further widening the gap between these two groups.[7]

Finally, there is the veneration that Kennedy enjoys among modern progressives and, in particular, the idea that his campaign energized a generation of liberal activists. There are surely many who viewed RFK's eighty-five-day run for the White House in inspirational terms. But in 1968 the antiwar organizers of the Democratic Party more readily migrated to McCarthy's upstart campaign. Even after Kennedy jumped in the race, few of McCarthy's college-aged supporters defected from the man who had convinced them that change could be achieved through the political system. In reality, Kennedy had a strained relationship with liberals, whom he considered unrealistic and too inclined to place political purity above political reality. To Kennedy and his staff, "the very word 'liberal'" became "a synonym for 'emotional,' 'doctrinaire' and, worse yet, 'ineffectual,'" wrote Kimball in a 1968 book on Kennedy's political appeal. "Middle class liberals baffle" him, said one of his aides. He viewed them as never "happier than when they are going down in certain defeat."[8]

If anything, Kennedy's ideological flexibility is what made him a uniquely compelling figure—and his untimely demise so particularly tragic. Rather than the embodiment of New Deal liberalism, Kennedy's politics represented a "third way" for Democrats, a generation before that term entered the party's lexicon. A blue collar–black coalition didn't exist in 1968, but the need to find a new political vocabulary for those who were being left behind (blacks, Hispanics, and the increasingly angry and anxious white lower class) could not have been more vitally important. Kennedy was ahead of his time in seeking to bridge this divide, even if he was an imperfect leader for such an effort. The hostility that existed between Kennedy and many in organized labor, for example, risked alienating the most mobilized and engaged constituency of any successful Democratic political coalition. Still, unlike other Democrats, he recognized that the party had to do a better job of responding to the larger political shifts taking place in American society, rather than simply falling back on familiar and increasingly tired liberal nostrums.

Indeed, it is nearly impossible to buttonhole Kennedy with static descriptions like "liberal," "moderate," or "conservative." He could be—and at various times was—all of the above. The saintly image of him created after his death is misleading as well (the paperback of Jack Newfield's 1969 biography of Kennedy, for example, shows the candidate in a contemplative moment perched under a picture of Jesus Christ). A politician he was, warts and all, even if he was capable of enormous courage in talking about the need for racial reconciliation. By the end of his life Kennedy found himself torn between two sometimes disparate impulses—a driving desire to win the presidency and an equally burning ambition to right the many injustices he believed plagued America.

On June 3, 1967, Robert Kennedy spoke at a packed Democratic fundraiser held at the Waldorf Astoria Hotel in New York City. His task that evening was to introduce the man who had succeeded his brother as president. As the state's junior senator and one of the nation's most prominent Democrats, Kennedy played the part of the loyal soldier. He hailed Lyndon Johnson for "the breadth of his achievements, the record of his past, the promises of his future." LBJ had "borne the burdens few other men have ever borne in the history of the world, without hope or desire or thought to escape them," said Kennedy. He pledged that a united Democratic Party would produce a victory in November 1968 on par with the one achieved four years earlier. The next day's *New York Times* ran a large picture of the two men standing next to each other, clad in tuxedos, with broad smiles on their faces. Yet only weeks earlier, in a conversation with Arthur Schlesinger, Kennedy revealed his true feelings about Johnson. He was a "crazy man," he said.[9]

This dichotomy between Kennedy's personal feelings and public statements about Johnson symbolized the political cross that he bore after the death of his brother. Robert Kennedy loathed Johnson. He hated his obsessive focus on politics and dealmaking. He hated his phoniness, his coarseness, and his deviousness. He came to abhor his stewardship of the war in Vietnam. Above all, he hated the fact that Johnson occupied his brother's seat in the White House. The feeling from Johnson was mutual. This fractured relationship bred constant speculation that Kennedy would challenge Johnson for the Democratic nomination in 1968. In fact, at the same time Kennedy sang the praises of Johnson at the Waldorf-Astoria, he was being publicly shamed by young antiwar activists, who held up signs at his public events that read "KENNEDY—HAWK, DOVE OR CHICKEN?" But Kennedy knew that even if he were successful in defeating Johnson in a primary fight—at best a long shot—it would tear the party apart. It would resuscitate the perennial charge that Kennedy was a hard and ruthless man, and he feared it would be "misinterpreted" as stemming from a vendetta against Johnson. "I can't do anything," he once complained to reporters, "without somebody questioning my motives."[10]

Kennedy's fears were not mere rationalizations. McCarthy might have been audacious enough to challenge Johnson, but as a Senate back-bencher with a low national profile and still able to joke, when he announced his candidacy, that he wasn't sure if he was engaging in "political suicide" or an "execution," he had less to lose. For Kennedy, the full weight of his political lineage made the risks that much greater. "If his name had been something else, I think Bobby Kennedy would have announced for President in 1967 and taken Johnson on without any question," said Kenny O'Donnell, a former JFK advisor and a close friend of his brother.[11]

The enmity between Johnson and Kennedy went back decades, but reached its height during the 1960 Democratic Convention when Jack

Kennedy offered Johnson the vice presidential slot, only to have "that little shitass"—as Johnson called Bobby—try and retract the offer hours later. In the White House, Kennedy, like many of JFK's advisors, saw Johnson as an unpleasant reminder of the grubbiness of the presidential campaign and a relic of Washington's sleepy past that had little place in Kennedy's Camelot. While the president went out of his way to soothe Johnson's ego, his brother made little effort to hide his disdain. He would barge in on their private Oval Office meetings and refuse even to acknowledge the vice president. He usurped the few meager responsibilities granted to Johnson, and stories of the vice president being mocked by partygoers at Kennedy's Hickory Hill estate would also end up being relayed to Johnson. All of it served to intensify LBJ's insecurity and distance from the White House.[12]

After the president's assassination in Dallas, the battle lines between the two men became even sharper. From each end of Pennsylvania Avenue, like boxers sizing up their opponents from across the ring, they kept close tabs on each other. Johnson feared that Kennedy would seek to reclaim his brother's office by challenging him for the Democratic presidential nomination. Kennedy, elected to the US Senate from New York in 1964—with Johnson's help—knew that any criticism of the president would result in screaming headlines and Washington melodramas. As a result, every public statement Kennedy made was carefully calibrated to avoid any intimation of a personal attack on Johnson.[13]

However, as Kennedy's frustration with Vietnam grew, it became increasingly difficult for him to hold his tongue. In February 1966, he offered his most provocative assessment yet of administration policy, floating the possibility of a coalition government in Saigon that would include the Vietcong. Kennedy and his speechwriters had labored over the words and, based on his own previous pronouncements about the war and even those of the Johnson administration, they believed his statement would spark little controversy.[14]

They were quickly disabused of this belief. "Ho Chi Kennedy!" newspaper headlines blared as reporters raced to cover the latest escalation in the Johnson/Kennedy feud. Chastened by the response, Kennedy kept quiet for the rest of the year, in part out of fear that if he spoke out more forcefully against the administration's prosecution of the war, it would harden the White House's resolve. Johnson, Kennedy complained to Newfield, "hates me so much that if I asked for snow, he would make rain." (McCarthy would ruefully note that he had made a similar proposal for a coalition government only weeks earlier and no one noticed.)[15]

However, as US involvement in the conflict continued to expand and opposition to the war grew within the Democratic Party, Kennedy found it impossible to remain on the sidelines. "The most powerful country the world has known now turns its strength and will upon a small and primitive land," he declared in a February 1967 speech from the Senate floor, "and still there is no peace." While Kennedy placed most of the blame on the North Vietnamese, he told his colleagues that they must look at themselves and America's role in "the unending crescendo of violence, hatred, and savage fury" being unleashed on the Vietnamese people. "It is we who live in abundance and send our young men out to die. It is our chemicals that scorch the children and our bombs that level the villages. We are all participants." Unsurprisingly, the chattering class portrayed the speech as a revival of the feud with Johnson. "Men at War" Newsweek blared, as reporters speculated that Kennedy's rhetorical broadside represented the first salvo in a bigger, perhaps more consequential fight to come.[16]

Already, "Citizens for Kennedy" groups, pushing the idea of a presidential run, began popping up around the country. Johnson's approval ratings were plummeting, and by the fall of 1967 head-to-head polls of Democrats showed Kennedy leading the president by a 52–32 margin. Behind closed doors, Kennedy's aides urged him to keep his options open. Joe Dolan, a staff member in RFK's Senate office, began compiling a list of filing dates for presidential primaries. Speechwriter Adam Walinsky sent Kennedy a series of memos with titles like "Gratuitous Advice Revisited," offering reasons for him to take on the "ignorant bully" in the White House.[17]

By the end of the year Kennedy agreed to a suggestion by Pierre Salinger, his brother's White House press secretary, to convene JFK's old allies for a strategy session. The usual suspects were in attendance—Sorensen, Schlesinger, Dick Goodwin, O'Donnell, and RFK's brother Teddy—but not Kennedy, who sought to preserve his "plausible deniability" should word of the meeting be leaked to the press. Besides a decision to conduct a poll in New Hampshire—and agreement among all assembled that Kennedy needed to get a haircut—nothing much was decided, except that support among Democrats for an RFK candidacy appeared to be tepid at best.[18]

After McCarthy's entry into the race, the group convened again in December. Kennedy was present this time, and while again little was decided, the battle lines had become clearer. Goodwin and Schlesinger strongly urged Kennedy to jump in; others like Sorensen and Teddy remained steadfastly opposed. Kennedy was torn. According to Salinger, he told the group, "It's not a question of my political future.... This country can't stand another four years of this man [Johnson]." Yet at the same time he reiterated his fear that a run would not only divide the party but do real damage to Democratic Senate doves who were up for re-election. But no argument resounded more loudly for Kennedy than the fact that getting in the race would likely be a pointless, unsuccessful effort. A November memo from Fred Dutton, a longtime, trusted political advisor to the Kennedys, suggested that challenging the president might be seen as an "act of conscience to some people," but nonetheless would likely be "political suicide."[19]

At the beginning of 1968 Kennedy traveled to California and met with Jesse Unruh, the powerful Speaker of the California State Assembly, who urged him to challenge Johnson and pledged his help in the state's Democratic primary. Kennedy also consulted with Walter Lippmann, who, while unwilling to offer direct advice, told him if he thought Johnson's re-election would be a "catastrophe" for the country, then the "question you must live with is whether you did everything you could to avert this catastrophe." Still, Kennedy resisted, telling friends and colleagues in early January that he would wait things out until 1972.[20]

At the end of the month, Kennedy sat down at the Sperling Breakfast at the National Press Club and made official his refusal to run. That at virtually the same moment the Vietcong launched the Tet Offensive made it seem as if the political gods had chosen the opportunity to mock Kennedy's vacillation. By closing the door on a run, RFK had made a tactical mistake, and he knew it. In the days afterward he moped in his office, refusing to return phone calls or answer his mail. A week later, in Chicago on a press tour for *To Seek a Newer World*, he unburdened himself, offering his most strident and stinging critique of the war: "Our enemy, savagely striking at will across all of South Vietnam, has finally shattered the mask of official illusion with which we have concealed our true circumstances." Kennedy argued that the country must "face the reality that a military victory is not in sight and that it probably will never come."[21]

The *New York Times* called Kennedy's speech "the most sweeping and detailed indictment of the war and of the Administration's policy yet heard from any leading figure in either party." The speech again raised an obvious question: How could he sit the '68 race out? His press aide Frank Mankiewicz told him pointedly, "I don't know how you can say those things about the major enterprise in which your country's engaged and then continue to support that leadership." Increasingly, Kennedy could muster no good answer.[22]

Robert Kennedy would not be the only person reassessing his position in the wake of Tet. Almost overnight, the North Vietnamese and Vietcong's risky military gambit had wiped away the two most powerful illusions about the war in Vietnam: that progress was being made in the war effort and that a military defeat of the enemy was still possible. Within twenty-four hours of the initial surprise attack, thirty-six of forty-four provincial capitals, five out of six major cities, and sixty-four district capitals in Vietnam were hit. In Saigon, enemy forces briefly overran the American embassy and attacked the presidential palace, the army general staff headquarters, and the national airport. North Vietnamese and Vietcong fighters even captured the imperial city of Hue and unleashed a bloody wave of massacres and reprisals against the civilian population.[23]

Yet the Communist offensive constituted a military failure. Its primary goal of sparking a nationwide revolt against the South Vietnamese government went unrealized. The Vietcong, in particular, suffered massive casualties, and within several days the US and South Vietnam forces recovered and were able to push the Communists back. Far more successful, however, was the offensive's secondary goal—to influence US public opinion. Photos from the initial wave of attacks—of dead American soldiers on the grounds of the US Embassy (as military policeman crouched nearby)—as well as the chilling video of a South Vietnamese general summarily executing a captured Vietcong guerrilla—would shake the American people like few other events in the three years of US escalation in Vietnam.[24]

Johnson initially called Tet a "complete failure" and claimed that "when the American people know the facts... [the Communists] will not achieve a psychological victory." McCarthy ridiculed Johnson's assertions. "If taking over a section of the American Embassy, a good part of Hue, Dalat and major cities of the Fourth Corps area constitutes complete failure, I suppose by this logic that if the Viet Cong captured the entire country, the Administration would be claiming their total collapse." Michigan governor and Republican presidential candidate George Romney chimed in as well. "If what we have seen in the past week is a Viet Cong failure, then I hope they never have a victory," he said.[25]

At CBS News headquarters in Midtown Manhattan, the network's news anchor, Walter Cronkite, expressed the sentiment of many Americans. "What the hell is going on? I thought we were winning the war!" A month later, Cronkite, after traveling to South Vietnam, delivered a nationally televised editorial eloquently declaring that the time had come to acknowledge a military stalemate in Vietnam and begin winding the war down. Only days before, the *Wall Street Journal* dropped its own hammer on the White House. "We think the American people should be getting ready to accept, if they haven't already, the prospect that the whole Vietnam effort may be doomed... We believe the Administration is duty-bound to recognize that no battle and no war is worth any price."[26]

Tet offered the American people clear evidence that the president and the military leadership had actively misled them about Vietnam. The more the public saw the president in an unfavorable light the more the stain of the nation's other problems—urban riots, rising inflation, and the nation's growing social disorder—began to adhere to him as well. For months Johnson had become the focal point of anger, disillusionment, and frustration about the country's direction. Tet solidified those views.[27]

For the first time both hawks and doves united in opposition to the president's policy in Vietnam. For the latter, Tet reinforced their view that the war had become a lost cause. For the former, it showed that Johnson did not have a plan for winning it. In the weeks to come, both groups—those who saw Tet as a reason for escalation and those who saw it as a reason to reduce the American presence—would coalesce to destroy Johnson's presidency. By the end of February, new polls showed a dramatic shift in public opinion. Only a third of Americans believed the United States was making progress in Vietnam, and now approximately a quarter said that the United States was losing—three times more than had said so in November.[28]

The bad news kept coming. The runaway costs of the Great Society programs and the war had created a nearly $20 billion budget deficit, and Johnson's efforts to pass a 10 percent tax surcharge, which he had proposed a year earlier, continued to be met with a cold shoulder from Congress. Growing concerns about the nation's trade deficit as well as a drop in US gold reserves—to the lowest level since 1937—heightened fears about the strength of the dollar. The precarious fiscal situation led Johnson to avoid seeking spending increases or significant new investments in his Great Society programs.[29]

Meanwhile, in late February, the hand-picked group that LBJ had asked to investigate the urban riots that had plagued American cities since 1964 dropped its own bombshell. The Kerner Commission report, named after the chairman, Ohio governor Otto Kerner, publicly claimed that America was on the path toward becoming "two societies, one black, one white— separate and unequal." The report's authors asserted that "the Negro can never forget" the fact that "white society is deeply implicated in the ghetto. White institutions created it, white institutions maintain, and white society condones it." The commission called for more government spending in the nation's inner cities and, "if necessary, new taxes" to pay for it.[30]

Of all the things that Johnson did not want to hear the year he faced re-election, foremost would be his blue ribbon commission on urban riots demanding more federal money for the nation's ghettoes. Johnson viewed the Kerner report findings as a personal indictment of his efforts to fight poverty in America. Incensed, he ignored them, which led Kennedy to derisively complain, "This means he's not going to do anything about the war and he's not going to do anything about the cities, either."[31]

Each of these developments fed a palpable and rising sense of helplessness in the country. Only months earlier, in an article that named Johnson the Man of the Year, *Time* noted that there was no segment of society immune to the national sense of dissatisfaction. "Housewives were alarmed by growing grocery bills, farmers by tumbling prices for their produce, parents by their alienated children, city dwellers by the senseless violence around them." Writing in the *New York Times*, James Reston said, "The main crisis is not Vietnam itself, or in the cities, but in the feeling that the political system for dealing with these things has broken down."[32]

At various times in his presidency, particularly after the death of John Kennedy and later in his spine-tingling "We Shall Overcome" speech to a joint session of Congress in March 1965, Johnson had demonstrated an exceptional capacity to bring Americans together and unite them in common cause. This success derived in large measure from the fact that for a short period Johnson kept his enormous ego in check. But by the spring of 1968 Johnson was no longer capable of acknowledging let alone grappling with the country's growing ennui. Locked into hardened political positions and fundamentally averse to any indication he was wavering on Vietnam, which he believed would be seized upon by Republicans or even the liberals in his own party, Johnson hunkered down.[33]

Speaking to US sailors aboard the USS *Constellation* in mid-February, he declared, "Men may debate—men may dissent—men may disagree and God forbid that a time should come when men of this land may not. But there does come a time when men must stand. And for America, that time has now come." Johnson was speaking about Vietnam, of course, but at the same moment that he offered his rousing words, in the snows of New Hampshire men and women were standing up as well—but with a very different goal in mind.[34]

Out Like a Lion

As winter gives way to spring, it is said that the month of March enters like a lion and leaves like a lamb. March 1968 would flip this proverb on its head. No month that year offered greater drama and surprises or more enduring political change than these thirty-one days. The month became a character in its own right in the story of 1968; the inflection point in a transformative political year.

March 1968 saw Johnson's teetering presidency finally collapse. Frustration on the home front mounted as America was buffeted by crises, both domestic and foreign. The entry of a new candidate into the presidential race further roiled the nation's politics (as did the decision of another not to run). Above all, in the aftermath of Tet, the US war in Vietnam, which by March 1968 had already taken nearly fifteen thousand American lives, began its slow shift toward de-escalation and de-Americanization. The offensive's political impact would be most acutely felt thousands of miles away, in the state of New Hampshire, site of the nation's first presidential primary. There, Eugene McCarthy's motley army of college students and antiwar activists engaged in their own political insurgency—one that before Tet seemed to be on a path to nowhere.

A January survey of Democratic delegates from the 1964 convention showed that 87 percent supported Johnson's renomination. McCarthy did little better among the rank and file; a February Gallup poll had him trailing Johnson by a 71–18 margin. John Roche, a White House aide, drafted a note to the president saying, "Eugene McCarthy is doing so badly that I am tempted to float a rumor that he is actually working for you to dispirit the 'peace movement.'"[1]

McCarthy initially resisted even entering the New Hampshire primary out of fear that the state's hawkish electorate would not warm to his antiwar message. At the urging of his campaign manager Blair Clark and two local activists, David Hoeh and Gerry Studds (a future congressman from Massachusetts), who argued that entering the primary would "reaffirm the seriousness" of his challenge to Johnson, McCarthy relented. It would be one of the few fortuitous moments in the entire campaign when he took the advice of his aides.[2]

Still McCarthy didn't make his first stop in the state until January 25—only six weeks before the March 12 primary—and his presence there sparked little excitement. He canceled dawn appearances at factory gates to meet voters because, as he told staffers, he wasn't really a "morning person." A photographer hired to take pictures of the candidate quit after five days because the only people in the shots were out-of-state volunteers. Richard Goodwin, who had joined the campaign on a whim after reading a newspaper story on the aftermath of Tet, recounted walking into the Sheraton Wayfarer Hotel in Manchester ("maybe the biggest dining room in the state of New Hampshire") with McCarthy, and "not a single head looked up."[3]

McCarthy refused to be bothered with the ins and outs of the campaign. He would barely talk to donors and failed to thank them for their support. His speeches sounded more like plodding lectures than rousing calls to arms ("People don't want to be shouted at," McCarthy explained). The national campaign infrastructure was basically nonexistent. There were no polls taken ("We don't want to get discouraged," McCarthy said); and the New Hampshire contingent was left largely to fend for itself, with no manager at first, no advertising, no campaign materials, and no slogan. (Studds and Hoeh would eventually come up with one on their own: "There Is an Alternative. McCarthy for President.") "Events will march in our favor," he told the increasingly exasperated Clark. *Newsweek* summed up the views of many when it described the New Hampshire effort as "hardly even an embarrassment."[4]

The candidate's laconic, indifferent attitude looked like laziness to many, but McCarthy adamantly wanted to make a measured and rational case for change, even at his own political expense. Days after the announcement of his candidacy, McCarthy traveled to Chicago to address an audience of Democratic antiwar activists. Though he had been speaking to such groups for months, the Chicago appearance offered him a coming-out party of sorts—and a chance to preview the key themes of his campaign. At the event he had been slated to follow Allard Lowenstein, who proceeded to rile up the audience with a personal attack on Johnson and a harsh denunciation of the war. As McCarthy stood backstage, his blood pressure began to rise in concert with Lowenstein's tone (Lowenstein's right-hand man, the future senator and presidential candidate Gary Hart, later described McCarthy as "visibly pissed"). Lowenstein's stridency represented precisely the sort of demagogic campaign that McCarthy did not want to wage. To prove his point, when his turn came to speak, he went into full poet-professor mode, with obscure references to the Dreyfus case and the Punic Wars, and no mention of Lyndon Johnson. The crowd politely gave McCarthy a standing ovation, but their disappointment was unmistakable.[5]

McCarthy had taken on Johnson, in large measure, because he believed the president and the war had coarsened the national discourse and bred "political helplessness." He refused to try to repair those wounds with more invective. Eight years earlier, in *Frontiers in American Democracy*, McCarthy wrote, "The Christian in politics should shun the devices of the demagogue in all times, but especially at a time when anxiety is great, when tension is high, when uncertainty prevails, and emotion tends to be in the ascendancy." This attitude would be reflected in virtually every aspect of the New Hampshire campaign. As he told a local radio station in early March, "The issues with which we are dealing are the kind that ought to be considered with some reservation and some restraint—somewhat moderately instead of in the atmosphere of shouting and emotion."[6]

While McCarthy's views on the war and US foreign policy in general departed from the political consensus, few who encountered McCarthy in New Hampshire would have easily drawn such a conclusion. In fact, his campaign downplayed his opposition to the war, and his local staff kept the shrillest antiwar voices at arm's length. The message of campaign advertisements and press releases—which were similar to McCarthy's own public statements since the fall—was focused on the larger question of whether America had lost it way. "What happened to this country since 1963?" asked one flyer, accompanied by a picture of a smiling McCarthy and President Kennedy. "The Bigger the War the Smaller Your Dollar," said another, which contrasted the prosperity of the Kennedy years with the higher cost of living that had resulted from Vietnam.[7]

"The great issue in this contest between President Johnson and myself is not Vietnam," McCarthy told voters. "It is not rising violence in the cities or rising prices. It is one of leadership and the direction of our nation." McCarthy targeted those who might not have agreed with his opposition to the war—or his overall foreign policy views—but who believed that Vietnam was taking a terrible toll on the nation as a whole. "It's not only the war," he reiterated in a February campaign appearance in New Hampshire, "but what it's doing to us at home."[8]

McCarthy's low-key demeanor, particularly in his television advertising, which would become his main source of contact with voters, gave his message even greater effectiveness. "Nobody could look at McCarthy and think that he was a radical," said Goodwin. "They saw that Midwestern face and the manner of speaking...and it was absolutely clear that they were looking at a man that, whatever his position on the issues, that in his heart he was a conservative." In a year of heightened political passion and social upheaval, there would be substantial electoral benefit in toning things down, rather than ratcheting up the rhetoric.[9]

McCarthy's "reasoned" approach to New Hampshire voters would also be reflected in the campaign's intensive ground game. Curtis Gans, a deputy of Lowenstein, and Sam Brown, a Harvard divinity student, developed and implemented the "Clean for Gene" canvassing effort, which took full advantage of the legions of college students who flocked to New Hampshire that winter. Gans and Brown made clear that no young men with long hair would lobby the state's famously conservative voters. Shave, they were told, or head to the basement of McCarthy headquarters to prepare campaign materials.[10]

The strict rules didn't stop the flow of volunteers. They came from college campuses across the Northeast, intent on fulfilling McCarthy's pledge to restore "a belief in the processes of American politics." In fact, few of those who were knocking on doors in snowy New Hampshire would have counted themselves among the more radical fringe. Serious and sophisticated, McCarthy's young supporters were far more likely to run for a position in student government then ask how many kids LBJ had killed that day. "We aren't the see-you-in-Chicago crowd," said Brown. "They want to tear it all down."[11]

Armed with rational, evidence-based arguments, young men in suits and young women in maxiskirts were set loose on New Hampshire Democratic voters. They were instructed to ask voters questions, listen politely to their answers, and under no circumstances argue with or berate them. They talked about the war in terms of its "endless nature," said Gans, rather than offering dovish solutions to end it. They received a far more positive response than anyone might have imagined. "Violet-eyed damsels from Smith are pinning McCarthy buttons on tattooed mill-workers," wrote the columnist Mary McGrory, "and Ph.D.s from Cornell, shaven and shorn for world peace, are deferentially bowing to middle-aged Manchester housewives and importuning them to consider a change of commander-in-chief."[12]

Over a six-week period, McCarthy's enthusiastic army of polite, well-scrubbed volunteers rang some sixty thousand doorbells—accounting for two out of three New Hampshire Democrats. These grass-roots efforts were backed by a near-constant stream of newspaper and radio ads (often voiced by McCarthy's legion of celebrity supporters, like actor Paul Newman) asking voters, "Won't you be happy to have a new change for America?" By mid-March it would have been nearly impossible for New Hampshire residents to ignore McCarthy's call for change.[13]

For his part, Johnson deliberately avoided the hustings in New Hampshire—and purposely limited White House engagement with the primary campaign—for fear that taking part would grant legitimacy to McCarthy's challenge. Johnson wasn't even an official candidate in the primary: voters had to write in his name on the ballot. Instead, he relied on nominal Democratic allies New Hampshire governor John King and Senator Thomas McIntyre to make his case to the voters. They hardly could have taken to the job with greater tactlessness. The Johnson camp openly accused McCarthy of providing aid and comfort to the enemy: a vote for the senator "would be greeted by cheers in Hanoi," claimed one campaign ad. Another praised Johnson for sticking with men like General Westmoreland and "not listening to those peace-at-any-price fuzzy thinkers, who say give up the goal, burn your draft card, and surrender." (Only a few weeks after the primary, Johnson announced that Westmoreland would be stepping down as commander in Vietnam.)[14]

Events in Washington would soon lend new impetus to the anti-Johnson effort. Americans for Democratic Action took the extraordinary step of endorsing McCarthy—providing clear evidence of the widening divisions on the left over Vietnam. The real test for Johnson, however, came not from those who thought the war was lost but instead from those who believed it could still be won. The Joint Chiefs of Staff had (with little success) been urging Johnson to increase US military efforts on Vietnam by mobilizing the US Army Reserves. After Tet, they made a new push. The chairman of the Joint Chiefs, Earle Wheeler, traveled to Vietnam in February and returned with a stunning and unanticipated request—another 206,000 soldiers for the war effort. "It's not possible to overestimate the degree of concern and even fear that possessed the heads of our government when Wheeler returned," Clark Clifford, who took over as secretary of defense at the beginning of March, later said. Johnson remained "as worried as [Clifford had] ever seen him."[15]

With the admonition that Clifford should give him "the lesser of evils," Johnson ordered an evaluation of Wheeler's proposal. Clifford had long been a hawk on Vietnam. In fact, when asked by LBJ (along with several other close confidants and advisors) to review McNamara's November 1967 memo calling for de-escalation, he sent the president one of the most forceful and dismissive responses. But as he undertook his assessment of Wheeler's troop request, what he found shocked him. The military leadership could provide him no guarantee that the additional soldiers they were re-questing would be enough to win the war or even bring about the de-Amer-icanization of the conflict. "All I had," Clifford later said, "was the statement, given with too little self-assurance to be comforting, that if we persisted for an indeterminate length of time, the enemy would choose not to go on."[16]

For Johnson to ask for a further expansion of the war, after his claims of progress the previous fall—and after his confident pronouncements fol-lowing Tet—would have been nearly impossible to explain to the American people. The president turned down the call for more troops, but the debate inside the administration would cast a dark political shadow. Two days before the balloting in New Hampshire, the *New York Times* revealed Wheeler's request. In a front-page blockbuster, the paper quoted a senior Pentagon official saying that Vietnam had become "a bottomless pit." On the same day a new Gallup poll showed that 49 percent of Americans now believed that the United States was wrong to have ever chosen to fight in Vietnam.[17]

Johnson called Roche, who was on the ground in New Hampshire the night before the primary to ask how things were looking. Roche had no good news for the president. McCarthy could get as much as a third of the vote, he predicted. "No, he'll get 40 percent, at least 40 percent," said Johnson. "Every son-of-a-bitch in New Hampshire who's mad at his wife or the postman or anybody is going to vote for Gene McCarthy."[18]

The next day, McCarthy won 42 percent of the vote to Johnson's 49 per-cent. He also won twenty of the twenty-four state delegates that would be sent to the Democratic convention in Chicago. After write-in votes were counted, Johnson's margin of victory was a mere 230 votes. Though LBJ had officially won, the result was seen as a clear repudiation of his administration.

McCarthy's strong performance, however, did not mean that voters had embraced his antiwar stance. Many New Hampshire Democrats didn't even know McCarthy's position on the war (his staff suspected that at least some of those who voted for him thought they were casting a ballot for Joe McCarthy)—and 60 percent of his backers believed Johnson should be fighting the war *more* aggressively. Neither Vietnam nor crime, the cost of living nor the Great Society united McCarthy supporters (in fact, an estimated one in five McCarthy voters would cast a ballot for George Wallace in November). Frustration with Johnson was their only true consensus position.[19]

Overnight, the presumed inevitability of Johnson's renomination had been punctured. McCarthy had given direct voice—and a political outlet— to the antiwar sentiment inside the Democratic Party. His success in New Hampshire inspired a crop of Democratic activists and future politicians to recognize the value and power of grass-roots organizing *within* the political system. This opening up of the political process would eventually lead to a host of party reforms that changed the way Democrats, and later Republicans, chose their presidential nominees. By energizing skeptics of the Cold War consensus, McCarthy's performance also led to a dramatic shift in how the party approached foreign policy and national security in general. Challenging Johnson when he seemed almost certain to be the party standard bearer in November fundamentally changed the direction of the Democratic Party. It would, contra Orville Freeman, be far more important than a mere historical footnote.

As McCarthy spoke to his delirious supporters on election night in New Hampshire, he seemed to sense the momentous nature of the vote. He went "through an almost physical change," said Goodwin, "You could see the color come into his face." A romantic campaign intended to reframe the national debate over Vietnam was on the verge of national legitimacy. McCarthy's backers could be excused, if only momentarily, for imagining their man standing in front of the assembled delegates in Chicago five months later, accepting the party's nomination for president.[20]

Like McCarthy's rosy glow, such optimism wouldn't last long. The primary-night victory hangovers had barely been medicated by black coffee and hot showers when reporters approached Robert Kennedy at Washington's National Airport and asked for his thoughts on the results in New Hampshire. Kennedy replied, "I am actively reassessing the possibility of whether I will run against President Johnson." Imagine waking up Christmas morning and finding that he had stolen all the presents from beneath the tree, one McCarthy supporter complained. By the time McCarthy had returned to

Washington on March 13, stories in late newspaper editions about Kennedy's likely entry into the race had already replaced those reporting McCarthy's performance in New Hampshire. "He wouldn't even let me have my day of celebration, would he?" McCarthy said bitterly.[21]

Yet Kennedy's "reassessment" did not mean that he'd made a final decision about running. Over the years, his supporters have claimed that even before New Hampshire Kennedy was poised to get in the race, but the historical record points as much to vacillation as it does certitude. "He never entirely decided to run," Fred Dutton later said. "He'd take two steps forward and one step backward, and pretty soon he found he was too far in the tunnel to get out." On March 8 Kennedy did an impromptu interview with Haynes Johnson of the *Washington Star*, in which he refused to reveal his plans, but which nonetheless convinced the reporter that Kennedy had made up his mind. "Certain he will run," Johnson wrote in his notebook. The next day Kennedy flew to California to offer support to Cesar Chavez and his hunger strike on behalf of migrant farmers. The experience seemed to further embolden him. He told close aides on the flight home that he would indeed challenge Johnson, though, at their urging, he agreed to wait until after New Hampshire before making an announcement.[22]

McCarthy's "win" upended those plans. The next day Kennedy sent a handwritten note to the *New York Times* reporter Anthony Lewis in which he ran down all the reasons for running and then asked, "So again what should I do?" Kennedy even invited Lewis to join him on a planned vacation to Ireland in May, if, he said, "I am not off in the California primary." When asked by an aide about his presidential intentions, Kennedy responded, "I'm going to go ahead with it unless you don't think it's a good idea." In a meeting with a group of congressional doves several days after New Hampshire, he paced back and forth, offering both pro and con arguments. "His face was that of a suffering man trying desperately to reach a solution to an enormously, complicated problem," reported McGovern, now feeling his own regrets at having turned down Lowenstein's offer the previous fall to challenge Johnson.[23]

Those inside the Kennedy camp leaned heavily toward running, but some aides still looked for an exit ramp. The day before New Hampshire,

Johnson had met with Sorensen and floated the idea of appointing Kennedy to an independent commission to review Vietnam policy. Kennedy saw the move as a trap, but one that he couldn't simply sidestep, particularly if it served as a legitimate avenue for achieving peace. Sorensen told Clifford that if the president would be willing to renounce his Vietnam policy and appoint a commission to offer an alternative policy, Kennedy would remain on the sidelines during the election. Johnson could not accept such a deal, and the idea died a quick death.[24]

Kennedy's own interaction with McCarthy didn't provide much clarity about his plans either. After the New Hampshire vote, the men met at the Capitol for an awkward twenty-minute meeting. Kennedy ran down his list of reasons for entering the race, though he never clearly stated his intentions. For his part, McCarthy told Kennedy that while he doubted he could win the nomination, he wouldn't drop out. In the closest McCarthy came to extending an olive branch, he did say that he would only serve one term if elected, which would leave Kennedy with a clear path to the presidency in 1972.[25]

Behind the scenes, Dick Goodwin, with support from Blair Clark and Ted Kennedy, ginned up the idea of dividing the remaining primaries between the two contenders and amassing a block of anti-Johnson delegates. The two men could then fight it out in the California primary in June. The younger Kennedy boarded a late-night flight to Wisconsin (where McCarthy was campaigning for the April 2 Democratic primary) to broach the plan. McCarthy summarily rejected it. McCarthy was already smarting over RFK's post–New Hampshire comments, and Kennedy's proposal left a bitter taste in his mouth. He told his wife, Abigail, who had been reluctant to even let the young Kennedy see her husband, "That's the way they are. When it comes down to it, they never offer anything real."[26]

Teddy returned to Washington to deliver the bad news. He found his brother surrounded by his top advisors, in the last surreal hours before Bobby became an official candidate. Arthur Schlesinger later recalled being awakened by Kennedy, who asked him point-blank, "What do you think I should do?" Schlesinger suggested endorsing McCarthy. Kennedy looked at him and "stonily" replied, "I can't do that. It would be too humiliating.

Kennedys don't act that way." Schlesinger went downstairs to find Teddy, Sorensen, and another aide, William vanden Heuvel seated around the breakfast table. "Where is he now?" asked vanden Heuvel. "Looking for someone else to wake up in the hope of finding someone who agrees with him," replied Sorensen. Finally, Kennedy appeared in his pajamas and announced he couldn't come out for McCarthy and he also couldn't sit the race out. "I'm going ahead, and there's no point in talking about anything else."[27]

So on March 16, a mere six and a half weeks since he had said that he could see no foreseeable circumstance under which he would challenge Lyndon Johnson, Kennedy stood in the same Senate Caucus Room where his brother Jack had declared his candidacy and announced his intention to seek the presidency. His wife, Ethel, stood by his side—but the presence of his slain brother was undeniable. "In every way possible," wrote *Time*, "Bobby subtly invoked the memory of his late brother—same room, same gestures, same table, same prose style, same age at declaration." He wore a PT-109 tie clasp (a World War II memento of his brother), and the first sentence Kennedy uttered was even identical to the one used by JFK eight years earlier.[28]

"I do not run for the presidency merely to oppose any man but to propose new policies," he said. "I run because I am convinced that this country is on a perilous course and because I have such strong feelings about what must be done, and I feel that I'm obliged to do all that I can." The message reflected the aspirational tone for which Kennedy's candidacy is remembered. "I run . . . to end the bloodshed in Vietnam and in our cities," he said, and "to close the gap that now exists between black and white, between rich and poor, between young and old in this country and around the rest of the world." It offered a resounding call for national unity at a time of national disunity. At the end of his remarks he declared, "At stake is not simply the leadership of our party and even our country. It is our right to the moral leadership of this planet." While Kennedy's goal was to evoke the better angels of the American spirit, his words had unintentionally reflected the national mindset that had entangled the United States in Vietnam in the first place—the belief that the country had a sacred responsibility and duty to serve as a global steward. This was a far cry from McCarthy's call for greater modesty in foreign policy—a difference between the two candidates that would become more distinct in the weeks and months to come.[29]

The assembled journalists, however, were far more interested in Kennedy's assurance that his candidacy would not be "in opposition" to McCarthy, but rather "in harmony" with it. Several reporters could barely conceal their skepticism. After all, Kennedy would be competing against McCarthy, not Johnson, on the campaign trail. McCarthy, who had once pined for Kennedy's entry into the race, was publicly unfazed. "I'm still the best potential president in the field," he said; "I committed myself to a group of young people and, I thought, a rather idealistic group of adults in American society.... I'll run as hard as I can in every primary."[30]

Less charitable was the response from the political class. Most national Democrats sided with the president. "Bobby-come-lately has made a mistake," blustered West Virginia senator Robert Byrd. While many Democrats had liked his brother, Byrd said, they "don't like him." President Truman reported he was 100 percent behind the president and called his challengers "a damned bunch of smart alecks." An anonymous Florida Democrat, quoted in the US News and World Report, summed up the views of many southern Democrats: "Bobby Kennedy is my second choice for President. Anybody else is my first choice." Even Alaska senator Ernest Gruening, one of only two senators to vote against the Gulf of Tonkin Resolution, chastised Kennedy for challenging Johnson.[31]

Prominent media columnists offered similar dismissals. Writing in the New York Post, Murray Kempton analogized Kennedy's run to coming "down from the hills to shoot the wounded. He has," he continued, "in the naked display of his rage at Eugene McCarthy for having survived on the lonely road he dared not walk himself, done with a single great gesture something very few public men have ever been able to do: In one day, he managed to confirm the worst things his enemies have ever said about him."[32]

Kennedy's first days on the campaign trail did little to quiet the criticism, or the fears that his candidacy risked doing serious damage to the party. New Hampshire had proven that Democrats were far from united, but his initial campaign events did more than widen the gap. In Kansas, Kennedy evoked Tacitus—"They made a desert, and called it peace"—to describe US policy in Vietnam. At Vanderbilt University in Tennessee, he attributed the country's growing divisions to Johnson's leadership and said that the president and his administration "have removed themselves from the American tradition, from the enduring and the generous impulses that are the soul of the nation." Departing from his prepared remarks, Kennedy exclaimed, "They are the ones, the President of the United States, President Johnson, they are the ones who divide us." The same day in Alabama he said America was "divided as never before in our history," a strange charge to be delivered in a former Confederate state. But Kennedy made his most serious attack at the Greek Theater in Los Angeles, as he accused Johnson of "calling upon the darker impulses of the American spirit." Years of bitterness toward Johnson were being uncorked. "I'm free. I'm a man again," he told aides.[33]

Kennedy seemed to be blaming every national infirmity on Johnson and, like the president, accusing his opponents of unpatriotic and un-American behavior. In the pages of *Time*, the *Washington Post*, and the *Los Angeles Times*, Kennedy's tactics were labeled as demagoguery. Reporters pointed out that Kennedy's harsh words gave the lie to his earlier statement that his candidacy reflected "no personal animosity or disrespect toward President Johnson."[34]

There was, however, a clear strategy behind Kennedy's tactics. His campaign staff knew that he could never get enough delegates to win the Democratic nod via the primary route. His only hope was to spark a popular political movement and bring so much enthusiastic support to his campaign that party leaders would feel obligated to give him the nomination. According to Kennedy's young Senate speechwriter Adam Walinsky, the campaign would "change the rules of nominating a President. We're going to do it a new way. In the street."[35]

In those early weeks of the campaign, the candidate remained loyal to this approach—perhaps to a fault. At the Kansas State University field house, fourteen thousand students, some of whom hung from the building's rafters, gave him a rapturous welcome. When Kennedy finished his remarks, hundreds of kids rushed the stage, "overturning chairs" and "raising a haze of dust from the dirt floor." The same day at the University of Kansas, twenty thousand supporters greeted Kennedy with an outpouring of emotion so relentless that his own advance man, Jim Tolan, expressed genuine concern for the candidate's safety. Kennedy took the excitement largely in stride. "They're here because they care for us and they want to show us," he said after an old friend pointed out that his hands were bloodied after a day of campaigning.[36]

Kennedy might have been trying to energize his supporters, but to many Americans he appeared instead to be sparking a riot. If voters were seeking a moderating force in American politics—a key element of McCarthy's success in New Hampshire—Kennedy's campaign strategy gave the opposite impression. The primal response of the crowds risked overwhelming Kennedy's message that the fight in 1968 was about more than just Vietnam; it was a fight for "a new birth for this country" and "a new America." But he could do little to tamp down the fervor. His presence on the campaign trail evoked for many the bygone era of Camelot. His supporters weren't simply hailing Kennedy; they were venerating the memory of his brother. For many, RFK's candidacy represented an opportunity for America to turn back the clock on its troubled present and return to the glorious and optimistic past—the calm before the storm unleashed in Dallas.[37]

Nowhere did Kennedy's appeal resound more loudly than among America's black and brown underclass. No politician of the era was more revered by the nation's minorities than Kennedy, an affection he had earned through his revitalization efforts in the black slums of New York's Bedford-Stuyvesant neighborhood, his championing of migrant worker's rights in California with Cesar Chavez, and his work in the Senate on behalf of Native Americans. Unlike McCarthy, Kennedy had no problem traveling to the nation's ghettoes, shaking hands, and above all raising hopes. His visits received "a sighing, near sexual orgy of exultation," said the legendary campaign scribe, Teddy White, who compared it to "being in the eye of the hurricane." Hundreds of hands reached out just to touch the candidate; and there would be regular refrains of "Bobby, Bobby, if you win, will you come back?"[38]

His aides warned him constantly about the potential for tragedy—a child could be caught under the wheels of his motorcade, or the candidate himself could be pulled off his car and seriously hurt (during the Indiana campaign this actually happened, causing Kennedy to break a tooth and cut his lip). But Kennedy—a chronic risk taker—refused to listen. When told on an April campaign trip to Michigan about reports of a man with a rifle on a neighboring rooftop, he demanded his hotel curtains be left open, insisting, "If they're going to shoot, they'll shoot." The reaction he received on the campaign trail energized him. "He'd just light up," said Dutton. "The physical touching was like a couple of drinks." "Those are my people," he'd say when he ventured into a black crowd. He embraced, even encouraged, their passion.[39]

Kennedy remained equally willing to speak unpleasant truths. Like his brother eight years before, he directly challenged his audiences. But unlike JFK, who focused his message on the Communist threat, RFK's attention remained fixated on the disease of poverty, fear, and hopelessness that he believed was destroying the country, but which remained an abstraction to most Americans. Kennedy would speak movingly of the children he had seen in Mississippi with distended stomachs, the Indians living on "meager reservations," the "proud men" in Appalachia who couldn't find jobs, and the blacks in inner cities whose children were mired in appalling poverty.[40]

Beyond the calls for social justice, Kennedy focused on the paucity of national spirit. Evoking his brother's 1960 campaign themes, he bemoaned the fact that the country had "surrendered personal excellence and community values in the mere accumulation of material things." At that chaotic University of Kansas event he offered a rhetorical flight of fancy—perhaps his finest of the campaign—that gave a glimpse of the kind of leader he might have been:

> Our Gross National Product, now, is over $800 billion dollars a year, but that Gross National Product—if we judge the United States of America by that—that Gross National Product counts air pollution and cigarette advertising, and ambulances to clear our highways of carnage. It counts special locks for our doors and the jails for the people who break them. It counts the destruction of the redwood and the loss of our natural wonder in chaotic sprawl. It counts

napalm and counts nuclear warheads and armored cars for the police
to fight the riots in our cities…and the television programs, which
glorify violence in order to sell toys to our children. Yet the gross
national product does not allow for the health of our children, the
quality of their education or the joy of their play. It does not include
the beauty of our poetry or the strength of our marriages, the
intelligence of our public debate or the integrity of our public
officials. It measures neither our wit nor our courage, neither our
wisdom nor our learning, neither our compassion nor our devotion
to our country, it measures everything in short, except that which
makes life worthwhile. And it can tell us everything about America
except why we are proud that we are Americans.[41]

It remained to be seen whether a message of hope would resonate more
deeply with the American people than one of fear. Lyndon Johnson prepared to wager on the latter.

The prospect of facing off against Bobby Kennedy in a battle for the soul of
the Democratic Party had always hung over Lyndon Johnson's presidency.
When it finally happened, he expressed little surprise. "I had been expect-
ing it," Johnson matter of factly wrote in his memoirs. He initially greeted
Kennedy's entry into the race with indifference; he joked about it in public
gatherings and expressed nonchalance about the challenges that lay ahead.
His staff had been gathering information on RFK for years, preparing for
just this moment. They pulled from the archives all the kind words both
Robert and Jack had previously uttered about Johnson and even unearthed
alleged sordid details about the family patriarch, Joe Kennedy. In 1964, the
Johnson political team had tagged Barry Goldwater as a madman intent on
launching a nuclear war with the Soviets. They had no intention of adopting a more restrained approach for the political figure that the president
despised more than any other.[42]

Only days after Kennedy's s announcement Johnson laid down a rhetorical marker. "If you think you can stop aggression by getting out of the way
and letting them take over, roll over you, you have another thing coming,"

Johnson warned in a speech in Minnesota. "We love nothing more than peace, but we hate nothing more than surrender." Pounding on the lectern and pointing his finger at the audience, he thundered, "Make no mistake about it. I don't want a man in here to go back thinking otherwise—we are going to win." He wasn't just talking about Vietnam.[43]

Unable to make a convincing case for his war policies, bluster and patriotic appeals were all that Johnson had left. He told Arthur Krim, a key political advisor and fundraiser, that it looked more and more like he was going to be "the Barry Goldwater of 1964, the war candidate of 1968." Early drafts of a major speech on Vietnam, planned for the end of March, show that Johnson initially firmly rejected any talk of a bombing halt. "I've heard every argument on the subject," Johnson told his aides, "and I am not interested in further discussion. I have made up my mind. I'm not going to stop."[44]

If Johnson hadn't been in a fighting mode before Kennedy announced, said one campaign aide, "He's in it up to his neck now. He will not turn this country over to Bobby—not a chance." Johnson, however, again misjudged both his party and the electorate. A memo from the old Democratic political hand James Rowe (who had once served as an advisor to FDR) suggested that the Minnesota speech had done Johnson real political damage— and that both doves and hawks reported outrage and frustration at his uncompromising tone. "The fact is," wrote Rowe, "hardly anyone today is interested in winning the war. Everyone wants to get out and the only question is how." Krim reported that "from every corner of the country...the party leadership was desperate for him to make some dramatic de-escalation move in Vietnam."[45]

Johnson's public zeal after Kennedy's announcement stood in stark contrast to the curious lack of organizational attention to the president's campaign. An October 1967, forty-four page memo from Larry O'Brien laying out the structure of a campaign organization and a potential strategy for Johnson's re-election went largely unimplemented. Few strategic decisions got made; the position of campaign director remained unfilled; and there was a decidedly halfhearted approach to even the most basic political outreach and logistical decision-making. A March 5 deadline to get Johnson's name on the Massachusetts ballot (or that of a stand-in) came and went without action from the president. By late March all signs pointed to a catastrophic primary defeat in Wisconsin, where Johnson's political organization looked moribund, a contrast to McCarthy's energized and confident foot soldiers. Nationally, Johnson's approval rating sank to 36 percent, and support for his handling of the war plummeted to 26 percent. Missouri senator Stuart Symington told a closed-door meeting of his Senate colleagues, "Lyndon Johnson could not be elected dogcatcher in Missouri today."[46]

Beyond his immediate political challenges, a larger emotional toll was being taken on the president. He regularly shuffled from his personal quarters to the Situation Room in the basement of the White House in his bathrobe and slippers. In a meeting with his old friend Senator Richard Russell, he began crying uncontrollably. In his own words, he felt "chased on all sides" by the growing dissent and anger over the war, the "inflationary economy," and the "rioting blacks, demonstrating students, marching welfare mothers, squawking professors, and hysterical reporters." Not since Lincoln had an American president faced as much domestic dissent as that which confronted Johnson in the spring of 1968. Now the event he had "feared from the first day" he had become president had come true. "Robert Kennedy had announced his intention to reclaim the throne in the memory of his brother," Johnson said later, "and the American people, swayed by the magic of the name, were dancing in the streets." Johnson wondered, "How is it possible that all these people could be so ungrateful to me after I had given them so much?" So deep was Johnson's need for adulation—and so vast was his ego—that he could only view the country's growing frustration through the narrow prism of how it personally affected him.[47]

On March 26, two weeks after the New Hampshire primary, the "wise men" who had reported to Johnson the previous fall that he must stay the course in Vietnam gathered again in Washington. What they heard from State Department briefers would shatter their confidence and set the course for the most dramatic shift in US policy since the war began. They were told the military and political situation in Vietnam was far worse than what was being publicly reported. Pacification had made little progress; the South

Vietnamese government remained years away from being able to right itself; and even after their heavy losses from Tet, the enemy appeared to be no closer to defeat. The next day they met with the president. Reflecting the views of a majority of the group, LBJ's former national security advisor, McGeorge Bundy, told Johnson, "There has been a very significant shift in most of our positions." It was now clear, said Bundy, that "we can no longer do the job we set out to do in the time we have left and we must begin to take steps to disengage." The men who had built and nurtured a two-decade-long policy of Soviet and Communist containment and, in the case of Acheson, had been present at the creation of US Cold War policy, now told a stunned president that the war on which he'd staked his presidency had all been for naught. Even significant military escalation, a step LBJ had rejected weeks earlier, could not save the situation. De-escalation—the course of action McNamara had counseled him to take five months earlier—was now being forced upon him.[48]

When and why Johnson decided to forgo re-election in 1968 has long been the subject of intense speculation. As is so often the case with Johnson, the historical record points to a conflicting set of statements and actions. He had flirted with the possibility of not running as early as his presidential bid in 1964. In the interim he spoke about it frequently and in the fall of 1967 began discussing it much more openly with his political advisors. At the time, he pointedly asked Westmoreland what the effect on the morale of the troops in Vietnam would be if he didn't seek re-election (the general had assured him they would understand). According to Marvin Watson, Johnson told him privately in January 1968 that he wouldn't run. He had even asked his speechwriters to write up an addendum to his State of the Union address, announcing his withdrawal from the presidential campaign, which he allegedly "forgot" to bring to the Capitol. In mid-February he revisited the topic and was, Krim said, "adamant" in his "determination to withdraw." Yet at the same time Johnson told Watson to remain focused on the campaign as if he still intended to run. While the president now appeared to lean toward dropping out, he also clearly had yet to make a final call.[49]

In the end, no single knock-out punch drove Johnson from the race. Rather, a steady drumbeat of body blows felled him: Tet; the Kerner

Commission; the capture of the USS *Pueblo* in February 1968 and the imprisonment of its crew by North Korea, which almost sparked a military incident; the near collapse of the gold market in March; the firestorm over the two hundred thousand additional troops for Vietnam; McCarthy's strong performance in New Hampshire and his likely soon-to-be win in Wisconsin; that son-of-a-bitch Bobby; a Congress that no longer bent to his will; and, finally, the Wise Men. It was what Doris Goodwin called "the total impossibility of his situation," a situation that Johnson had created by refusing for so many years to make a choice on Vietnam. Now events outside Johnson's control, events he could no longer manipulate, forced a decision upon him. With this steady accumulation of woes, it finally became clear that Johnson had only one option left: quit.[50]

The Philosopher versus the Evangelist

On March 31, 1968, Lyndon Johnson threw in the towel.

"With America's sons in the fields far away," he told the nation from the Oval Office in a deliberate and steady, but melancholy-filled tone, "with America's future under challenge right here at home, with our hopes and the world's hopes for peace in the balance every day, I do not believe that I should devote an hour or a day of my time to any personal partisan causes or to any duties other than the awesome duties of this office.... Accordingly, I shall not seek, and I will not accept, the nomination of my party for another term as your President."[1]

At his inauguration in January 1965 Johnson had radiated a presidential aura that suggested a singular mastery of the job. "Like the old-time Texas cattle barons on their vast domains, Lyndon Baines Johnson seems to stand a good 20 feet tall in these parts," wrote Tom Wicker in the spring of that year. "There is nothing in the capitol that can look down on him except the Washington Monument." Four years later, he appeared to be a much smaller man. The vigor and vitality with which he had once stridden across the national stage seemed like a faint memory. The pressures of the job had overwhelmed and ultimately defeated Johnson. Aides and friends described him as "exhausted," "battered," and "drained." "I'm tired," he told friends. "I'm tired of feeling rejected by the American people. I'm tired of waking up in the middle of the night worrying about the war. I'm tired of all these personal attacks on me." He feared the fate that had befallen President Woodrow Wilson, who suffered a massive stroke at the tail end of his second term. After his abdication that March evening, Johnson stepped away from the cameras, and his "shoulders temporarily lost their stoop," said one aide.[2]

Johnson's decision, which was known in advance by perhaps a dozen people, left many of the nation's most prominent politicians at an uncharacteristic loss for words. "I don't know quite what to say," stammered Kennedy. Said McCarthy, "I think I'm surprised," and, more drily, "Things have gotten rather complicated." Barry Goldwater had perhaps the most down-to-earth reaction. "I went and had another drink. I just couldn't believe my ears."[3]

"I doubt if any single speech in history has so abruptly turned feelings around on one man," said Eugene Wyman, a prominent California Democratic committeeman. On the morning of March 31, Johnson seemed to his political opponents (and to some of his political allies) a sick, even deranged, man not to be trusted or believed. On April 1, 1968, he had been transformed into a selfless American hero who had fallen on his political sword for the good of the country. His 57 percent disapproval rating flipped to a 57 percent approval rating practically overnight. Even the antiwar activists who had been plaguing Johnson for years declared a cease-fire of sorts. A group of young people gathered outside the White House and unfurled a banner reading "THANKS, L.B.J.," and sang "We Have Overcome."[4]

Days after what *Time* called "the renunciation," Johnson traveled to New York for the installation of the city's new archbishop. As he walked down the center aisle of Saint Patrick's Cathedral, the congregation of five thousand rose in a sustained standing ovation (an almost unheard-of occurrence inside a Catholic church). Equally euphoric were the crowds outside. Still, while the electorate might have appreciated Johnson's selflessness, they had no apparent second thoughts about his departure. Two days before, voters in Wisconsin provided him with the final and crowning humiliation to his political career: a crushing defeat in the Democratic primary at the hands of McCarthy, who won 57 percent of the vote.[5]

The outpouring of appreciation was about more than just Johnson's abrupt exit from national politics. In his March 31 speech he announced that he would be pursuing a policy of de-escalation in Vietnam and preparing to "move immediately toward peace through negotiations" with the North Vietnamese—a decision that in the fall of 1967 he believed would produce a terrific political backlash. Instead, it gave Americans hope that an end to the war was possible. For a brief moment it appeared that the seemingly relentless process of national disintegration that the country had experienced in the first three months of 1968 could be reversed.[6]

Four days after Johnson's speech, at approximately 6:01 PM, a forty-year-old drifter and petty criminal peered out from behind the window of a rooming house in Memphis, Tennessee. He carefully aimed a Remington 30-06 Gamemaster slide-action rifle, loaded with metal-jacketed bullets, at a figure chatting with colleagues on the second-floor balcony of the Lorraine Motel. He fired a single bullet. It entered the slightly built man's right cheek, severed numerous vital arteries, fractured his shoulder, and lodged in the left side of his back. An hour later Martin Luther King, Jr., died in an emergency room in Memphis's Saint Joseph's Hospital—and the momentary optimism spawned by Johnson's withdrawal died along with him.[7]

If the most transformative political event of 1968 was the Tet Offensive, the most traumatic would be King's murder by a white racist. Dozens of American cities exploded in violence. While New York avoided unrest (due in part to the personal intervention of Mayor John Lindsay), Chicago took a major hit. So many young black men ended up in city jails that many went more than twenty-four hours without food. Within a day of the killing, federal troops were deployed to Baltimore and Pittsburgh. Tens of thousands of soldiers would end up patrolling America's streets in the aftermath of King's assassination.[8]

The greatest brunt of black fury would be directed at Washington, DC. On the night of April 4, the U Street Corridor—the heart of the city's black cultural, commercial, and political establishment—bustled. When news of

King's death began to spread, the streets swelled with mourners. Grief and anger soon spiraled out of control, unleashing a spasm of violence that lasted for twelve days. Looting and rioting raged across the city. Aerial pictures showed large plumes of smoke alongside images of the White House and the major monuments as the nation's capital virtually shut down.[9]

King's murder brought to the fore the growing internal political strife within the civil rights movement. Ascendant Black Power figures saw in his death confirmation of the nation's inherent racism as well as the ineffectiveness of asking for, rather than demanding, full civil rights. Their harsh, increasingly violent rhetoric alienated even sympathetic whites. While the media focused on the repercussions of black disengagement from the political process and a potentially irreparable lack of trust between the races, whites responded in different ways. In the first weeks of April, pistol sales in Washington nearly doubled. In what the New York Times dubbed a "domestic arms race," residents of affluent, white areas such as the DC suburbs of Montgomery County quickly became newly minted gun owners. Ironically, polls showed perceptible spikes in white support for integration measures (particularly among northern whites)—anything to forestall another summer of rioting. For all of the multiracial public memorials in the wake of King's death, many Americans, both black and white, wondered whether the nation's tenuous experiment with a nonviolent civil rights movement had come to an end.[10]

For Kennedy and McCarthy the events of late March and early April transformed the presidential race. LBJ's departure and his call for peace talks with the North Vietnamese robbed both men of the key rationale for their candidacies. Kennedy, whose campaign speeches had become full-scale rhetorical assaults on the president, suddenly had no clear theme on which to run. McCarthy crudely noted, "Up to now Bobby was Jack running against Lyndon. Now Bobby has to run against Jack." For McCarthy the road ahead looked equally uncertain. No longer could he run as the iconoclastic challenger to Johnson. Now he faced off against a flesh-and-blood opponent with better name recognition and greater star power. Voters might have been willing to indulge the McCarthy insurgency when Johnson was the enemy, but with the nomination now in question he faced the prospect of greater scrutiny and skepticism.[11]

The Democrat's third wheel further complicated matters. While Vice President Hubert Humphrey initially remained mum about his plans, he was almost certain to jump in the race. When he formally announced his candidacy on April 27, he instantly became the front runner, inheriting the support of the Democratic establishment, which, to that point, had been in the president's corner. Had either Kennedy or McCarthy faced off against Humphrey, the contrast with the vice president would have made for a straightforward anti-incumbent campaign strategy. Now they each had to first muscle the other one out of the way.

Today, the battles for presidential nominations are long, drawn-out struggles waged in the small towns of New Hampshire, Iowa, South Carolina, and dozens of other US states. Primaries and caucuses are the main venues for choosing delegates to a party convention, which gives party members (i.e., voters) the opportunity to choose their party nominee directly.

Things in 1968 operated quite differently. Two methods existed for choosing delegates to the national convention—primaries and state conventions. There were, however, only a handful of the former, and not all were even binding. So, for example, under 40 percent of Democratic and Republican delegates were actually up for grabs in the primaries, but even that number was misleading. In many states, primaries were simply "beauty contests" that did not necessarily determine the makeup of a state party's delegation or how they were required to vote at the national convention. So while some delegations would be bound by the results of the primary (in Oregon the winner would get the support of all delegates on the first two ballots at the national convention), others would not be bound at all. Or in some cases, like New York and Pennsylvania, a second group of at-large delegates would be chosen by the state Democratic committee. One commentator at the time noted that for Democrats "the process of assembling the 2,989 men and women" whose job it would be to select the party nominee "follows not one but 55 sets of rules"—one for each of the states, plus the District of Columbia, Puerto Rico, Guam, the Virgin Islands, and the Panama Canal Zone. On the Republican side, the process was equally byzantine.[12]

So while the primaries served as important tools for assessing candidate strength and support within the party, the real action took place in state party confabs. There the most powerful Democratic officeholder in each state—a governor, big city mayor, senator, or state party head—generally wielded enormous influence, both in determining the makeup of the convention delegates and also in influencing the vote. In some cases those leaders would be so-called favorite son nominees, chosen by the conventions as the party's representative at the national convention and given control of the state delegation. In return for "releasing" their delegates, they could demand concessions from the likely party nominee.

This system gave party leaders ultimate control over who would get the party's presidential nod. Going into 1968, President Johnson held the advantage both because his key allies controlled a majority of the delegates through state conventions and also because there existed no clear way for a challenger to unseat him. Even if McCarthy or Kennedy won every primary, they would have nowhere close to a majority of the delegates. On the Republican side, the same situation existed. Richard Nixon largely ran the table in GOP primaries, but he still went to the national convention with far less than the majority of the delegates needed to win. By one estimate only about 150 of the delegates (out of a possible 1,333) were actually chosen by Republican primary voters.[13]

Kennedy's and McCarthy's hopes rested on doing so well in the state primaries that it would convince party leaders to abandon the president (and subsequently the vice president) and vote for them at the nominating convention. Having entered the race so late, the vice president missed all the deadlines for appearing on primary ballots. Considering he initially had no campaign infrastructure, no staff, and no money, it was just as well. As Kennedy and McCarthy gave speeches, cut TV ads, and pressed the flesh in the hopes of securing a handful of delegates to the national convention in Chicago, Humphrey directed his appeals toward the state Democratic conventions and, in turn, the party powerbrokers. These weren't the activists who had decamped to New Hampshire, knocking on doors and beseeching voters to cast a ballot for change but rather longtime party loyalists focused, first and foremost, on winning in November. They would be far more inclined to support Humphrey then either of these senatorial upstarts, which meant that as hard as it would have been for Kennedy or McCarthy to wrest the nomination from Johnson, the fight against Humphrey represented in some ways an even greater challenge. With the fleeting hope that they could build up the necessary political momentum—and accumulate enough delegates—going into the convention in Chicago the two men set out on the campaign trail in the spring of 1968.

Washington Post political reporter Richard Harwood dubbed the race between Kennedy and McCarthy "evangelist vs. philosopher." This apt narrative captured the contrasting political sensibilities of the two candidates: the unabashed liberalism of Gene McCarthy versus the more nuanced centrism of Bobby Kennedy. Such descriptions don't fit easily with the popular reputations of either man, with Kennedy remembered as the passionate and energetic liberal and McCarthy as the more sober and thoughtful conservative. But a closer look at their campaign positions—and their campaign strategies—shows the stark divide between their personal demeanor and their policy proposals.[14]

Kennedy's image as a political evangelist came about in large measure because of his words and deeds in the hours after King's assassination. Kennedy heard the news upon his arrival in Indianapolis, Indiana, the location of his first major primary battle with McCarthy. He had plans to speak that evening in the city's ghetto, but as word of the killing spread, his staff and wife Ethel begged him not to go. "I'm going to go there and that's it," he told them. If ever a moment demanded an appearance from Kennedy, this was it. No other white politician in America could have given the speech he delivered that night.[15]

Most of the assembled crowd had not yet heard what happened in Memphis, and the burden fell upon Kennedy to break the news. The overwhelmingly black crowd reacted to word of King's death with heart-wrenching wails. As a light rain fell on a chilly early spring night, Kennedy stood on the back of a flatbed truck lit only by a few footlights perched on the speaking platform. He wore an overcoat once owned by his brother and for the first time spoke publicly about JFK's death. "For those of you who are black and are tempted to be filled with hatred and mistrust of the injustice of such an act, against all white people," said Kennedy. "I would only say that I can also feel in my own heart the same kind of feeling. I had a member of my family killed, but he was killed by a white man."[16]

What American needed at this moment of profound tragedy, said Kennedy, who spoke extemporaneously, was not division or hatred, violence or lawlessness, but "love and wisdom and compassion toward one another," he told the crowd. Kennedy reminded them that "the vast majority of white people and the vast majority of black people in this country want to live together; want to improve the quality of our life; and want justice for all human beings that abide in our land." In the end, he asked that those present "dedicate ourselves to what the Greeks wrote so many years ago: to tame the savageness of man and make gentle the life of this world."[17]

The evocation of JFK's assassination, or perhaps the impassioned plea for racial unity, had a tranquilizing effect. No violence and no rioting took place in Indianapolis that evening. The civil rights leader and future congressman John Lewis, who worked for Kennedy and was present in Indianapolis, would later say that he found consolation in the fact that "we still have Bobby Kennedy. We still have hope."[18]

Kennedy's brief speech represented an accurate distillation of his feelings on the question of racial unity and reconciliation in America. That morning Kennedy had spoken at Ball State University, and there, before the country's divisions would be cruelly exploited once again, he was already talking about the urgent need to bridge America's racial fissures. After his speech a young black man stood up and said, "You are placing great faith in white America. Is this faith justified?" "Yes," Kennedy replied. "I think the vast majority of white people want to do the decent thing."[19]

While his own faith in the decency of white Americans would be consistently questioned and tested throughout the Indiana primary, Kennedy kept sounding this theme, to both black and white audiences. The day after his remarks in Indianapolis, Kennedy kept a scheduled appearance at the Cleveland City Club in Ohio. There, speaking before a group of business and local leaders, he decried the bloodshed, hatred, and "mindless menace of violence" in American society. "Only a cleansing of our whole society can remove this sickness from our soul," he declared.[20]

In tones reminiscent of Lincoln's Second Inaugural Address, Kennedy spoke of the broad national responsibility for the rot at the heart of America's soul. "There is another kind of violence, slower but just as deadly, destructive as the shot or the bomb in the night. This is the violence of institutions; indifference and inaction and slow decay." Unlike Johnson, Kennedy preferred the bully pulpit rather than the next government program to bridge America's divisions. "Surely, we can learn, at least, to look at those around us as fellow men and surely we can begin to work a little harder to bind up the wounds among us and to become in our own hearts brothers and countrymen once again."[21]

This language gave birth to the notion of Bobby the Uniter, the great white hope who would challenge the country to live up to its founding creed. Jack Newfield wrote that King's death opened Kennedy's eyes to the "deeper roots of America's internal disease" and that he began from that point forward "to imagine himself as the possible healer of that disease." Kennedy's rhetoric on the campaign trail certainly suggested as much. For the next two months he would be the only candidate openly preaching a message of racial reconciliation.[22]

However, while many liberals applauded when Kennedy declared that America could and must do better, many others believed that crime, not racial division, was the most important issue facing America in 1968. To them the burden of ending poverty fell as much on the shoulders of black America as it did on white America. Whites had pulled themselves up by their bootstraps. Why couldn't blacks? At the University of Indiana on April 26, Kennedy spoke to a group of mostly white medical students and doctors. When a black audience member yelled out, "We want Bobby!" a chorus of white voices shouted back, "No we don't!" When Kennedy talked about his plans to increase health care access for the poor, someone in the audience yelled out, "Where are you going to get the money?" Kennedy sternly and unapologetically responded, "From you." He lectured the group in moral, occasionally pedantic terms: "I look around this room and I don't see many black faces who will become doctors....I don't see many people coming here from slums, or off the Indian reservations. You are the privileged ones here....You sit here as a white medical student, while black people carry the burden of the fighting in Vietnam." David Halberstam would later write of Kennedy that nothing seemed to inflame him more than coming into contact with those who didn't feel the same sense of indignation as he did.[23]

It remained far from clear, however, whether white Indiana voters were interested in Kennedy's pleas. Harwood noted that when the candidate spoke to campaign audiences about "unmet social needs and the racial crisis," it became "obvious that many of them, particularly the young, [were] not listening." Rather, wrote Harwood, "everybody seemed to be smiling."[24]

The ambivalence of white voters would not be lost on Kennedy. Indeed, after a few weeks of campaigning his language subtly shifted. He began touting himself as the candidate of "law and order." He boasted that as attorney general he had been the "chief law enforcement officer" in the country and that he understood "the importance of obeying the law." As Kennedy toured Indiana's conservative white communities, the emphasis of his talks moved away from minority suffering and toward "lawlessness and violence and disorders." *New York Times* political correspondent Warren Weaver said of Kennedy's speeches, "There is very little said about civil rights outside the Negro communities of Lake County and in Indianapolis, but there is steady emphasis on putting down the riots, with force if need be, to preserve the public peace." Kennedy also began to speak less about the need for sacrifice from white Americans. He avoided talk of fully integrating blacks into white communities. He spoke, rather, of his plans to bring more private enterprise into the ghettoes and hand off responsibility for poverty-related issues to the states. "We can't have the Federal Government in here telling people what's good for them," he said. "We've got to get away from the welfare system, the handout system and the idea of the dole."[25]

Kennedy's conspicuous move to the right frustrated his liberal advisors, but he understood that he needed to play the old politics game when necessary—and that ideological purity must take a back seat to winning votes. "I'm the Negro candidate," he told campaign speechwriter Jeff Greenfield. "I have to tell white people I care about what they care about." The politics of the era also demanded it. "I'll talk racial reconciliation for ten minutes, and it's cold as can be," Kennedy told his staff. "I'll talk about [how] we've...got to enforce the law, and they'll break loose. Now are we trying to win votes, or are we trying to drop dead here?" By the spring of 1968, crime and social disorder topped polls as the most important domestic issues facing the country. No candidate could hope to win the White House without talking about them. But liberals consistently downplayed the issue. (Johnson in his memoirs would complain that voters "failed to understand" that law enforcement was handled, largely, by local governments.) This failure to more directly address legitimate concerns about crime and public safety would weaken the confidence of once-loyal New Deal Democrats and hamstring the party. Democrats ceded the policy ground on law and order to Republicans, which contributed to the politicized and punitive policy responses on crime that would predominate in the years to come.[26]

Kennedy's private enterprise boosterism, however, was a different matter. In the Senate, he had made the relocation of private companies into inner-city neighborhoods, like New York City's Bedford-Stuyvesant, a signature element of his legislative agenda. In the mid-1960s this represented an innovative idea, particularly coming from a Democrat, and it dovetailed closely with Kennedy's political philosophy, which looked very different from the liberalism traditionally associated with Democrats. Kennedy wasn't indifferent to the plight of the poor; few American politicians demonstrated more concern for America's underclass than he did. Rather, it reflected his long-standing suspicion of bureaucracies and his focus on deficits of spirit, as opposed to deficits of material resources.[27]

Using the free market as a tool for urban revitalization also brought political benefits: fewer tax dollars for minority communities and less inconvenience for middle-class whites. More jobs in black neighborhoods meant fewer blacks looking for work in and moving into white ones. There was a great deal of wishful thinking to Kennedy's middle course. And at a moment when activist government found itself under attack from emboldened conservatives, such proposals ran the risk of further undermining the case for government solutions to these challenges. Private enterprise would turn out to be an imperfect and far less committed tool for fighting poverty—and others would use an argument similar to Kennedy's for making the case against a stronger public role in rehabilitating America's slums. Indeed,

RFK's words did not go unnoticed by his Republican rivals. The presumptive GOP nominee, Richard Nixon, who gave a major speech in mid-May calling for a return of federal power to the states and greater black economic empowerment, said, "Bobby and I have been sounding pretty much alike." Reagan joked, "I get the feeling that I've been writing some of his speeches," and even suggested that Kennedy should perhaps be considered the most conservative figure in the campaign. Kennedy pushed back, claiming that his Republican critics had never actually proposed "any concrete measures to accomplish local control." It's hard to imagine many voters grasped the nuance of Kennedy's position.[28]

Kennedy's centrist appeals would make for one of the many ironies of the 1968 Democratic campaign. In the early primaries McCarthy ran as the sober, quiet, and thoughtful pragmatist. He didn't raise his voice or play on voter emotions, and his speeches sounded more like civic lessons than calls to action. But as the campaign evolved, his domestic policy positions became increasingly far-reaching. Schlesinger would later muse that McCarthy said "radical things in a temperate way," and on racial integration, fixing the ghettos, and the responsibility of government to tackle these challenges he went much further than RFK.[29]

In a major speech in late May at the University of California, Davis, McCarthy unleashed a blistering attack on the Johnson Administration for its inattention to the cities, but also at Kennedy's plans for fixing them. "Poverty in America is no accident, any more than Vietnam is an accident," he argued. For McCarthy such destitution reflected a lack of attention "to the misery of our cities," and, above all, national resources being diverted to a war being fought six thousand miles away. Early in the primary campaign, McCarthy had offered a similar complaint, decrying the White House's relentless focus on the war in Vietnam for taking money away from America's cities, the fight against poverty, and a host of domestic challenges. "We cannot spend over $26 billion a year in Vietnam and still have safe and beautiful cities, fully financed school aid programs, and adequate health care programs for our citizens," he said in a February speech in Miami.[30]

McCarthy was striking at the heart of the liberal consensus—namely the belief that government had a responsibility to expand economic and social opportunity, while also maintaining a global commitment to containing communism. Vietnam had not only taken resources and political support away from Great Society programs, McCarthy argued, but had so shaken American society, and in particular the left, that the energy to continue liberalism's grand project in social reform had been greatly reduced. As Martin Luther King, Jr., presciently noted in the spring of 1967, "the Great Society...has been shot down on the battlefields of Vietnam."[31]

McCarthy's argument struck a powerful chord with liberals who for two decades had, on a national level, acted as though the United States could indeed enjoy both guns and butter. Vietnam convinced many on the left that the time had come to turn inward. Four years later, McCarthy's message would find its way into the acceptance speech of the Democratic presidential nominee, George McGovern, who noted, "For 30 years we have been so absorbed with fear and danger from abroad that we have permitted our own house to fall into disarray." In words that could have come directly from McCarthy's 1968 campaign speeches, McGovern asked America to "come home" from "military spending so wasteful that it weakens our nation."[32]

McCarthy's take on race relations, which echoed the most radical language of black separatists, provided an equally unorthodox perspective. He compared the plight of American Negroes to that of a "colonial" people living under duress. His solution: massive government intervention and a host of new public programs. "The ghetto will not be fundamentally affected until a new politics in America addresses itself to our society as a whole," said McCarthy. He believed that Kennedy's plan for fixing the ghettos' problems through "private enterprise" would "never be sufficient" in rehabilitating America's slums. "The ghetto may have a few more factories and a few more jobs, but it will remain a colony." He considered the plan a "retreat from the ideal of integration in American life." Instead, he called for building more "modern mass-transit systems to enable the ghetto unemployed to reach the jobs in the outer metropolitan areas," and providing millions of new housing units, improved health care, educational facilities, and job training. What McCarthy proposed went beyond even what Johnson had contemplated with the Great Society. Rather than pacifying white middle-class voters worried about the impact of racial integration, McCarthy argued that the key to eliminating misery in America's inner cities lay in bringing minorities into white communities—and plunging more taxpayer dollars into the effort.[33]

McCarthy's recommendations were driven, in large measure, by the need to differentiate himself from Kennedy on domestic issues, and they rested on generalities rather than sketched-out policy ideas. Nonetheless, at a time when Kennedy was talking about using the private sector to rehabilitate the nation's slums and when Republicans were pushing to give the states more control over antipoverty monies, McCarthy boldly made the case for continued, even ramped up, federal spending and engagement.

In the immediate aftermath of the election Democrats would end up hewing more closely to McCarthy's moralizing vision of a strong governmental role in fighting poverty than to Kennedy's "third way." Nearly a quarter century would pass before Democrats would embrace Kennedy's call. McCarthy, who as a House member in the late 1950s helped found the Democratic Study Group, which pushed for more liberal legislation in Congress, represented more than a last gasp of New Deal liberalism. He offered a cri de cœur for the idea that the federal government had an active and affirmative role to play in solving the nation's most intractable social challenges.[34]

The greatest divergence between the two candidates, however, would come on the question of America's role in the world—and the conduct of its foreign policy. Both McCarthy and Kennedy were strongly opposed to the Vietnam War, but the latter, while a fierce critic of the conflict, kept his critique within a constricted framework. The war represented a moral outrage, but for Kennedy it did not necessarily signal a larger failure of US Cold War policy. His call, when announcing his candidacy, for Americans to assume "moral leadership" of the planet echoed the pledge in his brother's inaugural address to pay any price and bear any burden for the cause of liberty. In Indiana, Kennedy called for "no more Vietnams," and, unlike most other public figures, Kennedy took direct responsibility for his role in initiating the policies that led to war. But he also vacillated over how far he would take his critique of US Cold War foreign policy.[35]

McCarthy, on the other hand, directly challenged the fundamental tenets of American foreign policy thinking. Early on in the campaign he railed against a conflict he called contrary not only to American traditions, but also to Eisenhower's and JFK's resistance to direct US involvement in anti-Communist fights in the Caribbean and Southeast Asia. As he complained about the dangerously increased role of the military in American life—and the use of Orwellian euphemisms like "kill ratio"—he said US conduct in Vietnam could no longer be viewed as "militarily defensible or morally defensible."[36]

By late May, McCarthy's campaign rhetoric began to take a distinctly more radical turn. In a speech at the Cow Palace in San Francisco he offered a stinging rebuke to Kennedy, Humphrey, and the larger foreign policy establishment. His remarks, ironically, grew out of a near-disastrous gaffe. Speaking to reporters on his campaign plane days earlier, he suggested that he could support Humphrey over Kennedy provided the vice president shifted his position on the war. The statement risked alienating McCarthy's core supporters, who felt as much hostility toward the vice president as they did toward Johnson. Even worse, it made him look like a stalking horse for his fellow Minnesotan. It became essential that McCarthy clearly differentiate his position on the war from both Humphrey and Kennedy.

Echoing arguments he had laid out a year earlier in *The Limits of Power*, McCarthy told the audience at the Cow Palace that "involvement in Vietnam was no accident; it did not happen overnight.... It came out of the consensus of the policies which have long been the principal guidelines for American conduct in this world." McCarthy bemoaned the fact that "containment and a continuation of the Cold War" and assuming a "moral mission" as the "world's judge and the world's policeman" continued to define US foreign policy, just as it had in the 1950s and early 1960s. In McCarthy's view, no effort had been undertaken to better understand the world or American's key rivals. While McCarthy's strongest denunciations were aimed at Kennedy, Humphrey did not go unscathed. The vice president had become the war's "most ardent apologist," and remained in thrall to "the theory of monolithic Communist conspiracy, the susceptibility of political problems to military solutions and the duty to impose American idealism upon foreign cultures."[37]

McCarthy directly challenged the pretensions of global leadership and the inflated view of American power that dominated the nation's politics. This far-reaching critique kept pace with his increasing propensity for campaign-trail provocations. Early on, McCarthy remained somewhat circumspect about what he would do differently in Vietnam—a curious stance for a candidate whose main rationale for running was opposition to the war. But as time went on McCarthy increasingly unburdened himself and began arguing for the withdrawal of American soldiers from Vietnam. "The time has come when we must say that we shall take our steel out of the land of thatched huts," McCarthy would tell supporters. In Oregon, he said to an editorial board that he basically stood prepared to "surrender" in Vietnam.[38]

He seemed to delight in pushing political boundaries. During the Indiana primary, one of McCarthy's speechwriters, Jeremy Larner, gently mentioned to McCarthy that in light of the state's conservative electorate he might want to lay off criticism of FBI director J. Edgar Hoover. The next day McCarthy appeared on CBS's *Face the Nation* and demanded that Hoover be removed from office. Larner's speechwriting colleague Paul Gorman later recounted, "He probably did it just to ... show Jeremy that he wasn't going to be playing that kind of game, but also because he believed it." McCarthy spoke of establishing diplomatic relations with Communist China and returning Cuba under Castro "to the family of nations." He called the Cold War "a concept ... which has outlived its usefulness." His incitements represented the first serious criticisms of anti-Communist orthodoxy heard on the campaign trail since Henry Wallace's failed independent run in 1948. Behind McCarthy's taciturn and sober image lay one of the most radical Democratic presidential contenders of the Cold War era.[39]

While McCarthy increasingly tried to separate himself from Kennedy on policy grounds and Kennedy increasingly tried to distance himself from his earlier calls for racial reconciliation, it had little impact on their key bases of support. Even though he called for reversing the trend of Great Society programs and promoted private enterprise solutions over public spending in the nation's ghettoes, Kennedy lost none of his popularity among blacks and Latinos. "There's something about a Kennedy candidacy," Larry O'Brien later said; "there's a tendency to focus on the candidate, the image, the personality, and to a lesser extent on the issues." At the same time, McCarthy talked about moving blacks out of the inner cities—and yet suburban voters remained among his biggest supporters. But in a phenomenon that would become the norm in US presidential elections, what the candidates said on the campaign trail mattered far less than how they said it.[40]

Indeed, McCarthy's problem with black voters was not his policy prescriptions; it was that he refused to make a concerted effort to reach out to them. "Go look at my record," he would tell black audiences. "Record, hell!" yelled a black activist at a meeting in Washington, DC. "Tell us what you feel." McCarthy refused to engage in what he saw as pandering and identity politics and derided Kennedy for having "twenty-six separate committees to deal with twenty-six varieties of Americans—like twenty-six varieties of ice cream." Prone to speaking, as one McCarthy supporter put it, in "the lingo of a 1940s liberal" he was too reserved, too prescriptive, and too detached when he spoke to black audiences. "The cat [Kennedy] was able to relax," said one black leader in Indiana, "McCarthy didn't put himself in it." He could also come across as patronizing, sometimes using the expression "these people" in reference to the black community.[41]

In Wisconsin, McCarthy's press secretary (and later renowned journalist) Seymour Hersh and his assistant Mary Lou Oates quit the campaign because of McCarthy's refusal to venture into the black ghettoes of Milwaukee. To minimize the political fallout from their departure, the campaign cobbled together a speech on race and took a tour of black neighborhoods, where McCarthy spent as much time ducking reporters as he did meeting actual residents. At one point three black boys playing basketball saw the scrum of white reporters and campaign handlers coming toward them and fled as quickly as they could. While his press releases referenced the "cancer" of "white racism" and a "racist mentality" that had corrupted "our whole society," McCarthy could not find it within himself to make the same sort of emotional appeals on the stump.[42]

Kennedy did not have the same problem. Yet his strong support among minority voters, which was key to his political success in 1968, was a double-edged sword. In one California poll an overwhelming 61 percent of respondents agreed with the statement "Robert Kennedy spends most of his time courting minority groups." Seven in ten disagreed with the notion that he was a "man who can bring peace to the cities." Increasingly, there was a sizable racial divide in voter assessments of Kennedy. One late May poll showed that 94 percent of blacks believed that he had "many of the same outstanding qualities" as his slain brother; among the overall population, only 40 percent made such a positive comparison. In the Indiana primary Bobby dominated among the state's minority population, winning approximately nine out of ten black votes. Those numbers helped spur him to a plurality victory with 42 percent of the vote versus 27 percent for McCarthy and 31 percent for Governor Roger Branigin, running as a favorite son candidate and stand-in for Vice President Humphrey.[43]

With blue-collar white voters—the so-called backlash voters—the story is more mixed. Indeed, Indiana is the place where the myth of the Kennedy "coalition" was born, the result, in large measure, of a postelection article by Evans and Novak entitled "Kennedy's Indiana Victory Proves His Appeal Defuses Backlash Voting," which claimed that RFK had run 2–1 ahead of his opponents in some Polish districts. The *New York Times* also reported that Kennedy had performed well in the white working-class wards that had voted for George Wallace during the Democratic primary in 1964. "Some of these voters," said the *Times*, "indicated to reporters that although Mr. Kennedy had the Negro vote they looked upon him also as a tough-minded Irishman with whom they could identify." Reporters quickly seized upon the narrative because it matched what they saw with their own eyes on the campaign trail—the intense response to Kennedy from blacks in the ghettos and working-class whites in adjoining blue-collar districts. Kennedy represented, the liberal writer Paul Cowan said in the *Village Voice*, "the last liberal politician who could communicate with working class America" and attract white workers and blacks at the same time.[44]

But, in reality, reporters saw a mirage. While Kennedy did well among German and Italian Catholic voters as well as some blue-collar Protestants, he only won about 30 percent of the white vote in Indiana. He did the best in cities (home to most of the state's African American voters) and among

Catholics, and worst with affluent, white-collar, well-educated voters as well as those who lived in communities abutting predominately African American neighborhoods. In Lake County, Indiana, which included the gritty industrial city of Gary, Kennedy's dreams of a multiracial coalition came face-to-face with the reality of the white backlash. He lost fifty-nine out of seventy of the county's predominately white precincts—scoring 34 percent of their vote against 49 percent for McCarthy. According to vanden Heuvel and Milton Gwirtzman, two Kennedy advisors who wrote a postmortem of the '68 campaign, of the fifteen Lake County cities townships in which Wallace had won outright in 1964, thirteen went to McCarthy. In neighboring Porter County, McCarthy won outright—one of only four counties he won in the state. In all, 80 percent of Kennedy's vote in Gary—and nearly half of his backing in the state—came from African Americans.[45]

While the racial divide clearly played a role in Kennedy's low support among whites, his problems in Indiana ran even deeper. A Harris poll taken in mid-April showed Kennedy with 50 percent of the vote in Indiana. By Election Day he'd slipped to 42 percent, while McCarthy picked up an additional eight points. It suggested that, for all of Kennedy's energetic campaigning, he failed to bring many new voters into his column, and may have actually rallied votes for his opponents. While Kennedy's Indiana win gave a boost to the campaign, many of his aides considered it a "disappointment." He couldn't finish McCarthy off, which meant that the draining primary campaign would continue.[46]

Considering Indiana's conservative electorate, McCarthy should have been well positioned. But Kennedy dramatically overshadowed him—as did Branigin, practically the only candidate featured in the state's conservative newspaper the *Indianapolis Sun* (whose publisher, Eugene Pulliam, was the grandfather of future vice president Dan Quayle and no fan of the Kennedys). Two press buses followed Kennedy; McCarthy only got one, and it was half empty. Except for his well-received appearances on the state's college campuses, attendance at McCarthy events was sparse. Unlike in Wisconsin and New Hampshire, he lacked an effective state organization and the money to compete with Kennedy. Bogged down by an ineffectual campaign manager, too many communications advisors, a lack of coordination between the national and local campaign efforts, and a candidate serenely, even proudly, uninterested in the details of the campaign, McCarthy likely had it right when he later said, "Probably, we should never have gone into Indiana, and if we had to, we probably shouldn't have done anything more than play baseball."[47]

McCarthy's one advantage in Indiana would be the backing of middle-class suburbanites and affluent, highly educated voters. This would take on greater importance as the race moved west to Oregon—a state that Kennedy, not inaccurately, called "one giant suburb." When a Kennedy aide asked about organizing city ghettoes, Oregon congresswoman Edith Green, who coordinated the state campaign effort for Kennedy, responded matter-of-factly, "There are no ghettoes in Oregon." Politically independent, affluent and middle-class Oregon voters were more inclined to support a candidate who used reason rather than emotion to make his pitch, and less likely to rally behind a candidate whose appeal remained greatest among "people who have problems," as Kennedy put it. "He had no contact with, no rapport with, no feel for, the petit bourgeois, the suburbanites," said John Bartlow Martin, a campaign aide. With two vocal antiwar senators, Democrat Wayne Morse and liberal Republican Mark Hatfield (which made the electorate particularly sympathetic to the original dove in the race), Oregon was McCarthy country.[48]

McCarthy got an extra boost from the fact that his dysfunctional national staff descended on Indiana and Nebraska, the site of a May 14 presidential primary, and thus couldn't involve themselves as directly in the Oregon campaign. Instead, local organizers—many of whom had been part of the antiwar movement since 1965—imitated the tactics used to such great effect in New Hampshire and Wisconsin. By the time voters went to the polls in Indiana, forty-two McCarthy groups were operating in Oregon versus ten for Kennedy.[49]

Everything about the Kennedy campaign in Oregon seemed off: poor organization, a message badly out of tune with the state's voters, and a candidate more likely to be met on the campaign trail by blank stares than adulation. Days before the vote, he said, "If I get beaten in any primary, I am not a very viable candidate." It was the sort of first-category political error that one would hardly expect from an experienced politician. Later, when he stripped down during a walk along the coast with his wife and ran into the chilly Pacific water, Oregon voters came to see the move as a political stunt. (Kennedy's advisors had privately recommended a beach trip because they felt it would make him more appealing to Oregon's "great outdoorsman" and change the growing image of RFK as the candidate of "hip youth and giddy women.") During an event at a zoo in Portland, he was preparing to leave just as McCarthy arrived for his own campaign rally. Fearful of a head-to-head meeting, Kennedy jumped into his car to make a quick escape, but TV cameras caught the whole scene, panning directly from McCarthy's motorcade to Kennedy's departing one. Taking full advantage of the opportunity, McCarthy leaped on board Kennedy's press bus to kibitz with reporters.[50]

Kennedy badly underestimated his opponent. From the beginning of McCarthy's quixotic effort, Kennedy had consistently dismissed his rival in both personal and political terms. Privately, he levied a litany of criticisms against him, born of past political grievances, particularly McCarthy's support for Adlai Stevenson at the 1960 Democratic Convention in Los Angeles. "Gene McCarthy felt he should have been the first Catholic President just because he knew more St. Thomas Aquinas than my brother," Kennedy said to Newfield. Like many of McCarthy's contemporaries, Kennedy found him lazy, imperious, and flippant about legislating and politics. "Gene just isn't a nice person," he said at one point. When McCarthy began to aim his campaign jabs more directly at Kennedy, his response was resentment and annoyance. Kennedy, who had been the chief arm twister in the nasty 1960 campaign for the Democratic nomination of his brother, should have known better. His anger seemed to be grounded less in the specific nature of McCarthy's digs and more in the fact that he had the temerity to make them. McCarthy was a difficult man to like, and Kennedy would hardly be the first—or last—person to find him insufferable. His mistake lay in allowing it to affect his political judgment.[51]

Compounding Kennedy's personal dislike lay a deeper grievance— McCarthy had done what Kennedy could not. The night of his victory in the Indiana primary, Kennedy stopped in the Indianapolis airport to get a late meal and began chatting with two McCarthy supporters waiting for a flight home (one was the future civil rights historian and Martin Luther King biographer Taylor Branch). Kennedy acknowledged that while he admired his rival's courage for getting in the race first, he was just "toying" with them. McCarthy "really didn't want to be president," said Kennedy. He couldn't go into the ghettoes; he couldn't talk to poor people; he couldn't bring all Americans together the way that Kennedy believed he could. Still, neither activist budged in their support for McCarthy. "[Kennedy] had won in Indiana, but he couldn't win over those kids, and they really got to him," said Dutton. Loyalty to McCarthy, born during the lonely struggle against Johnson in New Hampshire, would not fade so easily.[52]

After the '68 presidential campaign, a voluminous oral history of McCarthy's staffers and volunteers was assembled. It is filled with accounts of activists and campaign aides who, while never quite sold on McCarthy the man, revered him for having the courage to challenge Johnson. "I don't think that I'll get over feelings of real gratitude toward Gene McCarthy for having run and for having made so many things possible," said Arthur Herzog, who coordinated McCarthy's efforts in Oregon and later wrote a memoir of the campaign. Joel Berger, who worked for McCarthy in Wisconsin, said, "I felt that those of us who were opposed to the war in Vietnam and had any political experience at all, had really, almost a civic duty to help this man because he was the only one who had stood up."[53]

Allard Lowenstein spoke even more glowingly of McCarthy. "We all had our heroes," said Lowenstein years later. "Jack Kennedy, Mrs. Roosevelt, but...none of them had ever been so heroic or had so many people owing him so much as Gene McCarthy." Lowenstein said it was something that Kennedy and his people could never fully appreciate. "They never understood the depth of feeling on the issues, and therefore, the depth of gratitude to McCarthy that he made the fight when Kennedy wouldn't."[54]

In between the Indiana primary in early May and Oregon at the end of the month, the race briefly sojourned to Nebraska for the state's Democratic primary. Kennedy ran aggressively; McCarthy did not, and the New York senator won a smashing victory. After the results Pierre Salinger, who had become a spokesman for the campaign, told reporters, "Senator McCarthy is no longer a credible candidate." His work had been done, and now the A team would take over, or so Salinger implied. "If there was one argument that was designed to make people stay with McCarthy and that was designed to make people furious, it was that," said Lowenstein. That he couldn't win had been the same excuse Kennedy made to beg off challenging Johnson in the fall. Such curt dismissals also served to enhance McCarthy's loathing of Kennedy and convince him to carry on. He would rarely miss an opportunity to remind voters that Kennedy had been "lighting bonfires" on the mountains while McCarthy and his army of volunteers toiled in the valley below. Nearly twenty years later, when McCarthy wrote his autobiography, *Up 'Til Now*, that looked back at his life in politics, contempt for Kennedy still permeated his recounting of the 1968 campaign.[55]

Beyond his personal animus, McCarthy loathed Kennedy's campaign style. "It's almost an offense," he said, to approach voters "as though you had to stir up their emotions to deal with problems which are as serious and as emotion-laden as issues like poverty and . . . the war." McCarthy, who found it difficult to ask people to vote for him, saw the insertion of emotional, personalized appeals into the campaign as precisely the sort of politics that were harming the country. "The last thing he wanted to do was be charismatic," said the poet Robert Lowell, who was a close confidante and traveling companion of McCarthy during the spring.[56]

While Kennedy chose to ignore his campaign-trail rival and devote his attention instead to Humphrey, McCarthy figured out how to spin his annoyance into an effective message: he focused on RFK's continued refusal to debate him. Since Indiana, McCarthy and his team had been trying to get Kennedy to meet, believing that their man would easily triumph in a head-to-head matchup. Kennedy demurred, intimidated in part by McCarthy's apparent intellect. Said Mankiewicz, "He never really did trust himself in that kind of give and take." The refusal to meet McCarthy left him on the defensive for the entire Oregon campaign, and fed the worst stereotypes about his candidacy—that he was trying to buy a primary win and that his idealism was tinged by ruthlessness and a win-at-any-cost mentality.[57]

Already a negative image of the candidate had started to take hold. According to a Harris survey in May, 67 percent of voters saw Kennedy as an opportunist; six months earlier only 46 percent had viewed him as such. In November 1967, 35 percent of voters thought he was too ambitious to be president; by May that number had jumped to 46 percent. In November, most voters compared him favorably to his brother; by May 1968, a majority found him to be a pale substitute for the slain president. In addition, a strong majority (55 percent) disagreed that his performance in the primaries to date proved he could win the presidency in November. His slippage in head-to-head polls with Humphrey and McCarthy was, however, the most dramatic sign of his political decline. Another early May Gallup survey found that only a quarter of voters wanted to see Democrats pick Kennedy as the standard-bearer in Chicago, placing him behind both McCarthy and Humphrey. In the fall of '67, Kennedy had led the president, among Democrats, by double digits. Such polling provides an imperfect snapshot. In November 1967, Johnson had been deeply unpopular, and Kennedy, unsurprisingly, appeared to be a more palatable alternative. By May 1968, public scrutiny had increased significantly. Nonetheless, Kennedy's months on the trail had clearly done little to improve his public image.[58]

In Oregon, McCarthy's TV and radio ads took on a decidedly more aggressive tone. One of the most effective spots showed a picture of the two candidates while a voice-over intoned, "This is probably the only time you'll see them together on television." During the last ten days of the campaign, Oregon voters were inundated with ads saying, "[Kennedy] wouldn't stand up to Johnson in New Hampshire. Now he won't stand up to McCarthy in Oregon." Kennedy had no good response. Caught between two competing impulses—to embrace the activist grass-roots politics of the era (as McCarthy did) or take the more traditional route of old-style politics—Kennedy chose the latter. In Oregon, it blew up in his face.[59]

On election night he netted 39 percent of the vote to McCarthy's 45 percent. Evans and Novak described the loss as a "disaster." In their conversations with party leaders they heard "great rejoicing over Kennedy's defeat" and a sense of "emancipation" allowing them to now "openly oppose" the powerful Kennedy clan. Above all, the defeat punctured the family's aura of political invincibility. Oregon was the first time, in twenty-six contests, that a Kennedy lost an election.[60]

Since the beginning of the campaign for the Democratic nomination, the California primary in early June had shone brightest on the electoral horizon. With 174 delegates at stake, the winner would receive an enormous burst of political momentum heading into the convention. For McCarthy and Kennedy it represented a crucial test, but especially for the latter. A Kennedy loss would almost certainly convince the party powerbrokers that sticking with Humphrey offered the safest path.

For McCarthy, even if he lost narrowly, he would stay in the race for the upcoming New York primary. There his strong local campaign team gave him a reasonable chance of besting Kennedy, who was unpopular among local activists. In fact, McCarthy needed Kennedy to do well enough in California that he would stay in the race, since his only real chance of winning the nomination would be a fractured Democratic convention—unable to choose between Humphrey and RFK—that instead turned to him. Not surprisingly, however, McCarthy wasn't about to curl up and play dead, especially for Kennedy.[61]

With poll numbers showing him down by as much as nineteen points in California, and Kennedy's own internal polling suggesting that it appeared "certain" their man would win, McCarthy made a remarkable comeback. In America's largest media market he put to good use his best and most underappreciated asset—his television presence. Goodwin, who masterminded McCarthy's media strategy in New Hampshire, called him the "best television candidate since Jack Kennedy." While pictures of Robert Kennedy being mauled by adoring crowds ran on nightly newscasts, McCarthy's TV spots offered a very different feel. They featured the dignified and composed Minnesotan, observing all his proper cues, speaking extemporaneously but coherently, presenting voters with a reasoned and unemotional argument for his candidacy. His local campaign—informed by the efforts in New Hampshire and Oregon and bolstered by the state's seemingly "inexhaustible supply" of college students and housewives—out-organized and out-canvassed the Kennedy forces.[62]

Kennedy, however, did not lack for political assets. California's large African American and Hispanic populations remained solidly in his camp. As with his first trip to the state in March, they gave him a rapturous welcome. A

daytime motorcade ride down the streets of downtown Los Angeles provided a memorable snapshot of Kennedy on the campaign trail. *American
Melodrama*, a remembrance of the '68 campaign by three British journalists,
recounts the response to Kennedy in both the business district and the
barrio: "Cheers, sobs, laughter, and cries of 'Viva Kennedy!' echoed off the
walls of the buildings. Women, with their lipstick smeared and hair disor-
dered, galloped along beside Kennedy's car. People reached out to touch
him: again his cufflinks vanished, his shirt soaked with sweat under the hot
sun." When Kennedy toured predominately Mexican American neighborhoods, one campaign aide said, it seemed like something "out of Viva
Zapata." There remained the risk that the adoration would turn off some
white voters—and campaign advisors tried to limit the candidate's appearances in black and Hispanic neighborhoods—but there was no escaping the
fact that Kennedy's best path to victory lay in energizing and mobilizing
minority voters.[63]

The intensity of the California campaign, however, produced further ill-
will between the two candidates. No longer able to ignore his opponent,
Kennedy took the surprising step of directly accusing McCarthy of "de-
meaning" American politics by turning his candidacy into nothing more
than a "campaign to distort me and to stop me." For his part, McCarthy
mocked Kennedy's declaration that he would quit the race if he lost in
California. He said it reminded him of a "child holding his breath unless
you do something for him."[64]

There would also be one other concession to political reality: Kennedy
could no longer refuse to debate McCarthy. The Saturday before the primary the two men met in a Los Angeles television studio for their only
face-off of the campaign. McCarthy gave a listless and uninspired performance. At the moment when he needed to highlight the key differences
between himself and Kennedy, he instead played them down. When asked
at one point about the distinctions between the two candidates, McCarthy
suggested that they "probably disagree some on Dean Rusk [Johnson's secretary of state] and on Robert McNamara and on some of the persons in
government." While McCarthy had been regularly calling on Rusk to resign,
this hardly covered the panoply of variances between the two men, and the
political value of pointing out differences over cabinet members was hard

to discern. Even worse, when given the opportunity to expand on his Cow Palace speech, McCarthy failed to take it.[65]

However, McCarthy's hesitancy on domestic issues did even greater damage. When questioned about rehabilitating the nation's slums, McCarthy echoed the position he had taken in his Davis speech. "Most of the employment is now in the belt line outside of the cities, and I don't think we ought to perpetuate the ghetto.... What we have got to do is to try and break that up. Otherwise, we are adopting a kind of apartheid in this country." Kennedy, who had been told by Unruh during debate preparation that he needed to use language that would appeal to the white middle class, pounced. "We have forty million Negroes who are in the ghettos at the present time. We have here in the state of California a million Mexican-Americans whose poverty is even greater than many of the black people. You say you are going to take ten thousand black people and move them into Orange County."[66]

Aside from the fact that this didn't reflect McCarthy's actual position, Kennedy's statement appeared to be an effort to play directly on white fears of integration. That Kennedy referred to the wealthy, all-white, and stridently conservative community of Orange County (which he later weakly claimed was not purposeful, but rather was the first California county that he could think of) made the attack bad enough. Even worse was the charge that McCarthy wanted to move minorities out of the ghettos and into largely white suburbs. In 1964, the state had been shaken by a ballot initiative to repeal the Rumford Fair Housing Act, which sought to end racial discrimination in housing. The act had sparked an angry response among white residents in the state, fearful of an influx of black neighbors, and the repeal effort not only represented a first volley in the emerging backlash against civil rights legislation, but it directly aided Ronald Reagan's election as governor two years later. For a candidate who prided himself on challenging white audiences about the urgent need for racial unity, it represented his lowest moment of the campaign.[67]

Inexplicably, however, McCarthy failed to respond. He meekly stumbled through an incoherent answer: "I didn't want to raise—I thought that you really—when this position was first raised, this was not your clear position of concentrating that much on the ghettos." Perhaps McCarthy had been confused by Kennedy's answer, or maybe the fumbling response reflected his oft-stated desire to avoid political confrontation. But whatever the reason, his nonrejoinder—and overall weak debate performance—stopped his political momentum dead in its tracks.[68]

Post-debate polling indicated that by a 55–38 percent margin, voters thought Kennedy had done the better job; internal polling for the Kennedy campaign told an even better story—undecided voters in the California suburbs where McCarthy had been gaining strength had swung back to his challenger. Three days later, the combination of those undecided voters and overwhelming support from African American and Mexican American voters propelled Kennedy to a narrow win—46 to 42 percent (ironically, Kennedy's Orange County gambit did him little good, as McCarthy won the suburb handily). Kennedy hadn't gotten the knockout that his camp had hoped for, but with the addition of a big victory that night in South Dakota (the state of Humphrey's birth), his campaign received a much-needed jolt.[69]

Around midnight, the candidate left his suite at the Ambassador Hotel in downtown Los Angeles to give his victory remarks in a sweltering ballroom packed with overwrought supporters and practically pulsating with energy. Gwirtzman recalled later that the scene had a "surreal quality" as Kennedy spoke. "I remember sensing almost a frightening suppressed violence in the way the crowd roared back at him. I remember feeling that this sort of mass crowd response, which had built up to such a fever pitch, was almost too strong, dangerously strong, the crowd an object for a demagogue. I had never seen an intensity, in one room, in one election night, before or since."[70]

Though Kennedy told ABC News earlier that evening that if he lost four out of five primaries (as McCarthy had done), "I'd be finished off," his remarks were among his most magnanimous of the campaign. He went out of his way to praise McCarthy and his followers ("All of us are involved in this great effort"), and he challenged Humphrey to debate in what direction each man wanted to take the nation. Privately, Kennedy told aides he intended to chase "Hubert's ass" all over the country. He decried the "divisions within the United States," and spoke in hopeful terms about the opportunity for his campaign to bridge those divides. "We are a great country, an unselfish country and a compassionate country," he said, one which "wants to move in a different direction." With a final nod to his campaign volunteers he told the crowd, "Thanks to all of you, and on to Chicago and let's win there." Kennedy gave the crowd thumbs up, flashed a "V" for victory, and ran his right hand across his drooping forelock. It was a gesture eerily reminiscent of his slain brother.[71]

Kennedy shuffled offstage and through a nearby pantry, shaking the hands of well-wishers and kitchen staff. He turned to find Ethel, who trailed behind him. At that exact moment a young, deranged drifter named Sirhan Sirhan, outraged by the senator's strong support for Israel, raised a snub-nosed revolver and fired a single shot. For an instant everyone in the cramped space froze—except Kennedy, who was hit in the back of the head. He raised his hands to his face, staggered backward and collapsed on the concrete floor. Pandemonium ensued. The football player and actor Roosevelt Grier, who was a member of Kennedy's entourage, joined with the author George Plimpton and others in trying to wrestle the gun from Sirhan's hand. More shots, sounding like mini-firecrackers, rang out in the dark, cramped room. Several others would be wounded, though none seriously. Ethel rushed to her husband's side and began stroking his face and chest as photographers snapped photos and aides tried to clear the space around the candidate. Kennedy turned slightly toward his wife and whispered, "Is everybody else all right?" A young Filipino busboy knelt beside him and pushed a rosary into his hand. While being lifted onto a stretcher by emergency workers, some reported hearing him cry, "Oh, no, no, don't." He soon passed out.[72]

In Washington, President Johnson, riven by an unimaginable set of competing emotions, picked up the phone every hour or so and demanded to know from his Secret Service team, "Is he dead yet?" The shot had entered the soft tissue behind Kennedy's ear and lodged in his brain. A few inches in a different direction and he likely would have survived, but Sirhan's bullet had done catastrophic damage. Kennedy's heart continued to beat strong until the early morning of June 6, when, surrounded by his family, he passed away.[73]

8

The "Politics of Joy"?

On the morning of March 31, 1968, returning from church services at the National Cathedral, and accompanied by his daughter Lucy and her husband, Pat Nugent, Lyndon Johnson arrived unexpectedly at the Washington apartment of Hubert Humphrey. The vice president was packing for an official trip later that day to Mexico City. After exchanging pleasantries with Humphrey's wife, Muriel, Johnson, along with his personal aide Jim Jones, took Humphrey into the den to speak with him in private.[1]

The president handed Humphrey a copy of the speech he would be delivering that evening from the Oval Office. Reading through it, the vice president praised Johnson's call for a bombing pause and the push for immediate political negotiations. Then Johnson showed Humphrey the ending. Jones recalled that the words "put a time-warp on Humphrey. His face flushed, and tears ran from his eyes." He urged Johnson to reconsider. "You can't do this; you can't resign from office. You're going to be re-elected." Though Johnson said the decision was not yet final, he spoke of his desire to move forward on negotiations with the North Vietnamese and his belief that he unless he appeared to be "non-political," talks would go nowhere. There were also more elemental concerns. "This is a terrible strain and men in my family have died early from heart trouble. I'd like to live a little bit longer."[2]

Sworn to secrecy, the vice president didn't even tell his wife what the president planned to do. At the residence of the US ambassador in Mexico City, Humphrey insisted on watching the president's speech live. As Johnson spoke, a phone call came in from Marvin Watson in the White House. The president intended to use the ending he had shown him earlier that morning, said Watson.[3]

The moment was bittersweet for Humphrey. He had longed for the White House from the moment he entered politics—and now the path to the Democratic presidential nomination had opened up before him. But Humphrey also understood that Johnson had handed him a poisoned chalice. "I was to fall heir to virtually all the animosity directed toward the Johnson administration and be beneficiary of practically none of the good-will due to an administration whose domestic accomplishments were historic," he later wrote in his memoirs.[4]

Johnson had urged his vice president to move quickly in preparing a presidential candidacy. "There's no way I can beat the Kennedy machine," Humphrey ruefully responded. Eight years earlier, as a badly organized and cash-poor candidate, he had been humiliated by the Kennedys in key Democratic presidential primaries, and had vowed never to get into a "political battle" with them again. But Humphrey dramatically underestimated his own political advantages, as well as the backlash that Kennedy had sparked in his two weeks on the campaign trail. As he parried reporter inquiries in Mexico City about his future intentions, Humphrey's top political operative in Washington, Bill Connell, made calls to hundreds of party officials, labor leaders, and Democratic officeholders, asking them to refrain from making any endorsements until Humphrey made his intentions clear. Connell quickly and dismayingly discovered that in most cases either Robert or Teddy Kennedy had already telephoned them. Yet the very fact that everyone he spoke to reported they were going to hold off on making a decision suggested that perhaps Kennedy's support within the party wasn't as strong as Humphrey initially suspected.[5]

"Has Bobby got it locked it up yet?" Humphrey asked aides after he stepped off the plane from Mexico. The answer was no. The failure to make a decisive case for his nomination and the chaos of his campaign-trail appearances had dimmed Kennedy's luster. Johnson's withdrawal came at the precise moment when Kennedy was at his most radicalized, as he accused the president of appealing to the "darker impulses" of American society. His populist attacks would produce for Humphrey no shortage of new friends who wanted nothing more than to stop Kennedy in his tracks. The day after Johnson's abdication Humphrey, not Kennedy, sat comfortably in the driver's seat.[6]

While Johnson remained frustratingly circumspect about who should succeed him, Democrats from across the country—and the political spectrum—showed far less reticence. Entreaties for Humphrey to run came from old southern bulls, such as Senator Russell Long, Congressman Hale Boggs, and Louisiana governor John McKeithen. Mayors Richard Daley in Chicago, Joseph Alioto in San Francisco, James Tate in Philadelphia, and Carl Stokes, the newly elected African American mayor of Cleveland, jumped onboard a Humphrey bandwagon that already included young and upcoming liberal senators like fellow Minnesotan Walter Mondale (a Humphrey protégé) and Fred Harris of Oklahoma. The latter two would eventually become co-chairmen of the Humphrey campaign. All those years of beating the hustings for Democratic candidates had earned the vice president dozens, if not hundreds, of political chits. In a year in which the New Politics of participatory democracy became all the rage, Humphrey seemed poised to show that old-school establishment politics still had some life left in it.[7]

At a meeting at the Waldorf Towers in New York in early April, Humphrey met with his old Minnesota political benefactor Dwayne Andreas, who would later become CEO of the agribusiness conglomerate Archer Daniels Midland. Andreas brought along Henry Ford II, Jacob Blaustein of American Oil, and Sidney Weinberg and John Loeb, investment bankers who had been supporting Johnson's now-aborted presidential bid. All of them urged Humphrey to run. In late April, Evans and Novak revealed that "a coalition of millionaire businessmen" was working to raise four million dollars not so much to help Humphrey but "to stop Robert F. Kennedy's drive for the presidency." One unnamed Democrat was quoted in *Life* magazine as saying, "I never thought I'd see the day that Hubert Humphrey is the most conservative candidate we've got."[8]

Days later, Humphrey traveled to Pittsburgh to speak to a local chapter of the AFL-CIO (the group's president, George Meany, had already urged Humphrey to enter the race). As a brass band played the old Democratic ditty "Happy Days Are Here Again," he was introduced as the "next president." Soaking up the applause, Humphrey played it cool. "A decision will come in due time," he told the crowd. To shouts of "Tell us now, Hubert," he took a stab at his likely Democratic opponent. "It's become a normal operation in America for most of us to 'reassess' our position," said Humphrey.[9]

With Kennedy and McCarthy beating each other up for a relatively small number of convention delegates, Humphrey could focus on building support in nonprimary states. Humphrey would later write in his memoirs that by not wrapping up the nomination within days of Johnson's withdrawal, Kennedy had squandered his chances. But, in reality, the strong support that Kennedy needed from Democrats simply didn't exist. Over the next few months the political fortunes of the two men would run on two very different tracks. Kennedy found himself on a rollercoaster, his prospects up in Indiana and Nebraska, way down in Oregon, and (briefly, before tragedy struck) sky-high in California. Humphrey's chances of winning the nomination traveled in only one direction—onward and upward.

Humphrey's announcement, on April 27, 1968, of his intention to seek the Democratic presidential nomination would serve as the perfect microcosm for the campaign he waged that year—and of the "old" politics he represented. The paragons of the Democratic establishment and the leaders of the New Deal Coalition, union bosses, civil rights leaders, and national politicians united for one last hurrah, filling the ballroom at the Shoreham Hotel in Washington, DC, to hear from the vice president.

In a none-too-subtle hit on his opponents Humphrey told the crowd, "I do not and will not divide either my party or my country." Instead, he asked those with him "who share a deep and abiding belief in the purpose and potentialities of this nation" to say, "I love my country." The rabble-rouser of 1948, whose pro–civil rights speech at the Democratic National Convention had pushed southern delegates to walk out in protest, had been replaced by, as he called himself in his speech, the candidate of "maturity, restraint and responsibility." Humphrey had already been making this pitch for several weeks. In Tennessee, not long after the King assassination and subsequent nationwide riots, he told an appreciative audience, "America doesn't need emotion, frenzy, demagoguery or false promises." Instead, the country needed to think "positively, affirmatively, creatively" and "stand proud and stop carping about America."[10]

Humphrey mentioned Johnson's name only twice in his announcement speech, and Vietnam not at all. *Newsweek* called the rather unmemorable address "effervescent, hortatory and dressed up with enough lovable platitudes to keep a ladies' embroidery circle busy for a month of Sundays." Three words from the speech, however, would resonate. Unfortunately for Humphrey, they were not among the thousands he had labored over for weeks with his speechwriters. Rather, they came in an off-the-cuff comment he made at the speech's outset: "Here we are the way politics ought to be in America, the politics of happiness, politics of purpose, politics of joy."[11]

Few people would have used the word "joy" to define much of anything about America in the spring of 1968—and Kennedy immediately took the vice president to task. "If you want to be filled with Pablum and tranquilizers, then you should vote for some other candidate.... If you see a small black child starving to death in the Mississippi Delta, as I have, it is not the politics of joy." He would spend the rest of the campaign using Humphrey's words to attack him. The vice president would later complain bitterly of being constantly forced to explain that he was, in fact, aware of "misery in our land and world." It didn't do him much good. Campaign reporters regularly mocked Humphrey's "incorrigible ebullience" and his constant wide-eyed "exuberance" (a word that showed up repeatedly in his press coverage). One British journalist joked, "Humphrey's tragedy is that whatever he does he has to do with enthusiasm."[12]

Yet Humphrey's eagerness and rectitude also played to his political advantage. He was the anti-Bobby. In late May he told a union convention that those who derided the president, the party, and country did a disservice to America. What the United States needed, Humphrey said, is "patience and steadiness" at a time of national dysfunction. "If you want a candidate that's got instant, miraculous solutions to everything, his name is not Humphrey. I'm not a miracle man." In a speech to dairymen in Kansas City he derided "spilt milk politicians." "If they would spend more time getting on with the job and less cussing out the cows or crying crocodile tears about everything in general we would all be better off," said Humphrey.[13]

Indeed, Humphrey's "politics of joy" gaffe did little to stop his drive to the nomination. Delegate counters estimated his likely haul to be 1,200 of the 1,312 needed to win the Democratic nomination in Chicago. More than half of those came from the South and border states, where neither McCarthy nor Kennedy had much hope of competing. Humphrey, long unloved in the region, now saw his political fortunes rise in direct proportion to the fear that his opponents instilled there. Five days after his announcement speech, a Harris poll gave Humphrey a double-digit lead over both Kennedy and McCarthy. Only a month earlier, the same poll had shown nearly the exact opposite result, with Kennedy at 37 percent, Humphrey at 24, and McCarthy at 22.[14]

In the last week of May 1968, Humphrey put a hammerlock on the nomination. On May 25 he captured fifty-three of Missouri's sixty delegates, a win that followed major delegate hauls in Maryland, New Jersey, and Alaska. The same week, *Newsweek* estimated that he stood thirty-two delegates short of clinching the nomination. CBS went further and claimed he already had enough to win. Two days later, on May 27, at a meeting of Pennsylvania's state Democratic Committee, two-thirds of the state's delegates were awarded to the vice president, even though McCarthy had won the state's nonbinding primary by a whopping 8–1 margin. McCarthy's discouraged followers denounced the loss as a "Pennsylvania railroad," to no avail. The victory offered validation for Humphrey's tireless politicking over the years on behalf of Democratic candidates. Earlier in the campaign, Kennedy had gone to Philadelphia mayor James Tate seeking his support. But Tate had a long memory. The previous year he'd asked both RFK and Ted Kennedy to help him get out the vote in his re-election campaign.

Both, believing Tate would lose, had refused, but Humphrey had been more than happy to fit a campaign visit into his busy schedule.[15]

On the twenty-eighth, Kennedy lost the Oregon primary to McCarthy. This ensured that McCarthy would remain in the race and at the same time deflated Kennedy's key argument to on-the-fence Democratic delegates that he had greater general-election appeal than the vice president. The next day Humphrey told reporters at a press conference that he felt "a sense of reasoned optimism about [his] possibilities." Days later, a new Gallup poll showed the extent of Humphrey's advantage: among Democratic county chairmen (who would be selecting the national convention delegates) he led 70 percent to Kennedy's 16 percent and McCarthy's 6 percent.[16]

A week later, on the evening of the California primary, Humphrey arrived in Colorado Springs to deliver the commencement speech at the US Air Force Academy. On the ride in from the airport he told speechwriter Ted Van Dyk he hoped for a big Kennedy win that would finally knock McCarthy out. In Humphrey's view, Kennedy had little hope of beating him for the nomination and was far more likely than the mercurial McCarthy to eventually fall into line and support his candidacy. "Bobby Kennedy and I understand each other. . . . If I am nominated he'll campaign for me without reservation," said Humphrey. "But if McCarthy stays in the game, he'll damage both of us. I know Gene and I have affection for him. But he's a spoiler." That evening, of course, everything would change.[17]

Since Kennedy's death many have posited that, had he lived, he would have been the Democratic nominee in 1968 and even possibly the next president. It is, however, a dubious notion—informed more by hagiography than history. There is little indication that McCarthy would have dropped out after his narrow loss in California. Soon after, in the New York primary, his army of volunteers orchestrated a major victory. There had always been significant hostility from local party activists toward Kennedy and strong support for McCarthy. In a head-to-head matchup against Kennedy, McCarthy might still have emerged victorious. Win or lose, however, McCarthy would have almost certainly stayed in the race and prevented Kennedy from turning the nomination fight into a two-man battle. Years later, he wrote that after their California debate he concluded, "I could not support Robert Kennedy for the presidency." It had little to do with the policy differences between the two men and far more to do with McCarthy's personal dislike for Kennedy, which had been nurtured during their time together on the campaign trail.[18]

Even in an alternate scenario in which McCarthy dropped out after California and New York, the advantage would have continued to lie decisively with Humphrey. "If Bobby had been able to go on to Chicago, he would have had an uphill struggle to be nominated," said Kennedy advisor and later Humphrey campaign manager Larry O'Brien. "Humphrey had the edge despite the California primary result." According to Goodwin, who had left the McCarthy campaign to work for RFK (only to return to McCarthy after the assassination), Kennedy thought he had at best an "outside chance" of beating Humphrey.[19]

There is also little reason to believe that the delegates in Chicago would have rallied around Kennedy. The unions and southern Democrats didn't trust him—and in more than a few cases couldn't stand him. Johnson's Democratic allies would have pulled out all the stops to prevent Kennedy from winning the nomination. And even had Kennedy been able to overcome all the opposition against him from fellow Democrats, winning the presidential election was no sure thing. Unlike Humphrey, he simply could not count on strong support from labor, a group with whom he had a deeply contentious relationship.

In the late 1960s, the unions remained the bedrock of the Democratic coalition and a group that Kennedy seemed to go out of his way to alienate. His interrogation of Jimmy Hoffa as a senate investigator in the 1950s would ensure Kennedy a cold shoulder from some in the labor movement, but he didn't make much effort to improve the relationship. RFK had made an enemy of AFL-CIO president George Meany (who derisively called him a "jitterbug") when in a 1964 speech he praised rival labor boss Walter Reuther, head of the UAW, for his help in the 1960 election and failed to recognize Meany's contribution. While Kennedy always felt closer to the UAW because of its more progressive racial views, the snub was a needless swipe that earned Meany's lasting enmity. In 1968 none of the AFL-CIO's twenty-nine international vice presidents endorsed Kennedy. Nor, as it turned out, did the UAW. In Oregon, the local chapters actively worked to defeat him in the primary.[20]

During the California campaign Kennedy canceled a last-minute breakfast with six hundred labor leaders. In Michigan, perhaps the most pro-union state in the country, a local political observer noted that Humphrey took the time to meet with party and labor bosses, while Kennedy spent his time in the state holding downtown rallies. "He's going to the people, but Hubert's going to the party." Had he won the nomination, Kennedy would have likely swallowed his pride and tried to patch things up with labor. But with the union leadership openly hostile, it would have been tough sledding. The views of AFL-CIO executive secretary Sam Ezelle reflected the gut reaction of many: "Bobby Kennedy, with his cocker-spaniel haircut, tries to tell us he's now our friend, but we remember."[21]

Kennedy's views on civil rights ensured that in the South he would be held in even lower regard. The segregationist governor of Georgia, Lester Maddox, said he'd sooner vote for Fidel Castro than Kennedy for the Democratic presidential nomination. The Kennedy campaign operated on the assumption that they would simply be shut out in the region. Things would not have been much better in the general election, especially with George Wallace on the ticket. Indeed, the myth-making that has evolved around Kennedy's campaign over the decades often minimizes the extent to which his strongest base of support in the Democratic Party, black voters, represented a significant political liability (and not just in the South).[22]

Finally, there is the issue of his backing among establishment Democrats. The week that he died, *US News and World Report* took a long look at Kennedy's chances of winning the nomination and argued that, based on their conversations with party leaders, he was unlikely to prevail. Switching to RFK would put congressional Democrats in the uncomfortable position of repudiating the Johnson administration, thus making it all the more difficult to run on the policy successes of the previous five years. Party bosses felt even more threatened by his promise to go over their heads directly to the voters. "You get two different approaches from some of the pros," said one. "They say they hate his guts, or they say he's trying to buy the election and they resent it." Quite simply, the evidence that Kennedy could have been the man to unify a fractured party heading into a tough general election is difficult to find.[23]

Regardless of what might have been, Kennedy's death cast an immediate and omnipresent pall over the nomination race. As Humphrey himself would later admit, "What I think the Kennedy assassination did was to sour the whole public, and particularly the Democratic party, on the election and on the political process. It was like a mental breakdown for the American political community." Humphrey noted that right after the assassination his polls slipped "drastically." "I think that the people really then turned against us.... They thought that all this violence and everything else was a kind of a byproduct of the way that the country had been operated, the way it had been managed, the way it had been governed. And I was caught up in that." Kennedy's death had ensured that Humphrey would win the nomination, but it also fundamentally weakened his chances of becoming president. "I said it and I meant it that the bullet that shot and killed Bobby Kennedy fatally wounded me," he later said. "I felt it from the minute it happened."[24]

Indeed, had Kennedy lived to continue his fight for the nomination, it would have put Humphrey, ironically, in a far better position to win the general election. With Kennedy and McCarthy still in the race, the pressure on Humphrey to distance himself from Johnson and the war would have been that much harder to resist. The need to mend fences would have been paramount—and nowhere more so than at the White House. Considering LBJ's abundant, and somewhat irrational, fear that the party would choose Kennedy as his successor, Humphrey would likely have been given greater leeway by the president to move closer to the antiwar camp on Vietnam. At the very least, Humphrey could have used the specter of a Kennedy victory to more aggressively push LBJ to accept such a move. He desperately needed the competition that Kennedy would have provided.

Instead, the pressure on Humphrey came in the opposite direction, from the president who demanded continued loyalty on Vietnam. As much as he tried to identify a middle-ground approach in the months after RFK's death, Humphrey could not find it within himself to disavow Johnson's position on the war. How Humphrey came away from perhaps the most significant intraparty insurgency in American history—nearly all of it revolving around the war in Vietnam—with a position that was indistinguishable from a president who had withdrawn in humiliation because of that conflict remains one of the great ironies of the 1968 race.

━━━━━━━

While Kennedy's death imperiled Humphrey's presidential aspirations, no candidate was more personally affected—and anguished—by it than Eugene McCarthy. Kennedy's murder was, for him, symbolic of the damage that Vietnam had wrought on the country. "It is not enough, in my judgment, to say that this is the act of one deranged man," he said in the hours after the shooting. "The nation, I think, bears too great a burden of guilt, really, for the kind of neglect which has allowed [the] disposition of violence to grow here in our land."[25]

The night of the assassination, McCarthy watched news reports on the shooting in muted disbelief. Eventually he retreated to his hotel room. An aide reported that the "gray glow of a television set burning from under the door" remained visible deep into the night. The next day he looked "white and ravaged" and broke down in tears when he learned that Kennedy was likely to die. He went to the hospital to offer condolences to the senator's family, but even that gesture created tension when Kennedy's campaign staff later complained about the sounds of sirens from his motorcade. As it was, McCarthy spoke briefly to Salinger and Goodwin and then headed out without saying a word to any member of the Kennedy family. On the flight back to Washington he dismissed any attempt to talk about next steps in the campaign. "It's all over you know," he told his new campaign manager, Washington lawyer Thomas Finney. "It's not going to make any difference."[26]

What had begun as a vital grass-roots political movement ended with a desultory whimper in the post-assassination haze of the summer of 1968. McCarthy's passion for campaigning had never been in great supply; after California it simply faded away. "It's as if someone gave you the football and you're running with it, but the field never ends," he told reporters. "There's no goal line. No opponent. You just run. And every time you reach a marker on the field, it's always the 50 yard line."[27]

McCarthy fluctuated between wondering whether he had contributed to the animus that led to the assassination or whether Kennedy, by stirring so much emotion on the campaign trail, had brought it upon himself. No matter the final verdict, Kennedy's death took a terrible personal toll on him. He "looked weary beyond belief, his skin used-up yellow, his tall body serving for no more than to keep his head up above the crowd," said Norman Mailer. McCarthy's wife, Abigail, would later write that "night after night he lay beside me sleepless, staring at the ceiling."[28]

McCarthy's campaign became an exercise in frustration and futility. Strategy meetings would end inconclusively, and even on the rare occasions when McCarthy would make a command decision, his orders would only occasionally be implemented. Three very different power centers emerged within the campaign: Curtis Gans, who wanted to continue his grass-roots mobilization campaign to build momentum before the convention; Finney, who nominally ran the campaign's operations and wanted to pursue a traditional preconvention strategy of using polls and a media blitz to make the case for McCarthy; and Steve Mitchell, a former DNC chairman who backed a more hard-edged approach of challenging the credentials of delegates and putting pressure on Humphrey to bend the party platform in McCarthy's direction. To add to the sense of chaos, Abigail McCarthy's brother, Steve Quigley, was also brought in to get control over the campaign's free-spending ways.[29]

Confusion and recriminations ran rampant. Many of McCarthy's youthful supporters viewed Finney with deep suspicion because of his ties to the Johnson White House. The candidate appeared to endorse Mitchell's hard-ball strategy, but in practice the campaign pushed ahead with all three approaches, with predictable results. "I never in all my life was in any operation in which so many people hated each other," said Pat Lucey, the future governor of Wisconsin who had joined McCarthy to help with his delegate operation. McCarthy's success to date had been the result of the local "Clean for Gene" teams purposely bypassing the national campaign and building their own organic grass-roots operations. Uniting all of these groups around a single strategy would have been difficult under any circumstances. That McCarthy did little to impose authority—indeed, he almost willfully rejected the task—made it impossible.[30]

McCarthy further weakened his campaign by his continued refusal to engage in the sort of glad-handing essential to modern politicking. After

Kennedy's death he told aides of his desire to "campaign the way he wanted to in the first place: without hoopla, without dealing in personalities, and—as much as possible—without organization." He believed that too much time and effort was being spent on public relations and the daily news cycle, and not enough on the policy issues, like the war, that had motivated him to run in the first place. No longer needing to parry Kennedy's moves, McCarthy believed he could return to the purist crusade he had always sought to wage.[31]

In reality, McCarthy needed to make the campaign more about personality, not less. Whatever hope remained of him winning the nomination depended on his convincing party regulars that he would be a more attractive general election candidate than Humphrey. Already most of the Harris and Gallup polls from the summer showed him outperforming the vice president in matchups against Nixon and Wallace. Beyond his own political future, McCarthy was also the only remaining candidate of the antiwar movement and, in the words of Larner, "the only man who was in a position to tell America what had happened, to tell us who we were and what we must now do."[32]

That job—that responsibility—appeared to be of little interest to McCarthy. While he still maintained a hectic travel schedule, speaking to fifty thousand supporters at Boston's Fenway Park and large, energetic crowds in Pittsburgh, Saint Louis, Richmond, and New York's Madison Square Garden, McCarthy offered his supporters a passionless message. He called on twenty-five separate state Democratic delegations, but to many it felt as though he was simply going through the motions. "These are not people who he particularly admires or whose intellectual or social attainments he particularly respects," said Finney, "and he went before them in the mood that 'I am obviously the best that you have and the following are the terms on which I will accept [the nomination].'"[33]

"He doesn't want to tell people what to do," said Dick Goodwin, "but to illuminate what should be done." McCarthy had once said of John F. Kennedy that he had the "perfect political mentality"—namely, "that of a football coach, combining the will to win with the belief that the game is important." McCarthy believed that the game mattered, but he simply lacked the determination to emerge victorious.[34]

As the summer wore on, McCarthy's ennui became even more pronounced. He canceled a meeting with Chicago mayor Richard Daley. He
refused to return phone calls from United Auto Workers president Walter
Reuther and ignored entreaties from prominent antiwar liberals like George
McGovern, both of whom were considering endorsing him. Eventually the
South Dakota senator decided to jump into the race himself in mid-August
in the hope of rallying the party's antiwar forces in Chicago.[35]

When McCarthy did campaign, he returned to his New Hampshire plea
for reasoned judgment. At a speech to a Jefferson-Jackson dinner in Oklahoma
City in late June, he made no reference to Humphrey, or to the late Kennedy,
or even to the likely Republican nominee, Richard Nixon. In fact, in remarks nominally intended to make the case for a McCarthy presidency,
there was no mention of Eugene McCarthy. According to the candidate, his
insurgent campaign had contributed to the creation of a "process" within
the Democratic Party "so that the people could pass judgment" on the war
in Vietnam and the country's domestic challenges. The Democratic Party,
he said, could "prove again that we can, as responsible participants in the
politics of this country, make the political system of America live and make
it work." The opportunity to exercise one's good judgment seemed to McCarthy
to be more vital than what that judgment actually happened to be.
Unsurprisingly, the assembled Democrats voted to give thirty-seven of the
state's forty-one delegates to Humphrey.[36]

McCarthy's political hesitancy reached near-comic proportions when
he met with former Kennedy supporters in California and then refused to
praise his slain rival or address the group's concerns. One commented,
"I was pretty much willing to accept the fact that McCarthy was the only
alternative now and that I could support him, but not work with him. But
because of the meeting, I'd have to think some more about it." Another
complained that McCarthy "actually reinforced the decision by our students to hold back support." In fact, McCarthy barely mentioned Kennedy
after the assassination. He even declined to strongly endorse new antigun
measures, expressing concern about political overreaction to the assassination. It was a statement that was both politically unhelpful and profoundly
insensitive.[37]

While McCarthy was loath to invoke Kennedy's name on the trail, he became even more disinclined to speak the name of the man who now blocked his path to the nomination. It had been obvious for quite some time that as much as he might have disagreed with Humphrey on Vietnam, McCarthy could live with him as the party nominee. McCarthy biographer Dominic Sandbrook has argued that financial assistance provided to his campaign by Humphrey's backers helped to silence McCarthy. While this can't be fully discounted, affinity for his fellow Minnesotan also clearly played a role. The two men were longtime friends and colleagues in Washington (they used to carpool together to their offices in the Senate). Jerome Grossman, a campaign aide to McCarthy, later noted that the candidate would regularly regale him with stories of how badly the president treated Humphrey. To Grossman it seemed that McCarthy felt not anger but sympathy toward Humphrey for the trauma he'd experienced as Johnson's vice president.[38]

"Had McCarthy thought it would turn into a two-way race with Humphrey," said Finney, "I don't think he ever would have gone into it." When Grossman put him on the spot at one point and asked when he was going to "attack Humphrey" in the same manner that he had targeted Kennedy, McCarthy replied that he wouldn't. The candidate stuck to his word; for the rest of the campaign he largely spared Humphrey from harsh criticism.[39]

McCarthy's message throughout the last few months of his campaign also remained consistent with the argument that he had been making since he announced his candidacy. He had never aspired to be the leader of an antiwar movement, but rather a vessel or "accidental instrument," as he put it, for those who sought to change the nation's politics via the ballot box. He almost seemed to delight in disclaiming any interest in actually being president. He said he would be "willing" to take the job, not that he actually wanted it. During the Indiana primary, Godfrey Sperling joined the candidate for an early-morning meet-and-greet at a local factory as he shook hands and bantered with the workers. Sperling couldn't help but notice that never once did McCarthy ask any of them to vote for him.[40]

One of the captions on a McCarthy campaign poster aptly summed up the role he played in 1968: "He stood up alone, and something happened."

It took a unique individual to challenge Johnson in the Democratic primary. But McCarthy's courage in taking that step accompanied a set of personal limitations that peeked above the surface throughout the hectic primary season only to emerge fully formed after Kennedy was killed. By the summer of 1968 the antiwar movement needed McCarthy to be more than a bemused bystander to the political process he'd helped to upend. While Eugene McCarthy might have been a hero simply by choosing to run, his behavior in the summer of 1968 provided compelling evidence that he was no leader.

For Hubert Humphrey, hesitancy in pursuing his political goals would be the least of his problems. Indeed, throughout the spring and summer of 1968 his pursuit of convention delegates looked like the furthest thing from the "politics of joy." The Humphrey camp instead played hardball politics as they strong-armed state conventions to secure as many delegates as possible, which further exacerbated the tensions between himself and McCarthy's supporters. In Indiana, Kennedy's death meant the delegates he'd won in the state's primary were back in play at the state convention. Party bosses ignored requests from McCarthy supporters to consider nominating his delegation to go to the national convention. Only Humphrey's people were recognized. Tempers flared when McCarthy backers tried without success to reach the microphone and place other names into nomination. Similar scenarios played out in Minnesota, Texas, Utah, Delaware, Connecticut, Washington, and Oklahoma.[41]

Humphrey's team was giving the "McCarthy people"—as he dismissively called them—little enticement to get on board. Humphrey aides (off the record) called McCarthy supporters "mean as hell," and complained, "You just cannot seem to reach any accommodations with them." Humphrey himself denounced the "abusive tactics" and "militant minorities" of those who believed they "had cornered the market in social justice and virtue." In July, he finally called on his supporters to back off the heavy-handed tactics, but the damage to party unity had already been done.[42]

The growing intraparty tension began to take a larger political toll on Humphrey. In the wake of Kennedy's death Democrats barely rallied around him. He was "popular with the generals and captains of his party" but was "a divisive figure among the troops," wrote Richard Harwood in the *Washington Post*. In late July, the *New Republic*, a longtime critic of Johnson and the war, even urged Humphrey to withdraw from the race.[43]

Reporters described Humphrey's crowds as "apathetic," "middle-aged and lethargic," and said the campaign had "an unmistakable whiff of mediocrity." Crowds of non–party loyalists responded to him with reactions ranging from indifference to outright hostility. In a visit to Watts, young blacks jeered him and yelled "Honky, go home." An estimated five thousand antiwar demonstrators surrounded his hotel in Los Angeles, pouring blood into the hotel's fountain and yelling "Dump the Hump." In Cleveland antiwar protesters called him a murderer, and at a poor people's solidarity rally in Washington he was lustily booed. Ever the optimist, Humphrey refused to publicly express frustration over the protests. Flying back to Washington, he told incredulous reporters, "A lot of the so-called pickets aren't really hostile. They'd have a sign saying, 'Peace in Vietnam' and I'd say, 'That's for me,' and I'll stick out my hand and they'd shake it. I was for peace before they could spell it."[44]

Humphrey's performance on the campaign trail only added to the sense of malaise surrounding his candidacy. His public statements were uninspiring and often contradictory. In a speech in Saint Paul he heaped praise on the auto industry and then said that cars were "choking our cities and polluting our air." He claimed that he and Kennedy had been in basic agreement on Vietnam—a statement that Kennedy advisors immediately and forcefully denounced. Humphrey fell back into his regular pattern of trying to be everything to everyone. In the *New York Times Magazine* Victor Navasky chronicled Humphrey's various political beliefs, as expressed on the campaign trail: in addition to the "politics of joy" there was the "politics of public service," "the politics of commitment," "the politics of service rather than noise," "the politics of happiness," "the politics of tomorrow," the "politics of personal sacrifice," "the politics of self-involvement," and, finally, "the politics of commitment, personal service and personal action." Humphrey had long been notorious in Washington for hiring staffers a notch below the best and brightest and it was evident from the campaign. His speeches meandered; the public events were poorly advanced, and the ads were uninspiring.[45]

Humphrey's biggest problem, however, was that when Americans looked at him, many saw Lyndon Johnson. Only a slim plurality of voters viewed the vice president as independent of the president, and one-third believed that he had previously backed policies "he hasn't really believed in." Humphrey's initial effort to distance himself from the White House was working about as well as Johnson's efforts to find a middle path on the war in Vietnam. The latter remained Humphrey's core "Johnson problem," and one that offered no easy or obvious solution.[46]

When Lyndon Johnson bowed out of the presidential race in March, it came at the tail end of a speech announcing a major shift in policy on Vietnam. For the first time, Johnson made clear a willingness to restrict US bombing of North Vietnam and to sit down with Hanoi for peace talks. Many Americans viewed Johnson's words with hope: perhaps there was a light at the end of the tunnel in Vietnam after all. As would soon become evident, however, Johnson had announced a change in strategy but not a shift in tactics. The overall goal of US military operations remained largely unchanged—maintaining an independent, non-Communist South Vietnam through the use of overwhelming American military force. Because of the heavy losses suffered by the enemy during Tet, US military leaders became convinced that a military solution to the war lay within their reach. West-moreland told his commanders there would be no letup in the "zeal and aggressiveness" with which the United States pursued the war. So even though three-quarters of North Vietnamese territory was now off-limits to US planes after March 31, fighting in Vietnam continued at a furious and deadly pace. B-52 missions tripled in 1968 as American bombers went after suspected insurgent bases and infiltration routes across the South, and the United States launched the largest search-and-destroy mission of the war, with one hundred thousand troops being sent into the provinces around Saigon. American casualties in the spring reached near-record highs.[47]

Peace talks didn't show much progress either. American negotiators, led by former New York governor Averell Harriman, continued to demand that in return for a full halt to the air war in the North, Hanoi had to de-escalate in the South and not take advantage of a military lull. This same stipulation had been rejected when Johnson dangled the idea in the fall of 1967, and the response, months later, was no different. Harriman urged Johnson to accept the North Vietnamese demand of a unilateral and unconditional bombing cessation, but the president rejected it out of hand and even contemplated reversing his bombing restrictions (a move the Joint Chiefs and hawkish advisors like Walt Rostow persistently lobbied for). As one US diplomat later ruefully noted, "Our most difficult negotiations were with Washington and not Hanoi."[48]

The lack of progress further strained the relationship between Johnson and Humphrey. The president, already concerned that his vice president would abandon him on Vietnam, told aides that when Nixon got the nomination "he may prove to be more responsible than the Democrats." LBJ's close aide George Reedy marveled at the complete lack of support that Johnson gave to Humphrey's campaign. "He wouldn't let anybody do anything for Humphrey." In conversations with prominent Democrats Johnson regularly accused him of playing politics with the war and letting "professors" dictate his position. When Nixon and Johnson spoke in mid-August, the Republican nominee pledged, "I won't say a damn word that's going to embarrass you," but also asked the president if he could "keep your Vice President firm" on Vietnam. "I'm going to do my best," Johnson replied.[49]

Part of the reason, amazingly, is that Johnson had begun to reconsider his own political options. Convinced that Nixon could be beaten but that Humphrey wouldn't be up to the task, he privately debated the possibility of re-entering the race. According to Joseph Califano, one of Johnson's top domestic policy advisors, "LBJ hoped, and probably anticipated, that the convention delegates in Chicago would offer to draft him to be their party's candidate." Califano added that he believed Johnson would have turned down the offer, but it would have given him the validation he craved.[50]

Marvin Watson took a similar view, claiming that Johnson "never wavered" in his decision not to seek re-election. He merely threw his name out, as Watson told Daley at the time, to stop the momentum of the antiwar delegates and to "scare some of these McCarthy people to death." McCarthy, however, wasn't the only person he wanted to frighten. According to Watson's memoirs, he told Humphrey directly that he must stick with Johnson on Vietnam, "if you expect to be nominated."[51]

But there is also substantial evidence that Johnson had bigger goals beyond just manipulating who the party chose as their nominee. On the eve of the Democratic Convention in August, Johnson and Watson pored over delegate counts in minute detail and discussed how they might get Johnson in range of winning the nomination. Plans were laid out for the president to travel to Chicago on August 27, his sixtieth birthday. Johnson's staff surreptitiously began drafting a convention speech, and potential supporters of a presidential draft, like Mayor Daley, were identified. Johnson's old Texas crony Governor John Connally, also in Chicago, began publicly assailing the antiwar wing. During platform negotiations the week before the convention, he unleashed a blistering personal attack on McCarthy and McGovern, accusing them of "appeasement and surrender" on Vietnam and of advocating an end to the war solely out of narrow political considerations. "The cause of peace should not be used as a vehicle for political favor or fortune," said Connally, whose words received a standing ovation from the Johnson-allied platform committee.[52]

Connally pestered the Humphrey camp with threats to put the president's name in nomination, but the vice president's aides came away unimpressed. They heard the same news as the governor—that party regulars had no interest in an LBJ reprise. Whether Johnson truly believed he could swoop in and garner the nomination is unclear, but once it became evident there was no support for a draft, he backed off his plans to fly to Chicago.

Still, Johnson forced Humphrey's hand on Vietnam. "The Vice President," he ruefully declared, "has very few guns in a battle with presidential artillery." In the months leading up to the convention, every one of Humphrey's efforts to publicly offer a more politically tenable position on the war was torpedoed by Johnson.[53]

At the end of July, for example, the Humphrey campaign's Vietnam task force crafted a statement that endorsed a reduction of US troops, called for a ceasefire, and intimated that a recent lull in fighting could "approximate the reciprocal action" that the United States had called for previously, leading to an "immediate halt in the bombing of North Vietnam." It was a tepid call for change, but it still differed qualitatively from the White House position. Humphrey prepared the new proposal as an overture to the peace camp. He took it to the president, confident that Johnson would approve. Instead, Johnson told him that the release of such a statement would "complicate and confuse the negotiations" with the North Vietnamese—and might lead to a new Communist offensive. Johnson said that such a shift from administration policy would not only "destroy" his chances of winning the election; it would endanger LBJ's son-in-law, future Democratic senator Chuck Robb, then serving in Vietnam. His "blood" could be on Humphrey's hands, the president darkly warned.[54]

"Did you believe him?" asked Humphrey's speechwriter Ted Van Dyk when the vice president recounted the story. "I had to believe him," replied Humphrey. Then, after a moment of reflection, he said, "I've eaten so much of Johnson's shit in this job that I've grown to like the taste of it." Two weeks later Humphrey traveled to the LBJ ranch in Texas with a new statement, one that directly linked a bombing halt to an "appropriate act of restraint and reasonable response from the North Vietnamese." This time Johnson agreed to the wording, though he urged Humphrey to hold off on releasing the document publicly. He hinted that a potential breakthrough in the peace talks could be just around the corner with a planned visit by Pope Paul to Vietnam. "You can get a headline with this and it will please you and some of your friends," the president said, "but if you'll let me work for peace, you'll have a better chance for election than by any speech you're going to make. I think I can pull it off."[55]

Humphrey didn't have the luxury of time. He needed to unite a deeply divided party, and quickly. This statement, as bland and unenthusiastic as it was, represented his only real hope for beginning that process. Nonetheless, he acceded to Johnson's request. A week later came a call from the president—the breakthrough hadn't happened. The North Vietnamese were bringing more troops into the fight. "Now do you want us to let 'em come though and hit our men?" bellowed Johnson. "Or do you want us to stop all we can?" Humphrey could barely get a word in before Johnson hung up the phone.[56]

Humphrey had one last way to separate himself from Johnson—the Platform Committee of the Democratic National Convention. If the vice president could craft wording on Vietnam that reflected the concerns of both the White House and the antiwar contingent, he might still be able to unite the party. Humphrey tapped David Ginsburg, an attorney and old Washington friend, to negotiate with the White House as well as the McCarthy and Kennedy camps on the platform's Vietnam language. The Saturday before the convention Ginsburg called Humphrey from Chicago with word that a deal had been reached. The key part of the statement involved the pledge of a full and "unconditional" end to the bombing of the North, which went further than the partial halt that Johnson had announced in March. "This action and its timing," the plank read, would "take into account the security of our troops and the likelihood of a response from Hanoi." Humphrey jotted it down and then immediately called Rusk and Rostow, the two biggest hawks in the administration, to get their sign-off. "We can live with it," Rusk told him.[57]

In fact, a diverse group of voices within the party approved the statement—Ted Sorensen, Kenny O'Donnell, and Fred Dutton from the Kennedy camp; the hawkish George Meany; the party platform chair Congressman Hale Boggs; and a host of southern governors. Dick Goodwin serving as a proxy for McCarthy, also signed off on the language. Humphrey could hardly have hoped to do much better in achieving consensus within the party on Vietnam.[58]

Johnson, however, remained unmoved. At first his complaints were nuanced, but as time went on he became unwilling to accept even the tiniest variation from the White House's position. "We do not favor any words that say we are ready to stop the bombing," Johnson told his man in Chicago, White House aide Charlie Murphy. "It puts a bunch of draft-dodgers and pacifists who've never seen a uniform in charge of telling us that we can't bomb the people until they get out of the DMZ." Ginsburg spent much of the Sunday night before the convention and the next day on the phone with Johnson's advisors. "They played with these words," recalled Ginsburg, "and the President at the other end of the line...just hung on to every inch as if he had nothing else to do."[59]

Johnson refused to provide Humphrey with even the most limited opportunity to stake out his own turf on the war. "That plank undercuts our whole policy," Humphrey later claimed Johnson told him, "and, by God, the Democratic Party ought not to be *doing this to me,* and you ought not to be doing it—you've been part of this policy." Johnson's fury was rooted in the fact that by taking this course of action Humphrey personally challenged him. Humphrey would later note that Johnson had shifted his views on talks with the Communists and bombing in the North—but on his own initiative. "For anybody else to recommend those changes," said Humphrey, "that was something he couldn't take."[60]

Humphrey mulled keeping the plank as worded, but after Boggs told him that, as chairman of the Platform Committee, he could not support it if the president was not on board, Humphrey relented. "I know, in retrospect, that I should have stood my ground," he later wrote in his memoirs. "I am not sure it would have made any difference in the election, but once we had arrived at that point, at some consensus with the Kennedy people, I should not have yielded."[61]

Humphrey's refusal to stick to his guns meant that when he arrived in Chicago at his nominal political coronation, he would be backing, on the record, a position on the war that he didn't truly support and which alienated a large segment of his own party. Failing to stand up to Johnson on Vietnam would turn out be Humphrey's greatest mistake—and as the Democratic National Convention began in Chicago during the last week in August, the vice president would experience firsthand the consequences of his decision.

Part III

The Republicans

The New, New Nixon

The mood in Room 724 of the Beverly Hilton on the morning of November 7, 1962, could best be described as funereal. After all, nine hours earlier Richard Nixon's political career had, from all appearances, died. Nearly two years to the day after his bid to be president of the United States had been narrowly rejected by the American people, California voters gave him a similar, if more stinging, rebuke—by re-electing his opponent, the state's liberal Democratic governor, Pat Brown.

Nixon stared blankly at the television, unshaven—although still wearing a tie—and with a drink in one hand. He fended off desperate requests from Herbert G. Klein, his press spokesman, to speak to the reporters assembled downstairs. "Screw them," said Nixon.

"They're still waiting," said Klein. "You've got to go down."

"Screw them, screw them, screw them." Nixon repeated the words like a mantra.

"I told them you'd make a statement," said Klein.

"You make the statement. You make it!" Nixon fired back.

Klein dutifully headed downstairs. When he tried to explain to the assembled journalists that his candidate wouldn't be conceding a race he'd
clearly lost, he was greeted with laughter. The response further embittered
Nixon, who was watching the proceedings upstairs. "I'm going down there,"
he announced. He jumped up out of his chair and strode down the hall
toward the elevator.

"He looked his worst," wrote Jules Witcover. "The small dark eyes, tight
mouth, rubbery nose and self-conscious demeanor that had made Nixon
the cartoonist's delight presented him at this moment in the least photo-
genic, most self-damaging aspect." Nixon's appearance would be the least of
his problems. Tired, angry, and quite possibly drunk, he prepared to tell the
world precisely how he felt.

"Good morning, gentleman. Now that Mr. Klein has made his statement,
and now that all the members of the press are so delighted that I have lost, I'd
like to make a statement of my own." What followed was a stream of frustration, pathos, and indignation directed at all those Richard Nixon believed had
done him wrong. He complained about his opponent: "I believe Governor
Brown has a heart, even though he believes I do not." He criticized the press: if
"they're against a candidate" and "give him the shaft," said Nixon, "they could
at least put one lonely reporter on the campaign who will report what the candidate says now and then." And finally, he spoke of his political future: "Just
think how much you're going to be missing. You won't have Nixon to kick
around anymore, because, gentlemen, this is my last press conference."[1]

At various points Nixon realized the depth of the hole he was digging
and fell back on insincere and formulaic platitudes: "I appreciate the press
coverage of the campaign," and "I congratulate Governor Brown," who, he
said, has "the greatest honor" of any governor in America. His back and
forth between sincerity and artifice offered the press conference's most revealing moment—a telling indication of the wide gap between the real
Nixon and the manufactured one. In 1956, Murray Kempton wrote, "Great
care had gone into the construction of the shadow which declares itself to
be Richard Nixon." But in a single morning of pique, all those many years
he had spent developing and honing the self-discipline and contrived earnestness that lay at the heart of his political success had been wiped away.[2]

"It had seemed the absolute end of a career," wrote Norman Mailer. "Self-pity in public was as irreversible as suicide." The loss to Brown not only christened Nixon a "two-time loser," but on live television, in front of millions of Americans, he had practically self-destructed. The vultures in the media didn't take long to swoop in. Nixon was, wrote James Reston in the days after his defeat, "unelected and unmourned," and just another "unemployed lawyer in Los Angeles."[3]

"Barring a miracle," said *Time* Nixon's "political career ended last week." After the embarrassment of his political defeat and the humiliation of the last press conference, few politicians would have dared venture back onto the political stage. But though Nixon's resentment burned bright that morning, so too did his desire to prove all his enemies wrong.[4]

His adversaries would soon give him plenty more incentive. Four days after the already infamous press conference, ABC broadcast a news special titled *The Political Obituary of Richard Nixon*. The host, ABC reporter Howard Smith, called Nixon a "savage political fighter" with an "un-subtle mind" that was "agile, but not deep." He even interviewed Nixon's old nemesis, the convicted Communist spy Alger Hiss. Calls from angry viewers and complaints from politicians and journalists inundated ABC. The show's advertisers received threats and, in some cases, requested police protection. Barry Goldwater called it "one of the lowest and dirtiest blows ever struck at a great American," and even prominent Democrats like Connecticut senator Thomas Dodd blasted ABC's decision to let Hiss "sit in judgment" on Nixon. Thousands of letters and telegrams praising Nixon for having the guts to tell off the press corps flowed in. Rather than write his obituary, the ABC broadcast planted the seeds of Nixon's political rebirth—and strengthened his connection to the disaffected, "forgotten" and disregarded Americans. Years later, after he had won and resigned the presidency, Nixon would write in his memoirs, with the singular benefit of political hindsight, "I have never regretted what I said at the 'last press conference.'"[5]

Over the next six years Richard Nixon would transform himself into the "new Nixon"—or, perhaps more accurately, the "new, new Nixon." The overwrought and emotionally coiled politician of old had disappeared. In his place emerged a patient, disciplined, affable, even self-effacing Nixon, who brought the two wings of a warring political party together under his leadership. During his years in the political wilderness, after the "last press conference," Nixon exhibited a self-discipline, energy, and single-minded devotion to winning the presidency that showed why he should be ranked among the most talented politicians of the twentieth century. He also had one other advantage working in his favor: a horseshoe lodged firmly on his back. As he traversed the road to 1968 he watched from afar as his fortunes were consistently—and unintentionally—boosted by the missteps of his enemies and allies alike. In the end, Nixon's political resurrection is the story of a politician both lucky and good.

Though it would have hardly seemed that way at the time, Nixon's good luck began when he lost that governor's race in 1962. He had previously spent eight years as Dwight Eisenhower's vice president and in 1960 came tantalizingly close to winning the White House over Jack Kennedy. That he had been prepared to go from debating Nikita Khrushchev over the benefits of Communism versus capitalism to bargaining with Democrats in Sacramento about agricultural policy in the Imperial Valley was a major step down politically. But Nixon and his advisors had seen the California statehouse as a safe harbor. It would be a way to re-establish his place in the national limelight and lessen the political pressure to challenge Kennedy in 1964—a fight that Nixon had no interest in waging and likely couldn't win. Instead he could make his second presidential run in 1968, against any Democrat other than Kennedy.[6]

But as Nixon would soon discover, becoming a private citizen brought with it a singular set of advantages. His presidential rivals would be serving in the Senate or in state houses across the county, casting difficult votes and negotiating with recalcitrant state legislators in ways that could come back to haunt them on the campaign trail. They would be forced to balance the interests of their political opposition with those of their political base. Nixon could instead dedicate himself to the task of reinvention out of the harsh glare of the camera's eye.

In May 1963, Nixon relocated to New York City, a move that put him at the center of national and international affairs and gave him the opportunity to establish himself as a "Republican Wise Man" on foreign policy. He traveled the world and met with everyone from Charles De Gaulle, Konrad Adenauer, and Generalissimo Franco to Abdul Nasser, Ayub Khan, Chiang Kai-Shek, and Pope Paul VI. During a trip to Finland he hopped on a twenty-four-hour train ride to Moscow in a failed effort to see his old sparring partner Khrushchev (the former leader wasn't home). Back in New York, as a partner at the (renamed) law firm of Nixon, Mudge, Rose, Guthrie, Alexander, and Mitchell, he enjoyed the lifestyle of a well-compensated corporate lawyer. He entertained casually in his twelve-room Fifth Avenue apartment, tastefully decorated by his wife, Pat. His attention, however, remained firmly focused on 1968.[7]

Nixon still had to contend with 1964. After Kennedy's assassination in November 1963, Nixon's political calculus changed. Extremism was on the outs. The conservatism of potential nominee Barry Goldwater suddenly seemed more dangerous than quaint, and New York governor Nelson Rockefeller remained a distrusted figure in the conservative camp. A February 1964 poll of Republican voters gave Nixon an eleven-point lead over Goldwater. Among the major Republican candidates, he was the favorite of independents.[8]

Publicly, Nixon denied interest in running. Yet somehow he kept finding himself in states that would be holding presidential primaries, or delivering major speeches with plenty of political journalists in the audience, or traveling to Vietnam, where he called for greater US effort in fighting the Communists. Soon he was surreptitiously raising money for Nixon write-in ballot efforts and declaring to reporters, "There is no man in this country who can make a case against Mr. Johnson more effectively than I can." In July he even found himself at the National Governor's Conference in Cleveland, involved in a behind-the-scenes effort to build momentum for an anti-Goldwater bandwagon that might deadlock the Republican convention and begin the search for a candidate who could unite the party—someone like Richard Nixon.[9]

For such a plan to work—and to keep Nixon's fingerprints off it—he needed a liberal Republican sacrificial lamb to challenge Goldwater. There were several to choose from in 1964: Governors Bill Scranton of Pennsylvania,

Jim Rhodes of Ohio, and George Romney of Michigan. Rockefeller, who had lost to Goldwater in the California primary, already had taken his best shot and missed. While each of them wanted to derail Goldwater, none were willing to announce their candidacy. Nixon also continued to remain on the sidelines, even as he publicly criticized Goldwater and said, in a press conference in Cleveland, that it would be a "tragedy" for the party if someone with his views "were not challenged and repudiated." Goldwater responded to Nixon's comments by telling reporters that the former vice president sounded "more like Harold Stassen every day"—a cruel but effective comparison to the perennial and hapless GOP presidential wannabe.[10]

Romney seemed the most likely candidate and in Cleveland gave Nixon a clear indication that he would take the plunge. But to Nixon's surprise he demurred. Instead Scranton jumped in the race. Though he outpolled Goldwater among Republicans, Scranton was no match for the Arizona senator's energized supporters, who would dominate the Republican National Convention in San Francisco. Nixon's long-shot hopes for a deadlocked convention began to fade away as it became increasingly apparent that no Republican could stop Goldwater's path to the nomination.[11]

Nixon, however, faced a more immediate challenge—repairing his political standing with conservatives. He asked Republican Party leaders to let him introduce the presumptive nominee at the party convention. That night, Nixon stood before the party's delegates and adopted the mantle of the loyal Republican soldier. "Before this convention we were Goldwater Republicans, Rockefeller Republicans, Scranton Republicans, Lodge Republicans," said Nixon. "But now that the convention has met and made its decision, we are Republicans, period, working for Barry Goldwater for President of the United States.... 'Let's grow up, Republicans, and go to work,' and we shall win in November."[12]

The delegates greeted these stirring words with cheers. But an elaborate parlor game was being played: Nixon didn't believe what he said, and the crowd applauded a sentiment it didn't share. Nixon's interest in party harmony existed insofar as it made him look like a unifying figure. He certainly didn't think Goldwater would emerge victorious in November—and it would have been the worst possible outcome for Nixon's own presidential aspirations. For their part, Goldwater's supporters cared little for party unity. They wanted to stick their finger in the eye of Rockefeller, Scranton, and the whole eastern establishment—and Goldwater did not disappoint them. He told the moderates they could essentially go to hell. "The Republican party is a party for free men. Not for blind followers and not for conformists. . . . Anyone who joins us in all sincerity we welcome. Those who do not care for our cause we do not expect to enter our ranks in any case."[13]

Throughout Goldwater's political career he'd made off-the-cuff comments that led many to view him as an extremist. He joked about lobbing nuclear bombs into the men's room at the Kremlin and sawing off the East Coast of the United States, and even suggested that Social Security should be made voluntary. In San Francisco, Goldwater embraced his divisive public image. "Extremism in the defense of liberty is no vice," and "moderation in the pursuit of justice is no virtue," said Goldwater in the most famous lines of his 1964 acceptance speech. Nixon later wrote that Goldwater's performance made him "almost physically sick." The consummate politician found it "terribly sad to see a man throw away his chance for something he wanted and worked very hard to get." Still, Nixon understood that someone would need to truly bring the conservative and liberal wings of the party back together again. And who better to perform such a task than the man who had stood by his party's nominee even as others abandoned him? That fall, Nixon crisscrossed the country, stumping for Goldwater: thirty-three days, thirty-six states, 150 stops, hundreds of thousands of miles traveled. Conservatives may not have fully trusted Nixon, but they now knew they could rely on him to show them the respect they craved.[14]

Goldwater, of course, was crushed in November, but there would be a lone bright spot—his performance in the Deep South, where his opposition to civil rights legislation won him five states. In these southern wins, the first hints of a possible political realignment—and opportunity for a Republican resurgence—could be discerned. This, however, was far from evident in the aftermath of Goldwater's trouncing. Instead, political journalists surveyed the wreckage and declared the Republican right dead. Goldwater not only lost the election, wrote Reston in the *New York Times*, he lost the "conservative cause as well. He has wrecked his party for a long time to come." In the *Los Angeles Times*, the Washington bureau chief Robert Donovan wrote, "Republicans must campaign as a modern party... or risk becoming a 'minority party indefinitely.'" Many prominent Republicans made the same argument. Kentucky senator Thruston Morton, a former Republican National Committee chairman and party moderate, warned that either the Goldwaterites had to accept the judgment of the voters or "there probably will be some blood spattered around."[15]

The moderates, however, missed the implications of what had happened in San Francisco. Goldwater's conservative supporters had done more than wrest the nomination away from the eastern Republicans; they had taken control of the party. They became the GOP's best and most energized organizers and the ones most dedicated to their political cause. Above all, they possessed the most effective political message. Goldwater's anti-civil-rights stance, though anathema in much of the nation, allowed the GOP to plant a flag in the South, a region traditionally dominated by Democrats. With the conservative embrace of the growing white backlash, it also created an opening in northern cities, one that would represent a new political opportunity if Democrats overreached with their grandiose plans for a Great Society. In suburban conservative communities like California's Orange County, the Republican right became the voice of an alienated community of Americans driven by anti-Communist, pro-business attitudes, and, above all, fears about rising crime rates. Elsewhere, attacks on the nation's growing crisis of authority and the loosening of social mores drew head nods from once-loyal Democratic voters. In short, far-right conservatism was not a passing fancy; it reflected the future of Republicanism. Nixon's task was to figure out how to make himself acceptable to conservatives while avoiding the extremist label. That political straddling would define the next four years of Nixon's pursuit of the presidency.[16]

Two days after the 1964 debacle Richard Nixon launched his 1968 presidential campaign. There would be no gaudy announcement, no brass band, and no screaming supporters. Instead, Nixon held a postelection press conference in New York City at which he accused Nelson Rockefeller of undermining the party's presidential nominee. "Spoilsport" and "party divider" were the epithets he lobbed at the moderate governor of New York, who had challenged Goldwater in the primaries and had been practically booed offstage in San Francisco when he decried the party's growing extremism. Rockefeller's refusal to work for Goldwater's election in the fall not only hurt the party in down-ballot races, said Nixon, but brought into question his ability to bring the fractured GOP together. "A man who runs for the nomination, pledges his support for the winner and then takes a walk, cannot come back and say he wants to be the leader," said Nixon.[17]

Tales of Rockefeller's absence from the campaign trail had been exaggerated, but Goldwater backers didn't need much evidence to make them believe the worst of him. Rockefeller struck back, accusing Nixon of the sort of "peevish, post-election utterance" for which he was all too well known. Nixon was unperturbed. Getting in a public fight with the New York governor would be a surefire way to solidify his support among conservatives.[18]

Nixon's next move would be to carve out a political identity that rested comfortably between the two wings of the party. In a front-page interview with the *New York Times* a week after the election, Nixon said, "There is a strong conservative wing of the Republican Party. It deserves a major voice in party councils, and the liberal wing deserves a party voice, but neither can dominate or dictate." The "center must lead," he said; "I'm perhaps at dead center." This represented an unusual position for Nixon, who had long been one of the most divisive figures in American politics. When Eisenhower had plucked him out of the US Senate to be his running mate in 1952 it was largely because of his strong connections to the conservative, anti-Communist wing of the party. But Nixon's role in the Eisenhower administration, his denunciation of John Birch Society extremists, and the fact that he was, in the words of conservative activist and longtime aide Pat Buchanan, "not one of us" left him a suspect figure on the right. His acceptance of demands from Rockefeller for policy concessions in the run-up to the Republican National Convention in 1960 had further deepened conservative misgivings. In 1962, the distrust had even led to a conservative challenge in his gubernatorial bid in California. So, in the months after Goldwater's defeat, Nixon sat down with prominent right-wing columnists and activists to reassure them that they could count on him.[19]

Conservatives swooned over his hawkish language on Vietnam, even if they remained wary of the fact that, like Eisenhower, Nixon had made peace with the post–New Deal welfare state. Though Nixon was a conservative-leaning politician, he was also the son of a Quaker mother and a pro-union father. Theodore Roosevelt and Woodrow Wilson were his political heroes, and he referred to himself as a "progressive conservative" (and later a Keynesian). His positioning between the liberal and conservative wings of the GOP, while politically motivated, also provided an accurate reflection of his ideological leanings. While it left conservatives dubious, Nixon could present himself to the American people as a far more tolerant version of Goldwater-style conservatism, while still being right wing enough to pacify the GOP rank and file.[20]

The various liabilities of his Republican rivals would provide him with even greater assistance. Within the party, Rockefeller's presence as the poster child for Republican moderation ensured that Nixon would be considered conservative enough for the Goldwaterites. To GOP liberals, Nixon was certainly preferable to a conservative like Ronald Reagan. "I know the liberal fringe and the conservative fringe have no use for me," he noted, "but they tolerate me, where they don't tolerate others." Toleration might just be enough to get Nixon over the hump.[21]

Ironically, Nixon's old "Tricky Dick" persona also helped, particularly among Southern Republicans. Goldwater's strong performance in the South in 1964 had swelled the region's delegate count, making it the new power center of the party. The eleven states of the Deep South plus Kentucky and Oklahoma represented a treasure trove of 356 delegates to the 1968 national convention. With only 667 delegates needed to win the nomination, capturing their support would put Nixon more than halfway toward his goal. Of course, appealing to the reactionary views of the Deep South meant risking the support of the party's northern liberals and effectively writing off black support. This required a deft balancing act, and none of the potential GOP candidates did it better than Nixon. He traveled to all the states of the former Confederacy, where he expressed his strong support for the Civil Rights bill and the Voting Rights Act. As he wrote in a monthly newspaper column in May 1966, "Southern Republicans must not climb aboard the sinking ship of racial injustice. They should let Southern Democrats sink with it as they have sailed with it." At the same time, however, he would sonorously note his strong backing for "states' rights."[22]

In May 1966, Nixon traveled to Jackson, Mississippi, to speak to the most virulently racist state Republican Party in the country. He told reporters that he would go to any state "to campaign for a strong two-party system, whether or not I would agree with the local Republicans on every issue." But he also made clear that he did not share the openly segregationist views of the Mississippi GOP. Southern Republican leaders wrote off Nixon's pro-integration statements as political posturing. As one famously said after hearing moderate Michigan governor George Romney speak about the importance of civil rights, "This fellow really does mean it." As for Nixon, he "comes down South and talks hard on civil rights," but he was just saying it "for the Northern press." Simply by showing his face in the region, Nixon provided reassurance to a group that he could never openly embrace. "Southern Republicans come in all varieties, from racist to progressive and all shades of in between, but, to a man, they crave the respectability of approval and acceptance by the national party and its leaders," wrote David Broder and Stephen Hess at the time. This regional inferiority complex resonated with Nixon's own feelings of resentment toward northern elites.[23]

Nixon's middle-ground strategy was already bearing fruit. But one more crucial step needed to be taken—rebuilding the party that had been so thoroughly defeated in 1964.

By the time of Lyndon Johnson's inauguration in January 1965, optimism about the Republican Party's chances for a near-term electoral comeback was in short supply. Democrats had huge majorities in Congress. Strong growth and low unemployment kept the economy humming. The liberal consensus appeared to be stronger than ever, pushed forward by a president whose passion for reform was matched only by his ambition.

Republicans, however, had one crucial factor working in their favor: the simple fact that everything that goes up must come down. In '64, Goldwater had been a millstone around the necks of countless GOP House and Senate candidates. Many viewed their defeat as a direct result of the destruction that he wrought on his own party. That meant there would be a host of Democrats up for re-election who were holding congressional seats in districts that leaned Republican—and were potentially vulnerable. Their political exposure would become even more pronounced as Johnson's approval ratings began to falter in 1966 and Democrats suddenly found themselves on the political defensive. Vietnam was seemingly spiraling out of control and doubts about the wisdom of LBJ's ambitious Great Society agenda were on the rise. Growing racial tensions and a national spike in crime rates only added to the sense of malaise.

More than any other Republican, Nixon had positioned himself to benefit from this shift in the political terrain. His main presidential rivals—Romney, Rockefeller, Charles Percy in Illinois, and even the emerging Reagan—were all on the ballot in the fall of 1966. They would be forced to stay close to home, which meant no countrywide campaigning and no political bases being built among GOP partisans. Nixon could ride what he believed was a coming Republican wave to become the head of the party.[24]

On his travels, Nixon made all the right friends: an Associated Press survey in the fall of 1966 showed that he enjoyed the support of three out of four Republican state chairman and national committeemen. He was also judicious about who he chose to campaign for. In the fall of 1964 he had worked tirelessly for Goldwater even though he knew from the outset that his presidential bid was doomed. This time, Nixon only associated himself with winning candidates—and it didn't matter if they were liberals or staunch conservatives, so long as they were potential victors. Two-thirds of those House candidates he stood with in 1966 won in November. Among Senate and gubernatorial hopefuls the numbers were even better.[25]

On his campaign trips, Nixon tested out the latest iteration of the "new Nixon." The tightly wound political slasher of years past had been replaced by an easygoing, self-deprecating pol who deftly spooned out platitudes and corny one-liners ("I'm a dropout from the Electoral College. I flunked debating"). In a late September trip to Fort Lauderdale he joked that the sign outside the speaking hall read "Nixon tonight—'Wrestling Next Week.'" Come back then, he said; "It'll be Bobby versus Lyndon." His suits fit better, his stubble was almost nonexistent (he shaved three times a day), and the candidate who had seemed so defensive and rudderless in his run for the presidency in 1960 now came across as self-assured and occasionally even charming.[26]

Beyond the new and more appealing persona was a dogged commitment to the task at hand. A typical day, September 14, 1966, began with a 9:00 AM flight from LaGuardia Airport in New York City to the Municipal Airport in Columbus, Ohio, followed by a meet-and-greet with GOP candidates, the local country chairman, and other prominent Republicans. Then there would be a quick press conference before leaving for an event at nearby Capital University, where Nixon offered brief remarks followed by Q&A. Then back to the airport for a flight to Athens, Ohio; a speaking engagement at a local fairground for a local congressional candidate; and a return to the airport for a flight to Cincinnati and an event across the border in Kentucky on behalf of another House hopeful. There was another rally at 8:00 PM and then a return to the hotel for a fundraising reception. The next day took him to more events in Ohio, Iowa, and Colorado. He kept up this exhausting pace for weeks until Election Day—and the press corps began to notice.[27]

Nixon is "better than ever" said the *New York Times*. Looking "tanned, fit and relaxed, he moves swiftly from town to town, parrying questions about his political future with his left, throwing hard rights and combination punches at the Democrats." *Newsweek* put Nixon on its cover under the headline "Can the GOP Come Back?" The crowds of loyal Republicans that greeted him on the campaign trail, said the magazine, would "guffaw at his jokes, applaud his punch lines [and] pump his hand with genuine affection and gratitude. 'He's become so much cuter,' coos a woman." Nixon's stump speech hit all the right political cues: call on Republicans to come together in support of the candidate with whom Nixon was appearing that day, knock Johnson for rising inflation and growing economic uncertainty, and above all attack Democrats for their unwillingness to stay the course in Vietnam.[28]

If "wavering" Democrats said that it was time to talk to the North, Nixon called it a "sign of weakness." Talking with North Vietnam, he wrote in the December 1965 issue of *Reader's Digest*, would be like "negotiating with

Hitler before the German armies had been driven from France." As for those "who want peace at any price," he said in a speech in 1966, "let's call them the appeasement Democrats." And no matter what Johnson did on Vietnam, Nixon always wanted more. If Johnson said bomb, Nixon said hit 'em harder. If Johnson sent more troops, Nixon asked why so few. The familiar battle lines of 1948, 1950, and 1952 returned.[29]

The one issue left unthumped in Nixon's fall stump speech was law and order. Thought it might have looked like an oversight to some, it was yet another example of Nixon's political deftness. The crime issue remained a powerful political card (and many Republicans were playing it) but also a divisive one, with overtones of racial bias. In August, Buchanan wrote a tough editorial under Nixon's byline for *US News and World Report*. In the piece, Nixon citied the national "deterioration of respect for the rule of law all across America," which meant riots, crime, and antiwar demonstrators. All of it could be "traced directly," said Nixon, "to the spread of the corrosive doctrine that every citizen possesses an inherent right to decide for himself which laws to disobey and when to disobey them." After this salvo, he didn't need to say much more, given that others—Reagan in California, Wallace in the Deep South, and plenty of Republicans around the country—were trumpeting the issue. For Nixon, coasting off the most caustic antigovernment and racially tinged rhetoric of the conservative right while keeping dirt off his shoes become a much used political tactic in the two-year marathon to come.[30]

Others would do the serious heavy lifting for him—including the president. In October 1966, the White House announced that Johnson would be traveling to Manila for a summit meeting with South Vietnamese strongman General Nguyen Cao Ky and other allied leaders. He would also visit US troops in South Korea and Vietnam. At the same time, word leaked out of the White House that upon his return Johnson would make a last-minute national tour on behalf of vulnerable congressional Democrats. An "October surprise" foreign policy success from Southeast Asia combined with the president rallying Democrats on the hustings might be just enough to neutralize the GOP surge at the polls.[31]

Hoping to counter any positive news coming out of Johnson's trip, Nixon offered a public "appraisal of Manila," that attacked LBJ for floating the possibility of reducing the US troop presence in Vietnam. "The effect" of such a move, said Nixon, "would be to leave the fate of South Vietnam to the Vietcong and the South Vietnamese Army, and almost certainly result in 'Communist victory.'" Nixon's critique was harsh, but not unfair. Johnson had indeed played up the potential for troop withdrawals with an eye toward the midterm elections. Nixon's politicization of the Vietnam issue was matched only by the president's politicization of the Vietnam issue.[32]

Nonetheless, after his return, Johnson unloaded on Nixon at an East Room press conference. "I do not want to get into a debate on a foreign policy meeting in Manila with a chronic campaigner like Mr. Nixon," said Johnson. "It's his problem to find fault with his country and with his government during a period of October every two years." Then the president got personal. "He never did really recognize and realize what was going on when he had an official position in the government," said Johnson. "You remember what President Eisenhower said, that if you'd give him a week or so he'd figure out what he was doing." Finally, Johnson challenged Nixon's patriotism. He accused him of purposely muddying the waters—and putting American soldiers at risk—over the possibility of troop withdrawals, and all for political gain. "Mr. Nixon," said Johnson, "doesn't serve his country well by trying to leave that kind of impression in the hope that he can pick up a precinct or two or a ward or two."[33]

A "savage swipe," *Time* called LBJ's remarks. Even the liberal *New Republic* held its nose and criticized the "impugning" of Nixon's devotion to his country. In a statement that no reporter found even remotely plausible, press secretary George Christian said that the president hadn't "showed any temper or personal attack toward Nixon," and added, "I know for a fact he rather likes Mr. Nixon personally."[34]

Johnson, however, knew exactly what he was doing. According to Joseph Califano, upon returning to the Oval Office, he "chortled" at the wire-ticker accounts of his tirade. "That ought to put him out front," he said. LBJ believed that Nixon would be the easiest candidate to defeat in 1968, and he wanted to elevate his public profile, said Califano. But Johnson had done more than that: he actually made people feel sorry for Nixon—again.[35]

Whatever Johnson's rationale, the attack delighted the Nixon camp. Buchanan met Nixon in Manchester, New Hampshire, where he'd been campaigning for Republican candidates. "You're not going to believe this. He hit us! Jesus did he hit us!" Buchanan gleefully told Nixon. Johnson miscalculated. By attacking Nixon he brought his own conduct and demeanor back to the political forefront. The "shadow" of Johnson already loomed over the midterm vote. Three days before the election Johnson elevated that specter again, with disastrous results for Democrats.[36]

Nixon had for years been predicting Republicans would pick up forty seats in the House, three in the Senate, six governorships, and seven hundred state legislative wins. His numbers were not far off. In the House, the GOP gained forty-seven seats, nine more than they had lost in '64. They picked up three seats in the Senate, eight governorships, and a whopping 540 seats in the nation's state legislatures, a full 171 more than they had given back in the Goldwater debacle. Not since 1938 had the nation witnessed a more dramatic electoral recovery. "In the space of a single autumn day," wrote *Newsweek*, "the 1,000 day reign of Lyndon I came to an end." While Johnson's political star continued to decline, Nixon moved in the opposite direction. Only months earlier he had been dismissed by one observer as "a pale political ghost who will venture out to lose in any weather." In the wake of the GOP comeback he became the leading Republican politician in the country and a frontrunner for the presidential nomination in '68. According to Buchanan, he didn't ever remember seeing Nixon happier than he was on Election Night 1966.[37]

Even more important for Nixon's presidential prospects, Republicans suddenly looked like a party revitalized. In the afterglow of the midterm triumph, the party's once-toxic image had been replaced, said *Time*, "with the vision of a cohesive, inclusive party broad enough to encompass men as ideologically diverse" as Rockefeller on the left and Reagan on the right. The 1966 results represented a popular backlash against Johnson and the Democrats, and the GOP's electoral success owed as much to what the party opposed as it did to what it was for. Nonetheless, Nixon's goal since

Goldwater's ignominious defeat in 1964 had been realized—a rebuilt and reunified Republican Party.[38]

Nixon took an outsized share of the credit for the win, which made his next move all the more unusual—the announcement of a self-imposed six-month "holiday" from politics. At the time of his greatest victory, Nixon ceded the presidential nominating stage to others, and in particular Michigan governor George Romney, who had just won an overwhelming re-election victory and seemed poised to take his political aspirations to the next level. Many found it hard to discern Nixon's motive for absenting himself. But during the 1964 campaign Nixon had gained particular insight into the Michigan governor's true political potential—or lack thereof—and understood better than most what would happen to him on the national stage. Few things could have helped Richard Nixon achieve his goal of the nomination better than an early frontrunner emerging, sucking up all the oxygen in the GOP race, and then crashing and burning. George Romney would be more than suited to the task.[39]

"Watching a Duck Trying to Make Love to a Football"

On paper, George Romney looked like the perfect Republican presidential nominee to emerge from the wreckage of Barry Goldwater's defeat. He was a charismatic moderate, a thrice-elected governor of an electorally important midwestern state, a successful business executive, and a devout man of faith with unimpeachable, if at times insufferable, integrity. Handsome with "silvering hair," he had the "bouncy optimism of a teen-age boy" and "the patient strength of a man who believes that sincere honest work will win over all adversity," wrote one biographer. "You would buy a secondhand car from Romney with happy confidence," wrote Stewart Alsop in the *Saturday Evening Post*. Like many Americans he was a social liberal, particularly on civil rights, but also an economic conservative. A plaque honoring Romney at Brigham Young University perfectly summed up his political philosophy, "A liberal in his treatment of his fellow humans, a conservative with other people's money."[1]

Yet Romney could not be so easily typecast. He complained about the "destructive centralism" of Democrats at the same time that he worked closely with labor unions in Michigan. He trumpeted the attributes of private enterprise and then lamented the fact that many saw the GOP as a pro-business party. He cultivated, quite purposely, an air of detachment from politics. In his first gubernatorial campaign in 1962, Walter DeVries, a top aide to Romney, wrote a fifteen-page strategy memo that described his greatest asset as the fact "that he is not perceived as a politician." The words took on a totemic quality for Romney and those around him. He was not merely the anti-Goldwater; he was also the anti-Nixon. Winning re-election in 1966, and carrying Michigan's Republican senator Robert Griffin and five GOP House challengers across the finish line with him, placed Romney at the head of the presidential pack. It didn't hurt that national polls showed Romney leading Johnson in trial runs for 1968—an advantage no other Republican could claim. For a party desperate to take back the White House, Romney's political appeal was obvious.[2]

Behind the glittering political résumé, however, was a man who lacked the political savvy and, above all, ruthlessness to be a serious candidate for higher office. Governor Jim Rhodes of Ohio famously said of him, "Watching George Romney run for the Presidency was like watching a duck trying to make love to a football." Even more problematic would be the fact that Romney remained a committed moderate in a political party that had lost patience for insufficiently doctrinaire Republicans. It made him the perfect stalking horse for Nixon, who was more than happy to "let Romney take the point," while he watched from the rear. "Let them [the national news media] chew on Romney for a while," Nixon told Buchanan, confident in what the results would be.[3]

When Romney began his quest for the White House in the winter of 1966–67, he did so with a clear blueprint (or so he and his advisors believed) for success: his experience as governor of Michigan. Romney had on three occasions convinced a Democratic-leaning electorate to elect him. Appearing to be a moderate Republican was a strategy born out of political necessity. But it also reflected Romney's personal frustration with what he saw as rising extremism within the Republican Party. Romney believed that the GOP's long-term success depended on becoming more "broadly inclusive" rather than kowtowing to a narrow rump of the party.[4]

In Michigan, Romney not only refused to pander to conservatives; he openly distanced himself from them. On the campaign trail he routinely played down his Republican affiliation and didn't even place the GOP label on much of his literature. "I'm a citizen who's a Republican, not a Republican who is incidentally a citizen," he said. In office, he attacked those he branded as "partisan Republicans" and embraced moderates who had worked with Democrats in supporting a state income tax. He piously declared that he would not become "identified with Welchism," a pointed attack on Robert Welch, the cofounder of the stridently anti-Communist John Birch Society—and he matched his words with actions, taking on Richard Durant, a conservative Republican leader with ties to the Birchers. He also wouldn't indulge the emerging white backlash on civil rights, instead adopting a position of strong support for racial integration.[5]

It was practically inevitable, then, that Romney and Goldwater would lock horns. The Arizona senator launched the first salvo. Only days after Romney announced his intention to run for governor in 1962, Goldwater arrived in Michigan for a party rally and took the unusual step of attacking his fellow Republican. Romney's soothing words about the need for a more welcoming party, said Goldwater, were "standard fare for politicians, like mother love, free beer and wide roads." Two years later, in 1964, when Goldwater was on his way to sewing up the presidential nomination, Romney returned the favor, announcing that he would "do everything within [his] power to keep him from becoming the party's presidential candidate"—though that did not include throwing his hat in the ring. "I accept it, but do not endorse it," he said of Goldwater's victory in San Francisco. Up for re-election as Michigan governor, Romney instructed voters on how to split their vote: "Johnson for President, Romney for Governor." This might have been a smart move in Michigan, but it was a more dubious decision for someone seeking the Republican presidential nod in 1968.[6]

Romney's moderation—like Goldwater's conservatism—was more than mere political gesture. In a letter exchange between the two men after the 1964 election, Romney took direct aim at Goldwater's vision for the party. "Dogmatic ideological parties tend to splinter the political and social fabric of a nation, lead to governmental crises and deadlocks, and stymie the

compromises so often necessary to preserve freedom and achieve progress," he wrote. The key to success going forward, argued Romney, was a
party that turned its back on the "Southern-rural-white orientation" that
had defined the GOP strategy in '64. Romney, like many liberal Republicans,
thought that courting segregationist southerners represented a betrayal of
the party of Lincoln's legacy on civil rights. Goldwater, who believed that
eradicating discrimination should be a matter of conscience rather than
government diktat, responded that Romney was the one being dogmatic
by insisting that conservatives compromise their principles to satisfy the
liberal wing of the party.[7]

Conservatives understood the need for pragmatism, but they also expected the next Republican standard-bearer to be broadly sympathetic and
attentive to their concerns. Romney never seemed to fully understand or
appreciate the importance of pacifying them. When he ventured into the
South, he steadfastly refused to indulge the region's parochialism and instead lectured his white audiences about the need for integration and racial
equality. Romney believed that Republicans should write off the South and
focus instead on the East, Midwest, and Far West in 1968, which according
to his internal campaign messaging played to his record in Michigan of appealing to "Dems, Independents and Republicans, Negroes, laborers and
young people."[8]

For GOP moderates, Romney looked like the best hope for getting one
of their ideological cohorts at the top of the ticket in 1968. Their backing,
however, couldn't make up for Romney's increasingly glaring political limitations. As he traveled the country in 1967 to build support within the
party for his candidacy, he spent much of his time trying to undo his latest
verbal gaffe. "The governor is the victim of his own candor," wrote the *Los
Angeles Times*, "a compunction that he must answer every and any question
thrown at him even when he doesn't have an answer." His comments and
inevitable clarifications became so frequent that the fabled *Baltimore Sun*
political writer Jack Germond joked that he had a special key installed on
his typewriter that typed "Romney later explained."[9]

No issue bedeviled Romney more than Vietnam. When Johnson first
sent combat troops to Vietnam in 1965, Romney, like most Americans,

rallied around the flag and backed the commander in chief. As the conflict intensified and the pictures from Southeast Asia failed to match the White House's confident assessments, his doubts grew. Yet he labored to find the right words to capture what he actually thought about the war—and in a way that wouldn't doom him politically. In his first major policy speech on Vietnam, in April 1967, he tried to carve out a position on the war that he said represented a middle path between "do we bomb" or "do we withdraw." The result was a speech awash in generalities and more focused on what Romney wouldn't do in Vietnam than what he would. Johnson sought to capitalize on Romney's vagueness by bragging that his potential GOP rival had given his war policies a "strong endorsement."[10]

In retrospect Romney's plight appears poignant. Nixon had a simple message on Vietnam: "No negotiation and no appeasement." He pushed for aggressive measures, like blockading North Vietnam's Haiphong harbor, which Johnson had rejected for fear that they would widen the war. Nixon faced no such limitations and risked little political consequences in constantly upping the ante. Romney could not match his rival's cynicism. Nor, as the country soon found out, could he match his discipline as a presidential candidate. On August 31, Romney was booked on a local Detroit news show, *Hot Seat*, hosted by a part-time TV and radio host and full-time lingerie salesman named Lou Gordon. The governor had appeared on the show many times and didn't see much need for major preparation. When asked about his shifting positions on Vietnam, and in particular a recent statement that the United States shouldn't "have been involved in it at all," Romney replied that his initial support was largely the result of a trip he took to Vietnam in 1965. "I just had the greatest brainwashing that anybody can get," said Romney, "not only by the generals, but also by the diplomatic corps over there, and they do a very thorough job."[11]

Although the comment attracted little immediate attention, it took only a few days for the national press to pick up the story. Today, of course, it is considered the defining moment of Romney's political career. The comment, however, illustrates the maxim that in politics a gaffe often occurs when a politician is being honest. While the Pentagon and civilian briefers didn't literally "brainwash" visiting politicians about the war, they certainly didn't tell the full truth either. Indeed, at the very same moment Romney made his ill-advised statement, the White House and the military were strategizing about ways to convince Americans that the war in Vietnam was going well.[12]

The problem for Romney was less what he said and more that it confirmed what political commentators thought of him already. *Time* magazine hinted that if Romney was really brainwashed, "it could have been because he brought so light a load to the Laundromat." Romney's hometown newspaper the *Detroit News* retracted its earlier support for his presidential bid and instead urged Rockefeller to get in the race. Romney went from matching Nixon in Gallup polls to trailing him by double digits.[13]

Though generally considered a turning point in the campaign, Romney's gaffe simply hastened a political decline that had been underway since the summer. Already two months earlier the *Wall Street Journal* had noted that Romney had "lost much of his early glamor and has been exposed...as a generally shallow thinker." In July, David Broder wrote in the *Washington Post* that Romney had "slipped seriously in the past six months," and had been overtaken by Nixon. In fact, Romney's support had always been something of an illusion. An April poll of GOP county chairmen, the local leaders who would likely determine the party nominee in 1968, indicated that by nearly a four-to-one margin they backed Nixon. When asked who they would support if Nixon were not in the race, the chairmen gave a plurality of their support not to Romney but instead to Reagan. A propensity for verbal miscues and a lack of political acumen certainly didn't help Romney campaign, but in reality the rightward shift of his party was the real problem.[14]

Not long after the "brainwashing" debacle, Romney, in response to the deadly riots that had occurred in Detroit earlier that summer, announced a six-thousand-mile tour of America's most impoverished slums and poorest rural communities. Romney wanted to "take the initiative on the key domestic issue of the day." But burnishing his credentials on fighting poverty rather than the more politically salient issue of reducing crime was of questionable value, especially since it would give Romney little opportunity to speak with actual Republican voters. Romney was running for president; his opponent, Nixon, was running for the Republican nomination.[15]

At the end of 1967, hoping to reclaim his lost momentum and strengthen his foreign policy credentials, Romney set out on another tour—this time a worldwide, twenty-nine-day fact-finding mission. It had the opposite effect; relatively minor gaffes, like finding himself "ruble-less" on a Moscow train, and slightly more serious ones, like saying to Jordanian officials that the West Bank of the Jordan River, captured in the 1967 Six-Day War, was "Israeli territory," were amplified by reporters looking to highlight the latest Romney misstep. In Vietnam he delivered a Christmas sermon to US soldiers with an oddly timed message about sacrifice: "Some of us have to lose our lives young and some of us when we are older." One would imagine that the assembled troops would have preferred the latter. At a field hospital in Da Nang he walked up to a wounded soldier who had recently undergone a tracheotomy and said, "I'm George Romney, where are you from?" *Newsweek* called Romney's "odyssey" an "exercise in embarrassment."[16]

In January, when Romney finally began active campaigning in New Hampshire, he would be greeted with an almost complete lack of interest. Round-the-clock phone calls and letters to potential supporters netted him crowds of two hundred people. "We flapped our wings and stood on our heads. Nothing happened," complained William Johnson, Romney's campaign manager in the state. News accounts actually praised Romney's ability to go several days without a verbal blunder. In one single February day of campaigning, three voters accused him, respectively, of being drunk, of letting his state of Michigan down, and being a crook—the latter charge nearly led the usually mild-mannered Romney to fisticuffs.[17]

By the end of February, campaign polls showed Nixon with such a huge advantage in the polls that Romney found himself in genuine danger of finishing third behind a write-in effort for Rockefeller. Romney huddled with a half dozen aides in a Ramada Inn as they laid out the bad news for him. Avoiding humiliation and providing the opportunity for another moderate to jump in and challenge Nixon appeared to be the only reasonable—and least mortifying—course of action for the candidate. So less than two weeks before the New Hampshire primary and just a hundred days after his official entry into the race, Romney withdrew. It was, the political journalist Jules Witcover wrote, the "first technical knockout in the history of presidential politics."[18]

In the end, what worked for Romney in Michigan didn't transfer to the national level, and certainly not in a party as fractured by its two dominant blocs as the GOP was in the mid-1960s. A politician who assiduously avoided parochialism and factionalism would, in the end, be felled by both. Romney's decline also highlighted one of the key political shifts that emerged from 1968: the growing power of the most doctrinaire and uncompromising wings of the two parties, groups that for much of the consensus period had been largely sidelined. For Democrats this meant the New Left; for Republicans, the reinvigorated conservatives. While Johnson pushed through significant victories on domestic policy, the counterculture and the increasingly assertive peace wing of the Democratic Party remained unsatisfied. By 1968, their frustration with Johnson and the war had reached a crescendo. On the Republican right, the sense of impotence ran even deeper. Since the 1940s conservatives had watched as one moderate Republican after another had betrayed what they saw as core conservative principles. Whether Dewey in 1948, the "dime store New Dealer" Eisenhower, or the "slippery" Nixon, who had been cowed by Rockefeller in 1960, the right heard in the party's leaders only a faint echo of the conservatism they longed for. Romney, and later Rockefeller, never fully appreciated the implications of this emerging political transformation, believing instead that the GOP's growing rightward tilt reflected a temporary development that could be overcome. Nixon, on the other hand, understood all too well that conservatives must be accommodated. So, long before Romney uttered the word "brainwash" on a Detroit television show, he was standing on political quicksand.

▬▬▬

While Romney sank further into the political abyss, Richard Nixon's prospects moved in a very different direction. As Nixon had suspected when he took his political sabbatical in the fall of 1966, Romney sucked up so much of the GOP's political oxygen that he discouraged any other moderate from joining the race. He also took attention away from Nixon, who could spend his time flying under the radar and positioning himself for the presidential race to come. In a December 1967 interview with Carl Greenberg of the *Los Angeles Times*, Nixon began to soften his position on Vietnam and distance himself from what he called the GOP "super-hawks" who wanted to escalate the war. At the same time he also dismissed "the wooly-headed doves" who wanted to bring US troops home. He instead argued—in words reminiscent of Romney's failed Hartford speech on the war—that the focus of US policy should be not "how we lose in Vietnam" but rather "how we win."[19]

Nixon's greater flexibility on the war stood in contrast to the hardening of his stance on law and order. In October 1967, he wrote in *Reader's Digest* that "permissiveness," "indulgence," and "sympathy for the past grievances of those who have become criminals" had spurred the nation's crime epidemic. The guilty parties, according to Nixon, were the judges who had made it harder for the police to do their job, the opinion-makers who made excuses for lawbreakers, and the "teachers, preachers and politicians" who promoted a doctrine of moral relativism with regard to breaking the law. By the time the new year rolled around, Nixon's tough talk on crime and slight moderation on Vietnam along with Romney's inevitable demise had solidified his position as the GOP frontrunner.[20]

On February 1, 1968, 150,000 New Hampshire residents opened their mailboxes to find a letter from Nixon, formally announcing his intention to seek the Republican presidential nomination. New Hampshirites read about the former vice president's fourteen years of experience in Washington and his eight years out of office when he had a "chance to reflect on the lessons of public office" and find "some answers" for the nation's challenges. At the same moment, copies of the letter were being handed out to reporters at Nixon's New York office. Nixon ran a well-oiled political machine, one made that much more effective by his focus on reaching out to voters directly, over the heads of national reporters (a focus that the campaign would maintain through the general election).[21]

Meanwhile, fortune again smiled on Nixon. On the same day his bid for the GOP nomination publicly kicked off, American TV viewers were bombarded by the images of Vietcong guerrillas attacking the US embassy in

Saigon. While the Tet Offensive might have vindicated Romney's antiwar views, it also lent implicit support to Nixon's call for experienced presidential leadership. Of course, Tet also made President Johnson further vulnerable to the antiwar insurgency already taking shape in New Hampshire. In April 1967, *Time* had called Nixon "the longest of long shots" for the GOP nod, but eight months later his keen political instincts—and an assist from George Romney—meant that his path to the presidency couldn't have been clearer.[22]

The "Doer" and the "Rising Star of the West"

On March 21, 1968, New York governor Nelson Rockefeller stepped before a podium in midtown Manhattan and announced that he would not be actively seeking the Republican nomination for president. His decision came, he said, after a "realistic appraisal" of his standing within the Republican Party. The news was a major surprise (and in a month in which major political surprises were practically daily events). A national figure with a legendary last name, Rockefeller was the moderate governor of one of most populous states in the country, a candidate for president just four years earlier, and the political champion of the liberal wing of the Republican Party. George Romney had bowed out of the presidential race three weeks earlier, and virtually every political observer in the country expected Rockefeller to take his place.[1]

In retrospect, Rockefeller's decision should not have elicited much shock. After all, announcing whether he would or would not be running for president had become a quadrennial rite of passage for Nelson Rockefeller—one accompanied by an uncanny ability to choose the wrong moment either to take the presidential plunge or stay on the sidelines. Indeed, few modern politicians would prove to be as dexterous at political self-sabotage as Rockefeller. And so, unsurprisingly, only six weeks after stunning political allies and adversaries alike, Rockefeller changed his mind—again—and jumped back into the race.

His vacillation in 1968, however, had been the product of a deeper and more enduring political obstacle, similar to the one that felled George Romney. More than just some garden-variety, "me-too" Republican—Rockefeller was a true believer. A technocrat and a reformer, Rockefeller brimmed with ideas for how to use the power of the public purse to alleviate hardship and create opportunity. As governor of New York, he had transformed the state, investing billions in new government-led projects and initiatives. During his years in office, the number of young people in New York state universities jumped fourfold. Miles of asphalt and track had been laid for new highways, railroads, and subway lines. Urban slums had been cleared and the state's polluted rivers cleaned. Hospitals and new housing complexes had been constructed. The minimum wage increased and civil rights legislation enacted. Quite simply, Nelson Rockefeller was a doer. Unfortunately for him, he sought to lead a political party ideologically opposed to doing.[2]

Across the country from New York State, another Republican politician with aspirations for the White House formulated his own bid for the presidency—the man *Newsweek* had dubbed in the spring of 1967 a "rising star in the West," California governor Ronald Reagan. Like Rockefeller, he too ran a halting and ultimately short-lived campaign for the White House in 1968. But unlike Rockefeller, Reagan's appeal to conservatives could not be questioned. It stemmed from both his ideological certainty and his political dexterity. When he campaigned for governor of California in 1966 (his first race for public office), Reagan figured out how the movement's underlying hostility toward big government could be merged with growing concerns about crime and social disorder to create a pathway to Republican power. While both men would lose the GOP nomination to Nixon, after election day there would be little question as to which of these two very different candidates, with very different philosophical views, represented the future of the Republican Party.[3]

Moderate Republicans like Rockefeller didn't simply disappear after 1968. They continued to play a leading role in the party for the next two decades. Only with rare exception, however, would the language of Republican liberalism, as championed by politicians like Rockefeller, feature prominently in the party's presidential nomination battles. In the years to come the Republican Party would be dominated by a new version of "me-too-ism"— namely, persistent competition among presidential hopefuls to move further and further toward the right. The trajectory of Republican politics that became more conservative in 1968 would gather speed in the years afterward—so much so that today moderate Republicanism is something read about in history books, not practiced by actual politicians. In the story of Rockefeller and Reagan, the Republican past and the Republican present are clearly illuminated. Though Nixon would ultimately win the Republican nomination, the post-1968 GOP became the party of Ronald Reagan.

The disappearance of the Republican Party's liberal wing would have seemed not just unlikely but fantastical when Nelson Rockefeller first ran as the Republican candidate for governor of New York in 1958. If anything, Rockefeller looked to many like the future of the party. The scion of perhaps the most famous (and certainly the richest) family in America, he was a politician without airs. During that 1958 campaign he visited every one of New York's sixty-two counties and gave more than 130 speeches. He famously ate blintzes on the Lower East Side of Manhattan, waded into crowds of Puerto Rican voters in Spanish Harlem, and slapped so many backs and yelled out so many "Hiya, Fellas!" that it quickly became his trademark. Even Harry Truman, no friend to the rich and well-connected, could not help but be impressed by Rockefeller's organic appeal. He "catches popular imagination à la Elvis Presley style and sweeps everything before it," said the former president. Though Republicans took heavy national losses in midterm elections that year, Rockefeller was one of the few exceptions, winning a comfortable victory over the Democratic incumbent Averill Harriman.[4]

Almost immediately Rockefeller entered the national spotlight. A believer in individualism and free enterprise but also government action,

Rockefeller had the ideal profile for a Republican presidential aspirant. He also had an ideal political perch. Teddy Roosevelt, Al Smith, Franklin Delano Roosevelt, and Thomas Dewey had each used the New York governor's mansion as a launching pad to becoming their party's presidential nominee. Rockefeller appeared poised to reach the same heights.

He had barely taken office before the rumblings began that the party might be better served by turning to this upstart rather than to the colorless frontrunner, Vice President Richard Nixon. Rockefeller had the potential to bring much-needed dynamism to the GOP ticket after six years of list-lessness with Eisenhower in the White House. He responded by dipping his toe into the political waters. Throughout 1959 he traveled the country to determine whether a New York Republican could win the party's nomi-nation. Another consideration drove his fact-finding tour: "I hate the thought of Dick Nixon being President of the United States," he told close aides.[5]

Rockefeller's meetings with Republican powerbrokers quickly deflated his presidential hopes. While the New York governor charmed the actual voters who crowded his events, party leaders showed far less interest in his potential candidacy. During a political trip to Los Angeles, a local Republican committeeman met him at the airport with a Nixon button prominently affixed to his lapel. Had Rockefeller found some way to wrest the nomina-tion from Nixon, he would have been a competitive candidate—John Kennedy once said that he probably would have lost the 1960 race had he faced off against him. But Rockefeller couldn't overcome his weak standing in the party.[6]

Part of this was due to his newness to the national political scene as well as traditional Republican fidelity to longtime party leaders such as Nixon. But larger issues loomed, ones that had first sprung up among New York conservatives and would plague Rockefeller for his entire political career: Rockefeller was a cosmopolitan. Gregarious and flirtatious, he immersed himself in extravagant cultural pursuits. He had worked for the hated FDR, and, above all, he was a reformer. These qualities stood in sharp contrast to the parochial, traditional conservatism of GOP decision-makers. By the late 1950s Republicans had largely acclimated themselves to the reality of the New Deal, the need for compromise with Democrats, and the necessity of choosing a presidential nominee moderate enough to have a chance at winning a national election. For many conservatives, a vote for Rockefeller, however, was simply a bridge too far. Rockefeller finished his two-month exploratory tour in December 1959, returned to New York, and announced his "definite and final" decision not to challenge Nixon for the GOP nomination.[7]

Nothing about Rockefeller's pursuit of the presidency, however, could be considered definite or final. Almost immediately, he came to regret the decision. Any leverage he had for influencing Republican policy debates and ensuring that his views would be taken into account at the national convention or in the party platform had disappeared. Rockefeller quickly began dropping hints that he was open to reversing himself. Finally, on May 25 he made clear his availability to be drafted by Republican delegates at the party's national convention that summer in Chicago. Rockefeller's move was provocative, but hardly a fatal one. That would come soon after.[8]

In the spring of 1960 Republicans found themselves increasingly on the defensive about Eisenhower's foreign policy stewardship. In early May, an American U-2 spy plane had been shot down over the Soviet Union. The White House initially claimed that the downed aircraft had been conducting weather research, a move that backfired badly when the Soviets revealed that they held the plane's pilot, Francis Gary Powers, captive. A superpower summit scheduled two weeks later with Eisenhower and Khrushchev was canceled; Cold War tensions heightened. At the same time, Democrats, sensing a political opportunity, went on the offensive, loudly claiming that the GOP had left the United States vulnerable to Soviet nuclear attack, via the infamous (and, as it turned, out nonexistent) "missile gap."

Rather than support his president and his party, Rockefeller piled on. On June 8, he issued a nine-point jeremiad that effectively repudiated Eisenhower's domestic and foreign policy positions. Calling for "plain talk" in a "difficult and testing time," Rockefeller accused the president (and in turn Nixon) of leaving the country in "dramatically weaker" shape than it was at the end of the Cold War. On domestic policy he blasted the administration for failing to push more aggressively for desegregation and national health care for the elderly. "We cannot, as a nation or as a party," said

Rockefeller, "march to meet the future with a banner aloft whose only emblem is a question mark." Unsurprisingly, Eisenhower was furious. The Republican-leaning *US News and World Report* said Rockefeller's "statement would appear to make him a more logical contender for the Democratic presidential nomination." Rockefeller argued that his intention was to shape the policy debate within the party. "Nelson felt he could be the conscience of the Republican Party," said advisor Emmett Hughes, a one-time Eisenhower speechwriter who had publicly broken with the president. But to many others, Rockefeller seemed to be playing the role of spoiler, and all for his own narrow political gain.[9]

Rockefeller was playing a dangerous game. Nixon almost certainly had the nomination sewn up, and Republicans were unlikely to turn to a man now openly at war with his own party. This wasn't 1940, and Rockefeller wasn't Wendell Willkie, the upstart businessman who outflanked the GOP establishment to win the party's presidential nod that year. Yet, ironically, it would be a miscalculation from Nixon that would do more immediate damage. Fearing dissension from the liberal wing at the Republican convention in Chicago, the vice president tried to pacify Rockefeller. The two men met at the governor's opulent Upper East Side apartment in New York City and agreed there to a series of relatively minor changes to the Republican Party platform that became known as the "Compact of Fifth Avenue." Conservatives responded with rage. Goldwater called the agreement a "surrender" and said it would "live in history as the Munich of the Republican Party."[10]

"It was," said Hughes, "a momentary triumph for which [Rockefeller] paid a high price." Rockefeller had needlessly antagonized conservatives, earned Nixon's enduring enmity by forcing him into a humiliating concession, and all the while provided political fodder for Democrats. Rockefeller's machinations suggested to many Republicans that he simply wasn't a team player. "The party never forgot or forgave his coming back in and being a spoiler for Nixon," said George Hinman, a longtime aide. "His mistake in 1960 was not getting out, but in getting back in."[11]

Four years later, Rockefeller's dalliance with the Republican nomination played itself out in a remarkably similar fashion. This time, however,

Rockefeller started off in a very different place on his way to winning over Republican hearts and minds. The party was desperate to win back the White House, and polls showed that Rockefeller fared better than any other potential nominee against Kennedy. Rockefeller, who this time showed no hesitation at getting in the race, had finally learned how to play the game of intraparty politics. He actively wooed conservatives with speeches that decried Kennedy's "appeasement in Cuba" and called for cutting burgeoning budget deficits, ending "domination from Washington," and providing new federal incentives for private enterprise. He even got Goldwater to tell the right-wing hardliners that Rockefeller was "more conservative than you would imagine." His path to the nomination seemed clear. "Nelson Rockefeller is running so far ahead for the Republican Presidential nomination in 1964 that he may have an unbreakable hammerlock on the prize even at this early date," wrote the *Wall Street Journal* in December 1962.[12]

However, if fate demanded yet another self-inflicted wound to end Nelson Rockefeller's dreams of becoming president, the candidate would not disappoint. In 1962, Rockefeller divorced his wife, Mary Clark, the mother of his five children. Many assumed that bachelorhood would mean a continuation of the incessant womanizing that had been a steady feature of their three-decade-long marriage. Rockefeller, however, had other ideas. In the spring of 1963, he announced plans to marry the newly divorced Margaretta Fitler Murphy (or, as she was better known, "Happy"). Adding to the public shock, she had also given up custody of her four children in the separation—a scandalous notion in the early 1960s. Rockefeller's advisors desperately urged him to wait. "If he marries Mrs. Murphy," said one Republican strategist, "he might as well take the gaspipe." But as willful as Rockefeller was in his pursuit of the nomination in 1960, so he was in regard to his personal life. On May 4, 1963, with Happy's children and Rockefeller's siblings (but only two of his five children) in attendance, the couple wed.[13]

The wedding scandalized the party's Protestant conservative base. Pre-wedding polls showed Rockefeller leading Goldwater for the GOP nomination by seventeen points. Three days after returning from his honeymoon, he trailed Goldwater by five. His hopes for the nomination never recovered.

Since he appeared to be the best bet to beat Kennedy, many conservatives had up to that point been willing to swallow their pride, acknowledge political reality, and back him for the nomination. His divorce and remarriage changed that equation. The anti-Rockefeller forces played up the moral outrage over his personal life and soon found that, in a party already wary of the New York governor, they were pushing against an open door.[14]

Rockefeller responded in kind. He told aides he was "off the unity kick" and issued a statement on July 14, 1963, that warned of a "radical, well-financed, highly disciplined minority" and of "purveyors of hate and distrust" who stood in opposition to the party's moderate, racially tolerant tradition. This direct attack on conservatives ensured Rockefeller would fight for the Republican nomination with a large segment of the party united against him.[15]

As Rockefeller's prospects dimmed, Goldwater watched his own brighten. Backed by a powerful base of conservative grass-roots support, he made his way through the Republican primaries with far greater momentum than the New York governor. While Rockefeller won the Oregon primary in May, by the time of the final primary showdown between the two men in California, Goldwater had far too much support within the rank and file of the party to be stopped. Yet Rockefeller trudged on, and he did so with a simple but blunt message: Goldwater was too extreme to win in November. "Who Do You Want in the Room with the H Bomb?" read one campaign mailer. Rockefeller was validating every Democratic attack that would be launched against Goldwater in the general election. It appeared to many Republicans that Rockefeller once again put his own personal aggrandizement ahead of what was best for the party and in the process drove a dangerous wedge between moderates and conservatives.[16]

More than just personal resentment or some insatiable need to win the presidency spurred Rockefeller on. He meant every negative word he uttered about Goldwater and the toxic effect that he believed his candidacy would have on the party. That such a stance incalculably damaged his hopes of winning the presidency hardly seemed to dissuade him. Robert Hartmann, who later worked with Rockefeller when he served as vice president, summed up his mindset well: "He always would rather be Nelson Rockefeller than President." Rockefeller's appearance at the 1964 Republican national convention in San Francisco exemplified his dogged commitment to personal virtue—even at the expense of personal ambition. Calling on his fellow Republicans to insert language into the party platform that would publicly "repudiate the efforts of irresponsible, extremist groups, such as the Communists, the Ku Klux Klan, the John Birch Society and others, to discredit our Party," Rockefeller declared war on the right. "These extremists feed on fear, hate and terror. They encourage disunity.... These are people who have nothing in common with Americanism," he declared, as boos and chants of "We Want Barry!" echoed across the hall. The angry responses from Goldwater partisans practically drowned out Rockefeller's words. Several times he had to stop speaking and wait for the din to die down. Yet he would not be deterred. "Some of you don't like to hear it, ladies and gentlemen, but it's the truth," said Rockefeller. Senator Thruston Morton, the convention chairman, pleaded for silence, to no avail. As the catcalls cascaded down upon Rockefeller, he stood serenely at the podium, looked out at the crowd, and a slight grin crept over his face. At this moment of conservative hysteria, as the members of his own political party subjected him to merciless abuse, Nelson Rockefeller very much appeared to be enjoying himself. The next morning he would say of the evening's festivities, "I had the time of my life."[17]

The glow, however, would fade. After once working so hard to win over conservatives, Rockefeller had gone out of his way to antagonize the segment of the party that held the key to the Republican nomination. His perceived abandonment of Goldwater during the general election further deepened hostility toward him. By the time jockeying for the 1968 nomination began, Rockefeller, immersed in marital bliss, seemed to have little interest in another presidential run. After a bruising come-from-behind re-election victory in 1966 for a third term in Albany, Rockefeller "unequivocally" declared that he no longer had any interest in being president. "Something happens in life and you lose ambition because you have a sense of fulfillment," Rockefeller told reporters at one point. "I just don't have the ambition or the need of inner drive—or whatever the word is—to get in again." The comment produced snickers from the political press. "I believe Rocky when he says he's lost ambition. I also believe he remembers where he put it," said journalist and former Johnson advisor Bill Moyers.[18]

While Rockefeller's presidential plans might have been unclear, his refusal to let the newly emboldened conservatives take over the party without a fight was more unambiguous. Behind the scenes he worked to unite the various liberal and moderate factions in the party in support of one candidate who could effectively compete against the conservatives. The recipient of this political largesse was George Romney. Rockefeller loaned the Michigan governor money and staff and gave him his political backing. But Rockefeller's familiar vacillation, and the widely held view that Romney served as a stalking horse for his own presidential aspirations, made it that much more difficult for him to build momentum. When Rockefeller traveled to New Hampshire to campaign for the Michigan governor, *Time* noted that he made as strong a case for "moderate Republicanism" as he did for the candidate. Then again, by that point there wasn't much Rockefeller could have done to weaken Romney's candidacy that Romney hadn't already done to himself. At the end of February when Romney finally threw in the towel, all eyes turned to Rockefeller. At this late juncture, no one else in the party could realistically hope to challenge Nixon. The names of Senator Charles Percy of Illinois and New York mayor John Lindsay, two nonconservative candidates, had been bandied around for more than a year by political observers, but neither had the name recognition nor the resources at this late juncture. Even Reagan had little hope of beating Nixon in a head-to-head primary battle.[19]

The Rockefeller camp, however, couldn't figure out a way to make it work. The combination of conservative antipathy, the absence of strong grass-roots support, and the lack of a campaign infrastructure made it difficult to see how Rockefeller could win a primary fight. When asked by an aide how many party leaders would welcome him into the race, Rockefeller responded, "I don't think any of them." As one unnamed Nixon advisor noted at the time, Romney's pullout was quite helpful for their man. "It forced Rockefeller to show his cards, and he didn't have any."[20]

Rockefeller did have his share of boosters. The first-term governor of Maryland Spiro Agnew set up a "Draft Rockefeller" movement in his state at the end of February. Several other moderate Republican governors, including Raymond Shafer in Pennsylvania, John Chafee in Rhode Island, and Tom McCall in Oregon, also counted themselves in the Rockefeller camp. Yet, while privately supportive, few wanted to go public, wary of being on the losing side if Nixon prevailed.[21]

While Rockefeller labored over whether to run, the upcoming primary schedule quickly forced his hand. The key challenge came with the Oregon primary, scheduled for late May. The site of his greatest primary victory in 1964, the northwestern state, with its moderate, technocratic Republicanism, was Rockefeller's natural environment. By a quirk of electoral law, however, once he appeared on the ballot in Oregon, he would then be placed automatically on the primary ballot in Nebraska—a far more conservative state and one in which Nixon would be heavily favored. Both Oregon and Nebraska had so-called free-for-all primaries in which the secretary of state could place any individual deemed to be a candidate for president on the ballot—unless they submitted an affidavit to the contrary. The deadline for the Nebraska primary was March 15, and for Oregon March 22. Theoretically, Rockefeller could have waited until after the fifteenth to make a decision, entered the Oregon primary, faced off against Nixon there, and then skipped Nebraska.[22]

Privately, Nixon's camp had been trying without success to get Nebraska's Republican governor and secretary of state to push up the deadline to match Oregon's. Fortuitously for them, Bobby Kennedy entered the Democratic race on March 16, and, though it was a day after the deadline, his name had been automatically placed on the Nebraska ballot. Clearly, if the deadline could be moved back a day, it could be moved a few more days to accommodate Oregon, the Nixon camp argued, this time with success. Rockefeller's deliberations suddenly became even more complicated. The Nebraska hijinks gave Rockefeller one more reason to stay out of the race, yet he still remained undecided. He couldn't simply cede the party nomination to the conservatives; but the odds for success could not have been lower. Why put his family and himself through what would likely be a pointless and draining struggle? Every day, it seemed, Rockefeller would make up his mind—and then change it the next.[23]

Respected national writers like James Reston and Walter Lippmann, who called him the "most qualified man available for the supreme task of reconstruction," beseeched him to run. Newspaper ads bought by liberal Republicans were making the same pitch. Even his in-state rival, New York City mayor John Lindsay, told him that, with the country increasingly "unhinged," he could not afford to sit the election out. On March 19, the *New York Times* reported that the wheels had been sent in motion for a presidential bid. The same day, however, Rockefeller traveled to Washington to meet with a group of Republican senators. To his horror, he discovered that most viewed his potential candidacy merely as a way to strengthen Nixon in upcoming GOP primaries by taking some of the spotlight away from the Democrats. It would be bad enough for Rockefeller to lose a chance at the nomination again, but to help Nixon in the process was too much to bear.[24]

So on March 21, when Rockefeller stepped before the microphones and three hundred expectant reporters at the Hilton Hotel in New York City, he dropped yet another of 1968's many political bombshells. "I have decided today to reiterate unequivocally that I am not a candidate campaigning directly or indirectly for the Presidency of the United States." He said that to get in the race would divide the party and guarantee its "impotence" in the general election. But there may have been another factor playing into his decision. For several months rumors had been circulating that Rockefeller had become romantically involved with one of his young female staffers (not an unusual occurrence for him). Word had leaked out not only to the Nixon campaign but also to the journalist Drew Pearson, who had written about the allegations in his private newsletter. In the wake of his marriage to Happy, news of an extramarital affair would be politically devastating. Indeed, when Nixon heard of Rockefeller's unexpected decision not to run, he turned to aides and said, "It's the girl." Whatever the reason, Rockefeller's political supporters felt blindsided by the announcement. When Agnew, who had brought reporters and friends to his office in Annapolis to watch Rockefeller's speech, heard the news, some present claimed that his "jaw dropped a full inch." Rockefeller's staff failed to give Agnew advance notice of his decision, a slip-up they would come to regret when their candidate later had a change of heart.[25]

In fact, Rockefeller's decision was not quite as "definite and final" as it might have seemed. Announcing that he wouldn't be "campaigning" meant he wouldn't be entering a primary fight with Nixon. It didn't mean that he had given up his dreams of becoming president. Asked at his March 21 press conference whether any Republican could win the nomination without actually running in the primary, Rockefeller responded, to laughter from reporters, "I suppose only time will tell." In the *New York Times* Tom Wicker intimated that Rockefeller's retreat had been "strategic." Now he wouldn't have to worry about being embarrassed in a primary election, and if Nixon faltered before the Republican convention, he could jump back in. Moreover, a Rockefeller candidacy would have rallied party conservatives who were playing coy, waiting to see what their preferred candidate, Reagan, would do. By remaining on the sidelines Rockefeller ensured that the conservatives would, for the time being, remain there as well.[26]

So it came as less than a shock when, six weeks later, on April 30, Rockefeller rejoined the race, announcing at an Albany press conference that he would indeed be a candidate for president at the Republican National Convention in Miami Beach. With Happy by his side, and flashing his ebullient smile, he said that he had been disturbed by the "dramatic and unprecedented events of the past weeks" and was being pushed to run by "men and women in many walks of life." This comment contained a kernel of truth. After his withdrawal in March, for perhaps the first time in his political career, Rockefeller had been swept up in a groundswell of public support for him to run for president. His change of heart, however, was likely due to a more essential conviction. "I'm a politician. That is my profession," he once said. "Success in politics, real success, means only one thing in America."[27]

For a brief moment that success seemed to be within his grasp. The day of Rockefeller's public return to the campaign would be capped by an unexpected win in the Massachusetts Republican primary over the state's favorite son candidate, Governor John Volpe. More broadly, the country's political terrain had dramatically shifted since Rockefeller initially dropped out of the race in March. At that time Democrats were in disarray. While Johnson still seemed to be the likely nominee, he clearly appeared

Figure 1: Throughout 1967, as opposition to the war in Vietnam grew, the number of antiwar protests increased. On October 21, 1967, demonstrators gather in Washington for a march on the Pentagon.

Courtesy of the LBJ Presidential Library, Austin, Texas. Photo by Frank Wolfe.

Figure 2: Johnson and Humphrey are briefed by the president's new military commander in Vietnam, Gen. Creighton Abrams (foreground), and the chairman of the Joint Chiefs of Staff, Gen. Earl Wheeler (obscured), March 27, 1968.

Courtesy of the LBJ Presidential Library, Austin, Texas. Photo by Yoichi Okamoto.

Figure 3: On March 31, 1968, Johnson stuns the nation as he announces from the Oval Office that he will not be seeking re-election.

Courtesy of the LBJ Presidential Library, Austin, Texas. Photo by Yoichi Okamoto.

Figure 4: Throughout the mid-1960s, President Johnson and Senator Kennedy eyed each other warily from opposite ends of Pennsylvania Avenue. Here they sit (peacefully) in the Oval Office, June 1966.

Courtesy of the LBJ Presidential Library, Austin, Texas. Photo by Yoichi Okamoto.

Figure 5: The cover of *Esquire*'s November 1966 issue captured the increasingly prevalent view of Vice President Humphrey as merely a mouthpiece for Lyndon Johnson.

Courtesy of George Lois and *Esquire* Magazine.

Figure 6: While McCarthy was often an ambivalent politician, he was uniquely skilled in the art of retail politics.

Courtesy of Special Collections, Rare Books, and Manuscripts, University of Minnesota, Anderson Library.

Figure 7: McCarthy's "Clean Gene" college-aged campaign volunteers became the symbol of his grass-roots political insurgency. Here, supporters take a catnap between canvassing.

Courtesy of Special Collections, Rare Books, and Manuscripts, University of Minnesota, Anderson Library.

Figure 8: A McCarthy campaign event in July 1968. Note the sign on the stage: "The Man the People Found"—a fitting description of McCarthy's relationship with his supporters.

Courtesy of Special Collections, Rare Books, and Manuscripts, University of Minnesota, Anderson Library.

Figure 9: Kennedy speaking at the Greek Theatre in Los Angeles, where he infamously accused President Johnson of "calling upon the darker impulses of the American spirit."

Courtesy of Sven Walnum, the Sven Walnum Photograph Collection. John F. Kennedy Presidential Library and Museum, Boston.

Figure 10: The key to Kennedy's success in Democratic primaries was the support of black and Hispanic supporters, especially in the crucial California primary. A young RFK supporter awaits his arrival at a campaign rally in the spring of 1968.

Courtesy of Sven Walnum, the Sven Walnum Photograph Collection. John F. Kennedy Presidential Library and Museum, Boston.

Figure 11: Kennedy addresses his jubilant supporters in the ballroom of the Ambassador Hotel in Los Angeles after winning the California primary. Only moments later he would be struck down by an assassin's bullet.

Courtesy of Sven Walnum, the Sven Walnum Photograph Collection. John F. Kennedy Presidential Library and Museum, Boston.

Figure 12: While George Romney's campaign in New Hampshire was an exercise in political futility, he enjoys a happier moment with supporters carrying a psychedelic image of the Michigan governor.

Courtesy of the Bentley Library, University of Michigan.

Figure 13: Ronald Reagan's victory in the 1966 California governor's race propelled him into the national spotlight and the '68 presidential campaign.

Courtesy of the Ronald Reagan Presidential Library.

Figure 14: Nelson Rockefeller barnstormed the nation in the summer of 1968, hoping to drum up support for his presidential bid. Here he rides a motorcade in New York City.

Courtesy of the Library of Congress, *US News and World Report* Archive.

Figure 15: Wallace campaign events in 1968 featured a combustible mix of supporters and detractors. At a rally in Albany, New York, one Wallace opponent holds up a sign declaring "We will never overcome with Wallace," October 9, 1968.

Courtesy of the Associated Press.

Figure 16: Nixon's political coronation at the RNC in Miami Beach featured the intent focus on image-making that became the hallmark of the '68 campaign. After his acceptance speech, Nixon and Agnew and their wives wave to the crowd, August 8, 1968.

Courtesy of the Richard Nixon Presidential Library, Yorba Linda, California.

Figure 17: Happy days are (briefly) here again as Humphrey and his running mate, Edmund Muskie, accept their party's nomination at the Democratic Convention in Chicago, August 29, 1968.

Courtesy of the Associated Press.

Figure 18: The Democratic National Convention in Chicago was marred by violence so severe it would later be dubbed a police riot. In this photo, officers beat demonstrators in Grant Park, August 28, 1968. Courtesy of the Associated Press.

Figure 19: After the lost month of September 1968, Humphrey's Salt Lake City speech gave him a burst of momentum that almost took him to the Oval Office. Only weeks before Election Day he rallies Democratic partisans, October 1968.

Courtesy of the Kheel Center for Labor-Management Documentation, Cornell University.

Figure 20: Nixon's advisors viewed campaign rallies primarily as an opportunity to create visuals for their omnipresent television ads.

Courtesy of the National Archives.

Figure 21: Nixon adopts a classic Nixonian pose, signalling V for victory.
Courtesy of the National Archives.

vulnerable. Now, with him out and Robert Kennedy looking to many like the potential nominee, Rockefeller could make the case that Republicans needed a more competitive national candidate, particularly one who could pull independents and Democrats to the GOP side. National polling backed him up. In March, Rockefeller led Johnson in a hypothetical matchup by seven points, while Nixon ran even with the president. Problematically, however, that same poll showed Rockefeller trailing Nixon by twenty-four points among Republican voters.[28]

Hughes later joked that "while the prospect of Nelson being nominated was appalling" to conservatives, it "was even more appalling that he might be elected." Rockefeller couldn't compete for the GOP rank and file against Nixon—and he barely even tried. Indeed, his entire campaign would be predicated on his weak standing inside the party. An internal campaign memo from late May 1968 described Rockefeller's dilemma in vivid detail: "While the current campaign obviously involves the Republican nomination and not a general election, the essential target of public policy is strength in the polls—and not the presumed preconceptions of GOP delegates." In other words, Rockefeller's pitch to Republican delegates would be to vote not with their hearts but with their heads. "Since the critical national polls are national and not partisan, the expression of policy must come from a man essentially sounding like a national, not just a party leader," the memo noted. Rockefeller's unorthodox strategy was best explained by the memo's reminder that "the candidate's own following outside the GOP is larger than within."[29]

While national Republicans, including Nixon, railed against wasteful Great Society programs that raised dangerous expectations among America's black population, Rockefeller tried to find a middle ground. In one lengthy campaign press release he spoke of making the "restructuring" and "streamlining" of the "federal establishment" a priority so that "the government is able to deliver on its major policy objective." Rockefeller didn't seek to get rid of the "big government" that Johnson had thrust on the nation; he wanted to make it more efficient.[30]

Two weeks before Rockefeller officially returned to the race, he delivered a major policy speech in Washington, DC, to the American Society of

Newspaper Editors. The address was an effort to raise his profile for a potential entry into the GOP race. But for a candidate intent on improving his standing among Republicans, he chose an odd topic—the urban crisis. According to Rockefeller's own internal polling, "rebuilding run-down sections of our cities," reducing poverty, and dealing with "Negro racial issues" ranked low on the list of concerns of average Americans. Nonetheless, Rockefeller made clear that the challenges of urban poverty, unemployment, and despair demanded "a profound act of national commitment" and "a readiness for sacrifice as the waging of a war for survival." He called for a massive new federal commitment of $150 billion over ten years in new spending for America's cities—$100 billion of which would come from an "aroused citizenry and a proud government." A *Washington Post* editorial about the speech, titled "Disappointing," captured the sentiments of many.[31]

Yet the campaign continued down the same path. In a speech at the Economic Club of Detroit in late May, Rockefeller bemoaned the plague of higher prices, which "cripples the buying power of those who have the least money and the least leverage to get money." Barely a mention was made in his prepared remarks about the impact on the middle class. While calling for a halt in some public spending, he also demanded a temporary increase in income taxes "at least as large" as the 10 percent increase that President Johnson had been lobbying Congress to pass. This might have been smart fiscal policy, but as political theater it fell flat. The *New York Times* described the response from the largely Republican crowd as "polite."[32]

Rockefeller's campaign advertisements, which inundated the country from early June until the Republican convention at the beginning of August, offered more of the same. One spot opens with the backdrop of a rain-soaked city street, as Rockefeller speaks in a voice-over about the need for black Americans to have an "equal chance" at the American dream. "They deserve decent housing. Decent jobs. And the schooling and training to fill these jobs. To those who cry, 'We can't afford it,' I say, 'We can't afford not to do it.' To those who cry, 'Law and order,' I say, 'To keep law and order there must be justice and opportunity.'" At this point in the ad a black man recently returned from Vietnam walks out of the shadows of the dark street. While it was an effort to dramatize Rockefeller's larger goal of repairing the ghettoes, the ad unintentionally evoked the fears that millions of white Americans had of the country's cities in the summer of 1968. It did, however, reflect Rockefeller's consistent refusal to make a play for backlash voters. In a speech that spring at Emory University he made clear that he had no intention of disguising his pride in his civil rights record. "This would insult not only my integrity, but your intelligence." For reasons of both politics and basic decency, Rockefeller believed that Republicans must not fall prey to the demagoguery of George Wallace or the inclination to use civil rights as a wedge issue.[33]

Rockefeller's move leftward became even more pronounced after the assassination of Kennedy. "I think the people who supported Bobby Kennedy are going to come to me now," he confidently told his staff. This meant new appeals to blacks and the counterculture youth, more calls for a solution to the urban crisis, and even greater moderation on Vietnam. In a speech at the National Press Club he pledged to complete Kennedy's "unfulfilled dreams" of peace and social justice and decried the "men of the old politics who do not understand change." Two days later he scheduled a Kennedy-esque walk-through in the predominately African American neighborhood of Watts in Los Angeles. Rockefeller was making a concerted and expensive effort to entice blocs of voters who would have absolutely no say in whether he would be the Republican presidential nominee in 1968. As Rockefeller's speechwriter Joseph Persico would archly note, "No Kennedy supporters were going to be delegates to the Republican convention."[34]

Rockefeller's persistent focus on public-sector solutions to tough domestic challenges like poverty, racial inequality, and lack of economic opportunity—rather than dog-whistle appeals to law and order—suggested a last gasp from Republican moderates, but also a last gasp of the 1960s liberal consensus. Rarely again would a GOP presidential aspirant take positions so supportive of activist government or devote so much attention to America's poorest citizens. On the campaign trail, Rockefeller would regularly tell voters about his many legislative achievements in New York State. He spoke of his ambitious plans for American cities and his determination to use government as a tool for eliminating poverty and expanding justice. And he challenged Nixon, albeit obliquely, over his law-and-order rhetoric.

"It is not straight talk to issue resounding statements on crime control, which wholly omit the slightest mention of gun control," Rockefeller declared at a campaign event in Atlanta. "It is not straight talk to place the overwhelming blame on the national government for our sharply rising crime rate, when we all know that criminal law enforcement is overwhelmingly in the charge of state and local government." Weeks later Rockefeller took a more direct line of attack. When a heckler yelled out "Nixon's the one!" he shot back, "That's right, he's the one who lost it for us in '60."[35]

Behind the scenes, Rockefeller tried to neutralize conservative opposition to his candidacy. A trip to South Carolina to woo the state's convention delegates produced mixed results. GOP state chairman Harry Dent noted that those present realized Rockefeller was "without horns or a forked tail" but they also found that, "as far as the Democratic choice goes...he was the preferable choice." Public opinion polls backed up Dent's acerbic comment. At the same time that Rockefeller steadily improved his standing among Democrats and independents, he was losing it among Republicans. "The closer he comes to demonstrating that he might be the one Republican to win in November," wrote pollster Louis Harris, "the weaker he becomes in his own party." Indeed, as Rockefeller tried to convince conservatives to choose a candidate whose views were antithetical to their core beliefs, one of his rivals for the Republican nomination was showing exactly what type of message appealed most directly to the party's right wing.[36]

In the waning days of the Goldwater disaster in 1964, one hopeful sign for the future of conservatism emerged. In a thirty-minute televised campaign speech, entitled "A Time for Choosing," Ronald Reagan catapulted himself into the national spotlight. The speech, though nominally intended to boost Goldwater's chances, offered a persuasive distillation of the conservative case against the centralized welfare state. David Broder immediately hailed it as the greatest rhetorical foray onto the political stage since William Jennings Bryan's "Cross of Gold" speech in 1896. Overnight Reagan went from being a B movie actor to a rising political star.[37]

But while Reagan might have been an effective communicator, he had a meager knowledge of public policy. For liberals he provided the quintessential example of style over substance. Even some Republicans had their doubts; the moderate Ripon Society called Reagan "unqualified for any national post requiring a high degree of administrative and diplomatic responsibility." He offered, they said, a "simplistic approach to domestic issues," an "inability to match rhetoric with administrative competence," and a "preoccupation with the role of military force in the conduct of foreign affairs."[38]

For conservatives, however, Reagan seemed a dream candidate. In his first run for public office in 1966, he had challenged Pat Brown for the governorship of California. Preaching traditional values, tarring Brown with the liberal label, and offering a forceful conservative critique of the evils of big government, Reagan crushed Brown by nearly one million votes. With his corny jokes and expressions ("Holy Toledo!"), his simple tastes (his favorite food was macaroni and cheese, and his favorite dessert, vanilla ice cream), and his hopelessly square demeanor, he was Goldwater without the intemperance and severity—a conservative ideologue in sheep's clothing. If you "peel away the plastic" with Reagan, said one aide, "you find more plastic." And while it was true that Reagan said his share of loopy things on the campaign trail in 1968 (like warning that Democrats were planning to divide the country into "administrative super-state districts" or comparing political hecklers to Hitler Youth), he generally managed to avoid Goldwater's more extreme rhetoric.[39]

In reality, Reagan didn't act much like a rigid ideologue. As governor he repeatedly broke with conservative doctrine on fiscal issues (within a few months of taking office in Sacramento he proposed the largest state tax increase in US history). He didn't fight to reverse open housing policies even though it had been the issue that helped springboard him into the governor's mansion. These apostasies were well known to conservative activists, but they were compartmentalized. Reagan's policy pragmatism could be taken with a grain of salt, because of the strength of his public defense of conservative values. "He has become the only decent salesman of conservative philosophy we have," said one Reagan aide.[40]

Above all, Reagan's political appeal was too dynamic to ignore. He understood how to match the antigovernment principles of conservatism with the tough-on-crime language that appealed to traditional Democratic voters. "Our city streets are jungle paths after dark, with more crimes of violence than New York, Pennsylvania, and Massachusetts combined," said Reagan, in a familiar refrain, during the 1966 California campaign.[41]

In his telling, not just left-wing politicians and judges but also the very existence of liberal social policies were to blame for the country's ills. Black migrants to California had been promised streets "paved with gold" by liberal reformers, said Reagan, and thus became disappointed and angry when their hopes were dashed. Instead of more government programs, he offered reasonable-sounding solutions to the problems of the ghetto that always adopted a very specific antigovernment spin: a dose of individual initiative and creativity, more volunteerism, the helping hand of the private sector, greater state control rather than federal, and, above all, fewer social programs and less bureaucratic involvement. Such calls appealed to voters who believed that a decline in responsibility and self-reliance served as the cause of ghetto riots and urban disorder. A heavy dose of implicit racial bias also clearly informed Reagan's campaign rhetoric. He joked at a fundraising dinner about the woman who called the welfare office and demanded a new crib. When asked where the baby slept now, the woman responded, "In the carton from the color TV." The line presaged his later, also racially tinged attacks on "welfare queens" who drove around ghetto streets in brand-new Cadillacs.[42]

Nothing better enhanced Reagan's value-laden sermons than the Free Speech Movement demonstrations that had begun on the Berkeley campus in 1964 and evolved into generalized antiwar and "anti-authority" demonstrations. The crown jewel of the California higher education system, Berkeley was accessible only to the state's elite students. These products of privilege thumbing their noses at social conventions created the perfect straw man for Reagan. The "malcontents" should go to class or get out, he said, as he regularly portrayed them as foul-mouthed, sex-crazed hippies who had brought shame to a great university. His admirers cheered lustily. Even after he became governor, Berkeley remained Reagan's most effective political punching bag. In language that Nixon would later use to great effect, Reagan claimed a "great silent majority of teachers and students— those who want order, who want to be free to teach and be taught unmolested—have not been heard from." Reagan oriented his political appeal around the growing sense that lenient judges, liberal social engineers, and leftist protesters were dragging America down. Conservatives would rely upon this narrative for decades to come to fuel their populist entreaties to white working- and middle-class voters. Even as social progress fundamentally shifted the basic mores of American society in support of civil rights, feminism, secularism, and tacit acceptance of homosexuality, Reagan found success in harkening back to a simpler era.[43]

Reagan's speeches also served as catch-alls for the right wing's increasingly aggressive attacks on government and liberal "elites." Fed up with teen pregnancies, pornography, homosexuality, drug use, or the "free love movement"? Liberal judges, feckless politicians, and authority-flouting hippies were to blame. Fed up with riots, crime, and "supporting too many families" on welfare that were not one's own? Liberal social policies that encouraged dependence and made law and order a secondary concern were responsible. Fed up with the war in Vietnam? The antiwar demonstrators unwilling to defend their country and the political leaders who refused to "use whatever power and technology we have at our command" to win clearly were the problem. Reagan's message was powerful, easy to digest, and asked little of its working- and middle-class targets.[44]

Yet, for all his us-versus-them rhetoric, Reagan also radiated an aura of hopeful optimism and authenticity. Nearly two decades before he ran for re-election as president with the slogan "Morning in America," Reagan understood that he had to temper even his dark ruminations with a sense that better days lay around the corner. "Our problems are many, but our capacity for solving them is limitless," he would tell audiences. Rather than a Great Society, he spoke of a "creative society" that relied less on government largesse and more on old-fashioned gumption and elbow grease. Reagan's combination of charisma, humor, and unpretentiousness made even his harshest attacks seem mild. "The government," he joked, "is like a baby's alimentary canal, with a healthy appetite at one end and no sense of responsibility at the other." Or, on another occasion: "We are told God is dead. Well, he isn't. We just can't talk to him in the classroom anymore." Though political writer Warren Weaver, Jr., referred to Reagan's ideological beliefs as "somewhat primitive" in the pages of the *New York Times Magazine*, he found himself smitten by the politician's obvious appeal. "Reagan almost always sounds reasonable," wrote Weaver, "earnestly serious or smilingly boyish.... No stretch of casting will make him sound like a kook."[45]

While Reagan's essential message contained little mystery, his presidential intentions, on the other hand, remained purposely and frustratingly opaque. In part, this was due to Reagan's own ambivalence about running. "He didn't want to embarrass himself," said longtime aide Lyn Nofziger. "He was a very careful guy." But it also had to do with the peculiarities of the Republican nominating process. In the early primary states a candidate often had to petition to have his name taken off the ballot. Reagan was already a favorite son candidate from his home state of California (and thus nominally controlled the state's eighty-six votes at the GOP convention), so he couldn't sign an affidavit saying he wasn't a candidate for president when, as far as the state of California was concerned, he was. At the same time, he had no campaign infrastructure and knew that if he entered any of the primaries, he'd likely be humiliated.[46]

Reagan was nowhere to be seen in New Hampshire and Wisconsin, and received a paltry percentage of the vote in a write-in effort. In conservative Nebraska he did better but still got only 20 percent. In the late spring, however, under the tutelage of Clifton White, the consultant who had guided Goldwater's 1964 campaign, Reagan began a national speaking tour before large and friendly partisan crowds excited by the prospect of a glimpse at the party's potential conservative savior. Reagan did not disappoint them. He trod an almost identical path to the one he had taken in California. "Today's youthful dissenters" sought "not to build a nation of laws, but to create a condition of tyranny," he claimed. At the University of Colorado, when he declared that the university administrators had a responsibility to maintain order on campus, loud applause greeted him. He quickly responded by asking "Have you ever thought about transferring to Berkeley?" In a speech in New Orleans he boasted that in his home state of California "we are trying to protect society from the lawbreaker instead of the other way around." In Indiana, he complained about a philosophy of "permissiveness from cradle to crime" and argued that "what were once considered privileges are now recognized as rights."[47]

Still, no issue animated Reagan more than big government. His speeches were peppered with statistics about the ever-expanding federal bureaucracy—the government spending that went up "eight and half times," the spending on health and welfare that was up "210 percent," and the "42 million Americans" now receiving checks from the federal government. In an interview with the *Christian Science Monitor* in late June 1968, he hit on themes that would become central to the modern Republican Party. "It is time government stopped telling people what to do—but, instead, to ask them what we can do to help them in solving their problems." Americans from across the political spectrum "had discovered they were not benefiting from the Great Society—but just paying for it." It was bad enough that the government issued diktats to the citizenry on who they could live next to or send their kids to school with, Reagan argued, but now it made them pay for the privilege while doling out money to the very people who were burning down their cities and menacing their communities.[48]

While Reagan called for a step back, Rockefeller's solution was still more: more social programs, more spending, and more government involvement. "It is folly to argue that the rebuilding of our cities, at the cost of many billions of dollars…, is merely a false hope," said Rockefeller in a speech in late May. "It is quite the contrary: it is true necessity and an urgent demand."[49]

Rockefeller's remarks highlighted the expanding divide in the party between moderates and Reagan's antigovernment, conservative populism. In their contrasting styles and views on the role of government, the two men offered two very different road maps for the ideological, programmatic, and, above all, rhetorical direction of the Republican Party. Though neither would come close to winning the GOP nomination in 1968, Reagan's value-laden message of smaller government—lubricated by healthy doses of political polarization—would ultimately be embraced by two generations of Republicans office seekers.

The dueling Rockefeller and Reagan campaigns, while historically significant, could do little, however, to weaken Nixon's increasing stranglehold over the nomination. Since Romney's departure at the end of February,

Nixon had plundered his way through the GOP primaries. After winning handily in New Hampshire he scored 79 percent of the vote in Wisconsin. In Indiana, running unopposed, he received more than half a million votes—180,000 more than the Democratic primary winner, Bobby Kennedy. In Oregon, a state where Reagan refused to travel to campaign on his own behalf, leaving matters to local backers, Nixon took 73 percent of the vote, and Reagan 22 percent. A week later, in California, things didn't go much better for Reagan; even though he ran unopposed as a favorite son, more than half of the state's Republicans failed to vote for him. The embarrassing numbers would be overshadowed by the assassination of Kennedy, but combined with Nixon's wins in Indiana and Oregon, which came after Rockefeller's entry into the race, offered convincing indication of his strength within the party. "The chances of my now being derailed are pretty well eliminated," Nixon claimed in a victory statement—and it would be hard to disagree.[50]

Although Rockefeller continued to spend millions for television and newspaper ads to move his flagging poll numbers, and Reagan maintained his stealth campaign, there was little evidence, as the candidates prepared to descend on Miami Beach, that Republican voters had any real interest in any presidential candidate other than Richard Nixon.

Part IV

Wallace

12

"We're Tired of This Mess"

On a warm October evening in New York, more than fifteen thousand people gathered in Madison Square Garden. The main event that night would not be a heavyweight fight, nor were the Knicks or the Rangers in town. The crowd waited excitedly beneath twelve outsized American flags as country pickers serenaded them with renditions of "The Star Spangled Banner," "God Bless America," "Yankee Doodle Dandy," and "Dixie." These ditties were interspersed with cries of "Niggers get out!" "Go back to Africa!" and "White power!" while the omnipresent protesters, primed for their role in the evening's proceedings, chimed in with "Pig! Pig! Pig!" and "Two-four-six-eight, we don't want a Fascist state!"[1]

Outside the arena shoving matches and fistfights broke out repeatedly as Birchers, Nazis, and Klansmen tussled with Trotskyites, Yippies, and Black Power activists. Confederate battle flags were flown, then wrested away and set aflame to chants of "Burn, baby, burn." Cries of "Sieg Heil!" were matched by chants of "Commie faggots!" Rocks and soda bottles, from both sides, pelted the cops, who were trying, without much success, to keep order. They responded with nightsticks and cracks to the heads of pro-testers.[2]

With the crowd inside at a fever pitch, the guest of honor arrived under the watchful eye of hundreds of police officers. George Wallace was greeted by a sound so overwhelming that even the jaded political reporters who had seen and heard it all were momentarily stunned. "It was uncontrolled release of frenzied, pulsating passion that seemed almost more sexual than political.... It may have been the loudest, most terrifying sustained human din ever heard in New York," wrote Robert Mayer in *Newsday*. "Wallace at MSG" was the dark-side equivalent of the Beatles playing Shea Stadium.[3]

Perhaps in honor of the venue's storied sporting history, Wallace, a former amateur boxer himself, thrust his arms upward in a victory salute, like a fighter who had just knocked out his opponent. He seemed to marvel at the fact that even in New York City a country boy from Alabama could be show-ered with such adulation. Then, with the traditional airing of grievances, the sermon began. Wallace fired broadsides against the "pseudo-intellectuals" and "theoreticians," "the "anarchists," "the liberals and left wingers," the "he" who looks like a "she," and the professors and newspapers that "looked down their nose...at the average man on the street." His pledges to "let the police handle" the country's rising crime problems and end the practice of "bus-sing your children where they don't want to be bussed" were met with bois-terous and sustained applause. "All you need is a good barber!" he yelled at the dozens of hecklers in the crowd. "Why don't you come down here...and I'll autograph your sandals!" As yet another fight broke out in the balcony, Wallace offered no quarter. "Well, you came for trouble and you got it."[4]

"You feel you have known this all somewhere," wrote the *New Republic*'s Richard Strout about the night's festivities. "Never again will you read about Berlin in the 30's without remembering this wild confrontation here of two irrational forces. The American sickness has finally localized; Wallace is the ablest demagogue of our time." In the *Village Voice*, Joe Flaherty diag-nosed the symptoms of that illness: the trepidation that millions of Americans felt about the social changes shaking American society in 1968. "Fear was what this evening was all about.... Black fear, hair fear, press card fear, busing fear, guideline fear, and endless other fears that make up the litany of right in America today. And the little man behind his bullet proof podium epitomized their anxieties."[5]

An extraordinary political manipulator, George Wallace possessed a unique ability to capture the resentments, frustrations, and fears of his listeners, whether they lived in the Black Belt of Alabama or the outer boroughs of New York. Political success, however (at least outside of Alabama), would not be Wallace's legacy. While his us-against-them, anti-integration rhetoric would define the politics of the 1960s and 1970s, when he renounced his segregationist ways in order to sustain his political career, it came largely because the resonance of those views—even in the South—had faded. Racial progress triumphed, despite his dogged efforts to stop it. Wallace's real political legacy would lie elsewhere. In the years that followed his 1968 run for the presidency, one would be hard-pressed to find a conservative politician who didn't speak in the populist and antigovernment idiom that he popularized that year. Wallace "laid the foundation for the conservative counter-revolution that reshaped American politics," wrote his biographer, Dan Carter. In an era of backlash politics, no voice would be more effective and influential.[6]

"Any cab driver in Montgomery knows more about why we're in Vietnam than a Yale professor sitting up there in his Ivory Tower," Wallace liked to say. The people everywhere, he claimed, are tired of the government telling them when to get up and when to go to bed. For Wallace, and for his supporters, this murky "establishment" became the enemy of the American people and perhaps the most effective foil in modern American politics. Wallace was hardly the first politician to speak of the government in harshly negative terms. But unlike Barry Goldwater, whose politics were grounded in ideology (often esoterically so), Wallace's rhetorical assaults featured more primal and openly racist appeals. While his bid for the national limelight began with a full-scale political offensive against civil rights legislation, it metastasized into a larger populist indictment of liberalism and government activism. This evolution allowed Wallace to turn himself from a regional agitator into a national figure.[7]

Indeed, the impetus for northerners who supported Wallace looked a lot like the motivation of those in the South who unfurled the Wallace banner.

"There are a lot of rednecks in this country," Wallace used to say, "and they don't all live in the South." "Theoreticians" and "bureaucrats" who sought to impose federal "guidelines" that threatened to upend union seniority and integrate all-white neighborhoods and segregated schools were taking direct aim at the advantages of white privilege that many northerners had long taken for granted. In Wallace they found a political outlet for their growing frustrations. Fearing social and cultural change, they yearned for an era when blacks knew their place, young people were respectful of authority, and the Feds were looking out primarily for *them*. It was, as one set of political scientists noted, "an ideology of preservatism."[8]

Wallace's racist past and his snarling personality also made him an imperfect messenger—and as the 1968 campaign neared its dénouement, the turmoil and violence that followed Wallace like a dark cloud became a genuine political liability. No matter how many white hands might have applauded when he railed against liberals, anarchists, "pointy-headed college professors," and bureaucrats who "can't even park their bicycles straight," there existed a hard cap on his support. But since Wallace would say practically anything, he laid a rhetorical path for others. Wallace's populist, antigovernment, antielitist rhetoric has become the template for American conservatism. The idea that the federal government does direct harm to the American people, that its expansion constitutes a usurpation of freedom, that it imposes its own values and moral conceits on ordinary people, and that states and localities are far better stewards of tax dollars is a pro forma critique out of the mouths of Republican politicians (and occasionally Democrats). In the 1960s it was just taking form, and George Wallace did more than any other leader to show how it could be utilized as a successful political tool. No candidate in 1968 had a smaller chance of winning the White House, and yet, arguably, no politician did more to change the narrative and language of American politics than Wallace.[9]

What you saw with George Wallace is generally what you got. There was little ambiguity or nuance in his political rhetoric, which was to be expected from a politician whose career would be sustained on an image of "telling it like it is." Yet he was not without contradiction, perhaps none more glaring than the fact that in his first major, statewide campaign in Alabama for governor in 1958 he had been branded a racial progressive. The charge was not without foundation. As a circuit judge, Wallace had demonstrated occasional bouts of racial sensitivity, even calling black lawyers in his courtroom "mister." He spoke out against the Ku Klux Klan and received an endorsement from the NAACP—in stark contract to his opponent, John Patterson, who boasted of his efforts as attorney general to fight the organizing effort of civil rights activists. Patterson swamped Wallace with charges that he was a racial progressive and nakedly racist appeals to white voters. Wallace's response to the defeat would reshape his political career. It was the equivalent of "If you can't beat 'em, join 'em." He told his aides on election night, "John Patterson out-niggered me. And boys, no other son-of-a-bitch will ever out-nigger me again." For as long as he was a national figure he remained true to this statement.[10]

When Wallace finally won the statehouse in 1962, his inaugural address offered compelling evidence that he'd learned his lesson well. The new governor pledged to an audience that included few of the state's 30 percent of black citizens "segregation now, segregation tomorrow and segregation forever." In words crafted by his speechwriter Asa Carter, a former Klan member, and dripping with the poisonous language of racial exclusion and prejudice, Wallace warned that just as "the national racism of Hitler's Germany persecuted a national minority to the whim of a national majority, so the international racism of the liberals seek to persecute the international white minority to the whim of the international colored majority." Six months later Wallace would make his defiant "stand in the schoolhouse door" at the University of Alabama. Before a national television audience he denounced the Department of Justice's demand that the school be integrated as an "unwelcomed, unwanted, unwarranted, and force-induced intrusion" on Alabama's sovereignty.[11]

This losing fight turned Wallace into both a regional hero and a national caricature. *Newsweek* sniffed that he was "a corn-pone redneck big-man-in-Alabama but nowhere else." The political establishment saw him as a creature of the South, representative of the region's prejudices, resentments, and peculiar psychosis of victimization. When Wallace embarked on a speaking tour of elite universities in late 1963, including Ohio State University, UCLA, and Harvard, he was routinely met with catcalls and protests, but the response hardly deterred him. Indeed, his detractors discovered that Wallace could not be dismissed merely as an ugly caricature. He was charismatic, funny, and adroit at parrying attacks from protesters. During one question-and-answer session at Harvard, a black student asked him whether he would consider running for president with a black man. He winked to the crowd and responded, "Between you and me we might get rid of the crowd in Washington. We might just run on the same ticket." Of course these college crowds, no matter how charmed, would never consider supporting him. While Wallace's appearances boosted his political prospects in Alabama, for northern audiences he served as a "grotesque amusement," wrote biographer Marshall Frady.[12]

Indeed, George Wallace's outsized influence on the nation's politics did not begin in Alabama, or on the lecture circuit in front of elite northern audiences. Rather, the first indication of how compelling Wallace's message of social resentment and cultural fear could be on a national level emerged in April 1964, at the Serbian Memorial Hall in Milwaukee, Wisconsin, at a campaign rally of white ethnic voters who had long been the mainstay of the Democrats' New Deal coalition. A month earlier Wallace had announced his intention to enter the Wisconsin Democratic presidential primary. Though he had no chance of winning the nomination, running in a few northern primaries would give him a platform to protest the civil rights bill that was winding through Congress (Wallace liked to call it the "civil wrongs bill"), while also building up his national reputation for a potential national run in 1968.

On the surface, Wisconsin did not appear to the most logical place for a racially charged appeal. Milwaukee's black population was relatively small, and the state had few of the serious racial divisions that existed elsewhere in the North. Nonetheless, the descendants of Polish, Yugoslav, Czech, and Hungarian immigrants packed Memorial Hall that evening, eager to see the Alabama governor. A makeshift band played off-key versions of "Swanee River" and "Dixie," to which the audience gamely tried to sing along. These traditional Democratic voters, wedded to their modest homes and close-knit communities and too poor to flee to the suburbs, had watched with growing anxiety as black families began to encroach on their ethnic enclaves. Living on the frontlines of the battle for racial integration they saw themselves as sacrificial lambs in the civil rights fight.[13]

As would often be the case at Wallace's rallies, hecklers and protesters loudly made their presence known. The Wallace camp would purposely pick small venues for their public events because, as Bill Jones, a Wallace staffer, later wrote, "Having mobs outside, we got a more favorable press than otherwise.... The more the pickets who appeared, the greater the favorable reaction for the Governor." On this night the anti-Wallace activists were black. Taunted by the white audience, one of the protesters, a minister, yelled, "Get your dogs out," a reference to the animals used by state troopers in Alabama to attack civil rights protesters. Bronko Gruber, a local tavern owner, rally organizer, and former marine, grabbed the microphone and delivered a fierce tirade. "I'll tell you something about your dogs, padre.... Three weeks ago tonight a friend of mine was assaulted by three of your countrymen or whatever you want to call them.... They beat up old ladies eighty-three-years old, rape our womenfolk. They mug people. They won't work. They are on relief. How long can we tolerate this?" The crowd roared its approval, practically drowning out Gruber's words. The black protesters beat a hasty retreat to the door.[14]

Gruber's outburst whipped the crowd into a frenzy, and soon after Wallace leapt onstage to rowdy applause. He pilloried the civil rights bill as an affront to the rights of hard-working Americans. For the heavily Catholic audience he ladled out attacks on the Supreme Court and its decision banning prayer in public schools. At the end, he told the crowd (which interrupted him thirty-four times with applause), "A vote for this little governor will let the people of Washington know that we want them to leave our homes, schools, jobs, business and farms alone." After he finished, it would take Wallace more than an hour to wade through the throngs of well-wishers and autograph seekers.[15]

For years afterward, Wallace would refer fondly to that night in Milwaukee. He boasted, "There were at least 100 confederate flags being flown," and they "played Dixie and 3,500 people stood and sung it in Polish."

As for the crowd that had menaced civil rights activists and hounded them out of the room, he said, "They had all been so friendly that I didn't want to leave." He recounted speaking to one young man who grabbed Wallace and said, "'Governor, I have never been south of South Milwaukee, but I am a Southerner.'" Wallace's response was telling. "Of course he was; the South is no longer geography—it's an attitude and a philosophy toward government."[16]

The electric response in Milwaukee would be replicated across the campaign trail in 1964. Though practically every major political figure in Wisconsin, as well as union and church leaders and major newspapers, decried Wallace's presence in the primary, he won a third of all ballots cast in the Democratic primary. His support would not be restricted to Milwaukee's ethnic voters; in fact, he did best among middle-class Republicans, many of whom had the same fear of blacks encroaching on their communities as did the working-class voters of Milwaukee.[17]

Wallace labeled his performance in Wisconsin a "tremendous victory." (Privately, however, he expressed disappointment, complaining that if Martin Luther King had run against him in Alabama he would have gotten a third of the vote too.) He next headed to Indiana, where he warned about the potential impact of civil rights legislation on union seniority and segregated white neighborhoods and won 32 percent of the vote. In Lake County, an area of traditional Democratic support, more than half the ballots went to Wallace. In Gary, Lake County's largest city, he garnered two-thirds of white support. Blacks represented a large percentage of the city's population; racial tensions were higher; and many white Lake County neighborhoods abutted black communities. As in Alabama, Wallace did his best in places where whites and blacks lived in close proximity. In the white communities along the southern border of Gary's black ghettoes, for example, Wallace received close to 70 percent of the vote.[18]

On May 19, in Maryland, Wallace withstood another round of attacks from labor, religious, and Democratic Party leaders to score his most impressive win that spring. He took 43 percent of the vote, including sixteen of the state's twenty-three counties. By one estimate he earned more than 90 percent of the vote from the Eastern Shore, an area of the state that had what amounted to de facto segregation. In fact, if not for what Wallace re-pugnantly called "the nigger bloc" in Baltimore, he almost certainly would have won the primary. At the very least he captured a majority of white votes, a result that exposed the fragility of the New Deal coalition in the face of black advances.[19]

Wallace turned the traditional political allegiances of the white working-class voters that supported him upside down. No longer did they see the federal government as the guarantor of the extraordinary economic gains they had made in the postwar years. No longer did they view it as the pro-vider of education for their children, or job security at work, or safe neigh-borhoods at home. Almost overnight, the push for civil rights legislation had turned the federal government into a threat to white interests. Many voters who were now willing to believe Wallace's claims that Washington was maliciously reaching into their homes, schools, and workplaces had benefited from the federal government's largesse. It provided compiling ev-idence of the shallowness of the popular support for the full realization of Johnson's Great Society. Wallace's performance in 1964 showed that fears of racial integration could move loyal Democrats away from their tradi-tional political home—and not just in the South. By painting a picture of an overzealous federal government that put the needs of blacks ahead of those of "hard-working Americans," Wallace was taking a wrecking ball to the lib-eral consensus.[20]

On July 2, 1964, Johnson signed into law the civil rights bill that Wallace had expended so much energy excoriating. Two days later, at a fairground in suburban Atlanta, he offered his response. Drenched in sweat from the ninety-five-degree heat, Wallace called the bill an "act of tyranny" that would "force us back into bondage." He said, "A left-wing monster has risen in this nation. It has invaded the government. It has invaded the news media. It has invaded the leadership of many of our churches. It has invaded every phase and aspect of the life of freedom-loving people." The address was directly tailored to his audience's racial chauvinism and fear of meddle-some liberal elites. The civil rights bill endangered the entire edifice of southern white privilege. Wallace offered the white suburbanites of Atlanta a last gasp of "Southern pride" before the walls came down around them.[21]

Though Wallace lost the fight against the civil rights bill, he had positioned himself to prosper after its passage, particularly as white opposition to the effects of racial integration grew. Wallace's political skills, after all, came not in marshaling a political agenda but in sowing discord and capitalizing on fear. His was always a political movement of "against" rather than "for." "Wallace offered neither palliative nor real cure; just a chance to scream into the darkness," wrote Garry Wills.[22]

In the immediate aftermath of the 1964 election, Democratic Party leaders tried to downplay Wallace's strong performance. Johnson's stand-in during the Maryland primary, Senator Daniel Brewster, said in his victory statement, "Maryland's 48 votes will be cast for President Johnson. It makes no difference about the percentages." Like Goldwater's historic defeat, Wallace's campaign appeared to be more of a last gasp of the revanchist right than the emergence of a new political movement. Johnson showed little inclination to trim his sails. Indeed, in the short term Wallace would actually play an essential role in helping further the president's agenda.[23]

On March 7, 1965, less than two months after LBJ's inauguration, several hundred civil rights demonstrators set out on a peaceful march from Selma, Alabama, to the State Capitol in Montgomery to plead their case for full voting rights. The governor didn't meet them. After crossing the Edmund Pettus Bridge on the way to Montgomery, they were greeted instead by Alabama state troopers, who, cheered on by white bystanders, who just as easily could have been at an Auburn-Alabama football game, proceeded to club, whip, and tear-gas the demonstrators. The scenes of police violence would be replayed that evening for a horrified national TV audience. Wallace was "as mad as I've ever seen him," said his press secretary Bill Jones—not because of the actions of his officers but rather because they forced him to defend the indefensible. Appearing on *Face the Nation*, a defensive Wallace farcically insisted that his police force was more tolerant of dissent than those in New York City.[24]

Johnson quickly took the offensive. In the wake of what became known as "Bloody Sunday" he convened a joint session of Congress to call for new legislation protecting voting rights. He declared that the cause of Negro rights "must be the cause" of all Americans, and, in a gesture that represented the fullest validation of the civil rights movement to date, Johnson evoked the words of the great Negro spiritual "We Shall Overcome" as he exhorted Americans to come together in pursuit of civil rights for all the nation's citizens. Less than five months later Johnson would sign into law the Voting Rights Act, effectively ending the era of Jim Crow in the Deep South.[25]

"George did more to bring about what he professed to oppose than any other three people I can name," joked William Dickinson, an Alabama Republican congressman. Such losses, however, had the perverse effect of strengthening Wallace, turning him once again into the most prominent southern leader willing to fight back against the dictates of an imperious federal government. But soon a more worrying political problem emerged: the Alabama state constitution forbade him from seeking a second consecutive term as governor. Becoming a private citizen might have made it easier for him to travel the country and run for president, but it would also have taken away his political base. Wallace's solution was to ask the Alabama legislature to rewrite the state constitution to allow him to run again—and, in large measure, so he could once again seek the presidency.[26]

In a statewide address Wallace said that the people of Alabama had "sent him north and east and west to tell the story of Americanism and the South," a trip on which he had braved "wild-eyed fanaticals" and "walked through stomping crowds of screaming leftists.... Their spittle has run down my face," said Wallace. At the same time that he asked voters for the chance at four more years as governor, he told them "I will go again," up north to run for president. Wallace presented his own personal ambition for political advancement as an issue of state and regional pride. The Alabama state legislature, many of whose members wanted Wallace's job and who already chafed at his overbearing character were unpersuaded. The succession amendment failed.[27]

The defeat left Wallace depressed and temporarily chastened. He had no hobbies, few vices, and zero interests outside of politics. Now suddenly he had no office to seek. But Wallace soon showed that anyone who doubted his political nerve would be proven wrong. If he couldn't run himself, he'd run a different Wallace for governor—Lurleen, his wife. Lurleen Wallace possessed neither political acumen nor Eva Peron–like charisma. Content in her role as a mother and housewife, Lurleen served as an adornment to her husband's political aspirations who became "practically mute in his company." Indeed, Lurleen had shown about as much interest in politics as her husband had shown in her—but she was far more pliable than the Alabama legislature. She "did it for George," said Bill Jones.[28]

On the campaign trail, Lurleen held fast to her role as the dutiful wife. She would offer a few opening words at rallies and then give the floor to her husband, who would deliver one of his grievance-filled addresses with the usual litany of attacks. "I'm not fighting the federal government," he would tell his cheering crowd; "I'm fighting this outlaw, beatnik crowd in Washington that has just about destroyed the federal government—and I'm trying to save it." The centerpiece of Wallace's remarks was his invocation of the southern inferiority complex. He would regularly point out the reporters in the crowd—some from northern outlets, some from critical newspapers in Alabama—and dismiss them as "liberal, left-leaning" socialists who look down their noses at the "common folk of Alabama." He would list all the ways in which the *Wall Street Journal* or the *New York Times* had insulted him or Lurleen because of their working-class roots. "You're just as cultured and just as refined as those New York reporters and editors," he would tell his audiences. After all, said Wallace, he himself had "spoke[n] at Harvard." Such ostentatious regional pride coupled with a crippling, yet unspoken, sentiment of cultural inadequacy remained a resounding feature of southern politics, and few spoke its language better than Wallace. Perhaps because he felt the same sense of personal alienation and insecurity, Wallace possessed an amazing ability to exploit his audience's core insecurities. As he would regularly say on the campaign trail, he desired nothing more than the opportunity to "shake his eyeteeth" at the "liberal pinkos." The crowds lapped it up.[29]

Lurleen's political opponents stood no chance against the Wallace juggernaut. Rather than destroying him, the events around the Selma march coalesced support behind his wife. After Bloody Sunday, federal marshals arrived in Alabama to protect thousands of black demonstrators, led by

Martin Luther King, marching from Selma to Montgomery. This enflamed and enraged white Alabamans, wrote pollster Samuel Lubell. They saw it as "a show of force by some foreign occupying power." Wallace's use of the government as a punching bag demonstrated anew that the art of politics, particularly as practiced by Wallace, lay in picking the right enemies.[30]

Wallace knew he could always count on the support of a certain segment of segregationist and racist voters, particularly in the South. But in order to turn himself into a national political figure he needed to win new converts. Growing national anxiety over the riots, antiwar protests, and urban crime created a febrile mix of fear and frustration that became the ideal breeding ground for another Wallace presidential bid. More important, it allowed him to move beyond an agenda narrowly focused on civil rights to a broader set of social and cultural issues. "George Wallace may speak for some large, unknown number of Americans—five million, ten million, more?—not necessarily racist, not necessarily reactionary, not necessarily stupid or vicious or ignorant, but human, concerned, determined," wrote Tom Wicker in a lengthy profile of Wallace for *Harper's* in the spring of 1967. In an interview from his office inside the Alabama State Capitol (he was officially an "advisor" to his wife), Wallace told Wicker that if the two parties didn't recognize that Americans were "fed up with crime in the streets" and "courts and politicians coddling these criminals" and were "tired of folks raising money and blood for the Vietcong...while our boys get shot at," then the American people were going to need another choice, and, he said, "I'll give them one." The key issues in 1968, Wallace told the *National Review*'s James Jackson Kilpatrick, were going to be schools ("The people don't like this triflin' with their children, tellin' 'em which teachers to have to teach in which schools"), busing (trying to achieve "the proper racial mix," he said, was "no business of the federal government"), and crime ("The people are going to be fed up with the sissy attitude of Lyndon Johnson and all the intellectual morons and theoreticians he has around him").[31]

The first indication that Wallace's new political strategy had promise came in California during the summer and fall of 1967. There the governor and his closest aides found themselves mired in what seemed like a hopeless effort to get Wallace's name on the ballot for the 1968 election. Intent on running as an independent rather than challenging Johnson for the Democratic nomination again, Wallace had created his own political party—the American Independent Party (AIP)—whose sole function was to serve as a vehicle for his presidential aspirations. Still, the AIP made it only slightly easier for Wallace to navigate the byzantine rules governing ballot access for third-party candidates. Virtually every state had a different set of requirements. In some places just a few hundred signatures would suffice to get him on the ballot. In California, he needed sixty-six thousand of the state's residents not merely to sign a petition but to become members of the AIP—all before January 1968. Magnifying the challenge was the fact that the state wasn't exactly Wallace country. Conservatism there was more ideologically grounded than Wallace's resentment-oriented populism. Nonetheless, there were still plenty of white Californians—many of whom had enthusiastically voted to repeal open housing legislation in 1964 or who had supported Ronald Reagan in 1966—drawn to Wallace's down-home appeal.[32]

In September, Wallace's young aide Tom Turnipseed traveled to the state to check out the petition drive and discovered to his horror that it had been taken over by a frightening collection of kooks and fringe figures, warning of Communist conspiracies and the pernicious influence of the Trilateral Commission. Wallace always attracted a fair share of conspiracy mongers, Ku Klux Klan members, American Nazis, and various right-wing fanatics, but his team usually kept them out of the limelight—not in charge of a crucial ballot drive. Turnipseed called home for reinforcements, and within weeks hundreds of volunteers from Alabama made their way to the West Coast. Wallace soon followed, as did Lurleen and many of the state's top officials, who sought to maintain the fiction that they were traveling west on state business. Surrounded by a retinue of Alabama State Troopers, Wallace spent four weeks traveling California, attacking the "pro-Communist, long-haired hippies" and the "pseudo-intellectuals" who excused arson and murder by "saying the killer didn't get any watermelon to eat when he was 10 years old." This was pure backlash politics—and it worked. By the first week of January, Wallace and his team had signed up more than a hundred thousand Californians for the AIP, nearly 65 percent of whom had been Democrats. Eventually Wallace would find his way onto the ballots of all fifty states.[33]

Wallace's national ballot drive offered what is perhaps the most notable example of the "New Politics" of participatory democracy that defined the politics of the era. Those who had long been on the outside of American politics—whether on the right or left—were demanding that their voices be heard. Antiwar activists, ignored by the Democratic Party's leaders and frustrated by the lack of a political outlet, had succeeded in toppling a sitting president. Even after Goldwater's 1964 debacle, conservatives continued to flex their muscles within the Republican Party. Another group of Americans, however, would have an even greater effect: those who, in the words of Teddy White, represented the "ignored, unheard and unlistened to." They constituted both haves and have-nots—those who believed they had been left behind and those who'd made progress into the middle class and didn't want to fall back. These were the Americans most deeply affected not only by rising black prosperity but also by the growing disorder of urban America. Wallace would be the only politician in 1968 who spoke directly to them.[34]

While they might not have agreed with everything he said, "When he's on 'Meet the Press'" said Lurleen, "they can listen to him and think, 'That's what I would say if I were up there.'" In his speeches he'd praise the beauticians, the garbage men, the farm workers, steel workers and textile workers, the pipe-fitters, the plumbers, the fireman and the policeman, the barber and the small businessman. Wallace, who had once driven a taxi himself, would regularly talk about the "cab-driving logic" of his working-class supporters—a rhetorical flourish that led one journalist to call him "the Cicero of the cab driver." Wallace's campaign literature asked if a former truck driver married to a dime-store cashier and the son of a dirt farmer could be elected president, and he would even go so far as to purposely mispronounce words in his speeches as if to bolster his populist credibility. In the years since, this kind of identification with the "ordinary American" has become the idiom of modern campaign messaging.[35]

Wallace's populist entreaties would not be restricted to venerations of the "common man." His message also featured a powerful economic component.

While governor of Alabama, Wallace acted like a New Deal Democrat, spending more public money than any of his predecessors, and much of it on public welfare. A majority of his backers identified themselves as Democrats and were far more likely to be supportive of government spending than traditional conservative voters. They just preferred the kind of spending that benefited them. When the American Independent Party issues its platform in October 1968, it bemoaned the "riots," "minority group rebellions," "domestic disorders," "student protests," and "loss of personal liberty at home," while also demanding that the government put more police officers on the streets and end the social activism of federal judges. Yet the document also called for greater government engagement in nearly every other facet of American life: more job training for "all Americans willing and able to seek and hold gainful employment"; more federal monies for transportation, education, and even the space program; a significant increase in Social Security benefits; and more support for elderly health care. The civil rights leader Julian Bond would later say, only partially in jest, that Wallace confused him, "because he's a liberal on a great many questions, except race." Wallace proposed a more broadly generous vision of the welfare state than that offered by Democrats—but it was one reserved for whites and those few blacks who had made the difficult journey to the American middle class.[36]

In an interview with *US News and World Report* in June 1968, Wallace nonetheless argued, "We are still against the philosophy of big government controlling every phase and aspect of our lives." In reality, Wallace wanted to redirect the flow from the government's spigot rather than turn it off altogether. Indeed, conservatives regularly attacked Wallace for his "collectivist" views. James Ashbrook, the head of the American Conservative Union, blasted his candidacy as "repugnant to ideals of American conservatism." The *National Review* decried Wallace's working-class populist message as "the radical opposite of conservatism." In fact, the overlap between Wallace and Goldwater voters was far less extensive than generally assumed. Only half of those who would vote for the Alabama governor in 1968 had voted for Goldwater four years earlier. Goldwater's strongest backing came from those who considered themselves economically secure, while Wallace did best among the working class. Even given the reactionary nature of Wallace's politics, his supporters were more likely to call themselves "liberals" than Nixon voters. Wallace voters had little apparent interest in the right's ideological dogmatism. For them politics had become a zero-sum game of resource allocation and government attention. More money and public programs for blacks meant less for them—and they wanted to protect what they had.[37]

Still, the major driver behind Wallace's support was fear. "You can't even walk the streets of this country without some black animal robbing or raping you," said one typical Wallace voter in Missouri. Wallace had a simple solution for such problems: "Enforce the law—all laws." He offered no technocratic suggestions for dealing with the "root causes" of crime or ghetto hopelessness. Instead, he held "a small minority of people . . . responsible for the breakdown of law and order"—anarchists, activists, militants, revolutionaries, and Communists. Deal with them, Wallace argued, and the crime problem in America would be solved. As for urban rioters, Wallace had an even more sure-fire solution, "The people know the way to stop a riot is to hit someone on the head." In a southern campaign swing in early June 1968, he offered the most apt slogan for his presidential bid that year, "We're tired of this mess."[38]

On Vietnam, Wallace's backers, like most Americans, were conflicted. They supported taking whatever military steps were necessary to win, but they were also most likely to believe that the United States should never have gotten involved in the first place. But their real outrage was directed at antiwar demonstrators—and Wallace happily fed that anger. Wallace said that those on college campuses "raisin' money, blood and clothes for the Viet Cong Communists and flyin' the V.C. flag" should be "dragged by the hair on their heads and stuck under a good jail." He liked to remind his followers that a "group of anarchists" had once lain down in front of Johnson's presidential limousine. Under his administration, he said, if "a group of anarchists lay down in front of my automobile it's gonna be the last one they ever gonna wanna lay down in front of."[39]

All of Wallace's speeches featured a Manichaean worldview—the precise opposite of Johnson's call, four years earlier, for shared sacrifice in pursuit of the greater good. America had rarely before seen a presidential candidate so willing to tap into the dark pools of popular alienation. When segregationist George Mahoney ran as the Democratic nominee for governor in Maryland in 1966 on a Wallace-like platform, fellow Democrats organized against him and supported the Republican candidate, Spiro Agnew. Even Ronald Reagan, with his strong anti-Communist views, sought to distance himself from Robert Welch, head of the John Birch Society. Wallace, on the other hand, relied heavily on the Birchers for organizational muscle for his presidential bid in 1968.

Wallace deliberately sought to ratchet up intense, racist emotions at his campaign events. While he kept up his pledge to never say the word "nigger" while on the stump, Seymore Trammell, a close aide to Wallace, later acknowledged that "the racial issue was the very basis of his campaign. He was really trying to reach the common, ordinary white person out there who did not like black people." The violence that would break out at Wallace events was a feature, not an accident. "We didn't want anybody killed or seriously injured," said Trammell, but his speeches would be "purposely...inflammatory" in order to draw wider attention and "play in the press." Not since the days of Huey Long or Joseph McCarthy had the country seen as menacing and dynamic a political demagogue—and certainly not one so willing to push his supporters so dramatically toward violence.[40]

Behind the scenes, the Wallace campaign gave new meaning to the words "southern efficiency." The candidate, said one aide, was completely uninterested in the "nuts-and-bolts" of campaign operations. When asked for advice or how to proceed on spending or advertising, Wallace would tell his staff, "Do the best thing and don't get in trouble and don't break the law." His advisors maintained tenuous control over the various state campaigns, many of which were stocked—in the words of Turnipseed—by "a motley group of segregationists, Southern rednecks, Northern ethnics, John Birchers, corporate executives, right-wing kooks and assorted bigots." The campaign seemed to operate flying by the seat of its pants—schedules would be revised with little notice; reporters would find themselves lodged in filthy motels and given no advance texts of the candidate's speeches or even drinks on the rickety campaign plane. "An almost total lack of organization" defined the Wallace campaign, reported Richard Cohen, a twenty-year-old Brown University undergraduate who followed the candidate for a week in the fall of 1968. Only the Secret Service men seemed capable of telling the press what was happening next. Cohen joked that, had he stayed with Wallace another week, he could have been appointed press secretary.[41]

Wallace's aides shined in one key area, however: maintaining the candidate's furtive fundraising efforts. These included twenty-five-dollar-a-plate dinners whose fare would have made rubber chicken seem like a step up. Supporters could purchase the ubiquitous bumper stickers, pins, tie clasps, and campaign paraphernalia hawked at every one of his appearances or give money to the pretty Alabamans known as "Wallace girls" who would pass collection buckets around like it was Sunday morning at church. Amazingly, even though many of those in attendance struggled to get by themselves, they opened up their wallets to help Wallace get his message out. Many others sent their meager contributions to the campaign offices in Montgomery, where it wouldn't be unusual for $100,000 to pour in during a single day. The placement of television and radio advertisement was done with an eye toward soliciting financial contributions as much as toward helping Wallace politically. More often than not, Trammell said, those locations would be "any place there were racial tensions." In all, an estimated 80 percent of Wallace's campaign dollars came from donations of less fifty dollars.[42]

The reporters who covered the campaign couldn't figure out what to make of Wallace's traveling roadshow. "Some newspapers, indeed, played down their coverage...as a deliberate policy, like parents who refuse to look when their child is doing something naughty for fear it might encourage him to show off," said one trio of reporters. Others dismissed Wallace as simply a backwater repository of racist impulses in the country. His rise, wrote Marshall Frady, "confirmed the suspicion of many that the nation, in its heart of hearts, is irredeemably, though elusively, racist."[43]

As it became more and more difficult to ignore his rising poll numbers, journalists resorted to crude characterizations about the man and his supporters to explain his support. Media reports would be replete with stories of Wallace's slick-backed hair, his indulgent eating style (like the way he would drench all of his food in ketchup), his uncouth personal behavior (like spitting in a handkerchief when he gave speeches), his constant fidgeting, his sharp southern twang, and his diminutive size. *Time* said he came across like a cross between Flem Snopes—a recurring character from the novels of southern writer William Faulkner—and Huey Long. Garry Wills said that he had "the dingy attractive air of a B-movie idol, the kind who plays a handsome garage attendant.... He comes rubbing his hands on [an] invisible garage rag...smiling and winking. Anything-I-can-do-for-you-pretty-girl?" Yet these same writers would marvel at his demagogic skills. With grudging respect they would remark on the "special hold" and "disturbing power" that he maintained over the "less educated," the "less affluent," and those "distraught by an age of complexities." Reporters couldn't decide if they were describing the village idiot or Elmer Gantry.[44]

His supporters didn't fare much better. Newspaper and magazine copy was filled with tales of their outlandish and racist statements. A June 1968 *Saturday Evening Post* article entitled "George Wallace: The Angry Man's Candidate" offered a telling example of how journalists viewed the Wallace hordes. The story featured a picture of a white, middle-aged man with a "Win with Wallace" sign raised high in one hand and a cigarette held to his mouth in the other. At the bottom of the man's tight-fitting black T-shirt one could quite clearly discern a protruding, pasty white belly tucked over his jeans. This image of white working-class excess and primitive loyalty to a southern demagogue captured the way that many reporters conceived of the typical Wallace voter.[45]

That image gathered strength as Wallace traveled the country in the summer of 1968. Though Wallace had first announced his intention to seek the presidency in February, his campaign received its biggest boosts from King's assassination in April and Kennedy's in June. Between these national traumas, Wallace had a tragedy of his own—Lurleen died of cancer in May 1968. Wallace took five weeks off from the campaign trail to mourn her death, but when he returned, not long after Kennedy's murder, he continued his focus on crime and disorder—and the bureaucrats, judges, and intellectuals aiding and abetting it.

By July, violence had become the norm at virtually every one of Wallace's public appearances. In Omaha, anti-Wallace demonstrators pelted the crowd with coins, placards, and chunks of wood, which led to a night of riots. "These are the free speech people," he mocked. In Minneapolis, police were forced to use mace and nightsticks to break up the dozens of fistfights that broke out. Max Frankel of the *New York Times* described a Wallace rally in July 1968 in Providence, Rhode Island, as "45 horrendous minutes" of "scream[ing] and squeal[ing] on hatred's brink" as black demonstrators yelled "Go home, Go home" and white Wallace supporters responded "Throw the niggers out." Indeed, cries of "Sieg Heil" and "Kill the niggers" became staples at Wallace rallies. All the extremes of late-1960s politics— the resentments of the white working class and the demands of energized and angry blacks and liberals—converged into one crowded and sweaty locale whenever Wallace spoke.[46]

The apparent mayhem did little to halt his political ascendancy, however. In April and May he scored in the high single digits in national polls. By July he moved up to 16 percent. While the majority of his support had been localized in the South, his backing in the North hovered around 10 percent. The reason for voter affinity for Wallace was not difficult to discern—83 percent of Wallace backers believed integration had been "pushed too fast," versus 45 percent of all voters; 82 percent wanted looters in riots shot on sight. Most troubling for Republicans, seven out of ten Wallace supporters had an unfavorable view of President Johnson, meaning the GOP risked losing a healthy chunk of the electorate inclined to vote for their candidate in November. Democrats didn't have much reason to be pleased either; they were losing more of their voters to Wallace (16 percent) than the Republicans (8 percent). The establishment of both parties became so worried that over the summer a bipartisan effort gathered steam in Congress to prevent Wallace from potentially throwing the election into the House of Representatives.[47]

But there was no eliminating the appeal of his message. As the country appeared to descend further into a spiral of violence and dysfunction, Wallace's "solutions" offered a way out. The events of the late summer of 1968 would only add more fuel to the national conflagration being stoked by Wallace.

Part V

A Tale of Two Conventions

A "Plastic Paradise"

n the politics of 1968, style and polished image-making trumped substance and grit, which made the host cities for the Republicans and
Democratic national conventions uniquely—and unintentionally—representative locales. For the two political parties it is hard to imagine a pair of
cities richer in symbolism than Miami Beach and Chicago.

Swayed by Latin beats and shaded by palm trees, with its pastel stucco
architecture and baroque, overstyled interiors, Miami Beach felt unreal to
the political reporters who had spent the past few months trudging through
the flinty conservatism of New Hampshire, the taciturn midwestern sensi-
bility of Indiana, the suburban sprawl of Oregon, and the ethnic melting
pot of California. A "plastic paradise"; the country's "grossest national
product"; and the "materialistic capital of the world," they wrote. What had
been once "predominately a winter haven for the wealthy and ostentatious,"
wrote one reporter, "over the years had become the year-round haven for
the merely comfortably well-off and ostentatious, and the convention-going
and ostentatious." Norman Mailer marveled at the irony that "the party of

conservatism and principle, of corporate wealth and personal frugality, the party of cleanliness, hygiene, and balanced budgets, should have set itself down on a sultan's strip." Yet all of this made it the perfect spot for the coronation of Richard Nixon, whose presidential campaign had become so clearly oriented around the projection of a political image. Americans wanted desperately to escape from the political gloom that had gripped the country since Tet. Miami Beach offered a welcome respite from the year's passion plays.[1]

The GOP delegates who gathered in south Florida were not necessarily typical Americans. Richer, WASPier, and better educated, they were more likely to have served in the military in the past and on the local Chamber of Commerce in the present. "They're nice people," said one unnamed northern senator, "but they've just never ridden a subway." Nonetheless, they looked, said Garry Wills, like "the people *we* the people want to be." Looking at Miami and the GOP delegates, one might easily conclude that if America seemed more like them, things would be better. Few would draw the same conclusion seven weeks later when the Democrats assembled in Chicago.[2]

When Nelson Rockefeller landed in Miami Beach on August 3, he brought with him the optimism and enthusiasm that had become his political trademark. Surrounded by television cameras, photographers, and reporters with a torrent of queries, he leapt off his charter plane and had a "Hiya, fella" for practically every outstretched hand he could find. Over the previous few months Rockefeller had traversed the country trying to convince as many voters as possible that the only Republican who could win in November was him. Electability had been the rationale for safe moderate nominees in the past like Willkie in 1940, Dewey in 1948, and Ike in 1952. Rockefeller's best—and only—chance was now the hope that such considerations would again be front and center in Miami Beach.

Rockefeller's strategy made logical sense. After eight years in the political wilderness, mainstream Republicans certainly yearned to reclaim the presidency, particularly in a year in which Democrats looked so vulnerable. But many conservatives wondered what would be the point of winning if it meant putting a liberal like Rockefeller in the White House. Nixon may not have sent Republican pulses racing, but at least they could trust him. For delegates like Vic Smith, the Illinois GOP state chairman, Nixon's fealty to the party proved to be his greatest attribute. "People who've been in the political process as I have are comfortable with Dick Nixon," he said in an interview. "I've always trusted and felt grateful to him. I could feel this way about Rockefeller or Reagan if I knew them better, but I don't."[3]

Having accumulated little goodwill from party leaders, Rockefeller relied instead on opinion polling to convince GOP delegates. He needed the numbers to show him not simply outperforming Nixon but also trouncing Humphrey by such a margin that Republicans would see nominating him as their only chance to win in November. A week before the convention, that strategy collapsed. The *Miami Herald* got an early copy of the latest Gallup national poll. "NIXON OVERTAKES HUMPHREY AND MCCARTHY; ROCKY RUNS EVEN AGAINST BOTH DEMOCRATS," read the paper's headline. Hearing the news on his campaign plane, Rockefeller slumped in his seat. "Nixon or John Mitchell [Nixon's campaign manager] must have gotten to Gallup," he told aides. Rockefeller would always believe that the poll had been rigged and prematurely leaked in order to derail any hope of him getting the party nod. For his part, Mitchell gleefully jabbed at Rockefeller by noting that the Nixon campaign tended to "discount the polls generally," but since Rockefeller had played up their importance, they could not be ignored now.[4]

The Rockefeller camp, realizing that their faint hopes had now become fainter, sent reporters a commissioned poll that showed their candidate beating Humphrey in eight key battleground states, and Nixon losing to the vice president in four of them. Two days later, shortly before his arrival in Miami, the Harris survey provided another sliver of good news: it had Rockefeller beating both Humphrey and McCarthy by six points and Nixon losing to each man. In fact, as delegates began gathering in Miami Beach both Gallup and Harris polls suggested that Rockefeller had opened up a lead over the likely Democratic candidates. The Nixon camp responded with its own numbers showing their candidate with the advantage over Humphrey. But the dueling results canceled each other out. Given that neither candidate had an obvious advantage, delegates could simply choose to believe whichever poll suited their preferences.[5]

For conservatives the decision was an easy one. When Reagan said, "It's inconceivable to me that anyone who could support Dick [Nixon] or me could support Nelson Rockefeller," he was voicing the thoughts of many on the right. Privately, Rockefeller vote counters heard much the same message. Alton Marshall, New York's lieutenant governor and "de facto governor" while Rockefeller was campaigning for president, recalled meeting delegates from Idaho and telling them, "'Nixon can't win. He's not going to win.' They'd say right back to me, 'We'd rather lose with Nixon than win with Rockefeller.'" Perhaps this was the same Idaho delegate who explained his support for Nixon by telling a reporter, "I like Nixon. He wipes his butt the way I do."[6]

A week before the convention, at the GOP's platform committee meetings in Miami Beach, Rockefeller's distance from the ideological direction of the party would be even more evident. John Lindsay, the liberal Republican mayor of New York City and a top Rockefeller backer, told the group, "If we are to eliminate crime and violence in this country, we must eliminate the hopelessness, futility and alienation from which they spring." Reagan took a different approach. "Order has broken down in the streets," he declared. "Organized rebellion has broken out on our campuses. The courts approve and often underwrite the very things our individual integrity rejects." The diagnosis offered by the moderates, said Reagan, reflected a "permissive attitude" that allowed crime and disorder to fester. "We must reject the idea that every time a law is broken, society is guilty rather than the lawbreaker." Nixon's written statement adopted a similar tone. Calling for a "militant crusade against crime," he said, "Poverty, despair, anger, past wrongs can no longer be allowed to excuse or justify violence or crime or lawlessness."[7]

Though the California governor received the most enthusiastic response of the three (the reaction to Lindsay was one of "marked coolness," as one journalist put it), the final version of the party's platform, which included proposals to deal with the direct roots of poverty and crime in the United States and a call for an expanded federal role in everything from job training and education to health care, would nonetheless give a nod to the moderates. These symbolic platform wins reflected a larger decision by moderates to organize themselves around policy rather than politics after 1964. They had spent the intervening years developing proposals for handling the most intractable social and economic problems facing the country. Conservatives, on the other hand, identified the political issues that would galvanize a grass-roots coalition of committed activists to push that message in the political venue where it mattered the most—the voting booth.[8]

By 1968, the right had yet to build a policy apparatus that could compete effectively with the moderates. But Miami Beach proved that, from a political perspective, conservative language dominated. "Somehow," *Time* noted, "Nixon manages to sound more forceful and specific in emphasizing the need for law and order than in pleading for social justice." Somehow indeed. Nixon's emphasis highlighted an emerging shift within the Republican party, toward a polarizing tone on social and cultural issues. This move would become more pronounced in the years to come, and would eventually merge with the creation of a conservative policy infrastructure, via think tanks, advocacy groups, and deep-pocketed donors that would provide the intellectual backbone for the antigovernment populism that emerged out of 1968.[9]

Victory in the platform committee, however, could not revive Rockefeller's dwindling hopes of winning the nomination. Still, he continued to maintain his confident public demeanor. He was picking up support in "bits and pieces," he told reporters. When asked if he might consider the vice presidential nod, he said that it might be better to pose such a question to Nixon, given that "he's had more experience at the job than I have." Rockefeller wasn't merely acting for the cameras. According to Ted Braun, a Rockefeller aide, his weeks on the road had left him "deluded" about his chances. "When I got to Miami the first thing he said to me, 'Oh boy, this is a real cliff-hanger.' He was convinced that the race was so close."[10]

Rockefeller threw more of his vast fortune into the fight: a reception on Saturday, a dinner for the New York delegation on Sunday, and a $50,000 event for all delegates on Monday at the Americana Hotel with eight bars, two bands, and enough food to feed the eight thousand guests who showed up. Each room had a bandstand with live music, and chants of "We want Rocky" could be heard down the corridors. The campaign also began employing a riskier set of tactics. On the first day of the convention, an advertisement appeared in the *Miami Herald* in the guise of a memo to RNC delegates that said the candidacies of Nixon or Reagan would not be "acceptable to black America." Some amateur sleuthing by the conservative magazine, and Rockefeller adversary, the *National Review* uncovered that the ad had been placed and paid for by a Rockefeller advisor. The most misdirected part of the ploy, however, was the belief that enough Republicans would care about alienating "black America."[11]

Nixon, on the other hand, continued to act like the front runner. Campaign minders determined that the nightly newscasts began their coverage of the convention at 6:38 PM. So, on the first night of the convention, after circling Miami International Airport, Nixon's plane hit the tarmac and disgorged its passenger at exactly that moment. He touched down to find a prized political gift waiting for him: a public endorsement from President Eisenhower, who was recovering from his fifth heart attack. Frail and clad in a bathrobe, he called reporters in to his hospital room and, in a far cry from his tepid endorsement in 1960, told them that Nixon was a man of "great intelligence," "great decisiveness," and "great experience" and that he had his full support. Another crucial endorsement came when Spiro Agnew announced his support for Nixon. The move reflected Agnew's recognition of political reality but also a desire for revenge against Rockefeller for having so badly embarrassed him the previous March.[12]

Rockefeller's last hope came from his ideological rival Reagan. If the California governor could steal away enough delegates to deny Nixon a first-ballot win, Rockefeller's camp believed that they could potentially swoop in on the second or third ballot. Reagan, however, still refused to announce his official candidacy. Rockefeller aide George Hinman later complained that "Reagan was sitting out in Sacramento in regal splendor waiting for the nomination to be handed to him." Reagan wasn't playing coy; he had the same strategy as Rockefeller. He too hoped for a convention deadlock and no first ballot winner, which would allow him to ride in as the party savior. By remaining a noncandidate he appeared to be above the political fray and also kept himself out of the crosshairs of his rivals. While perhaps a good strategy in theory, in practice potential backers could

hardly be expected to endorse Reagan without a clear signal of his intentions. Every day that Reagan waited, more southern delegates—his strongest
base of support—shifted into the Nixon camp. The more Nixon's nomination appeared to be a done deal, the more likely the remaining favorite son
candidates would join Agnew and get in line.[13]

In the late afternoon of the convention's first day, former California senator William Knowland walked out of the state caucus's meeting to announce that the group had passed a resolution recognizing that "Governor
Reagan in fact is a leading and bona fide candidate for President." After
months of wooing delegates, delivering speeches to loyal Republicans, and
creating the infrastructure for a run at the nomination, the announcement
was the worst-kept political secret of the year. New Mexico governor David
Cargo described it as akin to "a woman eight and a half months pregnant
announcing she's going to have a baby." Yet Reagan stuck to his part. "Gosh
I was surprised. It all came out of the clear blue sky." Then off he dashed to
more long-scheduled meetings with wavering delegates. Amazingly, in
Reagan's 1990 memoir, *An American Life*, he continued to adhere to this
fiction, claiming that he never actively sought the GOP nomination in
1968.[14]

Nixon took seriously the potential threat from Reagan. In fact, he viewed
him as a stronger challenger than Rockefeller. Reagan spoke the language of
southern Republicans with such passion, wrote Nixon in his memoirs, that
they "could be lured at the last minute by his ideological siren song." GOP
delegates, said Garry Wills, were like the "princess in her tower, torn by
doubt on the eve of her wedding, respecting the heir she is pledged to but
not loving him, [who] must be given a glimpse of the handsome young
knight riding by." Reagan was that young knight, the dreamier version of
Goldwater whose magnetic appeal just might convince millions of Americans
to vote their conservative impulses. His entry into the race immediately
energized conservatives. According to a CBS News report, he quickly
picked up sixteen delegates, while Nixon still remained forty-one votes
short of a first-ballot win. The Nixon campaign's key southern vote counter,
Harry Dent; Mitchell; and South Carolina senator Strom Thurmond sat
down with Nixon on Monday night and counseled the presumptive nominee

that if he did not offer greater reassurances to the party's southern contingent, his nomination might not be so presumptive after all.[15]

The presence of Thurmond in the Nixon camp was no accident. In the spring of 1966, Nixon had traveled to South Carolina and declared the arch-segregationist "a man of courage and integrity" and "no racist." This public endorsement solidified the relationship between the two men. Above all, it shored up southern support for Nixon's candidacy, as perhaps no southerner had greater influence among the region's Republican voters. With Thurmond by his side, Nixon made his final case to southern Republicans in Miami Beach. A Florida delegate recorded the entire meeting and handed it over to a reporter from the *Miami Herald*, which published it the next day. In a potential make-or-break meeting, Nixon expertly calibrated his words to play on the South's abiding need to be mollified and appeased.[16]

Nixon told the delegates that on the issue of the vice presidency he would not take "anybody that is going to divide the party." That meant no Mark Hatfield (the liberal Oregon senator), no Lindsay, and certainly no Rockefeller. On busing, Nixon said it was "a problem in the North too," a none-too-subtle allusion to George Wallace's repeated assertions that northerners were in no position to cast aspersions on the South. On his public support for recently passed federal open housing legislation, he claimed it represented nothing more than a tactical move, intended to "get the civil-rights issues and open housing issues out of our sight so we didn't have a split party over the platform when we came down here to Miami Beach." According to Nixon, such issues would be better decided at the local level—a position sure to resonate with white southerners who chafed at federal intervention in their affairs. Nixon's statements were implicitly intended to reassure the assembled delegates that he publicly supported open housing laws insofar as it placated moderates, but that he had no real intention of aggressively enforcing the legislation as president.[17]

This kind of inscrutability would be Nixon's greatest asset in 1968. Trying to identify any single Nixon proposal drove the reporters covering his campaign mad. But the political benefit could hardly be denied. He had turned himself into a blank screen onto which both wings of the Republican

Party could project their policy preferences. And on no issue did he play his cards closer to the vest than Vietnam. In the spring of 1968 he had considered delivering a major speech laying out his views on the war. He scheduled it for March 31, but canceled when the White House announced that Johnson would be speaking on the same night. After Johnson's withdrawal from the race that evening, Nixon declared a personal moratorium on commenting about Vietnam. He explained his silence by saying that he feared if he said too much he would give the impression to the North Vietnamese that they might get a better deal from one of the presidential candidates than they would from the current negotiations in Paris. "If there is a chance we get the war over before this election," he said, "that is much more important than anything I might wish to say to get you to vote for me." In reality, Nixon knew he had little to gain by talking about Vietnam. Doing so would give his opponents the ammunition with which to attack him; not doing so allowed potential supporters to believe whatever they wanted about his intentions. And if elected president he would enter office with no embarrassing campaign pronouncements to explain away.[18]

Six years of navigating between the two wings of the GOP had taught Nixon that the key to intraparty success was equivocation. Few truly loved Nixon, but he made them just comfortable enough that they could live with him. Tom Stagg, a member of the Louisiana delegation, pronounced Nixon's performance before the southern caucus the "greatest stand-up performance by a politician I have witnessed." He received a further boost from Thurmond's entreaty to southern passions. "I love Reagan," he told them, "but Nixon's the one." According to Thurmond, "We have no choice, if we want to win, except to vote for Nixon."[19]

Nixon's courting of the southern delegates—and the South in general—became a key aspect of his strategy in 1968 and beyond. More than any other Republican candidate, he understood that the backlash from civil rights legislation and integration had turned the South into a potential power center for the party. If Republicans would no longer be forced to concede the region's 80–110 electoral votes to the Democrats, they wouldn't have to fight for the big electoral prizes in the Midwest, Northeast, and Far West with such limited room for error. With the South in the GOP's corner, Republicans would have a clear path to becoming the nation's presidential party. And as the racial divide between the two parties grew more pronounced, the South shifted even more decisively toward Republicans, both electorally and ideologically.[20]

This had major implications for conservatives. A strong presence in the South eroded the control northeastern moderates had long maintained. For years conservatives had begrudgingly acquiesced to the notion that, because of the GOP's structural disadvantages in the Electoral College, the party must nominate a moderate candidate to compete nationally. But if the Republicans could rely on southern support, they would no longer have to defer to northeastern liberals or seek the support of the black vote, as Nixon had done in 1960. They could instead run campaigns tailored to conservatives on both sides of the Mason-Dixon line while also picking off just enough of the white working-class voters who had been casting a ballot for Democrats since the 1930s. Seizing the South gave Republicans the opportunity to nationalize their appeal while ensuring that the party spoke the same language and used the same political messaging across the country.

Democrats, meanwhile, would be faced with the challenge of maintaining support in the South while also trying to preserve the allegiance of blacks and northern liberals. And so, as the Democratic coalition began to break apart over regional, ideological, and generational differences, Republicans coalesced around a single, unifying political narrative. Four years after Goldwater's historic defeat, the outlines of the coming conservative takeover of the party—and of the nation's politics—were clearly evident.

The nominating speeches on August 7, the third night of the convention, would both provide a fitting end to the nomination fight and demonstrate Nixon's success in capturing the party's middle ground. Ivy Baker Priest Stevens, a former treasurer of the United States and the first woman to deliver a nominating speech for a presidential candidate, began the speechmaking on behalf of Reagan. She implored the delegates to support a "man who will confront the radicals on our campuses and the looters on our streets and say: the law will be obeyed." On foreign policy, Stevens pledged that Reagan would make it clear to all potential adversaries that "if we must fight for freedom, we will fight to win." The heated language set off a twenty-minute demonstration, with the loudest cheers emanating from southern and western delegates. Soon after, the moderate Pennsylvania governor Raymond Shafer endorsed Rockefeller, a man who he said "can build bridges across the deep and fragmented divisions that separate black from white, young from old, poor from rich." Rockefeller's dwindling band of moderate supporters exploded for a thirty-minute celebration that even topped Reagan's. Finally, Agnew delivered the nominating speech for Nixon. The 1960 GOP nominee would be the right man in 1968, the Maryland governor said, because of his "courage to rise up from the depths of defeat six years ago...to make the greatest political comeback in American history." Agnew's case for Nixon was nonideological and more pragmatic than Reagan and Rockefeller as he noted that his tireless campaigning in 1966 had led to one of the party's "greatest victories in the past two decades." Mailer wrote that Reagan's supporters had the look of "soldiers and state troopers" and Rockefeller's were more akin to swingers in "so far as Republicans had swingers"; but for Nixon "the mood on the floor was like the revel in the main office of a corporation when the Christmas Party is high."[21]

The speeches pushed the roll call vote back to 1:30 AM, though any suspense about the final result had long since disappeared. The ever-cautious Nixon even invited a camera crew from CBS into his hotel suite to record the moment when his six-year struggle for the nomination would be realized. With Wisconsin's votes, Nixon went over the top. He received a congratulatory call from Rockefeller, who complained to him that "Ronnie didn't come through for us as well as we expected." After the roll call, Reagan jumped onstage looking jovial and even relieved as he asked that the vote for Nixon be made unanimous. He would later write that he knew then that he "wasn't ready to be President." Still, whatever his true feeling, Reagan's effect on the delegates, his performance at the convention, and the direction of the party, which was moving to the right and the South, suggested that his future couldn't be brighter. Plus, as he told reporters upon his departure, "How can you lose when you go back to being governor of California?"[22]

Things were less cheery for Rockefeller. He had spent roughly $29,000 for each of the 277 delegate votes he received (for a total of approximately $8 million). "Maybe I was in the wrong party," he later admitted. It would be his last try to win the party nomination. In 1964 the moderates were defeated because of failure to organize effectively and an inability to rally behind a candidate who could stop Goldwater. By 1968, those problems had become far more acute, and went deeper than just the Republican Party. They hadn't simply lost support among the party's rank and file; their message of technocratic, conservative-lite governance no longer resonated with Americans more broadly.[23]

From the liberal Republican perspective, Romney's embarrassing collapse and Rockefeller's frustrating vacillation—along with the conservatives' greater effectiveness at mobilizing their supporters—had certainly done damage. But ultimately the moderate wing's long-standing preeminence within the GOP had been undermined by the country's rightward political turn. No longer did Republicans need a moderate to soften the party's harder edges. Even tactical genius from the liberal wing would not have been able to prevent that transformation in American politics.

"There can be a mystique about a man. You can look him in the eye and know he's got it. This guy has got it." So Richard Nixon described his decision-making in selecting the governor of Maryland, Spiro Agnew, as his running mate. When a reporter for *Time* asked voters in Atlanta what they thought of when they heard Nixon's choice, the reactions were less than reverential. "It's some kind of disease," speculated one. "It's some kind of an egg," offered another. Rockefeller had a harsher indictment: "It's just like Dick. He always blows the big one." Indeed, little about Agnew's experience or potential suggested that he merited consideration for being placed a heartbeat away from the presidency.[24]

Unlike Nixon, whose desire for respect and public admiration dominated his life, Agnew set lower goals for himself. It would not have been hard to imagine him as a suburban lawyer, perhaps vice president of the Kiwanis Club or president of the local Parent-Teacher Association. In fact, this had been precisely Agnew's career trajectory when he decided to enter politics. His political rise would be marked by many of in-the-right-place-at-the-right-time opportunities that had defined Nixon's own political rise. But Agnew was also a direct beneficiary of the GOP's increasingly conservative tilt. When he first ran for office in 1960—a circuit court judicial race in Baltimore—Agnew finished fifth out of five candidates. Undaunted, he ran two years later for Baltimore County executive, and would have lost again had the Democratic Party not been hopelessly divided.[25]

There seemed little chance that he could hold on to the seat—but then Democrats handed Agnew another gift. In 1966, the Maryland Democratic Party found itself mired once again in turmoil, and largely because of the rising power of George Wallace's acolytes after his impressive performance in the 1964 Democratic presidential primary. Out of a wide-open primary for governor emerged George P. Mahoney, a perennial segregationist, hyperconservative candidate. His slogan, the Wallace-esque "Your Home Is Your Castle—Protect It!" was pointedly directed at the most racially hostile impulses among Maryland voters. Agnew's unlikely victory in Baltimore had made him an immediate contender for the GOP nomination for governor, which in the heavily Democratic state meant that he would be a sacrificial lamb come Election Day. Mahoney's nomination changed that political equation. Black voters surely didn't intend to vote for a segregationist, and prominent Democrats saw little choice but to publicly support Agnew over the odious Mahoney. Agnew won handily. In only four years he'd gone from county executive to the governor's mansion, a political rise that had very little to do with any particular appeal of the man himself but rather the dearth of better alternatives.[26]

Since he'd run against Mahoney, many political observers viewed Agnew as a political moderate—an image he briefly cultivated as governor. He fought for the repeal of a three-century-old antimiscegenation law and passed the state's first open-housing law. Yet throughout his career Agnew had moved through the worlds of business, government, and politics without having much contact with black people or gaining much understanding of their struggles. In July 1967 the radical black leader H. Rap Brown traveled to the town of Cambridge in Maryland's still largely segregated Eastern Shore and in a fiery speech declared that "if Cambridge don't come around, Cambridge should be burned down." An hour later, police ex-changed gunfire with local residents, and the local public school was set ablaze. Convinced that the violence could only be the direct result of out-side agitators rather than genuine grievances, Agnew called for legislation expanding his power to corral rioters and pushed for a state budget filled with cuts to social programs and poverty reduction initiatives—an "East Coast version of the Ronald Reagan budget," Paul Sarbanes, the future Democratic senator from Maryland, called it.[27]

Agnew would take a similar approach a year later when widespread loot-ing and arson shook Baltimore after the assassination of Martin Luther King. Agnew invited the city's moderate black leaders—many of whom had spent the previous days trying to quell the uprising—to a meeting at the State Office Building. In front of television cameras he proceeded to blame them for the disturbances. "You were beguiled by the rationalization of unity; you were intimidated by the veiled threats," Agnew lectured. "You were stung by insinuations that you were Mister Charlie's boy, by epithets like Uncle Tom." Agnew's words infuriated the audience, which rose en masse to depart in protest. "We were talked to like children," complained one state senator.[28]

The outburst, however, further propelled Agnew's political ascendancy. Suddenly the Maryland governor had become a national expert on urban affairs and a speaker in demand on the subject of law and order. He told audiences that the police should have the right to shoot looters and ad-opted the rhetoric of Reagan on the true source of social disturbance: "If one wants to pinpoint the cause of the riots, it would be this permissive climate and the misguided compassion of public opinion." "Evil condi-tions" did not cause the riots, he said, but rather "evil men," and he further bemoaned the "national whining catharsis" that had taken over the country. No one was calling Spiro Agnew a moderate anymore.[29]

Agnew's defense of the "decent white community" impressed Nixon. In marrying tough law-and-order language to an image of political modera-tion, Nixon saw much of himself in the Maryland governor. By the middle of the summer Agnew had moved onto Nixon's short list for vice president. Still, on the last day of the convention, when Nixon announced him as his running mate, audible gasps could be heard from reporters. But the move made political sense. Picking an actual moderate risked alienating southerners. A conservative like Reagan would tilt the ticket too far to the right. Agnew would appeal to conservatives based on his April outburst (Reagan spoke approvingly of his "good record for dealing firmly with rioters"), and to others he would be seen as the moderate who had stood up to George Mahoney's toxic racism.[30]

As Nixon wrote in his memoirs, the campaign's focus on the border states that rimmed the South meant that "Agnew fit the bill geographically, and as a political moderate he fit in philosophically." Stephen Hess, who later would be conscripted to write speeches for Agnew, said of the decision, "If you put all the conflicting Republican elements into a computer, and programmed it to produce a Vice President who would do least harm to party unity, the tape would be punched SPIRO T. AGNEW."[31]

For Nixon, the journey to Miami Beach had been grueling and circuitous. He'd romanced and reassured moderates and conservatives and outlasted and outmaneuvered his potential rivals. But now on August 8, the last night of the Republican convention, Nixon had a different audience to woo: the American people. To win them over he would need to present, once again, a "new Nixon"—a man who would no longer be seen as the divisive, partisan, and sullen loser of the past but instead as a statesman who would calm fears and unite the nation. At no point in his campaign for the White House would that goal be realized with greater effectiveness than in Nixon's acceptance speech. Though Nixon's success in 1968 can be accurately viewed as a triumph of style and image-making, it is also true that even in the most seemingly platitudinous speech-making there is often real substance; such was the case in his convention address.[32]

Nixon eschewed policy specifics, relying instead on what one reporter called "oratory so evenhanded as to be meaningless." For example, he sounded his usual note of anger at "the loan sharks and the numbers racketeers," the "filth peddlers and the narcotics peddlers," and the "cities enveloped in smoke and flame." His underwhelming solution to this national crisis? Calling for a new attorney general to combat these contributors to national disorder. Instead, Nixon focused on Johnson's "deluge" of government programs. The time had come, he said, "to quit pouring billions of dollars into programs that have failed in the United States of America," programs that had reaped "an ugly harvest of frustration, violence and failure across the land." On Vietnam he argued that the Johnson administration had ineffectively utilized the country's "military and economic and diplomatic power" and had wasted "a record for courage and sacrifice unsurpassed in our history" by America's fighting men. His policy would be different: "The first priority foreign policy objective of our next administration will be to bring an honorable end to the war in Vietnam," he assured the convention crowd. Those seeking an answer to how he would achieve that goal would have to wait for another day.[33]

The heart of Nixon's speech, however, was directed toward the hopes and fears of those he called "the great majority of Americans." Given how crucial the message was to his campaign in 1968, it bears quoting in full:

> The forgotten Americans—the non-shouters; the non-
> demonstrators. They are not racists or sick; they are not guilty of the
> crime that plagues the land. They are black and they are white—
> they're native born and foreign born—they're young and they're
> old. They work in America's factories. They run America's businesses.
> They serve in government. They provide most of the soldiers who
> died to keep us free. They give drive to the spirit of America. They
> give lift to the American Dream. They give steel to the backbone of
> America. They are good people, they are decent people; they work,
> and they save, and they pay their taxes, and they care. Like Theodore
> Roosevelt, they know that this country will not be a good place for
> any of us to live in unless it is a good place for all of us to live in. This
> I say to you tonight is the real voice of America.[34]

Sixteen years earlier, when he successfully saved his place on the 1952 Republican ticket, Nixon had cast himself as the common man with a wife in a "respectable Republican cloth coat" and a cocker spaniel named Checkers for his two daughters. In Miami Beach he did it again. But this time, the common man was ensconced in the middle class, living in sub-urbia, and worried whether he could provide for his family.

Nixon's language always tacked back to the middle. Echoing the rhet-oric of Robert Kennedy, he said, "Black Americans, no more than white Americans...do not want more government programs which perpetuate dependency." They wanted the "pride," "self-respect," and "dignity" that came from an "equal chance" at economic opportunity. By balancing his tough talk on law and order with calls for black empowerment, he appealed to voters moved by Wallace's pseudo-segregationist message but who didn't want to vote for an overtly racist southerner. With Nixon they could have both—a candidate strong on crime but, outwardly, sympathetic to the Negro plight.[35]

Nonetheless, Nixon's words played on the same prejudices that animated Wallace's supporters. Implicit in his speech—and in his middle-ground positioning—was a darker and more divisive message. Those shouting and demonstrating, who didn't work, who hadn't served, and who didn't pay taxes were clearly not included in Nixon's vision of America. Nixon's de-scription of the "real voice of America" left out black voters—despite his Kennedy-like appeal—the hippies, the feminists, and the agitators. In time, this us-versus-them construct would become an explicit feature of Nixon's political rhetoric.[36]

More directly, Nixon wrapped himself in a powerful American my-thology. This would be particularly evident in the speech's conclusion, where he spoke of the children in America who were awaking to "a living nightmare of poverty, neglect and despair." For them, said Nixon, the "American system is one that feeds his stomach and starves his soul. It breaks his heart. And in the end it may take his life on some distant battle-field." He contrasted this present with a more glorious past, one swathed firmly in Nixon's own personal experience. He, too, dreamt "impossible dreams...of far away places where he'd like to go" as a child. He was helped along the way, not by government handouts, but rather a hard-working father, a "gentle, Quaker mother," a great teacher, a remarkable football coach, an inspirational minister, "a courageous wife," "loyal children," and, finally, "millions" who "worked for his success" so that he could stand before the American people, that night, "nominated for President of the United States of America."[37]

At a moment when millions of Americans felt the country slipping away from underneath their feet, Nixon's speech suggested that the American dream could be restored under his presidency. For all of the cynicism that one might see in his political machinations—and the myth-making of his personal narrative—Nixon spoke to very real and very raw emotions in the American body politic: a desire for simplicity, order, tradition, and, above all, tranquility. For the past seven months the nation had endured one national trauma after another. Nixon offered them hope of brighter and calmer days ahead.

"The Democrats Are Finished"

O n the surface, Chicago seemed the obvious gathering place for a political party determined to "dance with the one that brung it"— the white, working-class voters who had for decades served as the foundation of the New Deal coalition. Dominated by Mayor Richard Daley's powerful political machine, it was the quintessential Democratic metropolis. Vibrant neighborhoods of Irish, Polish, Czech, and Ukrainian immigrants crammed into modest wooden bungalows, separated from the city's restive blacks and the grinding poverty of the ghetto.

Chicago had escaped the deadly riots that had torn apart Los Angeles, Detroit, Newark, and Washington, DC, and compared to San Francisco or New York there were few hippies or "agitators." While not immune to the problems of urban America, the city's benevolent and iron-fisted leader had simply been more effective at keeping those forces at bay. Daley's control, however, would be lost in the late summer of 1968, and unlike the Republicans, who had been so successful at presenting a unified front, in Chicago the Democrats would find themselves caught in the crossfire

between the youth counterculture and the white backlash. "All the unmuz-
zled passions, inconsolable frustrations and polarizing hatreds plaguing the
republic surged to the surface" in Chicago, *Newsweek* wrote on the eve of
the convention. Miami Beach may have offered Americans a veneer of political harmony, but it would prove far more appealing than what Americans
were about to witness on the streets of Chicago.[1]

Lyndon Johnson purportedly once said that he never trusted a man "unless
I've got his pecker in my pocket." While perhaps apocryphal, the statement
is very much in keeping with the president's pronounced obsession with
the male phallus. Johnson, who held meetings while he sat on the toilet or
while skinny-dipping in the White House pool, became infamous for pull-
ing out his own member (nicknamed "Jumbo") when he sought to emphat-
ically punctuate a point during a conversation. During his decades in
Washington, Johnson had (figuratively) filled his pockets with many a
man's genitalia, but by the summer of 1968 none was more firmly ensconced than that of his vice president, Hubert Humphrey. Even as
Humphrey prepared to make his entrance onto the political stage as the
presidential nominee of this party in Chicago—and become his own
man—Johnson still refused to release his hold over him.[2]

On no issue would Johnson's grip on Humphrey remain tighter than
Vietnam. In the months after Robert Kennedy's death, Humphrey worked
exhaustively to craft a position that would satisfy all of the key constituencies
within the Democratic Party—the doves and the hawks, the McCarthyites
and the Kennedys. But only complete acquiescence to White House policy
would placate the president. "Johnson just doesn't give a damn about the
party or the nominee," said one administration official off the record. "He
just won't bend on Vietnam. He wants personal vindication, even if it
wrecks the party, which it may." These words would prove prophetic.[3]

On August 25, the Sunday before the Democratic National Convention,
Humphrey appeared on NBC's *Meet the Press* and essentially conceded
defeat. Endorsing LBJ's policies in Vietnam, he made clear that Hanoi "isn't
going to get a better deal out of me." Humphrey's surrender on Vietnam
epitomized his entire political strategy leading up to the convention in

Chicago. Despite the near certainty that he would be the Democratic nominee, Humphrey acted in constant fear that Johnson would use his influence to pull the rug out from underneath him. Rather than radiating the aura of a triumphant candidate, he instead looked like a scared politician seemingly willing to appease any party rival—except the antiwar contingent.[4]

While Humphrey believed these concessions would smooth his path to the nomination, his hypercaution had the opposite effect. When he arrived at the airport in Chicago on the Sunday before the convention, August 25, virtually no one greeted him. Mayor Daley, who had announced that he was withholding his endorsement of the presumptive nominee "to see if something develops," was notably absent. (In contrast, several thousand well-wishers greeted McCarthy, though the microphone at the airport didn't work—an apt symbol for the increasingly leaderless "Clean Gene" movement.) In his reluctance to fully throw his support behind Humphrey, who he called a "lousy candidate," Daley was not alone. According to a Gallup poll taken on the eve of the convention, barely over half—56 percent—of Democrats indicated a preference for Humphrey.[5]

With concern growing that nominating Humphrey would lead to disaster for Democrats in November, an incongruous combination of antiwar activists and seasoned political professionals began to cast their gaze toward Teddy Kennedy, the last of the Kennedy brothers and the heir to Camelot's political legacy. The antiwar activists saw him as the best hope for getting the country out of Vietnam. The politicos feared no other Democrat could win in November. For their part, the Humphrey camp viewed Kennedy as a possible running mate, believing that he could bring liberals back into the fold and give the ticket excitement and momentum heading into the general election. A June Harris survey suggested that running with Kennedy would add five million votes for Humphrey and turn what could be a tight race into a Democratic landslide.[6]

The day before Humphrey's arrival in Chicago, Daley breakfasted with Jesse Unruh, head of the California delegation and a strong Robert Kennedy supporter during the state's primary in June. The meeting sent ripples of speculation through the convention. When Daley called Ted Kennedy on Saturday in Hyannis Port to gauge his interest in a presidential draft, the once quixotic notion that he could be coaxed into making himself available for a convention draft suddenly seemed very real. With Kennedy emerging on the left, Johnson lurking, and McCarthy and George McGovern still publicly contesting his nomination, a divisive floor fight over the nomination now seemed possible. Humphrey surveyed the scene, assessed his position, and did what he had done repeatedly since he had entered the political arena in 1948: he engaged in a series of humiliating backtracks and capitulations to appease those who he believed held his political fate in their hands.

The first reversal came on the so-called unit rule, which required that all of a state's delegates vote for one candidate at the party convention. This was an issue of particular importance to southern Democrats, because it allowed them to keep a tight rein on their delegations. A delegate leader who controlled all his charges wielded significantly greater influence and, as a favorite son candidate, could demand significant concessions in order to release those votes for a prospective nominee. In an era of "New Politics" and calls for a more transparent nominating system, the unit rule had become a target of party reformers. Humphrey initially sided with them, which caused the southern caucus to explode in protest. Texas governor John Connally, who was already making noises about a "Draft Johnson" movement, offered the loudest criticism. Humphrey quickly returned to Dixie with hat in hand. He told Connally that he would push to keep the unit rule in place in Chicago (though not in the future). He also offered his help to the Texas governor in warding off a credential challenge to the makeup of the delegation and pledged to pick a vice presidential candidate whom the South considered acceptable. In the end the credentials challenge would fail, but the unit rule was dropped by voice vote—representing a critical party reform, the full consequences of which would only become obvious later.[7]

Next, Humphrey formally withdrew from consideration the minority plank on Vietnam that his counsel David Ginsburg had painstakingly negotiated but that Johnson had once again rejected. Humphrey would now be on record endorsing a war policy that had led McCarthy, Kennedy, and now McGovern to take on the party's leadership and sparked a full-scale insurgency within the Democratic Party. As McCarthy pointed out, "He asks the Democratic party to offer the people four more years like the last three years." Humphrey biographer Carl Solberg noted the "stunning" irony of his situation. "Twenty years before, as the fiery young challenger to the Establishment, he took a minority report before the Democratic Convention and won a famous victory for a civil rights plank.... Now as the cautious middle-of-the-roader who could not bring himself to 'step out from under,' he truckled to the president and relied upon old southern dignitaries and the relics of city machines to combat the restless and the discontented." Writing in *New York* magazine, Jimmy Breslin put it more succinctly: "In Chicago, with the smell of the White House so close to him, he turned into ectoplasm." In his march to the nomination Humphrey subsumed his ideals and his resolve to ambition. It was a microcosm of his entire political career. Two decades of concessions to political reality— from red-baiting and romancing Johnson in the Senate to keeping his mouth shut about Vietnam in the White House—had made expedience Humphrey's overriding political impulse.[8]

A more self-assured candidate might have surveyed the situation in Chicago and concluded that he held the political high ground. Humphrey repeatedly failed to appreciate his own political advantages—none more so than the fact that the only Democrats more unpopular than him were those seeking to unseat him as the party's nominee. While McCarthy had a committed base of enthusiastic supporters, party regulars viewed him as too dovish on the war and too much of a troublemaker in general. His entire approach to politics—emboldening young activists and opening up the party to new voices—represented a direct threat to traditional Democratic powerbrokers who relied on control over party machines and the power of patronage appointments. "Deep down they're afraid that if he wins the McCarthy supporters will replace them," said Pennsylvania congressman Milton Sharp. Although the *Washington Post*'s David Broder wrote on the eve of the convention that McCarthy's "New Politics" had made him the Democrats' best bet to win in November—and poll after poll showed him doing better than Humphrey against Nixon and Wallace—the party's rank and file had no interest in seeing him get the nomination. For Johnson's part, he would have sooner cut off his own arm than allow a candidate—either McCarthy, McGovern, or Kennedy, all of whom openly opposed his policies in Vietnam—to succeed him.[9]

Johnson could certainly make problems for Humphrey, but there was no support for a presidential draft, and ultimately LBJ still preferred his vice president to any other possible candidate. Southern Democrats might have been unhappy with Humphrey, but they had nowhere to turn either. If they withheld their support it could have paved the way for a more liberal candidate (particularly on civil rights) to get the party nod as a compromise choice. They could have backed segregationist Georgia governor Lester Maddox, who had briefly thrown his hat in the ring in late August, but a vote for Maddox, who had no chance of winning, would also have the practical effect of helping Humphrey's rivals.

Humphrey faced major challenges, of course. Upsetting the president by publicly disagreeing with his Vietnam policy, while highly unlikely to cost him the nomination, could have prevented him from winning on the first ballot in Chicago—and potentially created a major political embarrassment. Nonetheless, Humphrey possessed strengths that no other candidate could possibly match. The unions, African Americans, the South, and a majority of the delegates were in his column, albeit some more eagerly than others. None of these groups had a better alternative. While Nixon had exploited fears of what might come from not supporting him in Miami Beach, Humphrey failed to grasp the fact that he could play the same game.

Amazingly, the one group Humphrey insisted hold their nose and support him, the antiwar wing of the party, likely had most to gain by him being denied the nomination. They were also the one group within the party that had consistently shown no inclination toward compromise. Humphrey standing up to the president on the Vietnam plank or negotiating with the southerners to neutralize Johnson's opposition would have cooled talk of a Kennedy candidacy, ended McCarthy and McGovern's presidential dreams, likely brought the antiwar wing back, and above all reassured the delegates (and voters) that he had a backbone. His advisors said the convention would be a "Bar Mitzvah" opportunity—a chance for him to prove that he had become his own man. But rather than operate from a position of strength or take a risky, short-term step that had the potential to produce major political dividends, he took the path of nonconfrontation. His political antenna, so well calibrated in the past, was surpassed by his even better-developed penchant for playing it safe. By seeking to mollify Johnson, Daley, and the old power centers of the party, Humphrey ensured that he would be the nominee of a hopelessly divided party that had little enthusiasm for his candidacy.[10]

When it came to taking the path of least political resistance, however, Eugene McCarthy proved more than Humphrey's equal. His summer campaign, which had already gotten off to a poor start, went from bad to worse. He made odd and unhelpful pronouncements, such as musing that he would go to Paris to look in on peace talks with the North Vietnamese. He shrugged his shoulders when Warsaw Pact troops invaded Czechoslovakia on August 20, arguing that the episode barely registered as a "major world crisis." The same candidate who had purposely played down his antiwar views in New Hampshire was now being needlessly provocative. "His conduct both prior to and during the convention," wrote a British journalist, "suggested the frame of mind of a man who knew it was all over but the shouting—and was instinctively dreading the shouting."[11]

McCarthy's disengagement reached a crescendo on the second day of the convention when he, Humphrey, and McGovern met with the California delegation. McCarthy's disastrous appearance earlier in the summer had cost him an endorsement from the state's Kennedy delegates, so when they arrived in Chicago, the Californians were a wild card—wary of McCarthy but unwilling to side with Humphrey until he offered them an olive branch on Vietnam. The meeting would provide McCarthy his only opportunity to challenge Humphrey directly and, in a nationally televised event, make the case for why the delegates should choose him as the party nominee. As the candidates gathered in the Grand Ballroom of Chicago's La Salle Hotel on Tuesday morning, August 27, the presidential nomination, at least nominally, still hung in the balance.

The performance of a lifetime still would have been unlikely to stop Humphrey, but the Californians didn't even get an adequate one. McCarthy mentioned Kennedy only in passing, barely spoke about Vietnam in his opening remarks, and instead told the group, "You know my stand on the issues.... I do not intend to restate my case." Instead, he launched an attack on McGovern, of all people, who had angered him the day before by saying that McCarthy had adopted "the view that a passive and inactive Presidency is in order." (Privately McGovern went even further, bluntly stating that the biggest difference between the two men was that "Gene really doesn't want to be President, and I do.") McCarthy reminded the Californians that he had been "the most active candidate in the party this year," which though true was hardly relevant. For his part, McGovern wowed the delegates, as he offered an impassioned antiwar speech that received a standing ovation from the Californians. He later called the debate a personal turning point and one that helped convince him to run for president in 1972.[12]

As for Humphrey, his presentation offered little reassurance to already ambivalent delegates. When asked whether he disagreed with Johnson's position on Vietnam, he refused to distance himself: "I did not come here to repudiate the President of the United States." He claimed that the United States had not tried to impose a military solution on Vietnam and could not be held responsible for the war's intensification ("Regrettably, wars have their built-in escalation," he said). According to Humphrey the real "roadblock to peace" lay not in Washington but in Hanoi, and "we ought to recognize it as such."[13]

Given the opportunity to respond, McCarthy stood up, said, "The people know my position," and sat down. There would soon be more peevishness. On the first day of the convention, he turned to Dick Goodwin, who had returned to work on the campaign after Kennedy's death, and asked, "What about this Teddy thing?" Perhaps, he suggested, the two men could join forces. Events quickly gathered steam. In a meeting the next day with Kennedy's brother-in-law Steve Smith, McCarthy offered a magnanimous concession: so long as his name was placed in nomination (as a sign of respect to the young people who had pushed so hard for his candidacy), he would urge his supporters to cast their vote for Kennedy. Yet, still unable to hide the unrequited anger he felt toward Robert Kennedy, he told Smith, who only two and a half months earlier had buried his other brother-in-law, Robert, "While I'm willing to do this for Teddy, I never could have done it for Bobby."[14]

Word of the meeting soon leaked. *CBS News* reported that Smith and McCarthy had met for two hours (it was actually fifteen minutes) and that Smith had asked McCarthy to support Teddy's presidential bid (also untrue). To many it seemed as if Kennedy was actively trying to build delegate support. Spooked by the news, several of the southern delegation leaders, who had been debating remaining neutral on the first ballot, quickly endorsed Humphrey. The leak and subsequent response convinced Kennedy, already hesitant about running, to drop the effort altogether. He would later write in his memoirs that while he understood what was at stake in 1968, he "simply could not summon the will."[15]

Now only McCarthy and McGovern remained. On that same Tuesday the former once again sabotaged his candidacy. Only hours before his meeting with Smith, McCarthy sat down with the editors of the Knight newspaper chain and essentially conceded defeat. "I think it was probably settled more than twenty-four hours ago," he told the assembled reporters. "You mean it's wrapped up for Humphrey?" came the response. "I think so," replied McCarthy. That evening the news reached the hall, and completely deflated the dwindling optimism of McCarthy's backers. Though he later claimed that he didn't know the statement would be leaked before balloting began on the nomination, McCarthy had placed no restrictions on its use.[16]

With his key rivals out of the picture, Humphrey clearly had the nomination in his grasp. Some on his staff argued that the moment had come to formally declare his independence from LBJ. According to the campaign's polling, "The single reproach most frequently leveled against Humphrey is that he is 'too much like Johnson,'" and only 15 percent of voters wanted to see the next president carry on "nearly all" of the administration's policies. On Wednesday morning, Larry O'Brien, who had been advising Humphrey over the summer and would become his campaign manager for the general election, met with the candidate and on behalf of the staff, floated the idea of him resigning the vice presidency in his acceptance speech on Thursday night. Humphrey shot the idea down. "It would not look like an act based on principle or conviction," he told O'Brien. "It would look like a gimmick. It would seem strange. And it will enrage the President."[17]

As Humphrey prepared for the roll call on the convention's third day and his acceptance speech the next night, a new crisis would emerge to hobble his already tenuous candidacy. Mayor Daley, it turned out, was doing more than withholding his support for the vice president. His dedication to maintaining order was about to light a powder keg on the streets of Chicago.

Daley was the prototypical Democratic "boss," a one-man power center who ruled Chicago politics and the city's Democratic machine with both the force of his personality and the lucre of city patronage. Hosting the Democrats' quadrennial gathering had been a long-sought opportunity to show off the city he loved so dearly and ruled so completely. "Remember to impress on the visiting delegates that they are not just visiting Chicago, but Mayor Daley's Chicago," read the instructions to convention workers. It also allowed Daley to put his own personal stamp on the national party. Democrats weren't traveling to "some resort center, but...the very heart of a great city where people live and work and raise their families," he said in his welcoming address to the delegates. Doing so, he said, represented "an important sign of faith to the American people." Democrats didn't gather on beaches separated by causeways from cities and surrounded by glitz and glamour. They belonged in a great American city, meeting in an amphitheater where the speakers, the delegates, and the newsmen could smell whiffs of the slaughterhouse from the stockyards only a few miles away.[18]

Daley, who lived in the same modest bungalow he had resided in before he became mayor and remained a daily attendant at Catholic Mass, had deep affection for hierarchy. "Daley believes in authority—rigid, inflexible, unquestionable authority," wrote Teddy White. The counterculture, antiwar contingent that threatened to invade Chicago during convention week offended Daley on a personal level—just as they offended so many of his white working-class constituents. For Daley, demonstrating, even peacefully, was not a right to be exercised but a threat to public order. "This is his Chicago, and he simply doesn't dig anything else. Anything or anybody that wants to disrupt or tear down seems foreign, an invader," one unnamed political associate of Daley told *Life* magazine.[19]

Daley's fears went beyond the merely theoretical. Just four and a half months before the convention, in the hours after Martin Luther King's assassination, looting, robbery, and arson overwhelmed a city that had largely been immune from such racial disturbances. Eleven people had been killed, hundreds injured, and thousands arrested. Fires raged across the city, taking out twenty city blocks and causing millions in property damage. By one count, a new fire broke out every fifteen seconds. Chicago cops showed notable restraint in the face of such disorder—as befitting a police force considered among the most professional in the nation. The muted response, however, enraged Daley. At a City Hall press conference days after the violence, he said that in his opinion "policemen should have had instructions to shoot arsonists and looters—arsonists to kill and looters to maim and detain." He then openly criticized his police superintendent for failing to issue such edicts to his units. While Daley would later modify his harsh words, his angry declarations were clearly heard by cops already inclined to view antiwar demonstrators in the worst possible light.[20]

So at the end of April, when peaceful antiwar protesters held a peace rally in the city's downtown, the police were waiting—with chemical sprays and batons. It took only the slightest failure to follow police orders for the cops to attack, which they did with a primal intensity. Not content to merely beat demonstrators, the police also went after innocent bystanders merely watching the march from the sidelines. Anyone with long hair became a target—chased down city blocks and savagely beaten when caught. The march coordinator Clark Kissinger complained that "by making a non-violent protest impossible, [the police] made a violent one possible." Daley nonetheless backed the cops without reservation. "They only tried to enforce the law," he declared. A postdemonstration citizens commission report on the violence concluded that "the police were doing what the Mayor and Superintendent had clearly indicated was expected of them."[21]

As preparations began for the influx of convention delegates, Daley's adamancy that order must be maintained at all costs further heightened tensions. The security arrangements at the DNC looked like nothing seen before at a political convention. A thirty-thousand-person-strong security force patrolled Chicago. Manhole covers were sealed; the streets around the International Amphitheater, where the delegates would meet (which the press dubbed "Fort Daley"), were shut down; barbwire ringed the hall. Police were even stationed at the city's water filtration plants because one of the protest leaders had threatened to slip LSD into the water supply. Despite the fact that only a few thousand badly organized demonstrators were expected, no precaution had been overlooked. "Never before had so many feared so much from so few," wrote Chicago columnist Mike Royko. Antiwar groups were pushed as far away as possible from delegates and news cameras. Permits to march were denied; requests to sleep in city parks were refused; and dozens of undercover officers infiltrated antiwar groups.[22]

Daley's hard line on security naturally extended to the convention hall itself. Specially magnetized floor passes, which had to be inserted into a security box upon entering and departing the floor, tightly corralled the delegates. Violations of the rules were met with stern rebukes from security guards, occasionally followed by pushing, shoving, and fisticuffs. Signs were forbidden. The same went for handbills and propaganda, unless they were brochures positively describing the majority Vietnam report, color photos of Humphrey (once it was clear that he would be the nominee), or placards declaring "We Love Mayor Daley." And if the crowd broke out in chants, the band quickly drowned them out—unless the demonstrators screamed on behalf of Humphrey or, even better, Daley. Antiwar delegates from California, New York, New Hampshire, Wisconsin, and Oregon found themselves treated like wayward children as they were relegated to the back of the convention hall. Their microphones would be kept purposely underamplified to prevent disruption. McCarthy delegates reported finding it impossible to even stand up and have a conversation. To do so would immediately bring what one called "a squad of huskies ready to keep order." At one point, helmeted police dragged Alex Rosenberg, a member of the New York delegation, which was a hotbed of McCarthy support, out of the hall for failing to produce his floor pass.[23]

The press faced similar restrictions. Daley imposed rules preventing more than two reporters per network to walk the convention floor for fear they might find a dissident delegate to appear on camera. Television coverage was replete with scenes of security guards openly tussling with reporters. One punched CBS correspondent Dan Rather in the stomach; another CBS correspondent, Mike Wallace, got socked in the jaw. After a while the job of roving political correspondent had been broadened to include the responsibilities of both pugilist and ringside analyst.[24]

The scene inside the hall well illustrated the cultural clash that defined the Democratic Party in 1968. The defenders of the Cold War bipartisan consensus—confident that they understood the true nature of the Communist threat—squared off against the determined antiwar activists, who were just as sure that the old guard had it all wrong. The southern boosters of legal segregation did battle with the black activists demanding their place at the table, and the Democratic bosses tussled with the young reformers insisting that their voices be heard.

Yet the struggle between these competing forces paled in comparison to the scene outside, where on the streets of Chicago the counterculture faced off with the city's police, many of whom had been raised in the same working-class neighborhoods as Daley. Resentment ran deep. Demonstrators regularly taunted the cops as "pigs" or raised their right arms and screamed "Sieg Heil." These were not the idealistic antiwar activists who had rung doorbells for McCarthy in New Hampshire. Most of that contingent (encouraged in part by McCarthy) had stayed far away from Chicago, fearful of the potential violence. Those who did come represented the most radical wing of the antiwar movement, a subset of the youth counterculture that viewed participation in the political process as selling out. "Heightening the contradictions" was of far greater interest than changing minds. Two key protest groups descended upon Chicago. One was the National Mobilization Committee to End the War (MOBE), led by David Dellinger, Rennie Davis, and Tom Hayden, one of the authors of the Port Huron Statement, a manifesto that became the ideological basis for the New Left and the credo of the movement's calls for a more participatory democracy. MOBE openly offered support to the Vietcong and viewed the antiwar movement's failure to stop the war as a rationale for embracing more confrontational tactics. The time had come, said Hayden, to "risk our necks to take democracy back, a time no longer for visionary platforms but for suffering and physical courage." In their planning document for Chicago,

MOBE said that the demonstrations would serve to highlight the fact that "American society is being destroyed by its unrepresentative government." MOBE's participation in the protests, however, was about more than just opposition to the war in Vietnam, which they viewed as merely one manifestation of America's corrupted political system. "We are coming to Chicago," said Hayden, "to vomit on the politics of joy, to expose the secret decisions, upset the nightclub orgies, and ace the Democratic Party with its illegitimacy and criminality."[25]

The Yippies, led by Abbie Hoffman and Jerry Rubin, constituted the other protest group. Their radicalism far exceeded that of MOBE. To them the venality of the political system was obvious; by sparking outrage they hoped to expose it to the world. Hoffman's guiding principle of "We encourage everything"—as well as his adroitness at playing to the news media—led the group's members to make an escalating series of outlandish threats. Yippies claimed they would pose as taxi drivers and take delegates across the border to Wisconsin. They said they would drug delegates' food and have "hyperpotent" male Yippies seduce their wives, daughters, and girlfriends. They would burn draft cards to spell out "Beat Army," and they would nominate a pig for the nation's highest office (they actually tried to do the last one of these). For the Yippies, Chicago was as much performance art as it was politics. Not surprisingly, their antics garnered the most headlines and did significant damage to the image of genuine war opponents. Indeed, very little that happened on the streets of Chicago that August gave the American people any insight into the conscientious young men and women who had worked so tirelessly to end the war in Vietnam.[26]

Chicago instead became a battleground between two hardened groups committed to confrontation: one willing to accept violence to get their point across and the other more than willing to use overwhelming force to maintain order. Their showdown began in the shadow of tragedy. On Thursday, August 22, before delegates had even began to arrive, a seventeen-year-old runaway from South Dakota named Dean Johnson brandished a handgun in front of two policemen. Johnson's weapon misfired, but the cops' didn't. Johnson was shot three times and died. Amazingly, his death would be the only recorded fatality among the protesters at the convention.[27]

On Sunday the Yippies kicked off their protests/performance act with a "Festival of Life" in Lincoln Park, which they contrasted against the Democrats' "Convention of Death." Replete with music (the Detroit rock band the MC5), free food, and copious amounts of drugs, it also featured skirmishing between cops and bottle- and stone-throwing demonstrators yelling "Pigs eat shit! Pigs eat shit!" By the evening, the situation teetered on the knife's edge as more young people streamed into and a new shift of officers arrived on the scene, ready for battle. The flash point came when the police demanded that the protesters leave. Curfews in the park had rarely been enforced in the past, and the cops would have been well-served to simply let sleeping hippies lie. But with Daley's edicts in mind, there would be no concessions. At 11:00 PM a skirmish line of police began to walk through the park pushing demonstrators farther back until only a few thousand remained. Both sides eyed each other warily. Then a Yippie shouted out, "Your mother sucks dirty cock." That was all it took. Enraged cops instantly rushed the protestors. Those unlucky enough to be caught were beaten mercilessly with billy clubs. Even members of the demonstrators' medical contingent, dressed in white, were not spared. Police chased down those able to escape the initial melee just so they could beat them some more.[28]

The refusal to allow protesters the opportunity to demonstrate ensured that a tense situation would be made far worse—and far bloodier. Hoffman found it simply "inconceivable" that the police continued to make an issue out of protesters trying to bed down for the night. The Walker Report, a follow-up report to the National Commission on the Causes and Prevention of Violence that chronicled the week's fighting, concurred. It would conclude that the police's decision to enforce the curfew sparked the week of violence to come.[29]

To be sure, antiwar protesters provided the police with plenty of provocation. They hurled bricks and bottles, threw pieces of pavement and bags of feces, and taunted the cops with disgusting insults. Some of their leaders simply shrugged at the violence—or viewed it positively. "A movement cannot grow without repression," declared Jerry Rubin. After the first night of violence he said, "This is fantastic and it's only Sunday night.... They might declare martial law in this town." For Hayden, the fighting was a "100% victory in propaganda." People, he said, needed to be "faced with the existential question of giving their life" and "asked what they are willing to do to stop the war." Another Yippie, Stew Albert, spoke even more positively about the violence. It's "a revolutionary wet dream come true"—a view shared by many of the protesters.[30]

But none of that provocation excused the wanton cruelty of the Chicago police, many of whom threw away their nameplates as they waded into the defenseless and cowering crowds. "Individual policeman, and lots of them, committed violent acts far in excess of the requisite force for crowd dispersal or arrest," concluded the Walker Report. When Daley opened the convention with the declaration that as long as he remained mayor "there is going to be law and order in Chicago," police officers took his words to heart, firing tear gas canisters and yelling "Kill, Kill, Kill" as they charged into the crowds. It didn't matter whether demonstrators were male or female, aggressive or prostrate, or even if they wore a clerical collar. They all received the same treatment. Journalists in particular would find themselves singled out, especially photographers and cameramen. "Get the camera, get the camera," the officers would yell before swinging their billy clubs. Of the three hundred reporters assigned to cover the comings and goings outside the hall, more than one in five, said the Walker Report, would be arrested, injured, or have their equipment damaged. The situation became so untenable that the publishers of the *New York Times* and the *Washington Post*, the three major television networks, *Time*, and the local Chicago papers sent a telegram to Daley, accusing his police of deliberately beating journalists and trying to prevent them from covering the unfolding violence. Speaking on-air, NBC newsman Chet Huntley declared, "The news profession in this city is now under assault by the Chicago police."[31]

The violence reached its zenith on Wednesday, August 28, and it came in lockstep with the increasingly tense situation inside the convention hall. The nine-month antiwar insurgency had come to a head, as the antiwar activists finally forced the party to debate the war in a public forum. Even though Humphrey had already announced his support for the party platform's language on Vietnam, the antiwar contingent remained resolute in trying to insert a minority plank into the platform calling for a bombing halt. Such a move, said former Kennedy aide Ted Sorensen in a speech to the convention delegates, would give voters "some hope for an end to this miserable war." He pointed out (correctly) that Democratic primary voters overwhelmingly opposed US policy in Vietnam. In contrast, he said, the platform language supported by Humphrey represented a position "on which Richard Nixon and Barry Goldwater could run with pleasure."[32]

The one man who didn't speak up during the debate was McCarthy. While it would have been unheard of for a candidate to speak in person to the convention with the nomination still in doubt, McCarthy's advisors believed that the discussion over the minority plank offered the right moment to break with precedent. A McCarthy appearance in the amphitheater would have had an electrifying impact, both in lending a boost to the antiwar wing and giving fresh hope to his fleeting chances of winning the nomination. It was a long shot, but what did McCarthy have to lose? Three times Steve Mitchell called the candidate and implored him to come to the hall. Each time McCarthy refused. "I've always been running against Johnson; if he shows up I will," he told his increasingly desperate aides. The comment offered a revealing insight into McCarthy's view of the race. He never truly aspired to the presidency, but simply wanted to register his opposition to Johnson's policies. Once Johnson dropped out and his unlikely campaign had gone from the realm of a principled but futile challenge to one capable of reaching its goal, he increasingly lost interest in the entire endeavor. Inertia rather than ambition had brought him to Chicago. As he said the previous day to the California delegation, "The people know my position." And so a political movement that cultivated such promise and enthusiasm in New Hampshire, Wisconsin, and Oregon ended dispiritingly at the national convention, abandoned by its leader.[33]

The delegates instead listened as the supporters of the majority plank made their case. Maine senator Edmund Muskie argued that the differences between the two sides seemed starker than they were in reality. Louisiana congressman and House majority whip Hale Boggs, head of the party's platform committee, read from a declassified military briefing, which claimed that enemy capabilities in the demilitarized zone would increase 500 percent if the bombing stopped. Ohio congressman Wayne Hays took a different approach; he attacked the antiwar radicals who "would substitute beards for brains, license for liberty and riots for reason." They want "pot instead of patriotism, sideburns instead of solutions," he said to boisterous and sustained cheers. In the end, the majority position—with Humphrey's backing—won handily. However, the *New Republic* later analyzed the votes and noted that in no state where a presidential primary had been held did less than 63 percent of its delegate vote for the antiwar plank. In the states with the most tightly controlled delegations, such as Texas, South Carolina, and Illinois, the majority position won over-whelming support. The greater the openness of the political process in any particular state, the more likely its delegates were to support the minority plank.[34]

With defeat at hand, the New York and California delegations at the back of the hall began singing "We Shall Overcome" and chanting "We Want Peace" as they pinned black armbands on their sleeves in protest and waved two fingers in the air—the antiwar symbol for peace. The singing got so loud that convention managers ordered the band to strike up a tune. Their song selection: "Happy Days Are Here Again."[35]

While the Democratic Party was coming apart inside the convention hall, the action outside heated up again. Wednesday, August 28, was the only day antiwar groups received an actual permit to demonstrate, so on a steamy afternoon ten thousand demonstrators gathered in front of the band shell in Grant Park, not far from the Hilton Hotel, where the convention delegates (and three presidential candidates) were staying. The police, there in full force, insisted that demonstrators could not march at all or risk arrest. Once again the city's inflexible restrictions increased the potential for violence.

The day's events, punctuated by speeches from antiwar activists, Vietnam veterans, and such celebrities as Norman Mailer, William Burroughs, and Dick Gregory, began relatively smoothly. Though participants yelled the occasional "pig" at officers surrounding the park, the scene remained tran-quil. But in the late afternoon a young man climbed a flagpole to lower an American flag. The cops forcibly detained him, which led to further taunting, projectiles thrown by the protesters, and even an effort to raise a Vietcong flag in its place. The police needed no more provocation. Once again, those who had come simply to listen to the speeches were beaten alongside those hurling insults. Simply being in the park meant you were a troublemaker. MOBE organizer Rennie Davis tried to separate the police from the most hot-headed protesters and quickly became a target himself. "Get Davis!" yelled the cops as they rained blows down on him. He staggered away, covered in blood. For his fellow MOBE leader Hayden, the unprovoked attack was the breaking point. In a fiery speech he told the assembled crowd, "We must move out of this park . . . and turn this overheated military machine against itself. Let us make sure that if our blood flows, it flows all over the city, and if we are gassed that they gas themselves."[36]

Demonstrators proceeded, en masse, from Grant Park to the Hilton, where another line of police and national guardsmen wearing gas masks and toting bayonet-tipped rifles met them. They chanted, "Dump the Hump," "Fuck You LBJ," and "Ho Ho Ho Chi Minh." Provoked once again by flying objects and protesters who kicked and punched them, the police responded with a final burst of violence. It would later become known as the "Battle of Michigan Avenue." Teddy White, who stared down at the proceedings from inside the Hilton, had a different take. "At about 7:55 in my notes, I read that the demonstrators are now chanting: 'Fuck You, LBJ, Fuck You, LBJ, Fuck You, LBJ.' Ten minutes later, I find that my notes read, at 8:05, 'The Democrats are finished.'"[37]

White's description is memorable. "Slam! Like a fist jolting, like a piston exploding from its chamber, comes a hurtling column of police . . . into the intersection, and all things happen too fast: first the charge as the police wedge cleaves through the mob; then screams, whistles, confusion, people running off into Grant Park, across the bridges, into hotel lobbies." White went on to describe the police clubbing practically anyone they could get their hands on and then dragging them into patrol wagons any way they could. They lifted their own police barricades and used them as battering rams against the crowd. Hippies were again chased caught and then beaten with police batons. Journalists and bystanders were sent tumbling through the glass at the Haymarket Inn on the first floor of the Hilton. The officers then went trudging through the broken glass to pick up those hurt and bludgeon them some more before arresting them. Even bar patrons were set upon.[38]

Overcome by a seemingly primordial desire to inflict pain, the police were merciless. According to a reporter for the *Milwaukee Journal*, as quoted in the Walker Report, "In many cases it appeared to me that when police had finished beating the protesters they were pursuing, they then attacked, indiscriminately, any civilian who happened to be standing nearby." Said another witness, "To my left, the police caught a man, beat him to the ground and smashed their clubs on the back of his unprotected head.... As I stopped to help him, the police turned on me. 'Get that cock sucker out of here!' The police were angry. Their anger was neither disinterested nor instrumental. It was deep, expressive and personal."[39]

From their hotel rooms above Michigan Avenue, the three announced candidates for the Democratic nomination watched the violence below. McGovern was furious; "Do you see what those sons of bitches are doing to those kids down there?" McCarthy was somber. He compared the cornering of the marchers after first allowing them to protest to the treatment of Native Americans. "We always told them we were taking them to a happier hunting ground and then we surrounded them." His staff set up an ER unit for the injured in their suite. The next night they became victims of the violence themselves, when cops stormed their rooms and pulled campaign workers out of bed, claiming that the staffers had thrown items from their windows on the officers below. McCarthy came down to the lobby in his bathrobe to confront the police and escort his young charges back to their rooms. Later he would walk out to Grant Park and tell the demonstrators that he was "happy to be here to address the government of the people in exile." Humphrey was unsympathetic. From his hotel room he could clearly hear the protesters in Grant Park screaming in unison, "Fuck the Hump! Fuck the Hump." With eyes watering from the tear gas that wafted from the park below, he told reporters that the protesters "don't represent the people of Chicago."[40]

While the pitched battles would continue throughout the evening, those few violent minutes outside the Hilton would have an enduring political impact. News cameras recorded much of the mayhem, but because of an ongoing electricians' strike, it was not shown live. Instead, the recorded images of violence would be rebroadcast, over and over, on the TV sets of the eighty-nine million Americans watching from home. When the protesters taunted the cops with cries of "The whole world is watching," they didn't know how right they were. The pictures from the streets would end up being interspersed with live shots from inside the hall of satisfied, laughing, and smiling Democratic delegates cheering the nominating speeches and the evening's proceedings. Dan Rather managed to reach Daley on the convention floor to ask about what happened outside. The mayor assured him that the Chicago police would never use "undue violence" in dealing with demonstrations. They are, said the mayor, the "finest men in America." Rather's CBS colleague the veteran political correspondent Eric Sevareid had a different view. He said the situation on Michigan Avenue made it "the most disgraceful night in the history of American political conventions."[41]

Viewers would soon witness even more acrimony. As the delegates began viewing images from Michigan Avenue on portable TVs smuggled into the amphitheater, calls were made to adjourn the night's proceedings. The usually mild-mannered and generally uncontroversial Democratic senator from Connecticut Abraham Ribicoff gave voice to the growing anger. Tasked with putting McGovern's name into nomination, Ribicoff instead departed from his proposed remarks to tell the audience that if McGovern were to be nominated as president, "we wouldn't have Gestapo tactics on the streets of Chicago." The audacity of Ribicoff's words momentarily stunned the delegates into silence. Then the crowd exploded. Antiwar delegates rose to their feet in adulation. Mayor Daley stood too. Angrily pushing a floating balloon out of his way, he cupped his mouth and screamed at Ribicoff, "Fuck you, you Jew son of a bitch, you lousy motherfucker, go home." Others in the Chicago delegation, only twenty feet from the speaker's podium, joined in with similar taunts and catcalls. Ribicoff held his ground, staring down at Daley with a look of smug satisfaction and declared, "How hard it is to accept the truth. How hard it is."[42]

The conflict between the urbane, liberal Ribicoff and the profane, working-class Daley exposed another widening gulf among Democrats: white collar versus blue collar, college educated versus working class, socially liberal versus socially conservative. On one side stood a liberalism defined increasingly by an adherence to principle, expanded democratic participation, and an emphasis on social justice—and less on the economic populism of the past. On the other side resided the politics of order and parochialism, transactional to its core. This was precisely the divide clearly exposed by the appeal of George Wallace's antielite populism for once-loyal Democratic voters.

The Ribicoff-Daley showdown, however, had a more immediate effect. "Each battle is now beamed into the nation's rumpus rooms," said the *Wall Street Journal*. For those watching at home, the televised spectacle erased any doubt about the dysfunction within the Democratic Party, and it offered the best possible rationale to vote for Republicans in November. How could Democrats ask the American people to entrust them with the responsibility of running the country for four more years when they couldn't even run a national convention?[43]

The division and violence in Chicago was not, however, going to derail Humphrey. If anything, it strengthened the resolve of establishment Democrats to see him get the nomination. At a little after midnight that evening, Pennsylvania finally sent him over the top—the state where only a few months earlier McCarthy had won 90 percent of the vote in a nonbinding primary. Humphrey sprang to his feet and began clapping. He kissed the television screen when an image of his wife Muriel, who was in the hall, appeared. But Humphrey's brief moment of joy would be fleeting. "There was nothing to celebrate but wreckage. The night Vice President Humphrey was nominated was one of the most dismal that either he or any of us around him have experienced," said speechwriter Ted Van Dyk. "It was like a wake." Earlier that evening, during the balloting, Humphrey rose suddenly and walked alone into the suite's bedroom. When his doctor, Edgar Berman, followed after him a few minutes later, he found Humphrey weeping.[44]

The only major decision left for Humphrey would be his choice of a running mate. Rebuffed by Ted Kennedy, Humphrey went instead with Muskie, who he believed would help with Catholic voters and would represent a sober counterweight to his own exuberance. The pick would prove to be one of the best decisions that he made in the campaign, even though Muskie's home state of Maine did little to help Humphrey's chances in the Electoral College.

The next night, Thursday, August 29, Humphrey delivered his acceptance speech. He would later call it his most difficult assignment and one that "tested every nerve in [his] body," in part because of his fear that there would be a staged walkout by antiwar delegates. The speech went off without a hitch, but it was an uninspired effort, defined far more by what Humphrey didn't say then what he did. Although he declared that America stood on the cusp of a new day, his remarks felt grounded in the past—and the proud traditions of the party he now led—rather than his aspirations for the future. He spoke of "a state of law and order" rather than a "police state" and an America in which "neither mob violence nor police brutality have any place." But he gave little hint as to how he would achieve this goal. He refused to condemn the overzealousness of the Chicago police and instead blandly commented, "We have learned the lesson that violence breeds more violence." Stuck with a party platform that pledged more of the same on Vietnam and his abiding fear of adopting an independent course of action, Humphrey stuck to vague generalities. Though he acknowledged the "serious differences...within our party on this vexing, painful issue of Vietnam," he failed to offer any indication of how his policies would differ from those of Johnson.[45]

With the nomination secure, the speech represented Humphrey's best opportunity to reach out to the peace camp and soften his position on the war. No longer did he need to cower in fear of Johnson's wrath. As the presidential nominee of his party, the delegates and those watching at home would have expected nothing less. But he extended no peace offering. The closest he came was when he read a prayer from Saint Francis of Assisi: "Where there is hate, let me sow love; where is there injury, pardon; where there is doubt, faith; where there is despair, hope; where there is darkness, light." The touching sentiment reflected Humphrey's hope that the fractures exposed over the previous four days could be quickly mended. But

Humphrey's inability or unwillingness to reach out to those Democrats who viewed his nomination with apprehension was striking—and did not go unnoticed.[46]

When Humphrey finished, Muskie and McGovern joined him on the convention stage. McCarthy had refused Humphrey's entreaties to join him for the traditional postconvention demonstration of party unity. It would serve as a fitting conclusion to Humphrey's four days in Chicago. He had arrived poised to attain his lifelong goal of being the Democrats' presidential nominee. He left as that standard-bearer, but of a party that had torn itself apart.

Part VI

The General Election

"Overconfidence Is Not Our Thing"

n 1832, the French writer Alexis de Tocqueville traveled across the United States and witnessed firsthand the nation's eleventh presidential election, a fairly ho-hum affair in which the incumbent president Andrew Jackson handily defeated the Whig senator from Kentucky, Henry Clay. Yet the way in which the race captivated the nation amazed de Tocqueville. "As the election draws near," he wrote, "the activity of intrigue and the agitation of the populace increase" as the "citizens are divided into hostile camps, each of which assumes the names of its favorite candidate." With a touch of hyperbole, he wrote, the campaign is "the daily theme of the press," "the subject of every private conversation," and "the sole interest of the present." While "this ardor is dispelled" and "calm returns" once a winner is chosen, "who can refrain from astonishment that such a storm should have arisen?"[1]

Tocqueville words capture an essential element of the emotions that accompany an American presidential election, which, for a brief moment every four years, preoccupies the nation. On Labor Day weekend in 1968, as the candidates refined their attack lines, honed their calls for national unity, and prepared for the general election campaign, a very different sentiment could be felt across the land: most Americans wanted it to all just be over.

Given McCarthy's groundswelling grass-roots insurgency, Kennedy's rousing efforts to bridge America's racial divisions, and Rockefeller's dramatic national barnstorming, the primary season suggested American politics had taken on a new vitality. Yet by September the country found itself choosing between a presidential nominee who had never contested a party primary, a twenty-year political veteran whose most marketable political attribute was being better than the alternative, and a segregationist bomb thrower whose sole purpose in the race was to play the role of spoiler. "'Anything can happen' was the catchphrase of the spring," wrote Michael Janeway in the *Atlantic Monthly*. "In August, the world passed through a sort of looking glass and all the anythings seemed to add up to nothing much at all." The electorate grasped the underwhelming nature of their electoral options. Approximately half told pollsters they'd rather have someone else to vote for.[2]

The Democratic and Republican nominees embodied the political status quo. On Vietnam, little daylight could be found between their positions. On law and order the words they used to discuss the issue, rather than actual policy variances, most sharply defined their differences. Humphrey ran on the politics of nostalgia and the Democrats' New Deal legacy. Nixon castigated the "failures" of the Johnson years and called for political change without providing any sense of what that change might look like. Wallace offered voters the appeal of a quieter time when the blacks and the kids knew their place. An election once so full of promise became, as Wallace would say, a choice between Tweedledum and Tweedledee.[3]

———

Nominating conventions are historically the moment when the disparate constituencies within each of the nation's two major political parties come together, iron out their differences, and rally behind the party's chosen leader for the general election. The Democrats lacked any such comity in 1968. Hubert Humphrey had been subjected to perhaps the most divisive and humiliating nominating process in American history. He had needed to do two things in Chicago: separate himself from Lyndon Johnson and align the various wings of the Democratic Party—the unions, the South, the blacks, and, perhaps above all, the antiwar left—behind his candidacy. He failed on both counts. As the race kicked off, the vice president trailed Nixon by double digits and was barely ahead of Wallace.

The public image of Humphrey and the Democrats that emerged from Chicago could not have been more devastating. "The convention presented to the vast nation-wide audience," wrote James Reston in the *New York Times,* "a picture of division, of old-fashioned city bossism, of clashes between the young and old, of events out of control and of a party unable even to govern itself or maintain order." The Democrats' disunity would be magnified during the next four weeks. Humphrey's campaign seemed to operate under a cloud of dysfunction. Everywhere he went on the campaign trail antiwar demonstrators would be waiting, with chants of "Dump the Hump," and "Stop the War." His attempts at party fence-mending would be swiftly undercut by his comments on the violence in Chicago. "We ought to quit pretending that Mayor Daley did something that was wrong," insisted Humphrey, "He tried to protect lives." While this accurately reflected public opinion, which was overwhelmingly supportive of the police, it gave millions of liberal Democrats one more reason not to rally behind their party leader. Days later he tried to backtrack, and then reversed himself again, which only bolstered the increasingly popular notion—and one reflected in his internal polling—that Humphrey, while a nice man, had no core.[4]

Humphrey emerged from Chicago with no clear strategy for shrinking Nixon's lead. Even though Humphrey was almost certain to be the nominee of the party after the death of Kennedy, only at the tail end of the Democratic Convention did his advisors begin laying out a game plan for the fall. In an August 12 memo Larry O'Brien recommended creating a "politically oriented research team on Nixon"—a mere three weeks before the beginning of the general election campaign. Only days before the convention began, the Humphrey camp had still not settled upon the best message for the fall campaign. Not that they would have much luck in getting it out; Humphrey had no money, and Democratic donors, horrified by the violence in

Chicago, had little interest in squandering their resources on a candidate whose prospects appeared hopeless. "You launch a campaign with Gallup or Harris saying you're sixteen points down in the polls: political realists have a tendency not to reach into their pocket quickly," said O'Brien.[5]

Johnson, who had already done so much to undermine Humphrey's prospects, continued to be unhelpful. After the vice president said that US troops in Vietnam might soon begin to come home, Johnson declared, in an address to the American Legion in New Orleans, that "nobody can predict" when such a thing might happen. He recounted for the audience a conversation with General Creighton Abrams, his new military commander in Vietnam, about the potential peril of carrying out the suggestion "made by some of our enemies abroad and some of our friends at home to stop the bombing." It would, said Johnson, lead "to more Americans being killed."[6]

Humphrey also received little assistance from his own party. "With few exceptions," he wrote in his memoirs, "the Democratic party did not campaign for me with much enthusiasm until the very last days of the campaign." On a trip to California in early September Humphrey pulled Senate candidate Alan Cranston into a men's room at Los Angeles International Airport and begged him, at the very least, to "mention our names" in his stump speeches. The Humphrey-Muskie campaign would be reduced to sending out self-congratulatory press releases as fellow Democrats publicly endorsed the nominee of their own party.[7]

On September 19, Humphrey finally received a potential boost to the campaign when Ted Kennedy appeared at a rally with him in downtown Boston. The crowd, estimated in the low five figures, was one of the largest of the campaign to date. But any hoped-for momentum would be stifled by antiwar protesters who drowned out both men's speeches with cries of "Dump the Hump," "Stop the War," and "We Want Gene." One of the demonstrators even held up a papier mâché likeness of the vice president's head covered with blood. The constant interruptions came as a shock to Kennedy, who had never before been publicly booed on his home turf. It drew a furious response from the visibly angry Humphrey, who said the actions would "disgust" the American people and "injure the cause of peace." The front page in the next day's Des Moines Register offered evidence of the impact the disruptions were having: it showed the vice president and the antiwar contingent side by side with a headline that read "Humphrey and the Hecklers." (The Nixon campaign had its own strategy for dealing with such disruptions. The candidate asked his aide John Ehrlichman to get the Secret Service to "rough them up." When told that they would prefer not to take such measures, Nixon requested a "flying goon squad" be created. Instead, Ehrlichman enlisted local off-duty cops who were more than happy to "give the bum's rush to screamers and chanters.")[8]

The protesters and hecklers underscored the piteous nature of Humphrey's campaign. "Every stop from August through October, all the way through, that six or eight weeks there...was just disaster," said his close aide Bill Connell. Humphrey and Muskie told the few partisans who showed up to their events that a vote for the GOP would be a vote to roll back more than two decades of progress. But few listened. All they heard were the demonstrators, the hecklers, and an exasperated man trying and failing to pacify them. Columnist Stewart Alsop marveled at how Humphrey had been transformed from one of the most liked politicians in America ("Nobody hates good old Hubert") to a "sort of national whipping boy" blamed for all that had gone wrong with the country. Humphrey's image became so tarnished that the Nixon camp spoke internally of the need to define him more as "a subject of pity than scorn." Inside the campaign things weren't much better. State directors begged the national headquarters for the most basic campaign paraphernalia such as bumper stickers and buttons (Humphrey would make the same complaint to his staff, asking them, "Where the hell is the campaign?"). "I wish somebody would tell me the theme of the campaign," came a plaintive demand from Humphrey's Florida office. An NBC News correspondent quoted an unnamed Humphrey aide saying that the campaign didn't necessarily feel discouraged because "overconfidence is not our thing."[9]

Yet even as the election began to feel more and more hopeless, Humphrey still wouldn't turn on Johnson. In an interview with foreign reporters he declared, "I am not a prisoner of LBJ. Whatever you may accuse him, he has not captured me." No one found such words even remotely believable. Both publicly and privately, Humphrey's fellow Democrats were urging him to make a break with Johnson or risk being seen as an extension of his presidency. Humphrey's advisors needed little convincing that the road they were on would surely end in defeat. "As of now we've lost," O'Brien told the candidate. "It's on every newsman's lips.... Unless you change direction on this Vietnam thing, and become your own man, you're finished." Yet Humphrey refused to even entertain the idea. In addition to the disruption it would cause—and the angered response from the White House that it would almost certainly elicit—he continued to believe that it would do more harm than good. Ultimately, what kept Humphrey from breaking with the president is that he hadn't yet hit rock bottom. At the end of September, he did.[10]

First came a Gallup poll that showed his national support had dipped to 28 percent, only seven points higher than Wallace, and fifteen behind Nixon. This came on the heels of New York Times and Newsweek stories that suggested Humphrey could receive fewer electoral votes than Wallace. In California, a state with a huge registration edge for Democrats (and one that was essential to Humphrey's hopes for victory), Nixon was leading. (A Humphrey campaign memo from mid-August called the effort there "a vast political wasteland.") Even in Humphrey's home state of Minnesota the race was considered a toss-up. Humphrey expected wavering Democrats to return to the party they had supported for years, but more and more it appeared that many had drifted, in the words of the Washington Post editorial page, to the "redneck candidate." The same day the Gallup poll dropped, Humphrey spoke at Reed College in Portland, Oregon. Hundreds of students (by one estimate half the student body) walked out of his speech, shouting "Stop the War," "Murderer," and "Racist." At a luncheon later that day in Portland, a clearly exasperated Humphrey labeled the hecklers "American-style Hitler youth."[11]

The final straw came two days later in Seattle. That night at the city's Civic Center Humphrey experienced the single worst treatment of the campaign as demonstrators, brandishing a bullhorn, incessantly heckled him. "You've had equal time. Now shut up!" he shouted back. But it had no effect. He pleaded with the demonstrators to act like "ladies and gentlemen" and even interrupted the proceedings to allow the protestors to talk.

Humphrey's bullhorn-toting interlocutor responded, "We have not come to talk with you, Mr. Humphrey, we have come to arrest you." Humphrey's humiliation was now complete. Here stood the vice president of the United States, one of the great liberal leaders of his generation, six weeks from Election Day, barely nudging out a racist southern demagogue and arguing with a "shaggy-haired" hippie, who demanded that Humphrey be tried for "crimes against humanity."[12]

O'Brien later said that Humphrey was punished in 1968 for being a "good boy" to Johnson, but the wound went far deeper. He had long bent over backward to go along with the political currents of anti-Communism—and in the process paid a terrible price. The irony of course is that Humphrey understood better than most the political consequences of US involvement in Vietnam. In 1965 he had correctly predicted that the liberal wing of the party would be most vocal in its denunciation of the war and that escalation would risk undoing the Democrats' governing coalition. Upbraided by his commander in chief, however, he did what far too many Cold War liberals had done for twenty years: he got along to get along. At one point such political timidity had brought a temporary political benefit, but no longer. Humphrey told his staff that night in Seattle, "I'm probably going to lose this election ... but win or lose, I'm going to speak my mind, and I'm going to fight." Unable to defeat the antiwar activists who had tormented him for months, he made the decision he should have made in Chicago— to join them. The next day, in Salt Lake City, Utah, he finally offered his party and the nation what they wanted: a break with Johnson's policies in Vietnam.[13]

———————

Humphrey's Salt Lake City speech became the turning point of the fall campaign. Paid for with the last pennies of his dwindling financial resources, the speech was the political equivalent of a Hail Mary pass. Before it, the vice president's campaign had been an embarrassment. After it, he became a viable candidate with the political momentum that took him to the cusp of victory.

When the moment came for Humphrey to chart his own course on Vietnam, the disagreements inside the campaign mimicked the fierce debates that had roiled the party for years. O'Brien, Van Dyk, and Humphrey confidant Senator Fred Harris wanted a strong statement in support of a bombing halt. Connell and top aide Jim Rowe strongly opposed Humphrey even delivering the address. "There is only one interpretation that would be made," said Rowe, "and that is that you are a disloyal vice president." After hours of heated arguments, and after Humphrey was told, once again, that the draft remarks evoked the desultory spirit of a candidate who lacked the courage to stand up for himself, Humphrey finally exploded. "I am sick and tired of hearing this. I am insulted. I have guts. I am my own man." A few secretaries were brought in as Humphrey kicked everyone else out of the room and dictated the basic outline of his speech.[14]

Minutes before the address aired, Humphrey called Johnson to warn him what was coming. In his memoirs, he claimed that Johnson responded by saying, "I gather you're not asking my advice." In reality, White House tapes recorded a cordial phone call with no dramatic showdown. Nonetheless, for the first time, Humphrey did not ask for the president's permission.[15]

While the speech offered a general overview of Humphrey's foreign policy vision, all the attention would be focused on a few carefully constructed lines:

> As President, I would stop the bombing of the North as an
> acceptable risk for peace because I believe it could lead to success in
> the negotiations and thereby shorten the war. This would be the best
> protection for our troops. In weighing that risk—and before taking
> action—I would place key importance on evidence—direct or
> indirect—by deed or word—of Communist willingness to restore
> the demilitarized zone between North and South Vietnam. Now if
> the government of North Vietnam were to show bad faith, I would
> reserve the right to resume the bombing.[16]

Upon close examination, it is difficult to find much distance between Humphrey's position and Johnson's. LBJ himself said in a conversation with Senate Minority Leader Everett Dirksen, "A literal interpretation would show there's no great difference in it and our present policy." The fact that so many people came away from Humphrey's remarks convinced that he strongly supported a bombing halt, O'Brien joked, "proves again that people don't read." Nonetheless, in making even a half-hearted call to stop the bombing—and thus appearing to separate himself from Johnson—Humphrey had taken an essential step. "The great majority of people," read one internal pollster's guidance to Humphrey, "don't give a damn about HH having a position on any issue distinct from LBJ—what matters is the image of independence."[17]

His aides, including George Ball, who had resigned the post of US ambassador to the United Nations only days earlier to assist the campaign, convinced reporters that the vice president had decisively broken with Johnson. The *New York Times* charitably wrote that Humphrey's staff considered the speech's caveats about a bombing halt—which the vice president had once so painstakingly obsessed over—to be mere "window-dressing" for the larger message of independence from Johnson. Writing in the *Washington Post*, columnist Joseph Kraft called Humphrey's language itself "not very impressive," but nonetheless noted that by taking a tentative step away from the White House position on Vietnam he had exhibited "the kind of qualities required to make an effective fight for the Presidency." The same journalists who had practically buried the vice president only a few weeks earlier now called his Salt Lake City speech the engine for his political comeback.[18]

Johnson, not surprisingly, viewed Humphrey's gambit as a betrayal, and, when asked to hit the trail in early October for his vice president, he petulantly refused. "You know that Nixon is following my policies more closely than Humphrey," he complained to aides. In his memoirs he alleged that America's South Vietnamese allies used the vice president's words as an excuse to drag their feet on attending peace talks in Paris. Nixon, for his part, said Humphrey's speech would end "all chance" of a breakthrough in Paris, a claim publicly undercut by a statement from Averell Harriman, the chief US negotiator with the North Vietnamese in Paris, who said it would not jeopardize the talks.[19]

McCarthy was unimpressed too, calling the speech "good openers for twenty-five cent poker" but not much else. He still refused to endorse

Humphrey and instead spent the first week of October covering the World Series, between the defending champion Saint Louis Cardinals and the Detroit Tigers, for *Life* magazine. Among antiwar liberals, McCarthy would not be the only one unmoved by Humphrey's words. In mid-October, the *New Republic* sneered at the vice president's "break" with Johnson. "A partial bombing halt is as useful as a broken button," wrote the magazine's editors. Even mistrust of Nixon was not enough to convince them to support Humphrey's candidacy. "Sitting on the sidelines doesn't become a political journal of opinion and if we could endorse Humphrey (or Nixon) we would. We can't." The *Nation* followed suit, noting that by the time he had "belatedly broke the ice" on Vietnam, "the water was so shallow that he did not get his ankles wet." A week later, when the magazine's editors officially refused to endorse the Democratic nominee, they argued that "a lesser evil' is still an evil." Such statements would later contribute to the largely unproven charge that liberals stayed home on Election Day in 1968 and cost Humphrey the race.[20]

In retrospect, the Salt Lake City speech represented as much a turning point for the Democratic Party as it did for Humphrey. For much of the previous year Democratic mandarins had sought to marginalize antiwar voices in the party by refusing to allow their views on Vietnam to shape policy or political decisions. By the fall of 1968 that position was no longer tenable. The antiwar faction had become too vocal, their advocacy too significant, and their influence in the party simply too potent to be ignored. An emerging movement of antiwar activists and operatives who viewed American power with suspicion and even contempt would need to be accommodated if Democrats were to have any hope of retaining the presidency. For antiwar activists, Salt Lake City would presage a far greater victory. From that point forward, they, not the hawks, would dictate the foreign policy direction of the Democratic Party. McCarthy had dealt the first blow, but in a very real sense, the Cold War bipartisan consensus died in Salt Lake City on September 30, 1968.

More immediately, however, the speech resurrected Humphrey's candidacy. "The goddamn thing had a magical effect," recalled Connell. "Instead of the students getting up and raising hell...people were cheering him."

The "pickets, heckling, and hostility diminished and virtually disappeared from that moment on," wrote Humphrey. New signs began popping up at campaign rallies: "If You Mean It, We're With You" and "Stop the War—Humphrey, We Trust You." For the first time, money began pouring into the campaign. Humphrey's events were suddenly bigger and more boisterous. The return of Democrats started with a trickle in the days after Salt Lake City and became a tidal wave by Election Day.[21]

Behind the scenes, Humphrey told his staff to narrow the campaign's message to three core issues: "Who can you trust...who can get peace...who can hold this country together." On the stump Humphrey sounded like a new man, lambasting Nixon for his refusal to debate him and for his chronic fence-straddling on the issues. "Before I get through with him he'll have a blowtorch on his political tail like he never had before," said Humphrey in an appearance before ten thousand partisans in Jacksonville, Florida. He also aimed his sights squarely on Wallace, who was making inroads into Humphrey's base of union support. Labor leaders reported that surveys of their membership showed strong backing for the former Alabama governor; "Wallace for President" buttons adorned blue collars on factory floors across the industrial northern heartland. In early October, a poll of eight thousand members of a United Auto Workers (UAW) local in Flint, Michigan, showed Humphrey trailing Wallace by ten points (and the UAW had long been one of the more racially tolerant unions). In the steel plants around Pittsburgh, Wallace's numbers were even better. During a tour of "lily-white" Warren, Michigan, a UAW stronghold, the reporting team of Evans and Novak found, through their informal surveys, that support for Wallace could launch "a full-fledged political revolution."[22]

So, the day after Salt Lake City, Humphrey traveled to Wallace's backyard, Knoxville, Tennessee, to challenge him directly. Calling him an "apostle of the politics of fear and racism," he linked Wallace to hate groups like the KKK and John Birch Society and even compared his rise in prominence to that of Hitler. He recounted Wallace's antilabor and poor crime-fighting record in Alabama, his cronyism and corruption, his intimidation of political opponents, and what Humphrey described as a deliberate campaign "to bring this nation to the brink of broad-scale civil disorder." Seeking to link Wallace to Nixon, he accused his Republican opponent of aping Wallace in his "perfumed and deodorized" attacks on the Supreme Court. Though delivered in the South, Humphrey's speech was actually intended to sway white northerners still flirting with the Alabaman. That effort, it turned out, would be given even greater impetus by the third-party candidate himself, because on October 3, 1968—for the first time in anyone's memory—George Wallace found himself momentarily speechless.[23]

By the first days of October 1968, Wallace had reached the apex of his political rise. Featured on the covers of *Life*, *Time*, and *Newsweek*, Wallace, according to the *New York Times* led in seven states versus only four for Humphrey. According to a Harris poll, more than half the country thought he "would handle law-and-order the way it ought to be handled." His campaign rallies remained as enthusiastic, well-attended, and unruly as ever— twenty thousand greeted him at Boston Commons (far more than Humphrey turned out), and thirteen thousand in Fort Worth. The overflow crowds lapped up his paeans to the policeman and the firefighter, the beautician and the truck driver—and his harsh attacks on the anarchists, the hippies, and the meddling, liberal elite. Angry and bigoted taunting of reporters and demonstrators as well as fisticuffs between pro- and anti-Wallace forces was the norm.[24]

As his poll numbers began topping 20 percent Wallace suddenly became a major political problem for both parties. Humphrey worried about Wallace eroding his support among blue-collar workers. Nixon feared losing the votes of disaffected and resentful whites—people who without Wallace in the race were likely to vote Republican. If Wallace won just enough states, he could prevent Nixon from getting to 270 electoral votes. This would throw the election into the House of Representatives, where each state delegation would cast a vote for president. Since Democrats controlled the most congressional delegations—and they wouldn't be beholden to the electoral results in their state—it would likely have meant a Humphrey victory. So Nixon soon followed Humphrey's lead, though he muted his criticisms for fear of alienating Wallace's supporters. Instead, he reminded those mulling a third-party vote that they would be throwing away their ballot on a candidate who couldn't win, thereby indirectly helping Humphrey.

Nothing the two candidates did, however, could match Wallace's own self-sabotage in his choice of a running mate. All else being equal, Wallace would have preferred to run alone, but many states required a vice presidential candidate to be on the ballot with him. Wallace's close aides wanted a national figure, someone who might lend credibility to the ticket while also extending their electoral possibilities outside the Deep South and into places like Kentucky, Tennessee, the Carolinas, and Virginia. A. B. (Happy) Chandler, the one-time commissioner of Major League Baseball and former governor and senator from Kentucky, seemed like the perfect candidate. Wallace, however, was unconvinced. "Well, you know, that fellow's liberal now....He's the one...that integrated baseball." Chandler's tenure had indeed coincided with the breaking of color barrier by the Brooklyn Dodgers in 1947. As governor of Kentucky he had mobilized the National Guard to protect black students integrating previously segregated schools. Further complicating matters, Chandler was unrepentant in his pro–civil rights positions. As speculation mounted that he would get the vice presidential nod, Chandler told reporters, "I wouldn't change my record if I could."[25]

Sure enough, as Chandler's name began to leak, Wallace's backers publicly denounced the pick. His campaign chairman in Kentucky called Chandler an "out-and-out integrationist" and promptly resigned. Others threatened to follow suit, including Texas billionaire Bunker Hunt, one of the campaign's biggest financial contributors. Wallace quickly reversed course: Chandler was out. Hunt had been pushing for Ezra Taft Benson, a former Eisenhower administration official and prominent right-wing spokesman. But Benson was a leading figure in the Mormon Church, and while many Mormon leaders were privately supportive of Wallace, they worried about the public relations hit that the church would take and forbade Benson from accepting a place on the ticket.[26]

Wallace instead turned toward a candidate whose name had floated around the campaign for several weeks—General Curtis LeMay. Wallace, who believed that a military man would appeal to soldiers and veterans, could hardly have done much better than LeMay. During World War II and later as chief of staff of the air force, he became an infamous and, in some circles, heroic military figure. His decision to fire-bomb Japanese cities had killed hundreds of thousands of civilians but also helped to short-circuit an invasion of the Japanese mainland by American troops. In 1948 he had led the successful Berlin airlift during the Soviet siege of the city, and he had enshrined the nation's nuclear deterrent capabilities as head of the Strategic Air Command. With his square jaw; gruff, no-nonsense manner; and un-compromising views on the use of military force, he represented the ulti-mate foreign policy hawk.

LeMay, however, had one glaring liability. When it came to the use of American military force, he was something of a nut. "If you have to go [to war], you want LeMay in the lead bomber," John F. Kennedy said. "But you never want LeMay deciding whether or not you have to go." Practically no man in American public life spoke more loudly about the benefits of air power—and countenanced the use of nuclear weapons—than LeMay. Indeed, in the 1964 black comedy *Dr. Strangelove*, director and cowriter Stanley Kubrick used him as a model for the flamboyant and hawkish General Buck Turgidson. Unlike Wallace, LeMay was neither a segrega-tionist nor a doctrinaire conservative, but on war and in particular the use of nuclear power he was practically an evangelist. Indeed, LeMay, who be-lieved that the United States should tell the North Vietnamese to "stop their aggression, or we're going to bomb them back into the Stone Age," joined the ticket, in large part, because he thought Wallace would turn things in Vietnam over to the military. Unsurprisingly, then, even though Wallace's aides warned LeMay over and over against raising the nuclear issue when preparing for his introductory press conference in Pittsburgh on October 3, LeMay could not leave well enough alone.[27]

It took only one question after Wallace had introduced the general to the assembled reporters and the millions watching on live television to light the firestorm. As a potential vice president, one reporter asked, "What do you feel your experience can bring to the solution of the nation's domestic problems...and secondly, as a potential President, what would be your policy in the employment of nuclear weapons?" Unsurprisingly, LeMay chose to answer the second question first. "We seem to have a phobia about nuclear weapons," he replied. "I think to most military men that a nuclear weapon is just another weapon in our arsenal. . . . I think there are many occasions when it would be most efficient to use nuclear weapons." With the first words out of his mouth, LeMay had already begun to self-destruct.[28]

After playing down the contamination risks that came from nuclear testing, LeMay argued that while nuclear war would indeed be horrible, "It doesn't make much difference to me if I have to get killed in the jungle of Vietnam with a rusty knife or get killed with a nuclear weapon. As a matter of fact if I had the choice I'd lean toward the nuclear weapon." Many Americans at home likely preferred a third option, dying not by a corroded blade or an atom bomb. His efforts at reassurance did little to help. "I don't believe the world would end if we exploded a nuclear weapon," he told the increasingly slack-jawed reporters, cheerfully noting that after viewing films of Bikini Atoll, which had been the site of numerous nuclear tests, he had become convinced that people were not only exaggerating the dangers but also downplaying the positive side of nuclear weapons. "The fish are all back in the lagoons; the coconut trees are growing coconuts; the guava bushes have fruit on them; the birds are back." Even the rats had become "bigger, fatter, and healthier than they were ever before," LeMay said.[29]

Ed Ewing, a Wallace press aide, recalled that when he looked over at his boss, he had "never seen anybody angrier in his life." An ashen-looking Wallace finally edged up to the microphones. He tried to nudge LeMay aside to clarify matters. "General LeMay hasn't advocated the use of nuclear weapons, not at all. He discussed nuclear weapons with you. He's against the use of nuclear weapons and I am too." It was true LeMay hadn't actually called for the use of nukes in Vietnam—yet. But the reporters were not about to let LeMay off that easy. Jack Nelson, of the *Los Angeles Times*, kept pushing the point. "If you found it necessary to end the war, you would use them, wouldn't you?" LeMay rose to the bait. "If I found it necessary, I would use anything that we could dream up . . . including nuclear weapons, if it was necessary."[30]

Again Wallace tried to correct the record. LeMay preferred to use no weapon, he said, but if the "security of the country depended on the use of nuclear weapons," he would, like any national politician, counsel that they be used. Wallace began to walk away from the microphone, assuming—or perhaps hoping—the press conference had finally come to a merciful end. But the general was not done. "I know that I'm going to come out with a lot of misquotes from this campaign," said LeMay, demonstrating for the first time that morning actual self-awareness. "And I'll be damn lucky if I don't appear as a drooling idiot whose only solution to any problem is to drop atomic bombs all over the world."[31]

The damage had been done. "Anyone who can speak so lightly about the use of nuclear weapons has no conception of the reality of their terror," said Humphrey. Henry Reuss, a Democratic congressman from Wisconsin, more directly captured the sentiments of many. He called LeMay a "Neanderthal." Even Nixon hit the Wallace-LeMay ticket for its "irresponsibility and excessively hawkish attitudes." While noting that he shared Wallace's concerns over crime and the conduct of foreign policy in the Johnson administration, Nixon added, "I'm against a lot of these things. The difference is—I'm for a lot of things. And that's what we need now." It was a typically inscrutable comment from Nixon, but his willingness to directly confront his nominal anti-Humphrey ally—and risk alienating his supporters—showed how badly Wallace had been hurt.[32]

For weeks, the New York Times editorial page had been pillorying Wallace as a racist agitator and a figure so unqualified to be president that any American who voted for him would "bring shame upon this country." Picking LeMay had been the political equivalent of throwing chum in a tank full of sharks. The Times wrote that by choosing the general, Wallace had "underscored his total lack of qualification to have charge of this country's enormous nuclear arsenal." LeMay's selection had been intended to boost Wallace's standing on national security; instead, it reminded voters of the man they had rejected four years earlier, Barry Goldwater.[33]

The Wallace camp tried to argue that the general's words had been blown out of proportion, but they were so desperate to get LeMay away from reporters that they sent him on a "fact-finding" mission to Vietnam. In the airport in San Francisco, as he prepared to board a flight to the Far East, LeMay was cornered by reporters and somehow found himself saying that China never would have gotten involved in the Korean War had it not been for "traitors" in the United States. "Who are those traitors?" LeMay was asked. "You know who they are as well as I do," he snapped. Days after returning from his mission he gave a speech at Yale on environmental conservation, an issue, oddly, that was close to his heart. Though the address would be well received, news headlines were dominated by LeMay's statement in the question-and-answer period that he favored both birth control and abortion, comments sure to go over badly in the working-class Catholic enclaves in the North on which Wallace increasingly relied.[34]

LeMay's constant gaffes threw Wallace back on his heels. Compounding his problems, at virtually the same time as the disastrous Pittsburgh press conference, America's labor unions launched a massive campaign highlighting Wallace's antilabor record in Alabama. They distributed 125 million pamphlets, made four million phone calls, and sent one hundred thousand canvassers door to door in order to remind their members that Alabama was an anti-union, right-to-work state and that a vote for Wallace would be a vote against the financial future of the workingman. AFL-CIO head George Meany boasted that, after the convention, "All Humphrey had was us"—a comment that had more than a kernel of truth.[35]

In the end, Wallace became his own worst enemy. For four years he had reaped political benefit from campaign rallies that teetered on the brink of full-scale riots. After a while the disorder and chaos made him seem less like the man who could clean up America's problems and more like the person partly responsible for them. Wallace, who once reveled in the abuse he took from hecklers, began looking increasingly haggard and even frightened by the barrage of abuse being hurled at him on the stump. His frustration soon showed. "You're a little punk," he growled at one demonstrator. In San Diego, protesters who took the satirical approach of screaming "We Want War" drowned out his remarks. At a rally in Texas, demonstrators yelling "Sieg Heil" were so loud and persistent that he had to leave the stage without finishing his speech. In New Mexico schoolchildren booed him. When he did speak he complained that reporters were distorting his words and claimed that polls showing his numbers slipping had been "rigged by the Eastern Establishment moneyed interests."[36]

Though Wallace pressed on, his candidacy was clearly in decline. The combination of his own excesses; the counterattacks from Humphrey,

Nixon, and labor; and the traditional skepticism that third-party candidates generally receive at the tail end of presidential elections slowed his momentum. The race had become a two-man battle—between a newly reinvigorated Hubert Humphrey and Richard Nixon, whose efforts to run out the clock were slowly beginning to unravel.[37]

16

The Final Storm

When Richard Nixon began the 1968 presidential campaign, he did so with one advantage that none of his opponents could match: a clear, well-earned understanding of what not to do. Eight years earlier, he had faced off against John Kennedy, an opponent with a fraction of Nixon's political experience—and he made a complete mess of it. An ill-considered pledge to visit all fifty states, his tired and unshaven appearance at the first presidential debate with Kennedy, the selection of the listless Henry Cabot Lodge as his running mate, and, overall, a defensive and furtive campaign strategy—all contributed to a razor-thin loss. In a race that Nixon could have won, a calmer and more relaxed candidate beat him. "I spent too much time in the last campaign on substance and too little time on appearance. I paid too much attention to what I was going to say, and too little to how I would look," said Nixon a year after the loss.[1]

His 1968 campaign would be predicated on not making the same mistakes again. In a memo drafted by Bob Haldeman, the campaign's chief of staff, in the summer of 1967, he offered a preview of Nixon's strategy. "The

time has come for political campaigning—its techniques and strategies—
to move out of the dark ages and into the brave new world of the omnipresent eye," namely television, wrote Haldeman. Traditional campaign
methods—"six speeches a day, plus several handshaking receptions, a few
hours at factory gates and a soul-crushing travel schedule"—were tactics of
the past. "The candidate's time, energy and thinking will be programmed for
maximum possible benefit. And maximum benefit is defined as reaching the
most people most effectively. And this does not necessarily mean in the flesh."
On a practical basis, this meant Nixon would spend most of his time (and
advertising dollars) in seven of the states with the largest electoral prizes:
Pennsylvania, New Jersey, Ohio, Texas, California, Michigan, and Illinois (the
list would later be expanded to include New York). He would not schedule
multiple events on a single day or travel to the point of exhaustion. Instead,
Nixon would take on the mantle of de facto incumbency and focus on a few
well-controlled public appearances and regular days off from the trail.[2]

An almost obsessive emphasis on television replaced traditional campaign
outreach. Every day the Nixon camp choose one major news lead, picked
far in advance and designed to achieve maximum TV coverage. While it
would be necessary to occasionally "react" and "counterattack," Haldeman
had written the previous year, a "complete, preconceived plan" would be
essential. The campaign would not be thrown off kilter by the whims of
local GOP politicians or the daily grind of the news cycle. Instead, Nixon,
as much as he could, limited his public events to small town-hall meetings
in which a few local residents would lob softball questions at him, the answers to which he'd previously memorized. The campaign called it the
"Hillsboro approach," named after the tiny hamlet in New Hampshire
where it had been first executed during the Republican primaries. Nothing
would be left to chance. Everything—who posed the questions, what was
asked, who was in attendance, even what time the events took place, to
ensure maximum exposure—would be laid out in advance. A typical event
would include a housewife, a businessman, a blue-collar worker, and at
least one black participant, to demonstrate Nixon's embrace of diversity. A
reporter might also be asked to participate, but always a local one, awed to
be in Nixon's presence and unlikely to ask a tough question.[3]

When campaign rallies or speeches occurred, they followed a consistent script: minimal policy specifics, attacks on the Johnson/Humphrey administration, and declarations that new leadership in Washington would turn the country around. "Why should you hold a rally for 15,000 or 20,000 people when with TV you can get the whole state?" said one Nixon aide. The campaign tried to give the press corps not more but fewer visuals to work with and to make sure that what they got on film would shine only a positive light on the candidate. While Nixon attracted large crowds at rallies, his staff considered such gatherings useful mainly for the positive images they would produce for TV advertisements.[4]

Nixon's ads ran constantly, paid for by a war chest that dwarfed Humphrey's. Narrated by a stern-voiced Nixon and featuring jarring music and disturbing, occasionally psychedelic imagery of bloodied antiwar protesters, cities in flames, and soldiers in Vietnam under fire, the ads depicted a nation mired in chaos. One of the most effective spots, entitled "Convention," juxtaposed images of street violence with pictures of Humphrey and delegates on the floor of the Chicago convention. Another, called "Failure," asked, "How can a party that can't keep order in its own backyard keep order in our 50 states?" Others combined affecting images of smiling couples, happy children, laughing teenagers, dignified senior citizens, and nondemonstrating young people "who can change the world" (including, ironically, a stock photo of Grateful Dead guitarist Jerry Garcia).[5]

After the tumult of the previous year, Nixon's aides understood the importance of convincing Americans that a vote for Nixon meant a vote for what a half century earlier another Republican presidential candidate, Warren Harding, called a "return to normalcy." "The next President must unite America," went one ad. "He must calm its angers, ease its terrible frictions, and bring its people together once again in peace and mutual respect." Reflecting the key themes of his acceptance speech at the national convention (the ads often used snippets from the address), Nixon's message was simple: a vote for the Democrats meant four more years of anarchy, protest, and war; a vote for Nixon meant harmony.[6]

Nixon was hardly the first presidential candidate to micromanage his public image, but few had ever done it quite as brazenly. As Pat Buchanan noted in the fall of 1967 in a memo entitled "The Uses of Television," he would "rather see RN on Cronkite telling a joke about himself than being quoted on Vietnam." He went on, "If a guy doesn't know if RN can handle Vietnam, then a minute won't convince him. But a guy who thinks RN is a humorous S.O.B. might be stunned and convinced by a grinning RN telling about his 'getting stoned in Caracas'" (a reference to then–vice president Nixon being attacked during a trip to Venezuela in 1958). In September, the usually buttoned-down Nixon appeared on the popular sketch comedy show *Rowan and Martin's Laugh-In* and delivered the show's memorable catch phrase, "Sock it to me!" Democrats derisively called the unprecedented effort at media management "the Richard Nixon Show." National reporters, who were kept as far away as possible from the candidate, complained about Nixon's refusal to engage on the issues. But they could hardly refuse to cover his public events (though frustration with his refusal to talk with them repeatedly found its way into their coverage).[7]

A candidate who had straddled the divide between conservatives and liberals in the run-up to the nomination did the same in the general election. By the fall of 1968, the country had taken on a more conservative political orientation. Many Americans were distressed by the notion of welfare recipients collecting government checks but not working and began to believe that more federal programs meant an inexorable move toward socialism. Most believed that the best way to deal with crime was not more compassion but more police. None of this meant, however, that voters longed for the specific policy elements of a conservative revival. As Free and Cantril had written in 1967, while the electorate might have been ideologically conservative, it was operationally liberal. A majority of Americans favored Johnson's Great Society initiatives—and not just Medicare and Medicaid, education, Head Start, and environmental laws, but even the antipoverty programs that lay at the heart of the era's political backlash. This political division of labor in the minds of voters made it incumbent upon Nixon to say all the right things in the rhetorical direction of conservatism while also leaving the overall impression that when it came to prized government programs, voters had nothing to fear from a Republican president. Indeed, when confronted by Democratic accusations that he planned to cut Social Security and Medicare, Nixon said he wanted to increase benefits.[8]

At times, his vagueness reached almost comical proportions. "Shall we continue or shall we go forward?" he asked a partisan crowd in Ohio in late October. "I believe we must go forward." When asked by a high school student during an event in Saint Louis what new ideas the candidate was bringing to the table for young voters, Nixon genially responded, "All I can say is this: you've got to look at the man, and you've got to answer that question yourself." Humphrey aides joked that Nixon had gotten so evasive he wouldn't even offer a prediction on who would win the World Series.[9]

Pushed on the issue of whether he agreed with the Johnson administration's policy of withholding federal education funds from school districts that refused to desegregate, he managed to come down on both sides. In one breath he said he supported the Supreme Court decision to integrate schools, and in the next he said, "When you go beyond that and say it is the responsibility of the federal government and the federal courts to, in effect, act as local school districts in determining how we carry this out…then I think we are going too far." Nixon both confirmed his support for integration and criticized federal efforts to stamp out segregation. He had told southern delegates in Miami Beach practically the same thing. By refusing to take a clear position, Nixon allowed—indeed encouraged—listeners to draw their own conclusions about what he would do as president. On the war he took an even more enigmatic stance, constantly telling audiences that he couldn't say what he would do in Vietnam because "Hanoi is listening." Though it is often claimed that Nixon spoke of a "secret plan" to end the war, he never uttered those words. Even suggesting that he had a plan would have been too much for Nixon.[10]

This refusal to offer detailed policy proposals did little to hurt him with voters. After a late-September question-and-answer discussion in Cleveland, Frank Shakespeare, one of the campaign's top media gurus, drafted a memo to Haldeman, cheerily noting, "The viewers were far more impressed with Nixon than on the specifics of his answers." In characterizing their impressions, they used words such as "sincere," "honest," "straightforward," and "like the way he handles himself" rather than referring to a specific policy. The most common phrase, used by almost one in four, said Shakespeare, was "He has the ability to be President."[11]

Throughout most of 1968, the war in Vietnam agitated American politics more than any other issue. By the final leg of the presidential campaign, however, the salience of the war began to fade. Voters hadn't stopped caring (in many polls they listed it as their number one concern), but with Humphrey now talking about bombing halts and emphasizing the urgent need for peace—and Nixon saying very little about the war—voters would be hard pressed to identify any significant difference between the two candidates. (At one point in the spring Humphrey had even said that he didn't think he and Nixon were "too far apart" on Vietnam.) Both wanted to end the conflict; both were fuzzy about how; and neither appeared to be considering a LeMay-like solution. This dovetailed with public opinion. As a Humphrey polling memo from mid-August noted, "There is much more agreement (among Americans) about the importance of the Vietnam problem than about how to deal with it."[12]

Concern over events overseas increasingly had been supplanted by fears over chaos at home. The country, wrote Time, was "dominated by a pervasive and obsessive issue. Its label is law and order." The national anxiety and frustration over crime could be seen in "every conceivable category of race, religion, age, economic status, or political persuasion," wrote Humphrey's pollster Evron Kirkpatrick. "People are fed up," said Kirkpatrick. "There is more demand for federal action in the criminal area than any other area of concern" (and black voters expressed even greater support than whites). Republicans had their biggest advantage when it came to crime, and Nixon drew the sharpest lines between himself and Humphrey on the issue. His speeches and ads brimmed with terrifying statistics. "Crime and violence have increased ten times faster than population"; "daytime burglaries up by 187 percent"; "a murder rate that jumped 34 percent; an assault rate that increased 67 percent." He pledged to be a voice for "those who do not indulge in violence, those who do not break the law," implicitly linking Humphrey and the Democrats to the nation's disorder.[13]

Nixon's actual policy ideas continued to be underwhelming: replace the attorney general, increase wiretapping on organized crime, improve coordination of federal crime fighting policies, and create "a national academy of law enforcement for the training of local police." Crime was largely a local concern, and there were only so many tools at the federal government's disposal. But in truth, the substance of the proposals mattered less than Nixon's tone. He said little about the root causes of crime, like unemployment, poor living conditions, or the hopelessness of America's urban ghettoes. "Without progress," he instead darkly warned, "then the city jungle will cease to be a metaphor.... It will become a barbaric reality and the brutal society that now flourishes in the core cities...will annex the affluent suburbs." These images were racially charged and directly pitched to white audiences—though it must be noted this represented more of an exception than the norm. Nixon's campaign, by and large, avoided the kind of hard-edged racial language of Wallace or even Republicans like Reagan in 1966—and quite deliberately. Doing so risked upsetting the candidate's image as a uniting figure. Indeed, to deflect the accusations that he was playing on racist fears, Nixon would regularly note that blacks wanted law and order just as much as whites, because, after all, "They were the main victims of disorder and illegal activities." Many blacks might have noted that when they were the victims of violence in the Deep South, calls for law and order had not been quite as forthcoming.[14]

Nixon had little interest in winning over black voters (even though he'd won 30 percent of their votes in 1960). In a campaign memo, Buchanan argued that Nixon had far more to gain from ignoring blacks and Jewish voters and instead aiming for working-class Catholic voters. "The power of the Negro and the Jew to damage RN in this election lies in this: The Negro loud-mouths are given access to the public communications media by a guilt-ridden establishment—and the Jews control that communications media," wrote Buchanan. "They're not our voters; and if we go after them, we'll go down to defeat chasing a receding rainbow." Far better to focus on the Irish, Italian, and Polish Catholics of the big cities, said Buchanan, as well as the "white Protestants of the South and Midwest and rural America."[15]

While no other advisor would state the campaign's demographic approach as crudely and bluntly as Buchanan, this had in essence become Nixon's strategy. When asked by reporters why so few blacks attended his rallies, he conceded that while he wanted every vote, "We haven't been going to areas where there are many black faces to be had." Considering that a mid-September Harris poll showed Nixon with a seventeen-point lead over Humphrey among those Americans who held particularly negative and stereotypical views of blacks, the decision shouldn't have come as a surprise. For Nixon, ignoring black voters was a case of addition by subtraction.[16]

Humphrey had no such luxury. Without strong black turnout he had no chance of winning. But if he decried Nixon's and Wallace's focus on law and order as veiled racism, he risked alienating those white voters whose number one concern was the possibility that they or someone in their family would become a crime victim. Conversely, if he started talking tough, he would risk upsetting liberals and black voters. Trying to satisfy both whites and blacks on crime became as difficult for him as talking about Vietnam. In mid-September Humphrey unveiled an eighty-four-point program to "halt riots" and "protect liberty" that sought to cover every crime-fighting base and ended up mollifying few. While Nixon and Wallace painted vivid and frightening pictures of urban lawlessness, Humphrey used generalities. "There are two kinds of politics," he said when asked if law and order was the most important issue in the '68 campaign. "There is the politics of fear and despair, which I do not indulge in, and then there is the politics of hope and inspiration. That is more my kind." When he argued that there existed a clear link between continued economic deprivation and the crime epidemic, Nixon hit back, declaring that "contrary to what this Administration believes and preaches, the war on poverty is not a war on crime and it is no substitute for a war on crime."[17]

While Nixon would regularly conflate civil rights protesters, antiwar demonstrators, urban rioters, and "the criminal and the depraved" as the sources of disorder in America, Humphrey struggled to differentiate between legitimate dissent and crime. When he tried, such as by linking an "escalation of protest" with an "escalation of violence," he was angrily rebuked by liberals who argued that the former enjoyed far greater legitimacy than the latter. When he suggested at one point that if he were dealing with the same conditions that blacks faced in the ghetto, he'd have enough "spark left in" him to "lead a mighty good revolt," conservatives accused him of encouraging law-breaking. His vacillation on the issue meant, according to Kirkpatrick, that "Humphrey's soft image in the area of law and order" hurt the campaign "more than anything else." Indeed, Humphrey was seen as less tough than Nixon and Wallace, less tough than the electorate, and even less tough than his own supporters. Wallace further complicated the crime issue for Humphrey. Anything he said about it would immediately remind voters of the White House's, and in turn Humphrey's, failures. Nixon might have talked in harsh tones but he wasn't threatening to run over antiwar protesters with the presidential limousine as Wallace regularly did. Once again, the presence of a more extreme candidate made Nixon look more palatable.[18]

Since Nixon and Wallace weren't that far apart on law and order, the Nixon campaign believed—not unreasonably—that when Wallace's supporters eventually realized that a third-party candidate couldn't win, they would turn to their man as the next-best option. But by October the ticked off union men, and the embittered white working-class voters who had flirted with the Alabaman weren't moving to Nixon. They were returning to the Democratic fold.

In 1968, just under half the nation's voters were registered Democrats. Less than 25 percent were registered as Republicans. For twenty-eight of the previous thirty-six years, a Democrat had been in the White House. Congress had been in the party's hands for much of the previous four decades, and the tenor of national policymaking favored a liberal vision of government.[19]

In the last two weeks of October these centrifugal political forces reasserted themselves. Though Humphrey still lagged in the polls, the Salt Lake City speech had been transformative. No longer could he be so easily typecast as Johnson's toady. He had reclaimed the mantle of Hubert Humphrey, liberal icon. Overnight, his message got sharper and his attacks on Wallace and Nixon more pointed. "What has Richard Nixon ever done for old folks? Nothing! What has Richard Nixon ever done for schools? Nothing! What has Richard Nixon ever done for working men? Nothing! So what are you going to do for Richard Nixon?—Nothing!" he asked his suddenly large and enthusiastic crowds. Humphrey preached the old Democratic revival sermon—and there were promises galore: a call for doubling the federal investment in education; expanded Medicare; more money for jobs, housing, and health care; a Marshall Plan for the cities; more generous Social Security benefits. But Humphrey wasn't trying to convince the electorate there would be happy days ahead, but rather far worse ones if Republicans won the White House. He reminded the party faithful that Democrats had fought for them while Republicans opposed "every piece of social legislation that has benefited this country." Under Johnson and Kennedy there had been "eight years of good times," said Humphrey. A Nixon win would mean "you won't have to worry about what color you are, you'll be out of work." He raised the specter of the old Dick Nixon, the one who had delighted in calling Democrats "traitors" and "communists." He told them that a vote for Wallace would be a vote for the apostle of American hate and that "any union man who votes for one of them is not a good union man."[20]

He also went after Nixon for his continued refusal to debate, going so far as to label him "Richard the Chicken-Hearted." Publicly, Nixon opposed a debate because under the equal time doctrine Wallace would be allowed to participate (which might increase the chances of the election going to the House of Representatives). Privately, the Nixon team had no interest in providing Humphrey with the political oxygen that a head-to-head meeting could potentially create. Still, the cumulative effects of Humphrey's resurgence and Wallace's decline began to show in the polls. A Harris survey had the race within five points in mid-October. Gallup still had Nixon ahead by double digits, but by October 21 the margin had fallen to eight. In several must-win states for Humphrey, like Michigan, New York, Massachusetts, and Pennsylvania, polls had him in the lead.[21]

Nixon, however, continued to follow the same game plan—do no harm. Still the odds-on favorite, he and his campaign maintained its air of self-confidence. Personal appearances became rarer, as Nixon regularly took days off from the trail to devote attention to what the campaign considered the deciding factor—radio talks and TV commercials. When he did appear in front of actual voters, he delivered, in the words of David Broder, "the same speech to the same group of Americans and answered the same questions." But as Humphrey's surge became more pronounced, Nixon took the gloves off during a late-October swing through Ohio. On a day that the campaign dubbed "Law and Order Day," Nixon unloaded on Humphrey, calling him a "do-nothing candidate" and an "adult delinquent." He mocked his statement that if he had lived in a slum, he "might have started a pretty good revolt," and declared that "freedom from fear" could only be restored in America if Humphrey was defeated. The next day's *Los Angeles Times* offered a lesson about the risks of such an approach. "It was the Richard Nixon of old Tuesday . . . heaping scorn on Vice President Humphrey," said the *Times*. "Who gave Buchanan the keys to the mimeograph machine?" asked the *Associated Press*. "Tricky Dick," the partisan persona of the old Nixon that was supposed to be kept locked up until Election Day, had returned. Nixon quickly backtracked.[22]

The campaign instead decided to break out of its pattern of canned television appearances, and turned instead to a series of canned speeches. Dubbed "Operation Extra Effort," the plan was to deliver ten policy speeches for radio coverage. One of the first sets of remarks dealt with Nixon's claim that a "security gap" with the Soviets was growing. Nixon asserted that the Kennedy and Johnson administrations had decided that America "would no longer try to be first" in national defense, but simply be content "to stay even." He even expressed fears of a "survival gap" with the Communists. The next morning, Humphrey hit back, offering a statement to reporters based on Defense Department information that showed Nixon's estimates of Soviet strength were simply wrong. In fact, said Humphrey, the United States possessed far greater military capabilities, and he derided Nixon's charges as "irresponsible" and "threatening" to the cause of peace. The counterpunches showed how little Nixon had to gain from getting into a policy fight with Humphrey. Once he took a position that rose above the level of generality, he made himself a target for Democrats. The Nixon campaign has often been criticized for appearing flat-footed at a moment of peril for their candidate, but they possessed few better options. They had made their strategic bed and now they were going to have to lie in it.[23]

Humphrey's surge also brought with it another benefit. Up to this point the campaign had basically no television presence at all. But as Democratic supporters began opening up their checkbooks, the campaign got its TV ad campaign going. Their most effective spots highlighted Nixon's increasingly blunder-prone vice presidential pick. One ad showed the upper right corner of a television while in the background a man cackled hysterically. As the camera pans closer, "Agnew for Vice President?" appears on the screen. It is followed by the words "This would be funny if it weren't so serious." Agnew had by October become the running joke of the campaign. "It didn't take long to conclude that this fellow had a soft underbelly," O'Brien would later comment.[24]

Early in September, Agnew said that Humphrey had been "soft on inflation, soft on communism…soft on law and order," and "squishy soft" on the war in Vietnam. He then compared the vice president to Neville Chamberlain because, like the discredited former British prime minister, Humphrey sought "peace at any price" in Vietnam. These were scurrilous charges, for which Agnew was pilloried (including by prominent congressional Republicans, such as Dirksen and House Minority Leader Gerald Ford). Forced to apologize, Agnew claimed he hadn't been fully aware of the historical implications of the Nazi-appeasement phrase, a statement that, had it come out of the mouth of any other politician, would have been considered preposterous, but in the case of the incurious Agnew seemed quite plausible.[25]

Things with Agnew quickly went from bad to worse. When asked why he didn't spend more times in urban areas—especially since the Nixon campaign had billed him as an expert on cities—he said, "If you've seen one city slum, you've seen them all." In a press conference in Chicago, when asked about the lack of black faces at his events, Agnew responded, "When I am moving in a crowd, I don't look and say, 'Well, there's a Negro, there's an Italian, and there's a Greek and there's a Polack.'" When forced to apologize—again—he confessed ignorance that the term "Polack" was viewed as a slur and said that even in the heat of a presidential campaign it was important that Americans "don't lose our sense of humor."[26]

Agnew's "talent for sticking his foot in his mouth clear up to his patella" was worthy of admiration, joked the *Washington Daily News*. "What will he do next? What will he say?" wondered the *Washington Post*. They wouldn't have to wait long. After a mid-September trip to Las Vegas, as reporters on the Maryland governor's plane slept off their hangovers, Agnew spotted Gene Oishi, a Japanese American reporter who had covered his gubernatorial career for the *Baltimore Sun*. He turned to another scribe and asked, "What's the matter with the fat Jap?" Agnew claimed to be merely expressing friendly concern about Oishi's health—an assertion that none of the journalists took seriously. Amazingly, Agnew used the "fat Jap" line again, this time while traveling in Hawaii, a state with a large Japanese American population. Agnew later joked he had Nixon's "permission to reveal my secret role in our battle plans. I'm assigned the task of insulting all groups equally."[27]

While campaign aides increasingly viewed Agnew as a liability, Nixon was less concerned. When his running mate attacked antiwar protesters as "spoiled brats who never have had a good spanking" and said they "take their tactics from Gandhi and money from Daddy," he was clearly following the Wallace playbook. Nixon would later write that he admired Agnew for standing up to the "vicious onslaught of national political exposure." But Nixon appreciated more than just Agnew's thick skin. His assaults on permissiveness and liberal programs and his racially tinged calls for harsher anticrime measures might have led to the occasionally inappropriate comment, but they played well in the South, in the border states, and among the now wavering white working class up north.[28]

The contrast, however, between Agnew and Edmund Muskie could not have been greater. The Maine senator had turned almost overnight into a political superstar. He brought a critical asset to the Democratic ticket in 1968: a calming and serious presence. Low-key and restrained, Muskie had made few enemies, even in the rough and tumble of American politics. At a campaign rally in Pennsylvania, he invited a persistent antiwar heckler onstage to make a statement. Once the young man finished telling the crowd why they should stay home on Election Day, Muskie patiently explained to a now hushed audience why he was wrong. The press corps swooned. "The man nobody really knew" at the start of the campaign "progressively became the man nearly everybody was talking about," wrote William White in the *Washington Post*.[29]

In the face of Wallace's demagoguery and Nixon's winks and nod to the same, Muskie implored his audience to reject the "apostles of division" and come together in national purpose. "We are being told it is no longer safe to trust each other. People have a responsibility to protect themselves, their families and their property," said Muskie in a speech in Camden, New Jersey. But the real question for the nation, he said, is "whether we can do it with understanding and compassion or with a policeman's club." His optimistic demeanor—and his hard line on Nixon and Wallace—struck a chord with loyal Democrats. The *Associated Press* reported that at practically every campaign stop voters talked about voting Democratic solely because of Muskie. Some polling even suggested that if the Democratic ticket were switched, it might have a better chance of winning in November.[30]

Even with Muskie and Humphrey making up ground, the individual state polls still showed them lagging. For Nixon, Election Day could not come soon enough—especially when word began leaking that peace in Vietnam might be at hand. It seemed inconceivable, but in the last days of the campaign, the issue that had divided, diminished, and destroyed the Democrats now suddenly appeared to be the party's salvation.

Lyndon Johnson had been a Democrat for his entire political life. In his formative years he genuflected before the altar of the New Deal and its patron saint, Franklin Roosevelt. He maintained that reverence throughout his career. Yet as president he'd done little to further his party's fortunes. His domestic policy advisor Joseph Califano recalled, "Never once did I hear him say that he wanted to leave behind a strengthened Democratic Party." Under his watch the Democratic National Committee fell into disarray. The party's voter registration programs were cut, and, according to Larry O'Brien, by the fall of 1968 the committee had not been "staffed or equipped to conduct a successful presidential election." On the state level, Democrats largely fended for themselves. Johnson called himself a "free man first, an

American second, a public servant third, and a Democrat fourth—in that order." His presidency became a tribute to that hierarchy.[31]

Nowhere would his lack of attention to party politics be more pronounced than on Vietnam. As concern about the war grew among the party's rank and file, Johnson made little effort to mend fences. He viewed the dissenters as misbehaving children rather than legitimate voices of opposition, further widening the divisions within the party and feeding the combustible mix that exploded in Chicago. In the weeks after that mayhem, he did little to help Humphrey. He offered almost no public support to the nominee of his party and even prevented him from accessing campaign dollars raised for their re-election before Johnson dropped out of the race. Privately, he complained that Hubert needed to show "he had some balls," oblivious to the fact that Humphrey's efforts to demonstrate fortitude on Vietnam had been held back by the president.[32]

Yet in the last days of October, as talks in Paris between the United States and the North Vietnamese began to heat up, Johnson found himself in the position of providing a substantial boost to Humphrey's electoral chances. The breakthrough in negotiations was not a result of an eleventh hour decision by Johnson to help his vice president. In fact, the president went out of his way to avoid any appearance of assisting him. The benefits of a possible deal would be to burnish LBJ's political legacy. Helping Humphrey was an afterthought.

Since spring the talks in Paris had been stalled by the unbendable preconditions of both sides. The United States demanded that the Communists stop allowing Vietcong rebels to infiltrate the demilitarized zone that divided North and South, end the shelling of South Vietnamese cities, and agree to let the South Vietnamese government join peace talks. Hanoi wanted an unconditional bombing halt and a role for the National Liberation Front (the political wing of the Vietcong) in the negotiations. Neither side showed any willingness to budge.[33]

In the fall, however, with the election only a few weeks away, signs emerged that the North Vietnamese were prepared to take a first step toward getting the talks moving. Soviet diplomats, on behalf of the North Vietnamese, told the White House that if the United States unconditionally declared a bombing halt, it "could create a turning point at the meetings in Paris." The role of the Soviets added a wrinkle to the negotiations. They had unpleasant memories of Nixon's virulent brand of red-baiting, and had concluded, like Hanoi, that their interests would be best served by Humphrey winning in November. The Soviet ambassador to the United States, Anatoly Dobrynin, told by his superiors that he should do everything in his power to ensure a Democratic victory, even offered to provide money to the cash-starved campaign in a face-to-face meeting with the vice president. Humphrey, unsurprisingly, refused.[34]

For the first time, the United States and North Vietnam were engaged in serious negotiations. Press reports suggested that Johnson was on the verge of announcing a bombing halt. Still, he was unwilling to do anything that would be seen as directly assisting Humphrey. On October 16, Johnson held a call with all three candidates, in which he provided an update on the talks, but insisted that they refrain from talking publicly about them for fear of undercutting negotiations. Humphrey's best hope for victory would be a breakthrough in Paris, and now Johnson forbade him from speaking hopefully about the prospects for peace. Johnson seemed to be going so far in trying to avoid accepting a deal that Clark Clifford, for one, wondered whether the president actually wanted to prevent a Democratic victory on Election Day. Faced with a unanimous view among his foreign policy advisors that the deal represented a clear victory for the United States, however, Johnson relented. On October 31, he went on national television to announce a bombing halt over North Vietnam. This had the potential to be the October surprise that Humphrey needed. Coming only two days after McCarthy had finally endorsed him, it looked to many like he just might pull off a win after all.[35]

However, the South Vietnamese government, led by strongman Nguyen Van Thieu, balked. They refused to send negotiators to Paris. Ostensibly, Saigon's intransigence was predicated on its opposition to the National Liberation Front being included as an equal partner at the peace talks. A crucial part of the story lay elsewhere. In the most sordid tale of the 1968 campaign, the Nixon team had lobbied Thieu to reject Johnson's deal and hold out for a better one when their candidate took the White House.

Throughout much of 1968, Nixon worried that Johnson would spring a political trap on him by making peace in Vietnam. A breakthrough in Paris had the potential to boost Humphrey, convince Americans that the end of the war might be at hand, and, above all, cost him the presidency. So when the news first broke of progress in Paris, he did his best to put as negative a spin as possible on a potential deal. He told the press that while he was aware of the ongoing negotiations, "I am also told that this spurt of activity is a cynical, last minute attempt by President Johnson to salvage the candidacy of Mr. Humphrey. This I do not believe." A transparent attempt to look magnanimous was, of course, really a cynical ploy by Nixon to play up the notion that the whole peace project most certainly could be described as an attempt by Johnson to assist Humphrey.[36]

His public pronouncements notwithstanding, Nixon worked behind the scenes with a shadowy political operator named Anna Chennault. For Chennault, the Cold War was not just a geopolitical and ideological struggle, but also something of a vocation. Born in China, she had worked as a journalist and war correspondent, but had been forced to flee her homeland after the Communist takeover in 1949. She married General Claire Chennault, the American commander of the legendary Flying Tigers, a group that ran volunteer missions in Burma and China against the Japanese during World War II. The marriage catapulted her into the world of the "China lobby," a loose alliance of American conservatives, Chinese nationalists, and anti-Communist activists who vociferously cast blame for the "loss" of China to Communism on President Truman, George Marshall, and the Democratic Party as a whole. Chennault quickly became one of the lobby's most appealing members—a well-connected Washington hostess who threw lively parties at her penthouse apartment atop the city's exclusive Watergate complex.[37]

She maintained close ties to the city's key players, particularly those in the Republican Party, for whom she fundraised prodigiously. Her devotion to the GOP was predicated on the goal of maintaining the bipartisan anti-Communist consensus. Alarmed at the possibility that a Humphrey victory in November would mean the end of American support for the regime in Saigon and would provide a boost for the Chinese Communists, Chennault volunteered for Nixon and raised a quarter million dollars for his campaign.

But it would be her political connections that would provide the greatest benefit to the Nixon camp. She introduced the candidate to South Vietnamese ambassador Bui Diem and became the conduit between the campaign, the ambassador, and in turn the South Vietnamese government. In her 1980 autobiography, *The Education of Anna*, Chennault wrote that in a secret meeting with Nixon and Diem, the GOP candidate made clear to the South Vietnamese ambassador that Anna was his "good friend" and urged him to "rely on her from now on as the only contact between myself and your government." What this meant in practical terms is that when Chennault spoke to Diem—and he in turn spoke to his colleagues in Saigon—they could safely assume that she spoke for Nixon.[38]

The Nixon camp also relied on updates from Henry Kissinger, who had close contacts on the US negotiating team in Paris and would later become Nixon's national security advisor and secretary of state. Kissinger, who had been a foreign policy advisor to Nelson Rockefeller, quickly ingratiated himself with the Nixon team (he also attempted to make inroads with the Humphrey campaign, just to ensure he covered every base). But the Chennault connection proved far more crucial. Even under steady pressure from the US government, the South Vietnamese leadership remained deeply reluctant to go to Paris. Chennault and Diem did everything in their power to keep it that way and to convince Saigon that a Nixon victory would mean a better deal than the one Johnson was offering. "Many Republican friends have contacted me and encouraged us to stand firm," Diem cabled Saigon on October 23.[39]

Histories of the '68 campaign—from Teddy White's *The Making of the President, 1968* and *American Melodrama*, written by three British reporters for the London *Observer*, to Jules Witcover's *The Resurrection of Richard Nixon*—have played down Nixon's contact with Diem and Chennault. White wrote that Chennault's actions actually hurt the Nixon campaign. "At the first report of Republican sabotage in Saigon, Nixon's headquarters had begun to investigate the story; had discovered Mrs. Chennault's activities; and was appalled," wrote White. "The fury and dismay at Nixon's headquarters when his aides discovered the report were so intense that they could not have been feigned simply for the benefit of this reporter."[40]

History, however, offers more clarity—and less sympathy—for the Nixon camp. After the later declassification of FBI intercepts, the Chennault/ Diem channel took on a more sinister hue. There had been, in fact, regular contact between the campaign and the South Vietnamese. In reality, the only panic inside the Nixon camp was that their efforts to influence the talks would be found out and revealed on the eve of the election. LBJ, as it turned out, knew about the Chennault channel (he privately called her "that damn little old woman"). Not only did he have Diem under surveillance; Johnson had ordered the FBI to begin tracking Chennault and tapping her phones as well. Agents from the bureau reported that she made regular trips between her Watergate apartment, the Nixon campaign office, and the South Vietnamese embassy. Before his speech announcing the bombing halt, Johnson tried to shut down her efforts. During a conference with the three candidates—on the eve of the bombing halt—he made a veiled reference to Nixon's actions. "Some of the old China lobbyists, they are going around and implying to some of the embassies and some of the others that they might get a better deal out of somebody that was not involved in this. Now that's made it difficult and it's held up things a bit. And I know that none of you candidates are aware of it or responsible for it."[41]

The evidence of Nixon's connection to Chennault created what Clifford called an "extraordinary dilemma" for Johnson. In addition to the enormous diplomatic impact, LBJ had evidence that could turn the election in Humphrey's favor. "Can you imagine what people would say if this were to be known; that we have all these conditions met and then Nixon's conniving with them kept us from getting it?" Johnson asked at one point. Still, such revelations would not come without consequences: the wiretapping of Chennault, an American citizen, while legal on national security grounds, hardly shined a positive light on the White House. If Johnson wanted to play down the notion that the bombing halt in Vietnam had been intended to assist Humphrey, revelations that he was listening in on the conversations of Nixon aides weren't going to help in that process. Larger political and legal questions also loomed. To leak the story to the press or announce it publicly, wrote Walt Rostow in a confidential memo to Johnson, could "gravely damage the country whether Mr. Nixon was elected or not. If they get out in the present form, they could be the subject of one of the most acrimonious debates we have ever witnessed." The thought that Nixon would be elected president—which was the assumption inside the White House—and yet be publicly charged with activity that bordered on treason gave Johnson and his advisors pause.[42]

Johnson's oblique reference to old China hands didn't have the desired effect. In a call with Chennault the night of Johnson's bombing-halt speech, John Mitchell made clear that he was "speaking on behalf of Mr. Nixon." It is "very important," he told Chennault, "that our Vietnamese friends understand our Republican position and I hope you have made that clear to them." At the height of the campaign, Chennault reported that she spoke to Mitchell "at least once a day" and, on his insistence, often from a pay phone. The contacts continued even after the October 31 bombing-halt speech. She told Diem on November 2 to inform Saigon that her "boss" wanted to tell "Diem's boss" to "hold on, we are gonna win." The identity of Chennault's shadowy "boss" has never been established. FBI wiretaps recorded Chennault telling Diem that her "boss had just called from New Mexico," the same day that Agnew's campaign had traveled to the state, but the exact timing of Agnew's visit doesn't quite line up, and Chennault later claimed that she misspoke. Moreover, it seems impossible to imagine that such a sensitive operation would be entrusted to the vice presidential nominee. According to Tom Charles Huston, a young Nixon White House aide tasked with investigating the circumstances around Johnson's bombing halt, it was clear to him that the Nixon campaign played a direct role in the Chennault Affair, and that this involvement went all the way to the top. It is, Huston said in a 2008 interview, "inconceivable to me that John Mitchell would be running around...passing messages to the South Vietnamese government...on his own initiative."[43]

Whether Nixon had been directly involved still remains unknown. It is also unclear whether the contacts convinced the South Vietnamese to stay away. After all, Saigon didn't need to be told they'd be better off with Nixon rather than Humphrey in the White House. Nonetheless, as Clifford would later write in his memoirs, it "constituted direct interference in the activities of the executive branch and the responsibilities of the Chief Executive" and was a "gross, even potentially illegal, interference in the security affairs of the nation." Johnson used another word to describe what was happening— "treason." Even so, he remained reluctant to expose Nixon's behavior.[44]

For Humphrey, the last days of the 1968 campaign became a stomach-churning rollercoaster. The prospect of peace provided him with a jolt of electricity. On the trail, a newfound excitement was in the air; the polls showed the race dramatically tightening (Gallup reported that Nixon led by a mere two points). "Two-three weeks ago I was reading the election was all over," Humphrey told an overflow crowd in Peoria, Illinois; "Mr. Nixon was taking afternoon naps, his campaign cool and efficient. We've cooled it off plenty, and there's going to be a Democratic victory on November 5." Then, just as quickly, the optimism was dashed. As Humphrey was speaking, Johnson had the Secret Service pull Jim Rowe out of the rally for a call. He asked Rowe to tell Humphrey to stop sounding "jubilant" and "enthusiastic" about Vietnam, because, with the South Vietnamese wavering on going to Paris, he might need to "order [US planes] back to bombing tomorrow."[45]

Nixon, in contrast, trumpeted Saigon's reluctance to attend the talks in Paris. A close aide, California's lieutenant governor, Robert Finch, complained to reporters, "We had the impression that all the diplomatic ducks were in a row" and that the South Vietnamese were on board (Nixon knew this to be a lie, having been told the opposite by Johnson). It meant to encourage the notion that the president had been playing politics with the war. Nixon went a step further on the Sunday before the election. Appearing on *Meet the Press*, he said, "I will cooperate in any way President Johnson determines will be helpful," and even volunteered to go to Saigon or Paris to "get the negotiations off dead center."[46]

After being briefed on the details of the Chennault affair—and of Nixon's possible involvement—only days before Election Day, Humphrey was beside himself. "What kind of guy could engage in something like this?" he exclaimed. He privately railed against the "China lobby" and the "little bastards" in Saigon who "wouldn't be alive, if it wasn't for us." While he tried to get his aides to pass a message to the South Vietnamese telling them to either show up in Paris or be publicly denounced by Humphrey, he remained fearful that publicly revealing Nixon's role would boomerang against him. No clear evidence existed definitively linking Nixon to the affair, and he didn't want to be seen to be playing "cheap politics," said Connell. Humphrey was "persuaded that it would be considered by the American people as a last minute, last-ditch kind of thing and that it would be perhaps a lie." As a result, Humphrey "swallowed it," even though practically all of the vice president's aides, as well as Johnson, thought he should go public. Van Dyk later wrote that "ninety-nine out of a hundred men with the Presidency at stake would have had no inhibitions." Once again, Humphrey took what he believed to be the safer path.[47]

On Saturday, huge crowds in New York welcomed Humphrey; on Sunday, in Texas, Johnson gave him an enthusiastic endorsement at a rally in Houston's Astrodome. In one of the few exceptions to his indifference about Humphrey's plight, Johnson delivered a strong speech, one that defended their record and called Humphrey "a healer and a builder" who stood in contrast to "divisive men on both sides" who were "trying to play upon fear and grievances in this country." On Monday, in California, a state where the Humphrey effort had faltered from a lack of organization and grass-roots support, cheering crowds greeted the candidate. In his memoirs Humphrey described a noon parade in Los Angeles as one of the high points of the campaign. "Noise. Enthusiasm. Crowds. Thousands of people packing the streets. A feeling of victory. Ed Muskie and I in the convertible, looking at one another from time to time, sensing that victory was possible." The final Gallup poll showed him behind, but narrowly. The Harris poll had him ahead.[48]

On Election Day, as Nixon flew cross-country from his final rallies in California back to New York, he took his family and key aides aside and warned them that they might have to prepare themselves for yet another crushing defeat. This time, however, would be different. Humphrey had rallied to the very edge of victory; Nixon declined to the very cusp of defeat. In the end, by a popular vote margin of five hundred thousand votes, Nixon was elected the thirty-seventh president of the United States. The storm had passed.[49]

Part VII

After

"They Have Just Elected a Papier-Mâché Man"

F ew men in American history have devoted more time to the pursuit of
the presidency than Richard Nixon. By November 5, 1968, he had
traveled to every state in the country, gone to state fairs and rotary clubs,
and met with Jaycees, businessman, veterans, and policeman. He'd shaken
thousands of hands, repeated the same corny jokes, ate countless rubber
chicken dinners, and delivered the same applause lines. In 1960, he had
driven himself relentlessly, only to fall short. In 1962, he had set himself a
lesser political goal and suffered even greater humiliation. Yet he was undaunted. From the moment he left the last press conference, for six long
years, everything Nixon did came in pursuit of a singular political goal.

At approximately 3:00 AM on the morning of November 6, Nixon sat
down with his close aides to go over the latest returns in his hotel room on
the thirty-fifth floor of the Waldorf Towers in midtown Manhattan. Many
of the same men had been with Nixon—at practically the same hour—
eight years earlier when he realized that Jack Kennedy had bested him. This
time, however, would be different. Though he won the popular vote by only

half a million votes, he defeated Humphrey in the Electoral College 301–191, with Wallace winning forty-six electoral votes. A thousand miles away, in a hotel room in Minneapolis, Hubert Humphrey came to the same realization. As he fought back tears, he turned to an aide and said, "The American people will find that they have just elected a papier-mâché man."[1]

Humphrey had made an extraordinary comeback. Political folklore holds that with one more week to campaign Humphrey might have pulled off the greatest upset since Harry Truman defeated Thomas Dewey in 1948. In reality, Humphrey didn't need more time; he needed more courage. Had he delivered the Salt Lake City speech from the podium at the International Amphitheater in Chicago in late August, he probably would have won. No strategic misstep in 1968 loomed larger. Taking this route would have likely united the party behind him, rallied Democratic donors, put Nixon on the defensive, perhaps brought Eugene McCarthy on board earlier, and given Humphrey the momentum he needed for a tough general election campaign. The economy remained strong, unemployment was low, and he was, after all, the nominee of a party that was still viewed by a majority of Americans as the defenders of the workingman. And in Nixon, Humphrey had the ideal opponent for energizing wavering Democrats.[2]

Despite the fact that practically everything had gone wrong for the Democrats in 1968, Humphrey still almost pulled it off. Had a mere forty-two thousand votes in New Jersey, Missouri, and Alaska shifted from Nixon's tally to Humphrey's, no candidate would have won the 270 electoral votes needed to win the presidency. The election would then have been decided in the House of Representatives, where Humphrey and the Democrats enjoyed a sizable advantage and likely would have prevailed. Still, Humphrey's late rally—and the narrowness of his defeat—could not mask the scope of his loss. In 1964, he and Johnson won forty-three million votes and 61 percent of the popular vote. Four years later, nearly twelve million of those same voters abandoned Humphrey. The Democrats' tally fell to 42.7 percent. LBJ's win in 1964 was never going to be replicated in 1968. Migration from Johnson to a less frightening Republican was inevitable. The size of the flight, however, was remarkable. Forty percent of Johnson voters in 1964 cast a ballot for Nixon in 1968. In all, 57 percent of the

American electorate voted against the Democrats and chose a conservative or center-right candidate. Not since Hoover's loss in 1932 had an American political party seen such a four-year reversal of fortune.[3]

Though it was Humphrey who lost the race, the 1968 election, at its core, represented a fundamental repudiation of Lyndon Johnson. As Humphrey presciently noted at the outset of the campaign, as the nominal incumbent all the dysfunction in American society that rose to the fore that year would be blamed squarely on him. Compounding the misery of his defeat, however, would be the larger toll it took on Democrats as a whole. Humphrey's rejection at the polls came at the same time that a deeper set of political, economic, social, and even generational factors were conspiring against the party, all of which combined to ensure that the party would not quickly recover from their loss.[4]

For Nixon, the margin of victory would be as narrow as the campaign he ran. In the beginning of September, he was polling at 43 percent, and he ended up on Election Day with the same percentage of the popular vote. His win brought with it no coattails, and he became the first president-elect since Zachary Taylor in 1848 to see his party fail to win one house of Congress. While Republicans picked up seats in the Senate, they barely dented the Democratic majority in the House, and state legislative races ran fairly even. Nixon's victory, therefore, did not immediately herald a major electoral realignment. The American people had not embraced the GOP or the party's rightward turn. But just as Johnson's middle path on Vietnam would result in a political muddle, so too would the verdict of the electorate. In ways that would only become evident years, even decades, later, Nixon's triumph ushered in Republican presidential dominance, but also four decades of division, incoherence, and parochialism in American politics.[5]

No single issue did more to ensure Nixon's victory than Vietnam, but the war had an indirect impact on the outcome. Voters saw Nixon as the candidate best able to manage the war and more likely than Humphrey to end it. Yet few Americans reported that Vietnam had been the key question on which they decided how to cast their ballot. Americans were deeply conflicted: only 22 percent backed a pullout from Vietnam, and 37 percent supported further escalation. The rest preferred a cake-and-eat-it-too position of peace and US troops continuing to fight. That Humphrey and Nixon coalesced around similarly opaque positions on the war added to the electorate's confusion. In one postelection study voters were asked to indicate where they believed each candidate stood on Vietnam and then place them on a scale of one to seven, with one representing unconditional withdrawal and seven all-out war. Not surprisingly, Wallace (with LeMay as his running mate) and McCarthy fell on opposite ends of the spectrum. LBJ and Reagan leaned toward the escalation side, and Rockefeller was closer to McCarthy. Humphrey and Nixon, however, were rated almost identically: right in the middle, in virtually the same place that Americans placed themselves.[6]

Vietnam's real impact came far before Election Day. From New Hampshire, to Chicago, to the hecklers who plagued Humphrey throughout the fall campaign, the war divided and dispirited the Democratic Party. The antics and excesses of war opponents became closely linked to the Democrats, further undermining the party's national image. Postelection polls showed that vocal antiwar activists were among the most unpopular groups in the country—even among those who opposed the war. Those who were both against the war and also sympathetic to war protesters made up less than 3 percent of the electorate. Four years later, when many of those same activists appeared as delegates at the Democratic National Convention the political damage would be even greater. It must be said, however, that the mischief of the antiwar contingent was a direct response to Johnson's far more damaging stubbornness and Humphrey's timidity. As frustration over Vietnam grew, LBJ refused to take any steps to bridge the chasm among Democrats, and while Humphrey understood the necessity of bringing the war's opponents back into the party fold, he waited far too long to try to do so.[7]

Thus Democrats intraparty fight over Vietnam would contribute to a substantial erosion of the party's image on foreign policy. In 1964, by a three-to-one margin, voters agreed that Democrats were more likely to keep the nation out of war. Considering that Johnson ran against Barry Goldwater, this was hardly surprising. Nonetheless, it represented a major political shift that reversed a long-standing Republican advantage. Four years later, the numbers told a very different story. Postelection polling indicated that

Americans believed the country's standing in the world had suffered under Johnson's watch, and Republicans now held a two-to-one advantage in polls asking which party would be more likely to keep the country safe. Precisely as Humphrey predicted, escalation in Vietnam divided Democrats and squandered the party's positive standing on foreign policy. It would end up being one of the great unforced errors of American politics, and it would haunt Democrats for decades to come.[8]

Vietnam also came at a moment of maximum political peril for Democrats, as the party's positions on civil rights fueled anger and frustration among northern working-class whites and southern Democrats. Rather than focus their energy on addressing these concerns, party leaders became transfixed by the conflict abroad and immersed themselves in an internecine battle that left little time or energy for other policy matters. "Imagine the sixties without...the Vietnam War," wrote the activist and scholar Todd Gitlin, "and you can imagine an enduring era of reform...a reasonably successful wave of racial integration, a modestly successful War on Poverty, a weakened black power strain." The war ruined those possibilities.[9]

Instead, the nation's crime epidemic and growing racial divisions received far too little attention from Democrats. The result of that negligence could be seen in the demographic makeup of the electorate. The 1968 presidential election was, up to that point, the most racially polarized election in American history. By one estimate, more than 90 percent of African Americans voted for Humphrey, compared to approximately 35 percent of whites. It would begin a trend of Democrats consistently failing to win a majority of the white vote in presidential elections, leading to a further dividing of the electorate along racial lines.[10]

This shift in racial support could be seen most dramatically in the Deep South. The Democrats, who had once been able to rely on about half the southern vote, saw their share of the region's electorate fall to 31 percent in 1968. Only Texas stayed in Humphrey's column (Johnson's one political gift to his vice president). Among southern whites, identification with the party dropped to 57 percent, after being as high as 88 percent in 1952. No longer could Democrats count on a solid bloc of southern electoral votes, which meant that they would enter future presidential campaigns at a distinct disadvantage to Republicans. The emerging outlines of the GOP's so-called Southern Strategy, a phrase popularized by Nixon aide Kevin Phillips in his 1969 book, *The Emerging Republican Majority*, were now apparent. Over the next four decades the country's politics would move steadily rightward, due in large part to the shift of the once solidly Democratic South to the Republican column.[11]

The Democratic decline among white voters would not be restricted to the South. Humphrey relied on heavy union support to narrow the race, but he still only won half of organized labor's votes—a marked decline from the 66 percent that John Kennedy received—and he fared poorly in the white ethnic neighborhoods where JFK did well enough to win in 1960. Explicit racism offers only a partial explanation for this deterioration. By 1968, Americans had become more supportive of civil rights and desegregation efforts than they had been four years earlier. In fact, at no time during the campaign did Nixon suggest that the process of racial integration—and the expansion of civil rights for black Americans—should be reversed. Instead, he spoke of a desire to slow the process down. His message on crime, schools, and housing offered, in the words of one aide, a "subliminal appeal to the anti-black voter." In effect, he played both sides, and in the process ensured the support of both conservatives as well as racial liberals.[12]

Democrats, on the other hand, increasingly came to be seen as a party of black interests. Phillips's take in *The Emerging Republican Majority* sums up the dilemma well. The GOP was fortunate, said Phillips, "not to be weighted down with commitment to the political blocs, power brokers and poverty concessionaries of the decaying central cities of the North, now that the national growth is shifting to suburbia, the South and the West." In that demographic shift lay the GOP game plan on race and national politics for the next forty years—make nods to civil rights, while also subtlety playing on white fears about the costs of racial integration. For Democrats, their deep reliance on minority voters made it virtually impossible to craft a political message that appealed to anxious white voters.[13]

In the end, the white backlash did more than undo the Democrats' governing coalition; it undermined the cause of liberalism. To be sure, suspicion of the nation's governing institutions and leaders did not emerge in

1968; it had long defined American political culture. In the middle part of the twentieth century, however, voters balanced those traditional sentiments with a broad acceptance of the need for greater governmental activism. This uneasy tension between ideology and practicality was the basis of the liberal consensus. Beginning in the mid-1960s, however, that relationship fundamentally changed. The presidential election of 1968 would be the first modern campaign in which the conservative counternarrative that portrayed government as more disruptor than positive force began to dramatically reshape the nation's politics.

The shift would be a gradual one. In 1964, when voters were asked if "Washington is getting too powerful for the good of the country," 52 percent of Americans disagreed. Four years later, 55 percent now answered in the affirmative. By 1972, 60.5 percent of Americans embraced this fearful view of federal power, and after another four years the number rose to 72 percent. At the same time, confidence in government's ability "to do what is right" began a steady and rapid decline, as did the number of Americans who expressed "a great deal of confidence" in either the executive branch or Congress.[14]

These numbers spoke to a generalized fear of federal power, not specific distaste for government programs, most of which remained broadly popular. The key messenger for these attitudes was, of course, George Wallace. In 1968, he won 13.5 percent of the vote—with half of his votes coming from the South (where he won five states). But those nearly ten million votes changed American politics. Traditionally, as we've seen, the Wallace vote is portrayed as an articulation of the nation's racial animosities. In the South there is certainly evidence that race was a decisive issue, as was, it must be noted, regional solidarity (albeit for whites, not blacks). But in the North, a combination of racism, financial anxiety, anger over social disruption, and perhaps above all a sense that middle- and lower-class whites were losing ground drove his support. A strong sense of alienation dominated American politics in 1968, but the antiwar movement did not represent the largest and most influential bloc of disconnected voters; rather, it was those who felt their lives were being negatively affected by black advancement, urban disorder, and diminished economic prospects. Wallace spoke the most directly of any of the candidates to those concerns.[15]

However, Wallace backers could not be pigeonholed as traditional conservatives. Indeed, the Wallace vote did not represent an anti–big government ballot in the way that we think of such things today. Rather, it was specifically focused on the fear that the federal government's increased focus on helping black people took benefits away from whites. Plenty of Wallace voters held deeply prejudiced views of black Americans, but many viewed racial integration in largely parochial, zero-sum terms, in which one group's gain meant another's loss. This fear ensured that the backlash would be not just racially based but also class-based.[16]

As Wallace railed against the federal bureaucracy while simultaneously calling for an expansion of the elements of the welfare state that benefited whites, he played to the nation's ideological contradictions. Wallace provided ordinary white Democrats who disagreed with the racial and cultural liberalism of the national party—but still embraced its focus on economic fairness—with a weigh station on their way to becoming Republican voters. In 1968 he showed the GOP how conservative populism could move once-loyal Democrats away from their traditional political home. But Wallace also demonstrated to Republicans that they should not stray too far from the operational aspects of economic liberalism. Few understood this key lesson of '68 better than Nixon, who governed in his first term as the combination of a Humphrey liberal and a Wallace conservative.

George Wallace's appearance on the national stage came at a crucial inflection point for the Republican Party—and ensured that the GOP's already-commenced rightward tilt would continue. The obvious political benefits of Wallace's populist appeals hastened the decline of the GOP's moderate, pro–civil rights wing. After 1968, no Republican would be able win the party's presidential nod without offering a full-throated endorsement of the right's antigovernment platitudes. However, from a policy perspective, conservative victories are more difficult to discern. Post-1968, Republicans were unable to put a serious dent in the New Deal welfare state or even LBJ's Great Society.

During Nixon's first term, domestic spending, as a share of GDP, rose more rapidly than it had under Johnson. Part of this was due to the fiscal hangover from programs enacted during the Great Society years, but it also spoke to Nixon's inability to significantly roll back federal expenditures. At the same time, government regulation grew noticeably. Nixon's presidency saw the establishment of the Environmental Protection Agency and the enactment of regulatory initiatives like the Clean Air and Clean Water Acts. Nixon signed legislation creating the Occupational Safety and Health Administration, the Consumer Product Safety Commission, and the National Transportation Safety Board. At the end of 1969, he supported legislation that raised the tax on capital gains, lowered taxes for the poorest Americans, and abolished tax breaks for business. Later Nixon would go even further by imposing wage and price controls and taking the United States off the gold standard. Businessmen at the time openly questioned whether the "free enterprise" system could survive the onslaught.[17]

In order to erase the negative reputation of reactionary conservatism, Nixon—on policy issue after policy issue—tried to position the GOP closer to the left. He embraced (but failed to pass) key liberal priorities like universal health care and a welfare reform measure with a generous guaranteed minimum income tied to a work requirement. "Looking back on the budget, economic and social policies of the Republican years," Pat Buchanan lamented in 1976, "it would not be unfair to conclude that the political verdict of 1968 had brought reaffirmation, rather than repudiation, of Great Society liberalism." Many on the right shared this perspective, and saw Nixon as a sellout to conservative orthodoxy. If not for Nixon's tough stance on Vietnam and his attacks on antiwar protesters, the right-wing backlash against him would likely have been much greater.[18]

This didn't mean that Nixon could be classified as a closet liberal with a strong reformist impulse, as some revisionist historians have argued. Throughout his career, Nixon adopted positions of political convenience. His embrace of liberal measures stemmed from a realistic appraisal of the country's clear preference for government programs like Social Security and Medicare as well as education, health care, and transportation funding. In seeking to create a new Republican majority, Nixon followed the herd as much as he tried to lead it. But backlash politics were never far from his mind. In 1970, for example, Nixon proposed the so-called Philadelphia

Plan, the first federal affirmative action program. Intended, in part to soften the GOP's increasingly hard edge on racial issues and even win some support in the black community, there was another, more perverse, rationale: the measure created tension between blacks and union members—two key Democratic constituencies.[19]

Nixon's first term policy zigzags contributed to the development of an odd, incoherent dynamic in American politics—voters came to hate "big government" in the abstract while at the same time loving big government in its specifics. This had been the Wallace template. For Nixon—and the Republicans who followed in his footsteps—it meant engaging in an unceasing effort to delegitimize liberalism and its social justice aspirations while trimming around the edges of the modern welfare state.

As a candidate for president Nixon had eschewed the harsh conservative language of Wallace and Reagan. As president he embraced it. In November 1969, he spoke from the Oval Office and, harkening back to his RNC defense of nonshouters and nondemonstrators, asked "the great silent majority" of Americans for their support against a "vocal minority" opposed to Vietnam that Nixon claimed threatened the nation's future as a "free society." Nixon's stigmatizing of his enemies became central to his administration, and to the conservative ascendancy in American politics. His much-maligned vice president, Spiro Agnew, took the rhetorical point. In speeches throughout 1969 and 1970, Agnew regularly and loudly complained about "students," dissidents, and "professional protesters" who "mock the common man's pride in his work, his family, and his country." They could be separated from society, said Agnew, like "discarding rotten apples from a barrel." Nixon followed Agnew's lead as he attacked what he called "a small group in this country that always tear America down . . . that hate this country, actually, in terms of what it presently stands for; who see nothing right with America." The GOP so clearly utilized the Wallace playbook that at one point Wallace grumbled to reporters, "I wish I had copy-righted or patented my speeches. I would be drawing immense royalties from Mr. Nixon and especially Mr. Agnew." In California, Ronald Reagan took the administration's language a step further by saying of campus hooligans "if it takes a bloodbath" to deal with them, "let's get it over with. No more appeasement." Some translated these words into action. In the spring of 1970 an antiwar rally near Wall Street was met by hundreds of construction workers who did their best imitation of Chicago's finest and beat up protesters.[20]

Even Nelson Rockefeller, who in 1970 sought a fourth term as governor of New York, and still holding fast to his dream of one day becoming president, started attacking "welfare chiselers" and "liberal extremists" in a naked play for blue-collar support. The man who had run for president in 1968 on a platform of rehabilitating the cities and attacking the root causes of urban decay would later lead the charge in New York State for draconian new mandatory drug laws that would dramatically expand the prison population in the state and would eventually be imitated elsewhere.[21]

Republicans were now perfecting a simple but powerful message that cast their party as the defender of the working man and traditional values, all the while playing on growing white resentment and anxiety over social disorder and racial integration. Above all, they had an antigovernment, socially conservative message that, unlike Goldwater's ideological rigidity, spoke to the most essential concerns of ordinary Americans. "We never really won until we began stressing issues like busing, abortion, school prayer and gun control," said the New Right's media guru Richard Viguerie. "We talked about the sanctity of free enterprise, about the Communist onslaught until we were blue in face. But we didn't start winning majorities in elections until we got down to gut level issues."[22]

For Democrats, the years immediately after 1968 took the party from bad to worse. If Humphrey's defeat had been a disaster for the party, 1972 was a catastrophe—the poorest showing by the nation's modern presidential party since Warren Harding routed James Cox in 1920. The debacle would be a direct result of what had happened four years earlier—and, in particular, Eugene McCarthy's challenge to Lyndon Johnson.

McCarthy's insurgency brought immediate and far-reaching changes to the party that went well beyond his role in contributing to Johnson's withdrawal from the 1968 race. His odyssey through the Democratic primaries highlighted the fundamentally undemocratic nature by which the party chose its presidential nominee. In response, Democrats appointed a reform commission, chaired by George McGovern and Congressman Donald Fraser, to look at opening up the nomination process. McCarthy's fingerprints would be all over the group's work. Its final report directly echoed his declaration in November 1967 that he hoped his candidacy would alleviate the "sense of political helplessness" in the country and the "tendency to withdraw from political action" and "become cynical and...make threats of support for third parties or fourth parties." Ultimately, the commission's conclusion led the party to adopt statewide party primaries and caucuses in which the delegates for the national convention would be chosen. Going forward, the voters rather than the bosses would select the party nominee. Democrats also required that minorities, women, and young people be included in a state's delegation to the national convention. The setting of numeric targets for previously marginalized groups would broaden this mandate even further.[23]

So while Humphrey left Chicago with the begrudging support of southern democrats, the unions, machine politicians, and foreign policy hawks, by 1972, all these groups saw their influence within the party significantly curtailed. African Americans, women, and peace activists, focused more on social rather than economic justice, had taken charge. Nixon's strategy was, as he later wrote, to target "disaffected Democrats...blue collar workers...and working-class white ethnics." The Democratic Party played directly into his hand. Indeed, in light of Nixon's strategy, they could not have found a worse possible candidate in 1972 than McGovern. A passionate opponent of the Vietnam War and heavily reliant on support from the party's liberal wing, McGovern symbolized all the ways Democrats were becoming increasingly out of touch with the electorate.[24]

Edmund Muskie had initially emerged as the early Democratic front runner in 1972, but after he faltered in early primaries, Wallace, now back in the Democratic fold, picked up the mantle. "What did these so-called lib'rals bring us?" Wallace would ask his angry followers on the campaign trail. "Drugs. Riots. Bureaucrats. Contempt for the average citizen, taxes that crush them and leave no freedom. We have already become a government-fearing people instead of a God-fearing people." Wallace's reserved his sharpest condemnations for busing, a program to send white children to predominately black schools and vice versa in order to spur educational integration. By 1972, it had become the most divisive issue in the country. School buses were firebombed, white parents protested, and opinion polls showed that among whites it was universally unpopular and among blacks it barely had majority support. Busing, said Wallace, was the work of the "so-called intelligentsia," "the intellectual snobs," the "tyranny of the Federal Courts," and the "hypocrites who send your kids half-way across town while they have their chauffeur drop their children off at private schools."[25]

In the Florida Democratic primary, on the strength of his antibusing message, Wallace won 42 percent of the vote, and by some estimates, six out of ten nonblack primary voters pulled the lever for him. In clear evidence of the growing alienation among rank-and-file Democrats toward the party establishment, which uniformly opposed Wallace, he next finished second in the Wisconsin and Pennsylvania primaries. In the end, however, it was not voters but violence that ultimately stopped Wallace. On May 15, 1972, at an event in Laurel, Maryland, a twenty-one-year-old loner and publicity hound named Arthur Bremer approached him with a 38-caliber revolver and fired five bullets. One of them lodged in Wallace's spinal cord, paralyzing him. The next day Wallace won the Maryland and Michigan primaries, but his injuries were too serious for him to continue in the race. In all, Democratic primary voters cast more than 3.7 million votes for the Alabama governor. Per the guiding principle of his campaign, the voters had "sent a message." It was unclear, however, if Democrats were listening.[26]

In the wake of Wallace's shooting the fight for the nomination became a two-man contest between McGovern and Humphrey, who launched a sad, last-ditch campaign for the Democratic nod. Humphrey blasted McGovern for his connection to the same radical fringe that had wreaked such havoc on his presidential bid in 1968. (Two years before, he had been approached by Sy Hersh, who had briefly worked for McCarthy, and said that while he felt no antipathy toward him, as for the "kids who marched around saying, 'Hey, hey, L.B.J., how many kids did you kill today?' I say, 'Fuck 'em, fuck 'em, fuck 'em,'" his voice growing louder at each phrase.) He criticized McGovern's plans to cut the defense budget; he wooed Jewish voters by claiming his opponent's policies would leave Israel defenseless against its enemies; and he savaged his opponent's welfare-reform proposals, telling voters that "people in this country want jobs, not handouts." As Wallace later complained, "When I talked about the urban welfare mess in '68, Humphrey called it demagogic. And yet the first thing he said in '72 was he wanted to get the welfare chisellers and loafers off the welfare rolls." Humphrey showed all the hallmarks of a man watching his last chance to win the presidency slip out of his hands and taking every desperate step to stop it from happening. It would be a pitiable coda to a great career. And in the end would be for naught, as McGovern narrowly defeated him in the decisive California primary.[27]

When the Democrats gathered for their annual convention in Miami Beach in the summer of 1972, it looked quite a bit different than four years earlier. Mayor Richard Daley failed to abide by the new delegate rules and saw his delegation replaced by one led by the Reverend Jesse Jackson. Upon seeing the New York delegates, George Meany sneered, "What kind of delegation is this? They've got six open fags and only three AFL-CIO people" (though New York had more union members than any state in the country). Actress Shirley MacLaine complimented the California group, of which she was a member, by saying it "looked like a couple of high schools, a grape boycott, a Black Panther rally, and four or five politicians who walked in the wrong door."[28]

Affluent and well-educated, the Democratic delegates in 1972 seemed to have little interest in the economic plight of the middle class. The party platform read like a liberal wish list—an end to capital punishment, guaranteed income for the poor, more money for the ghettoes. On Vietnam, McGovern bemoaned a US war that rained down "a terrible technology of death on helpless people below." He told voters that they "must change those things in our character which turned us astray, away from the truth that the people of Vietnam are, like us, children of God." Still, even though he was openly running as the peace candidate, poll after poll indicated that voters overwhelmingly viewed Nixon as better able to end the war in Vietnam and more likely to bring the world closer to peace. When asked if "McGovern's ideas are impractical and too far out," 72 percent of Americans either completely or partially agreed.[29]

In the fall campaign Nixon lacerated McGovern's "big government" plans—even as he signed legislation to raise cost-of-living allowances for Social Security recipients and proposing a host of new spending measures intended to lead the country toward full employment in the run-up to Election Day. Greater consistency, however, came in Nixon's moralistic and nationalist attacks that portrayed Democrats as unpatriotic, permissive, feckless, and disrespectful of traditional values. This line of attack would prove to be Nixon's most effective, as economic issues didn't undo McGovern; instead, his liabilities on foreign policy and social issues caused the most damage.[30]

McGovern lost the 1972 election by eighteen million votes. Thirty-five percent of self-identified Democrats voted for Nixon, who also won 70 percent of the southern vote, 80 percent of the '68 Wallace vote, and more than half of the nation's blue-collar voters. The McGovern loss would resonate for a generation. It became a cautionary tale of what Democrats should not do when running for president. The problem, however, was that the party had no idea what they should do to win back the allegiance of their once-loyal supporters.[31]

"It's Never Stopped Being 1968"

Within one presidential cycle, the 1968 election had fundamentally altered America's political trajectory. The GOP's antigovernment populism had replaced the Democrats' economic populism as the nation's dominant political construct. Even in the wake of Watergate and the Democrats' strong performance in the 1974 congressional elections, the signs of conservative ascendancy were impossible to ignore.[1]

On the Republican side in '76, President Gerald Ford, who took office after Nixon resigned in disgrace over the Watergate scandal, initially outraged conservatives by choosing Nelson Rockefeller to be his vice president and barely fended off a primary challenge from Reagan. Rockefeller was thrown off Ford's presidential ticket for the more conservative Kansas senator Bob Dole. He served out his term as vice president and died of a heart attack in 1979. He would not be the only veteran of 1968 to see his political luck run out in 1976. Humphrey flirted with the idea of a presidential draft at the 1976 Democratic National Convention but ultimately decided against it. Having been re-elected to the Senate in 1970, he remained in office until his death from bladder cancer in 1978. His old rival McCarthy had briefly entered the '72 primary race, but fared poorly. In 1976 he launched an independent bid for the White House and won less than 1 percent of the vote. He remained something of a political gadfly, endorsing Ronald Reagan in 1980 and entering the New Hampshire Democratic primary in 1992. He died in 2005.

Instead, a fresh political face would emerge in 1976: Georgia governor Jimmy Carter, who ran not just as the anti-Nixon but also as the anti-McGovern. Steeped far more in the emerging evangelism of the new South than in the working-class appeals of FDR and Truman-style Democrats, and fearful of being seen as big government liberal, Carter ran against traditional Democratic issues. He opposed abortion and forced busing. He called for a balanced budget and tax reductions; he took jabs at the "confused and bewildering welfare system" and the "complicated . . . and wasteful federal bureaucracy." At the party's 1976 nominating convention in New York City he even spoke of the need for less government intrusion in "our free economic system."[2]

Though Carter would go on to narrowly defeat Ford, the victory was a poisoned chalice for the party. Democrats hadn't yet figured out a governing agenda, a post-1968 economic message, or a new vision for liberalism. On virtually every domestic issue Carter found himself caught between liberal interest groups on one side and the increasingly conservative direction of congressional Democrats (not to mention the American people) on the other. Labor, which had largely refused to support McGovern because of his opposition to the war in Vietnam, increasingly found itself alienated from the party's powerbrokers. Their key economic priorities, like Humphrey-Hawkins, a bill intended to promote full employment, would be so badly watered down by Congress that it barely made a mark. Labor-law reform, also strongly backed by the unions died in the Senate. Neither legislative effort received strong White House support. Instead of focusing on economic growth or strengthening the social safety net, Carter made fighting inflation his key economic priority. This led to more restrictive monetary and fiscal policies, which exacerbated the country's economic downturn, but also lent credence to the notion that the so-called party of the people had moved in a very different direction. Democrats, who had once dreamed big and offered a hopeful vision for the nation, were increasingly talking about "limits" and a national "crisis of confidence."[3]

After 1968, the issues with which Democrats had long been associated—civil rights, "activist government," fighting poverty, and social welfare—became political liabilities. In other areas where they had previously enjoyed an advantage, like protecting Social Security and support for labor, Nixon used his first term to position Republicans in a far more positive light on each of them. At the same time, voters showed greater interest in national security, crime-fighting, cutting taxes, smaller government, and the amorphous but potent question of morality and values. On these issues Republicans had long enjoyed an edge, and the party was intent on increasing it.[4]

But nowhere did the post-1968 Republican advantage loom larger than on the economy. In the years after World War II, the economy hummed along at a strong pace with low unemployment. Real incomes, for example, rose by 37 percent in the 1960s. As a result neither party had a wide lead on the issue—the rising tide tended to lift all boats. In the 1970s, however, this nearly twenty-five-year period of consistent growth began to fade. Incomes and wages fell, foreign competition began to erode the country's manufacturing base, tax burdens increased, and unemployment and inflation went up as the cost of living began to rise. Voters were now either treading water or falling behind. As a result, economic unease became the nation's dominant political issue. For the three decades following World War II, the economy had been a dominant public concern only 17 percent of the time. From 1973 to 2004, public opinion surveys indicated that the economy was considered the "most important problem" in the country 76 percent of the time. For much of the post-1968 era Republicans would be seen as the party most likely to produce the best economic outcomes. The root of GOP success lay in a simple, oft-repeated refrain that became the party's mantra—lower taxes, decreased regulation, and smaller government. Republican politicians—from president to congressman to dog catcher—spoke with one unified voice, castigating the excesses of the federal bureaucracy while declining to do away with the government programs enjoyed by middle-class Americans. The Wallace/Nixon playbook endured.[5]

Powerless to defeat Republicans—and wary of being tarred by the GOP's tax-and-spend label—Democrats began to join them. The party shunted aside the economic populism that had kept them in power for so many years and even embraced the traditionally GOP position of balancing the budget. This shift would be most visibly apparent in 1984, when presidential nominee (and former Humphrey aide) Walter Mondale called—disastrously—for raising taxes in order to reduce the deficit in his acceptance speech at the Democratic National Convention. In 1988, Michael Dukakis, fearful of running on an overtly liberal economic platform, stressed competence over ideology—and then watched helplessly as George Bush, drawing on the Nixon playbook, portrayed him as an unpatriotic, soft on crime, tax-and-spend liberal.[6]

Underpinning the GOP's increasing political advantage was race. While the Democratic focus on civil rights became a growing political liability, the 1968 election also showed that voters responded poorly to overtly race-based appeals. To be effective, racial signaling must be done subtly. "Welfare," "special interests," "law and order," "soft on crime," "affirmative action quotas," and "busing," all became part of an emerging political lexicon and the dog-whistle politics of the era.

In 1976, as he sought the Republican presidential nomination, Reagan made clear his support for civil rights, while also evoking the image of "welfare queens" driving Cadillacs and slum dwellers living in subsidized public housing that was a virtual urban palace. Four years later, Reagan kicked off his general election campaign in Philadelphia, Mississippi (near where three white civil rights workers were murdered in 1964). There he used the term "states' rights," but as time went on it would no longer be necessary even to invoke these code words. Republicans merely had to criticize free-spending and tax-loving Democrats or government programs writ large. Most voters quickly picked up the message—Democrats wanted to tax white Americans to pay for more government spending that benefited blacks. Racial and economic anxiety remained intermingled, and grew even stronger in the years after 1968. It got so bad for Democrats that in 1984 Mondale spent part of his general election campaign sounding a message of "fairness"—a populist notion that Democrats were the only party that could level the playing field and give working- and middle-class Americans a fair shot. Many white voters heard something different—"fairness" to them meant handouts to blacks.[7]

Democrats finally begin to reverse the tide in 1992, helped by a poor economy and a presidential candidate who ran under the populist slogan "Putting people first," as he attacked the special interests that he claimed frustrated their economic prospects. Bill Clinton, however, balanced his call for addressing the needs of the middle class with a bow to the nation's changed post-1968 political narrative. He boasted of his plan to end welfare "as we know it." On law and order he pledged to put more cops on the street and reiterated his support for the death penalty. Most famously, he distanced himself from African American interest groups by denouncing the antiwhite bigotry of a black rapper named Sister Souljah—and he did so with the nation's leading civil rights voice, Jesse Jackson, prominently seated a few feet away. While Clinton's approach won him the White House, his strategy spoke to a larger, unresolved political dilemma for Democrats: the party spent as much time shielding their vulnerabilities as it did focusing on their political advantages.[8]

In a 1992 study of presidential campaigns, three political scientists, John Petrocik, William Benoit, and Glenn Hansen, found that Republicans devoted two-thirds of their campaign appeals to issues they owned. Democrats also emphasized those issues that favored Republicans. Going back to 1952, they found, "Democrats...effectively promoted a Republican agenda." This phenomenon was in part structural. During the Cold War, national security played a dominant role, giving Republicans, who were generally viewed as tougher and more resolute in international affairs, a natural electoral advantage—one that Democrats tried to neutralize with the sort of hawkishness displayed by Kennedy, Johnson, and Humphrey. After 1968 and particularly 1972 the weakness meme became a far greater liability for Democrats—one made worse by the antiwar violence in Chicago and the dovish turn of the national party, as represented by McGovern.[9]

Democratic TV ads became more focused on the party's "owned" issues only after 1988, a period that coincided, not surprisingly, with the end of the Cold War. No longer did they need to overcompensate on national security. However, the GOP edge reappeared with a vengeance in 2004, the first election after 9/11. The Democratic nominee, Senator John Kerry, enjoyed a polling advantage on virtually every domestic issue and still lost, in part, because of the GOP's residual strength on foreign policy and national security.[10]

The problem for Democrats, however, was bigger than just an image of national security meekness. The party couldn't shake the political stereotypes that emerged after 1968. As Republicans began to increase their support among religious voters, they merged traditional GOP individualism with a value-laden agenda that looked askance at the cultural, racial, and social changes that had come to the fore in the election of 1968 and that increasingly came to define America in the 1970s and 1980s. Attributes like "individual responsibility," "respect for authority," "hard work," and adherence to traditional norms around sex, language, and family—all reflecting a spirit of social conservatism that had long defined American society—became powerful weapons in the hands of GOP office seekers, and they had their antecedents in the national tumult of the late 1960s. At the same time, conservatives turned the dominant public image of Democrats as compassionate, empathetic, and "liberal" in both politics and values against them by painting such virtues as evidence of weakness. When Democrats tried to co-opt Republican issues, it was inevitably described by the GOP as clear evidence that Democrats, unlike uncompromising Republicans, lacked a political core.[11]

These distinct party traits materialized in ways that are all too familiar. Republicans regularly portrayed Democrats as unpatriotic ("blame America firsters" became the foreign policy refrain in 1984, conjuring images of antiwar protesters from the '60s) or beholden to "special interests." They played on images of fecklessness in fighting crime (the infamous Willie Horton ads used against Michael Dukakis in 1988), and consistently described Democrats as unprincipled or guided by the changing winds of public opinion. In 2000, Republicans used the Monica Lewinsky scandal—and subsequent impeachment of President Clinton—to make the case they would be the party to restore "honor and dignity" to the White House. In

2004, George W. Bush brought virtually all of these stereotypes together, attacking John Kerry for looking to the United Nations for permission when deciding to go to war and for flip-flopping on whether he supported the American troops fighting in Iraq. Republicans even went after Kerry's greatest national security asset—his status as a decorated war veteran—by insinuating that he lied about or exaggerated his military record in Vietnam. The epigraph to this book came in a May 2004 preview of the election to come, when an unnamed White House aide, discussing John Kerry's dilemma in how to talk about the war in Iraq, gleefully noted, "It's never stopped being 1968" for Democrats.[12]

In a 2012 Republican presidential debate, former House Speaker Newt Gingrich provided an illuminating example of how Republicans continue to utilize the accumulation of post-1968 stereotypes. Referring to President Obama's decision to block support for a proposed gas pipeline, Gingrich imagined himself as the president: "I'm now going to veto a middle-class tax cut to protect left-wing environmental extremists in San Francisco, so that we're going to kill American jobs, weaken American energy, make us more vulnerable to the Iranians, and do so in a way that makes no sense to any normal, rational American." All of it was there: Democrats were soft; they didn't understand the threats facing America; they didn't care about jobs for hard-working Americans because they cared more about their special-interest extremists; they loved higher taxes, especially when the money could go to supporting their plans for social engineering; and, in his reference to San Francisco, they were tight with the gays and the fringe left.[13]

There is a real question as to how much this truly influences the way Americans cast their ballots. Political punditry in the United States is replete with talk of "turning points" and "decisive moments" in presidential elections, when in reality most Americans have long before decided who they will vote for. But like the liberal consensus of the 1950s and 1960s, politicians and their advisors assume that it matters. So all too often the response of Democrats has been to overcompensate as a way of neutralizing potential Republican attacks, from Dukakis's ill-fated tank ride in 1988, intended to burnish his national security bona fides, and a steady stream of liberal Democrats in the 1970s, 1980s, and 1990s calling for more deregulation so as to blunt their "big government" image (including liberal lion Ted Kennedy in his legendary "dream will never die" speech at the 1980 Democratic convention), to Bill Clinton's support for a middle-class tax cut and his "reinventing government" initiative to defend against the perennial label of "tax-and-spend, big government liberal." In 2008, Barack Obama took up the baton with his campaign-trail pledge to escalate the war in Afghanistan and ramp up the use of drones against terrorists in Pakistan. All of them can be traced, in some way, to the politics of 1968.

For Democrats, the need to make up for their perceived shortcomings became a virtual political credo, and continued to influence them even after they took office. Clinton may have run for president on a message of economic populism, but after his election he focused on fiscal stewardship and discarded a laundry list of domestic investments in order to pass a deficit reduction bill. When he tried to push a more liberal (but less populist) agenda, like health care reform, it ended in disaster. That failure reflected another key lesson of 1968: Americans were increasingly wary of sweeping reform measures, fearing they would do them more harm than good. The focus on health care for the uninsured rather than more direct populist appeals helped contribute to the Democrats losing control of Congress in 1994.

Though Clinton would be re-elected, his ambition had been curtailed. Deregulation of the financial services and the tele-communication industries became top presidential initiatives, as did reforming welfare, forcing single mothers to work for their benefits, and trade policies that were vehemently opposed by labor. His 1996 re-election campaign combined a defense of traditional Democratic programs like Medicare, Medicaid, public education, and environmental protection with small-bore initiatives like school uniforms and keeping kids away from disturbing content on television. It offered a telling indication of liberalism's new outer limits.

While Barack Obama would enact the most far-reaching piece of social policy since the Johnson years (the Affordable Care Act, better known as Obamacare), he would do so not by appealing to the better angels of Americans' nature but rather by depicting the legislation as a way to trim costs and cut the deficit. Pledging repeatedly that insured Americans would see no change in their own health insurance coverage, Obama's message was, at least initially, one of minimal sacrifice. In short, as confidence in government faltered, Democrats, rather than trying to arrest its decline, gave it a push.[14]

Yet, even though there was a rightward shift in the country's political narrative after 1968, conservatives failed to translate it into direct policy gains. When Ronald Reagan won the presidency in 1980, it appeared that conservatism had finally fulfilled the potential that had first become evident in 1968. His landslide victory, which came on the heels of nationwide tax revolts, seemed to augur a major change in governmental priorities.

While Reagan fulfilled his key campaign promises of expanding the Pentagon's budget, pushing through a massive tax cut, and loosening regulation, larger efforts to curtail government spending or do away with Johnson's Great Society programs failed. The man who had once proposed allowing Americans to opt out of Social Security eventually signed legislation that ensured the program's financial viability well into the twenty-first century. During Reagan's eight years in the White House, not one major spending program was eliminated. Rather than zeroing out the Department of Education, federal education spending increased by 47 percent under his watch. "The Reagan years appear to have been little more than a mild speed bump in the progress of ever-larger government," wrote Stephen Hayward, a conservative biographer of Reagan.[15]

George H. W. Bush continued this pattern. Even though he'd long been the embodiment of the party's WASP-y eastern Republican contingent, he ran as a fire-breathing conservative, echoing the same hard-on-crime, patriotic appeals of Wallace twenty years earlier. As president, however, he repeatedly frustrated the right. He signed the Civil Rights Act of 1989 and the Americans with Disabilities Act of 1990, extending greater rights and legal protection to the disabled. Even worse, he went along with Democratic demands to raise taxes in order to cut the deficit—a move that inflamed conservatives and led to a primary challenge from another '68 denizen, Pat Buchanan.

Under Bush's son, George W. Bush, the size of government continued to grow, with legislation expanding the Medicare entitlement to include prescription drugs, a heightening of the federal role in education policy, and the creation of the Department of Homeland Security. Aside from an unceasing effort to lower the regulatory burdens on big business, Bush's conservative policy triumphs were few and far between. Underpinning all of this would be a national sea change in attitudes on race, gender, and morality. Same-sex marriage, racial integration, and the expanded role of women in the workplace all came to enjoy far greater acceptance in American society. "Traditional values" would be challenged in virtually every corner of American society, from movies, television, and music to sports and fashion. On the cultural front, liberalism's successes seem almost impossible to deny. In short, even in an era of apparent conservative dominance, Republican presidents, and party leaders in Congress, did little to shrink the size of government or reverse the tide of social change. On the latter, they barely even tried; on the former, they surrendered without a fight. In 1968, Republicans had found the words and the images to reclaim a political advantage, but it was a hollow victory. They had won the political support of Americans, but not their hearts.[16]

Conservatives succeeded not in rolling back the welfare state but instead in containing it. Rather than offer a helping hand to the increasingly struggling and anxiety-ridden middle class, the federal government after 1968 took the opposite approach—often with the assistance of Democrats. Government benefits became less generous and more conditional. The minimum wage declined in value by 40 percent between 1968 and 2002. Income volatility increased dramatically; traditional pensions were replaced with more unpredictable 401(k)s; job protections were weakened, personal bankruptcies rose, and so did personal debt. Republicans actively pursed policies that undercut the influence and bargaining power of unions. The push for greater government regulation was stymied—with both parties playing a role. Taxes were cut, which benefited the GOP's affluent base of voters, but also shrank the government pie for ambitious new initiatives. When the red ink would flow from such profligate policies, Republicans would suddenly become fiscal conservatives, calling for federal spending to be reduced while holding the line on taxes.[17]

In the nearly half century since 1968, Republicans could take solace not in what they accomplished but in what they stopped. Since the late 1960s, wages decreased, inequality and economic anxiety rose, and more and more Americans found themselves without healthcare, affordable child care, or hopes for an easy retirement. Yet government had been almost completely neutered in its ability to respond. Any effort to craft a public response was met with Republican counterattacks that portrayed federal initiatives as detrimental to "ordinary Americans." By encouraging voters' fears about what new programs might mean, Republicans made it politically untenable for Congress to do much of anything.

This larger policy of treading water would be enabled by the increasingly harsh rhetoric of Republicans toward the federal government, as well as procedural tricks like the Senate filibuster that obstructed legislation and made government appear even less effective. It brought a radicalized and uncompromising group of conservatives to political power who refused to give up hope of rolling back the Great Society and the New Deal. Even after being stopped in the 1990s by Clinton—and seeing little progress in the Bush years—the conservative war against government took on an even more extremist tone during the Obama years. In 2011 Wisconsin congressman and 2012 vice presidential candidate Paul Ryan would put forward a budget proposal that was among the most radical effort ever conceived by Republican lawmakers to shift the country away from operational liberalism. Its failure, however, was emblematic of a larger conservative weakness. They couldn't kill the beast of the American welfare state.[18]

Conservatives achieved greater success on foreign policy, in large measure because Democrats initially embraced McGovern's antiwar conceits. Even Carter, who so assiduously ran away from McGovern on domestic policy, embraced many of his foreign policy views, in particular focusing on human rights as an overarching national security priority. Doves would maintain a tight hold on the direction of the party, as Democrats strongly opposed the arms buildup of the 1980s, the proxy wars fought by the Reagan administration in Central America, and the Gulf War against Iraq in 1990. Noninterventionist influence became so pervasive that the party's remaining hawkish members largely abandoned the Democrats for Reagan's GOP. As had been the case on welfare, crime, and taxes, Democrats would eventually reverse course on foreign policy too—adopting many of the same martial rhetorical tropes as Republicans and largely abdicating any serious challenge to the ever-mushrooming military budget or the national security state in general.

In the end maintenance of the status quo became the new "consensus," and 1968's most lasting contribution to the nation's politics. Arguably, rather than settling anything politically, the election created tighter gridlock—and further polarization. It pushed Republicans to embrace conservatism's hard edge for its electoral benefit and then reap the whirlwind of an increasingly radical brand of right-wing ideology. It led Democrats to move further to the political left, getting crushed in the process, and then spend years flailing for an effective political message—and finding one far removed from the hopeful spirit captured by Lyndon Johnson in his 1965 inaugural address.

In 2012, however, there came reason to believe that the tide had begun to shift back. That year's presidential election was one that spoke directly to the legacy of 1968. Republicans again ran on racial fear and against "big government." They divided the country into "makers" and "takers" and described the political choice facing Americans as that of the free market economy versus socialism. And they portrayed the Democratic incumbent as weak and spineless when it came to protecting America's national security interests. These rhetorical attacks fell flat, done in by Republican overreach and the nation's inevitable demographic shift. More than four decades after one of the nation's most polarized elections, racial schisms in American politics had come full circle as blacks, Hispanics, and Asians made up a far larger segment of the population. The Democrats now held the political trump card. No longer could the Republican Party run successfully on the template of anxiety, resentment, and white backlash fashioned out of the election of 1968.

Still, while the nation's electoral politics has evolved, the ideological shift toward antigovernment and antielite populism that emerged that year maintains its stranglehold over the country's politics. The Wallace-like impulses that Nixon had co-opted to help deliver him the Republican nomination and then the presidency has eroded the very foundation of American democracy. The antiwar activists had toppled a president and transformed their party in 1968, but they left subsequent generations of Democrats ill-equipped to lay out a politically popular vision for the future of liberalism. The 1968 election, by confirming and endorsing the ideological conservatism and operational liberalism of the American voter, fed the country's political incoherence—hatred of "big government" in the abstract and a fervent embrace of its specific elements.

In ways both large and small, that divergence remains the abiding legacy of the nine men who sought the White House in 1968. At a perilous moment in American history—when that which divided the nation was seemingly stronger than that which united it—their actions laid the foundation for a new political order. While the maelstrom that formed in 1968 is far closer to its end than its beginning, it continues to roil American politics.

Nixon takes the oath of office as president. Courtesy of Oliver Atkins, National Archives.

ACKNOWLEDGMENTS

American Maelstrom took more than five years to write, and so many people have generously given their time and support to make it possible.

First, I must thank David Greenberg, who was literally "present at the creation." More than six years ago he sent a note to a listserv that we were both members of asking for possible submissions for a series he was editing for Oxford University Press on pivotal moments in American history. The rest, as they say, is history. David has, from the beginning, provided essential guidance on this project, and while we've disagreed at times, he is a brilliant student of history and one whose insights have informed my thinking. This is likewise true for my editor at OUP, Timothy Bent, whose close editing has enormously strengthened and improved the book you hold in your hands. It's also because of him that this book is a lot less weighty than it could have been!

I must also thank my indefatigable agent, Will Lippincott, who has been a friend, therapist, and source of support throughout this roller-coaster experience.

The folks at Oxford University Press have been fantastic to work with, but none more so than Alyssa O'Connell, who has quite patiently put up with my numerous questions, no matter how obscure.

So many other people—far more knowledgeable about this subject matter than me—helped me along the way. I struggle to remember all of their names, but here it goes:

Mitch Lerner generously took time out from his schedule to read some of the early chapters and offer advice as I tried to solve the riddle of Lyndon Johnson. George Herring and Gian Gentile did the same for me on LBJ and Vietnam, as did Fred Logevall, who is not only a brilliant writer and thinker but also a top-notch human being. Carl Prine was a fount of knowledge in recommending source materials for my research on Vietnam.

Michael Flamm, whose book *Law and Order* deeply influenced my thinking about the role of crime in the 1968 election, was another great source of assistance. Richard Skinner and Tom Schaller read various iterations of the chapter on Nelson Rockefeller and provided helpful comments. Marcia Barrett generously shared with me her own doctoral research on Rocky, which helped fill in many of the holes in my research. Rich Yeselson gave a close read to some of the early chapters. He is a wise man and in our numerous conversations he helped me think through some of the key questions of 1968. Greg Anrig and Jordan Michael Smith both took the time to read the entire manuscript, and I am deeply indebted to them for their thoughts on the book.

Geoff Kabaservice, David Karol, and Jack Bohrer helped me wade my way through the Republican Party's evolution in the 1960s. Jeet Heer did the same with my chapter on George Wallace. Ed Kilgore was a great source on the particulars of southern politics. Michael Kazin helped me think through the larger historical issues raised by the '68 election. Jonathan Zasloff read an early draft of the backlash chapter and offered comments that steered me in the right direction on it. Others who played small but meaningful roles include Rob Mickey, Arthur Goldhammer, Eric Rauchway, Julian Zelizer, Matt Dallek, Josh Rovner, Robert Mann, Michael Crowley and Greg Veis, Mark Schmitt, Doug Schoen, Cal Morgan, and Neil Bhatiya who read some of the early chapters on McCarthy and Vietnam. Michael Landsman and Silvia Liu were excellent research assistants. John Buntin read several chapters of the book, gave me wonderful advice along the way, and, as always, has been a great friend though this entire process.

I didn't spend a significant amount deal of time doing personal interviews for the book, but several people who played supporting roles in the 1968 election provided me with much-needed context—Jeremy Larner, Stuart Eizenstat, Paul Gorman, Pat Buchanan, Jonathon Moore, and Thomas Hughes, who spoke to me at length about his old friend Hubert Humphrey.

Much of my research was focused on presidential libraries, and I am deeply indebted to the staff of the Richard Nixon, JFK, and LBJ libraries. In addition, I am grateful to Tom Rosenbaum and the staff at the Rockefeller Archives, outside New York; Timothy Johnson and his colleagues at Anderson Library at the University of Minnesota; the staff at the Minnesota Historical Society, the Bentley Library at the University of Michigan, the Library of Congress and the New York Public Library; and Kathleen Shoemaker at Emory University. I've been very privileged to be an adjunct professor at Columbia University for much of the period in which I wrote this book. I literally could not have completed this book without access to the books, online materials, and periodicals that are housed at the school's many libraries. I cannot thank each staffer personally who helped me, but I owe a debt of gratitude to each of them.

As I slogged through my research, I was able to write up some of my early conclusions about the race—and receive feedback—in a number of publications, including the *Guardian* and *Foreign Policy*, where I worked as a columnist; *Politico*; and the Ideas section of the *Boston Globe*, where I am now honored to work as a columnist.

My dad, Eugene Cohen, read some of the early drafts of the manuscript, and while his thoughts were of course helpful, I am far more indebted to him and my mom, Helen Cohen, for imparting in me such a deep and abiding love of history. Their recollections of the campaign and the historic moments that took place that year are ones that I remember vividly from my childhood: my father telling me that he jumped out of his seat on March 31, 1968, to exclaim, "He's not going to run"; my mother reminding me of her suspicions about the ruthlessness of Robert Kennedy and her frustration at her liberal friends for refusing to vote for Humphrey.

Finally, there is my wife, Sarah, who remains both the best editor and the finest person I know. She stuck with me on this journey, even as my nights and weekends—and practically every waking thought—became consumed with 1968. It is a cliché that I could not have done this without her support, but this is one cliché that rings true. My children, Isadora and Scarlett, were born as this book was being written, and I dedicate it to them in the hope that they will grow up with the same curiosity and passion for history that led me to write *American Maelstrom*.

NOTES

Introduction

1. "Record-Breaking Crowd of 1.2 Million Watches Ceremonies and Parade," *Washington Post*, January 21, 1965.
2. Roper Center for Public Opinion Research, University of Connecticut, Gallup, "America's Mood in the Mid-Sixties, February 1965."
3. *Time*, January 29, 1965; "Record-Breaking Crowd of 1.2 Million Watches Ceremonies and Parade," *Washington Post*, January 21, 1965; "'Great and Wonderful Day' Is Enjoyed by the President from Morn till Night," *New York Times*, January 21, 1965; "President's Way," *New York Times*, January 24, 1965; "Lyndon Johnson's Pledge," *Newsweek*, February 1, 1965; *American Experience: The Presidents: LBJ*, http://video.pbs.org/video/1049331248/.
4. Roper Center for Public Opinion Research, University of Connecticut, "America's Mood in the Mid-Sixties, February 1965"; Gallup Poll, January 1965; Gallup Poll, November 1964.
5. Lyndon B. Johnson, "Remarks at the University of Michigan," May 22, 1964, online at *The American Presidency Project*, http://www.presidency.ucsb.edu/ws/?pid=26262,
6. Ibid.
7. "The Johnson Landslide," *New York Times*, November 4, 1964; "Lyndon Johnson's Pledge," *Newsweek*, February 1, 1965.
8. Mary C. Brennan, *Turning Right in the Sixties: The Conservative Capture of the GOP* (Chapel Hill: University of North Carolina Press, 1995), pg. 20.
9. Lyndon B. Johnson, "The President's Inaugural Address," January 20, 1965, online at *The American Presidency Project*, http://www.presidency.ucsb.edu/ws/?pid=26985.
10. Ibid.; also see *Time*, January 29, 1965.
11. "The Big Show," *Newsweek*, January 8, 1968.

Chapter 1

1. Doris Kearns Goodwin, *Lyndon Johnson and the American Dream* (New York: St. Martin's Griffin, 1991), 226.
2. Stephen Skowronek, *The Politics Presidents Make: Leadership from John Adams to Bill Clinton*, rev. ed. (Cambridge, MA: Belknap Press of Harvard University Press, 1997), 356; Hugh Sidey, *A Very Personal Presidency: Lyndon Johnson in the White House* (New York: Atheneum, 1968), 114; also see Fred Dutton, memo to Bobby Kennedy,

November 3, 1967, "The Underlying Situation," box 491, Schlesinger Papers, New York Public Library, for a smart take on Johnson's weaknesses as a politician. I am also indebted to Mitch Lerner for his thoughts on this question.

3. As quoted in G. Calvin Mackenzie and Robert Weisbrot, *The Liberal Hour: Washington and the Politics of Change in the 1960s* (New York: Penguin, 2008), 93; Eric Goldman, *The Tragedy of Lyndon Johnson* (New York: Knopf, 1969), 332–33; Robert Dallek, *Lone Star Rising*, vol. 1, *Lyndon Johnson and His Times, 1908–1960* (New York: Oxford University Press, 1991), 6.

4. Irwin Unger, *The Best of Intentions: The Triumphs and Failures of the Great Society under Kennedy, Johnson, and Nixon* (New York: Doubleday, 1996), 104; Bruce J. Schulman, *Lyndon B. Johnson and American Liberalism: A Brief Biography With Documents* (Boston: Bedford/St. Martins, 1995), 81 and 91, 94; Goodwin, *Lyndon Johnson,* 218 (also see 216–20); Skowronek, *Politics Presidents Make,* 341.

5. Nicholas Lemann, "The Unfinished War," *Atlantic,* December 1988; Mackenzie and Weisbrot, *Liberal Hour,* 328; also see Goodwin, *Lyndon Johnson,* 286–95; James L. Sundquist, *Politics and Policy: Eisenhower, Kennedy and Johnson Years* (Washington, DC: Brookings Institution, 1968), 494; Maurice Isserman and Michael Kazin, eds., *America Divided: The Civil War of the 1960s,* 3rd ed. (New York: Oxford University Press, 2007), 196; see also the chapter titled "Things Go Wrong" in Goodwin, *Lyndon Johnson,* on implementation issues.

6. Roper Center for Public Opinion Research, University of Connecticut, Harris Survey, October 1965, Harris Survey, December 1965.

7. LBJ Commencement Address at Howard University, "To Fulfill These Rights," July 4, 1965, Lyndon Baines Johnson Library and Museum, http://www.lbjlib.utexas .edu/johnson/archives.hom/speeches.hom/650604.asp.

8. Michael W. Flamm, *Law and Order: Street Crime, Civil Unrest, and the Crisis of Liberalism in the 1960s* (New York: Columbia University Press, 2007), 59.

9. Ibid.; "Officials Divided in Placing Blame," *New York Times,* August 14, 1965; Rowland Evans and Robert Novak, "Negro Riots in Watts Create Backlash," *Free-Lance Star,* October 9, 1965.

10. "New Negro Riots Erupt on Coast; 3 Reported Shot," *New York Times,* August 12, 1965; "Officials Divided in Placing Blame," *New York Times,* August 14, 1965; Evans and Novak, "Negro Riots in Watts"; Unger, *Best of Intentions,* 148–49, 166.

11. Irving Bernstein, *Guns or Butter: The Presidency of Lyndon Johnson,* Kindle ed. (New York: Oxford University Press, 1996), 321–22; "LBJ Delivers State of the Union," January 1966; Miller Center, University of Virginia, http://millercenter.org/ president/speeches/detail/4035.

12. Robert Dallek, *Flawed Giant: Lyndon Johnson and His Times, 1961–1973* (New York: Oxford University Press, 1998), 400–403; Sidey, *Very Personal Presidency,* 162.

13. Goodwin, *Lyndon Johnson,* 296; Bernstein, *Guns or Butter,* 323.

14. Allen J. Matusow, in *The Great Society: A Twenty-Year Critique,* ed. Barbara C. Jordan and Elspeth D. Rostow (Austin, TX: Lyndon Baines Johnson Library, 1986), 143–47; Godfrey Hodgson, *America in Our Times: From World War II to Nixon—What Happened and Why* (Princeton, NJ: Princeton University Press, 2005), 174.

15. Kevin Phillips, *The Emerging Republican Majority* (New Rochelle, NY: Arlington House, 1969), 37; Ben J. Scammon and Richard M. Wattenberg, *The Real Majority*

(New York: Primus, 1992); also see Hazel Erskine, "The Polls: Demonstrations and Race Riots," *Public Opinion Quarterly* 31, no. 4 (Winter 1967–1968): 665–67.

16. Bil Gilbert, "The Great World and Millersburg," *Saturday Evening Post*, April 20, 1968.

17. American National Election Studies (ANES), 1964 and 1968; Trust in Government Index 1958–2008, http://www.electionstudies.org/nesguide/text/tab5a_5.txt; also see "Public Trust in Government," Pew Research Center, http://www.people-press .org/2014/11/13/public-trust-in-government/.

18. See E. J. Dionne, *Why Americans Hate Politics* (New York: Touchstone/Simon & Schuster, 1991); Kazin and Isserman, *America Divided*, 303.

19. Lloyd A. Free and Hadley Cantril, *The Political Beliefs of Americans: A Study of Public Opinion* (New York: Simon & Schuster, 1967), 8 and 22, and see chapters 2 and 3.

20. Kazin and Isserman, *America Divided*, 302.

21. See Ira Katznelson, "Was the Great Society a Lost Opportunity?" in *The Rise and Fall of the New Deal Order, 1930–1980*, ed. Steve Fraser and Gary Gerstle (Princeton, NJ: Princeton University Press, 1990), 185–211; Stewart Alsop, "Can Anyone Beat LBJ?" *Saturday Evening Post*, June 3, 1967.

22. Roper Center for Public Opinion Research, June 1965 Gallup Poll; September 1966 Gallup Poll, July 1967; "The Polls: Speed of Racial Integration," *Public Opinion Quarterly* 32, no. 3 (Autumn 1968): 522.

23. See Kevin M. Kruse, *White Flight: Atlanta and the Making of Modern Conservatism* (Princeton, NJ: Princeton University Press, 2005); Wallace Frady, "Gary, Indiana," *Harper's Magazine*, August 1969; Thomas J. Sugrue, *The Origins of the Urban Crisis: Race and Inequality in Post-War Detroit*, Kindle ed. (Princeton, NJ: Princeton University Press, 1996), 2.

24. Hazel Erskine, "The Polls: Negro Housing," *Public Opinion Quarterly* 31, no. 3 (Autumn, 1967): 493; this theme is explored at great length in Sugrue, *Origins of the Urban Crisis*.

25. Richard N. Goodwin, *Remembering America: A Voice from the Sixties* (Boston: Little, Brown, 1988), 259, 270, 306.

26. Allen J. Matusow, *The Unraveling of America: A History of Liberalism* (Athens, GA: University of Georgia Press, 1984), 214.

27. Flamm, *Law and Order*, 9; and Sugrue, *Origins of the Urban Crisis*.

28. *US News and World Report*, January 29, 1968.

29. Schulman, *Lyndon B. Johnson*, 241; see Jacob S. Hacker and Paul Pierson, *Winner-Take-All Politics*, Kindle ed. (New York: Simon & Schuster, 2011).

30. Pete Hamill, "The Revolt of the White Lower Middle Class," *New York*, April 14, 1969.

31. Flamm, *Law and Order*, 125–28; Scammon and Wattenberg, *Real Majority*, 40; Sourcebook of Criminal Justice Statistics Online, "Table 3.106.2010: Estimated number and rate (per 100,000 inhabitants) of offenses known to police," http://www.albany .edu/sourcebook/pdf/t31062010.pdf.

32. Erskine, "The Polls: Demonstrations and Race Riots," 760; Jeremy D. Mayer, *Running on Race: Racal Politics in Presidential Campaigns: 1960–2000* (New York: Random House, 2002), 71.

33. "Can Riots Be Stopped," *US News and World Report*, August 8, 1966; *Esquire*, July 1967.

34. "Crime and the Great Society," *Time*, March 24, 1967.

35. Richard Nixon, "What Has Happened to America," *Reader's Digest*, October 1967, 49–54; "Wallace in the North: Friends and 'Anarchist' Critics Cheer and Scream," *New York Times*, July 26, 1968.

36. Scammon and Wattenberg, *Real Majority*, 95; Flamm, *Law and Order*, 47, 125.

37. Flamm, *Law and Order*, 4; Jonathan Rieder, "The Rise of the 'Silent Majority,'" in Fraser and Gerstle, *Rise and Fall*, 258.

38. "Man of the Year: The Inheritor," *Time*, January 6, 1967; Matusow, *Unraveling of America*, 306–8.

39. Hazel Erskine, "The Polls: Demonstrations and Race Riots," 655–59; David Steigerwald, *The Sixties and the End of Modern America* (New York: St. Martin's, 1995), 243–71.

40. Dallek, *Flawed Giant*, 406; Flamm, *Law and Order*, 135.

41. Scammon and Wattenberg, *Real Majority*, 21.

42. Sundquist, *Politics and Policy*, 497; Rick Perlstein, *Nixonland: The Rise of a President and the Fracturing of America* (New York: Scribner, 2008), portrays the '66 election as the first sign of a rising conservative backlash—his most telling example being the defeat of liberal Illinois senator Paul Douglas, in part because of the issue of open housing. This view is disputed by Geoffrey Kabaservice, *Rule and Ruin: The Downfall of Moderation and the Destruction of the Republican Party from Eisenhower to the Tea Party* (New York: Oxford University Press, 2012), among others. The debate between Perlstein, Paul Krugman, Nolan McCarty, Paul Pierson, and Eric Rauchway, moderated by Henry Farrell at the 2008 American Political Science Association Annual Meeting provides a useful perspective on the two views of the election; transcript available online at http://www.henryfarrell.net/nixonland.pdf.

43. McKenzie and Weisbrot, *Liberal Hour*, 331, 360.

Chapter 2

1. Lyndon Baines Johnson, *Vantage Point: Perspectives of the Presidency, 1963–1969* (New York: Holt, Rinehart & Winston, 1974), 443.

2. Goodwin, *Lyndon Johnson*, 252.

3. William Conrad Gibbons, *The US Government and the Vietnam War: Executive and Legislative Roles and Relationships, Part III, January–July 1965* (Washington, DC: Government Printing Office, 1988), 457.

4. See Bernstein, *Guns or Butter*, 370.

5. Robert Dallek, *Lyndon B. Johnson: Portrait of a President* (New York: Oxford University Press, 2004), 318.

6. Mackenzie and Weisbrot, *Liberal Hour*, 308.

7. Fredrik Logevall, *Choosing War: The Lost Chance for Peace and the Escalation of War in Vietnam*, Kindle ed. (Berkeley: University of California Press, 1999), 76–77.

8. Dallek, *Flawed Giant*, 462; William L. Lunch and Peter W. Sperlich, "American Public Opinion and the War in Vietnam," *Western Political Quarterly* 32, no. 1 (March 1979); Edward J. Drea, *McNamara, Clifford, and the Burdens of Vietnam, 1965–1969* (Washington, DC: Department of Defense, 2011), 173; *The Gallup Poll* (Wilmington, DE: Scholarly Resources, 1980), 2073, 2075; also see Don Oberdorfer, *Tet!* (Baltimore: Johns Hopkins University Press, 1971), 82–83.

9. "The President in Trouble," *Newsweek*, September 4, 1967.

10. Ibid.; "LBJ Under Fire," *Wall Street Journal*, October 6, 1967; also see "Consensus of a Different Kind," *Time*, October 13, 1967.

11. Lunch and Sperlich, "American Public Opinion," 27.

12. Oberdorfer, *Tet*, 82; Bernstein, *Guns and Butter*, 414; Mark K. Updegrove, *Indomitable Will: LBJ in the Presidency* (New York: Crown, 2012), 239; Randall B. Woods, *LBJ: Architect of American Ambition* (New York: Free Press, 2006), 808–9.

13. Stewart Alsop, "Can Anyone Beat LBJ?," *Saturday Evening Post*, June 3, 1967.

14. "The War: Thunder from a Distant Hill," *Time*, October 6, 1967; "Non-Interventionism, 1967 Style," *New York Times Magazine*, September 17, 1967; "Johnson Assailed in Senate by Case for War Conduct," *New York Times*, September 26, 1967; *New York Times*, "Vietnam: Johnson Under Political Pressure," October 1, 1967; Robert Mann, *A Grand Delusion: America's Descent into Vietnam* (New York: Basic Books, 2001), 553 on declining Senate support.

15. "The War: Thunder from a Distant Hill"; Mann, *Grand Delusion*, 549–50; Dallek, *Flawed Giant*, 485; "Mansfield Fears New World War in Asia Conflict," *New York Times*, July 12, 1967.

16. R. W. Apple, "Vietnam: The Signs of Stalemate," *New York Times*, August 7, 1967.

17. Dallek, *Flawed Giant*, 471; Mann, *Grand Delusion*, 547; *Pentagon Papers:* Part IV C6 B Volume 2, 214; "Bottomless Pit in Vietnam," *New York Times*, August 6, 1967.

18. "The War: Thunder from a Distant Hill"; "Consensus of a Different Kind," *Time*, October 13, 1967; "The Case for Bombing Pause Number 7," also see *Life*, October 20, 1967.

19. Clark Clifford and Richard Holbrooke, *Counsel to the President: A Memoir* (New York: Random House, 1991), 449–51.

20. Ibid.

21. See David Halberstam, *The Best and the Brightest* (New York: Ballantine, 1992), 645.

22. Robert S. McNamara, *In Retrospect: The Tragedy and Lessons of Vietnam* (New York: Times Books/Random House, 1995), 269; "Draft Memorandum From Secretary of Defense McNamara to President Johnson," May 19, 1967, in *Foreign Relations of the United States, 1964–1968*, vol. 5, *Vietnam 1967*, ed. Kent Sieg (Washington, DC: US Department of State, 2002), Document 177; "Report of the Office of the Secretary of Defense Vietnam Task Force," *Pentagon Papers*, Part IV C 7 B, "Evolution of the War: Air War in the North: 1965–1968," National Archives, 100–104; George Herring, *America's Longest War: The United States and Vietnam, 1950–1975*, 2nd ed. (New York: Alfred A. Knopf, 1986), 177.

23. McNamara, *In Retrospect*, 308.

24. Ibid.; "A Fifteen Month Program for Military Operations in Southeast Asia," in Sieg, *Foreign Relations*, Document 375; "Implications of an Unfavorable Outcome in Vietnam," September 11, 1967, available online at http://www.foia.cia.gov/sites/default/files/document_conversions/89801/DOC_0001166443.pdf; Halberstam, *The Best and Brightest*, 645.

25. Mann, *Grand Delusion*, 562; Clifford and Holbrooke, *Counsel to the President*, 455; Walter Isaacson and Evan Thomas, *The Wise Men* (New York: Simon & Schuster, 1986), 680.

26. Lyndon B. Johnson: "Address on Vietnam Before the National Legislative Conference, San Antonio, Texas," September 29, 1967, online at *The American Presidency Project*, http://www.presidency.ucsb.edu/ws/?pid=28460; *Pentagon Papers*, Part IV C 7 B; "Evolution of the War: Air War in the North: 1965–1968," 101.

27. "Notes of Meeting," Washington, September 26, 1967, in Sieg, *Foreign Relations*, Document 336.

28. "Notes of Meeting," Washington, October 4, 1967, in Sieg, *Foreign Relations*, Document 346.

29. "Memorandum For the File by President Johnson," Washington, December 18, 1967, in Sieg, *Foreign Relations*, Document 441.

30. Logevall, *Choosing War*, 146; Dallek, *Flawed Giant*, 460–61.

31. Dallek, *Flawed Giant*, 469; Larry Berman, *Lyndon Johnson's War: The Road to Stalemate in Vietnam* (New York: W. W. Norton, 1989), 45; Mann, *Grand Delusion*, 557.

32. L. Berman, *Lyndon Johnson's War*, 84; George C. Herring, *LBJ and Vietnam* (Austin: University of Texas Press, 1994), 143; Stanley Karnow, *Vietnam: A History; The First Complete Account of Vietnam at War* (New York: Viking, 1984), 513; "Notes of Meeting," October 23, 1967, in Sieg, *Foreign Relations*, Document 363; Oberdorfer, *Tet*, 102; Edgar Berman, *Hubert: The Triumph and the Tragedy of the Hubert I Knew* (New York: G. P. Putnam, 1979), 116; also see Dallek, *Flawed Giant*, 492.

33. "President and Vietnam: Johnson Comes Out Fighting," *New York Times*, November 19, 1967.

34. Herring, *LBJ and Vietnam*, 147; *Evans & Novak Report*, November 29, 1967.

35. Philip E. Converse, Sidney Verba, and Milton J. Rosenberg, *Vietnam and the Silent Majority* (New York: Harper & Row, 1970), 38.

Chapter 3

1. Nick Thimmesch "McCarthy Makes His Move," *Newsday*, December 2, 1967; "Unlikely Challenger," *Wall Street Journal*, November 16, 1967; Arthur Herzog, *McCarthy for President* (New York: Viking Press, 1969), 60.

2. Lewis Chester, Geoffrey Hodgson, and Bruce Page, *American Melodrama: The Presidential Campaign of 1968* (New York: Viking Adult, 1969), 68; Eugene McCarthy, *Up 'Til Now: A Memoir* (San Diego: Harcourt Brace Jovanovich, 1987), 53; Dominic Sandbrook, *Eugene McCarthy: The Rise and Fall of Postwar Liberalism* (New York: Knopf, 2004), 90; the argument that McCarthy was primarily motivated by LBJ's snub is made prominently by Sandbrook in his biography of McCarthy.

3. "Dissenter on Vietnam," *New York Times*, October 16, 1967; "Straws in the Wind," *Time*, November 19, 1959.

4. Eugene McCarthy, *Frontiers in American Democracy* (Cleveland: World, 1960), 13.

5. Richard T. Stout, *People* (New York: Harper & Row, 1970), 112–13; Sandbrook, *Eugene McCarthy*, 162.

6. Eugene McCarthy, *Year of the People* (New York: Doubleday, 1969), 3.

7. Woods, *LBJ*, 485; Harry S. Truman: "Special Message to the Congress on Greece and Turkey: The Truman Doctrine," March 12, 1947, online at *The American Presidency Project*, http://www.presidency.ucsb.edu/ws/?pid=12846.

8. Roger Morris, *Richard Milhous Nixon: The Rise of an American Politician* (New York: Henry Holt, 1989), 613; Mann, *Grand Delusion*, 47.

9. Albert Eisele, *Almost to the Presidency* (Blue Earth, MN: Piper, 1972), 258; Sandbrook, *Eugene McCarthy*, 131.

10. McCarthy, *Up 'Til Now*, 128; Eisele, *Almost to the Presidency*, 162; Sandbrook, *Eugene McCarthy*, 124; "McCarthy Urges People to End Political 'Cult of the Presidency,'" *New York Times*, January 24, 1960.

11. McCarthy, *Year of the People*, 22; McCarthy, *Up 'Til Now*, 173.

12. Congressional Record—Senate, January 27, 1966, 1324.

13. Recording of Telephone Conversation between Johnson and Eugene McCarthy, February 1, 1966, WH6602.01, online at http://millercenter.org/presidential-recordings/lbj-wh6602.01-9601.

14. See Nicholas Thompson, *Hawk and the Dove: Paul Nitze, George Kennan, and the History of the Cold War* (New York: Picador, 2010), 203–5; also see Campbell Craig and Fredrik Logevall, *America's Cold War: The Politics of Insecurity* (Cambridge, MA: Belknap Press of Harvard University Press, 2009), 242; Randall Bennett Woods, *Fulbright: A Biography* (New York: Cambridge University Press, 1995), 403 and 719; Roper Center for Public Opinion Research, University of Connecticut, Harris Survey, December 1965, Harris Survey, February 1966.

15. Congressional Record—Senate, March 25, 1964, 6227–32.

16. As quoted in Woods, *Fulbright*, 388; also see Eisele, *Almost to the Presidency*, 261.

17. Eisele, *Almost to the Presidency*, 261; Congressional Record—Senate, September 30, 1965, 25, 622; also see Sandbrook, *Eugene McCarthy*, for his look at the influence of Fulbright on McCarthy's foreign policy thinking.

18. Senator Eugene J. McCarthy, *The Limits of Power* (New York: Dell Books, 1967), 21 and 171.

19. As quoted in William C. Berman, *William Fulbright and the Vietnam War* (Kent, OH: Kent State University Press, 1988), 88; George Rising, *Clean for Gene: Eugene McCarthy's 1968 Presidential Campaign* (Westport, CT: Praeger, 1997), 56–57.

20. Sandbrook, *Eugene McCarthy*, 162.

21. Chester, Hodgson, and Page, *American Melodrama*, 59; "Reminisces of Gary Hart": Oral History, 1988, Allard K. Lowenstein Project, Columbia University Center for Oral History, 16; William H. Chafe, *Never Stop Running: Allard Lowenstein and the Struggle to Save American Liberalism* (New York: Basic Books, 1993), 264.

22. Eisele, *Almost to the Presidency*, 277–78; Chafe, *Never Stop Running*, 264–71.

23. Stout, *People*, 74–76.

24. Eisele, *Almost to the Presidency*, 277–79.

25. "Press Conference of Senator Eugene J. McCarthy," November 30, 1967, http://www.4president.org/speeches/mccarthy1968announcement.htm; Stout, *People*, 112.

26. Stout, *People*, 112; "Unlikely Challenger," *Wall Street Journal*, November 16, 1967.

27. Ronald Steel, *Walter Lippmann and the American Century* (Boston: Atlantic Monthly, 1980), 587; Jesse Stellato, *Not in Our Name: American Antiwar Speeches 1846 to the Present* (University Park: Pennsylvania State University Press, 2012), 145.

28. David Charles Hoeh, *1968, McCarthy, New Hampshire: I Hear America Singing* (Rochester, MN: Lone Oak Press, 1994), 89.

29. "Eugene McCarthy Hits the Road," *New Republic*, November 25, 1967; Ray Boomhower, *Robert F. Kennedy and the 1968 Indiana Primary* (Bloomington: Indiana University Press, 2008), 17; Andrew Kopkind, "The McCarthy Campaign," *Ramparts*, March 1968, 50–55.

30. *Evans & Novak Report*, November 29, 1967.

Chapter 4

1. Robert A. Caro, *Master of the Senate* (New York: Vintage, 2002), 450; Hubert H. Humphrey Oral History Interview 3, June 21, 1977, LBJ Library, 5.

2. Chester, Hodgson, and Page, *American Melodrama*, 149; Harry McPherson, *A Political Education* (Boston: Little, Brown, 1972).

3. Humphrey Oral History, LBJ Library, 19.

4. Carl Solberg, *Hubert Humphrey: A Biography* (Minneapolis: Borealis, 2003), 271; E. Berman, *Hubert*, 90–91; Hubert H. Humphrey, *The Education of a Public Man: My Life and Politics* (Garden City, NY: Doubleday, 1976), 302.

5. "Memorandum from the President's Special Assistant for National Security Affairs (Bundy) to President Johnson," Johnson Library, National Security File, Memos to the President, McGeorge Bundy, vol. 8, online at http://www.presidency.ucsb .edu/vietnam/showdoc.php?docid=37.

6. Logevall, *Choosing War*, 318.

7. Gibbons, *US Government and the Vietnam War*, 50–51, 86; *Pentagon Papers*, Part IV C3, 1.

8. Humphrey, *Education of a Public Man*, 318–19; Eisele, *Almost to the Presidency*, 233; E. Berman, *Hubert*, 103.

9. "Memorandum from Senator Hubert H. Humphrey to the President," in *Foreign Relations of the United States, 1964–1968*, vol. 1, *Vietnam, 1964*, ed. John P. Glennon (Washington, DC: US Department of State, 1992), Document 208; Logevall, *Choosing War*, 169–70.

10. "Humphrey Calls for Popular Elections in South Vietnam," *Los Angeles Times*, August 18, 1964; Humphrey, *Education of a Public Man*, 318–19.

11. Gibbons, *US Government and the Vietnam War*, 92; author interview with Thomas Hughes.

12. "Memorandum from Vice President Humphrey to President Johnson," Washington, February 17, 1965, in *Foreign Relations of the United States, 1964–1968; Volume II, Vietnam, January–June, 1965*, ed. Glenn W. LaFantasie (Washington, DC: US Department of State, 1992), Document 134.

13. Ibid.

14. Ibid.

15. Ibid.

16. E. Berman, *Hubert*, 88.

17. W. Marvin Watson with Sherman Markman, *Chief of Staff* (New York: Thomas Dunne, 2004), 254; Thomas Hughes, "The Running Mates," unpublished draft provided to author; Fredrik Logevall, "Structure, Contingency, and the Vietnam War," SHAFR 2014 Presidential Address, available online at http://shafr.org/content/shafr-2014-presidential-address-structure-contingency-and-vietnam-war-fredrik-logevall.

18. Joseph A. Califano, Jr., *The Triumph and Tragedy of Lyndon Johnson: The White House Years* (New York: Touchstone, 1991), 64–69; Ted Van Dyk, *Heroes, Hacks and Fools: Memoirs from the Political Inside* (Seattle: University of Washington Press, 2007), 43–44; Humphrey, *Education of a Public Man*, 242; Eisele, *Almost to the Presidency*, 233–34; Thomas Hughes Oral History, July 7, 1999, *The Foreign Affairs Oral History Collection of the Association for Diplomatic Studies and Training*, available online at http://www.adst.org/OH%20TOCs/Hughes,%20Thomas%20L.toc.pdf; William Connell Oral History, March 18, 1985, LBJ Library, 23–24.

19. Robert Sherrill and Harry W. Ernst, *The Drugstore Liberal* (New York: Grossman, 1968), 1; "Summary Notes of the 553d Meeting of the National Security Council," Johnson Library, National Security File, NSC Meetings File, vol. 3.

20. Solberg, *Hubert Humphrey*, 240; Ambassador Max M. Kampelman, Oral History, June 24, 2003, *Association for Diplomatic Studies and Training Foreign Affairs Oral History Project*, 67; also see Max M. Kampelman, *Entering New Worlds: The Memoirs of a Private Man in Public Life* (New York: Harper Collins, 1991), 147–48.

21. "The Dogged Loyalty That Dogs HHH," *New Republic*, May 4, 1968; David English and the staff of the London Daily Express, *Divided They Stand* (Englewood Cliffs, NJ: Prentice-Hall, 1969), 216.

22. "Report Card on Humphrey the Traveler," *New York Times*, February 27, 1966.

23. Eisele, *Almost to the Presidency*, 243; Jack Richardson, "Who Is Hubert, What Is He?" *Esquire*, November 1966.

24. "The Vice Presidency: The Bright Spirit," *Time*, April 1, 1966; Solberg, *Hubert Humphrey*, 290; also see "Hubert Humphrey: The Peter Pan of Politics," *Baltimore Sun*, April 10, 1966; "Politics and People: Hubert the Helper," *Wall Street Journal*, April 29, 1966; Eisele, *Almost to the Presidency*, 246.

25. "Two From Minnesota," *New Republic*, June 8, 1968; Richardson, "Who Is Hubert?"; "Humphrey Says Meaning of Honolulu Talks Is a Sweeping US Commitment for Asia," *Wall Street Journal*, April 20, 1966.

26. E. Berman, *Hubert*, 116.

27. Solberg, *Hubert Humphrey*, 159; Sherrill and Ernst, *Drugstore Liberal*, 76; Winthrop Griffith, *Humphrey: A Candid Biography* (New York: William Morrow, 1965), 221.

28. Dan Cohen, *Undefeated: The Life of Hubert Humphrey* (Minneapolis: Lerner, 1978), 174; Griffith, *Humphrey*, 221; also see Allan H. Ryskind, *Hubert* (New Rochelle, NY: Arlington House, 1968), 206–9; Solberg, *Hubert Humphrey*, 159; Robert W. Griffith, *The Politics of Fear: Joseph McCarthy and the Senate* (Amherst: University of Massachusetts Press, 1987), 293.

29. Griffith, *Humphrey*, 222; "Hysteria on the Hill," *Washington Post*, August 19, 1954; Ryskind, *Hubert*, 204; Ellen W. Shrecker, *The Age of McCarthyism: A Brief History with Documents* (New York: Bedford/St. Martin's, 2002), 99; Solberg, *Hubert Humphrey*, 159.

30. Tom Hughes, interview with author, October 6, 2011; "Humphrey and Maddox See Room for Both in Party," *New York Times*, April 15, 1967.

31. Sherrill and Ernst, *Drugstore Liberal*, 12; "Conversation between Humphrey and [Kenneth] Harris [London Observer], post-August 1968," 150.F.18.5, University of Minnesota Historical Society; also see Griffith, *Humphrey*, 211.

32. "The Man Who Quit Kicking the Wall," *Time*, September 4, 1964; Tom Hughes, interview with author, October 6, 2011; Eric F. Goldman, *The Tragedy of Lyndon Johnson* (New York: Alfred A. Knopf, 1969), 263.

33. Solberg, *Hubert Humphrey*, 149, 345–46.

34. David Halberstam, *The Unfinished Odyssey of Robert Kennedy* (New York: Bantam, 1969), 165.

Chapter 5

1. Chester, Hodgson, and Page, *American Melodrama*, 106; "Kennedy Repeats: No Johnson Fight," *New York Times*, January 31, 1968.

2. Jules Witcover, *85 Days: The Last Campaign of Robert Kennedy* (New York: Putnam, 1969), 16; Chester, Hodgson, and Page, *American Melodrama*, 106.

3. Robert Kennedy, *To Seek a Newer World* (New York: Bantam, 1968), 232–34.

4. Jack Newfield, *RFK: A Memoir* (New York: Nation Books, 2003), 193–96; David Halberstam makes this argument more directly in *Unfinished Odyssey*; Witcover, *85 Days*, 20.

5. Robert F. Kennedy Conference, John F. Kennedy Library and Museum, November 18, 2000, transcript available online at http://www.jfklibrary.org/~/media/assets/ Education%20and%20Public%20Programs/Forum%20Transcripts/2000/2000%20 11%2018%20Robert%20F%20Kennedy%20Conference.pdf; Thurston Clarke, *The Last Campaign: Robert F. Kennedy and 82 Days That Inspired America* (New York: Holt Paperbacks, 2009), 2.

6. Penn Kimball, *Bobby Kennedy and the New Politics* (Englewood Cliffs, NJ: Prentice Hall, 1968), 53; Arthur M. Schlesinger, *Robert Kennedy and His Times* (Boston: Houghton Mifflin, 1978), 865, 876; Rick Perlstein, "Boston vs. Austin: The Political Rivalry That Split the Nation," *Slate*, November 5, 1997, http://www.slate.com/ articles/arts/books/1997/11/boston_vs_austin.2.html.

7. Newfield, *RFK*, 253.

8. Kimball, *Bobby Kennedy*, 67; also see Evan Thomas, *Robert Kennedy: His Life* (New York: Simon & Schuster, 2000), 316.

9. "Johnson, in City, Vows to Maintain Peace in Mideast," *New York Times*, June 4, 1967; Jeff Shesol, *Mutual Contempt: Lyndon Johnson, Robert Kennedy, and the Feud That Defined a Decade* (New York: W. W. Norton, 1997), 397; Schlesinger, *Robert Kennedy*, 836.

10. Kimball, *Bobby Kennedy*, 63.

11. Kenneth O'Donnell Oral History, April 3, 1969, Robert F. Kennedy Oral History Program of the John F. Kennedy Library, 6.

12. See Shesol, *Mutual Contempt*, 75–87.

13. Witcover, *85 Days*, 22; Thomas, *Robert Kennedy*, 332.

14. Edwin O. Guthman, ed., *RFK: Collected Speeches* (New York: Viking Adult, 1993), 285.

15. Thomas, *Robert Kennedy*, 315–16, Guthman, *RFK*, 289; Newfield, *RFK*, 126; Robert Sherrill, "The Faith of Eugene McCarthy," *The Nation*, December 4, 1967.

16. Schlesinger, *Robert Kennedy*, 773; "Men at War: RFK vs. LBJ," *Newsweek*, March 13, 1967.

17. Roper Center for Public Opinion Research, University of Connecticut, Harris Survey, November 1967; Decision to Run, "Gratuitous Advice Revisited," box 491, folders 4–5, Schlesinger Papers, New York Public Library; also see Thomas, *Robert Kennedy*, 358, on Dolan.

18. Shesol, *Mutual Contempt*, 406; Pierre Salinger Oral History, May 26, 1969, Robert F. Kennedy Oral History Program, JFK Library, 37–40; also see Pierre Salinger, *P.S.: A Memoir* (New York: St. Martin's, 1995).

19. Pierre Salinger Oral History, 46 and 53–54, 56; Richard Goodwin, McCarthy Historical Project, Oral History Interview Series, Eugene J. McCarthy Papers (SCRB 0014), University of Minnesota Libraries, Special Collections and Rare Books; "The Underlying Situation," Fred Dutton memo to Bobby Kennedy, November 3, 1967, box 491, folder '68 Campaign—RFK's Decision to Run, Schlesinger Papers; also see Theodore Sorensen Oral History, July 23, 1970, Robert F. Kennedy Oral History Program, JFK Library, 8.

20. Arthur M. Schlesinger, *Journals, 1952-2000* (New York: Penguin, 2007), 275; Clarke, *Last Campaign*, 34.

21. Newfield, RFK, 204 "Excerpts from Text of Kennedy Speech," *New York Times*, February 9, 1968; "Kennedy Asserts U.S. Cannot Win," *New York Times*, February 9, 1968.

22. "Kennedy Asserts U.S. Cannot Win," *New York Times*, February 9, 1968; Clarke, *Last Campaign*, 35.

23. Mann, *Grand Delusion*, 572–76.

24. Ibid.

25. Oberdorfer, *Tet*, 158, 167, 175.

26. Ibid., 158; "The Logic of the Battlefield," *Wall Street Journal*, February 23, 1968.

27. Clark Clifford and Richard Holbrooke, "Serving the President II: The Vietnam Years," *New Yorker*, May 13, 1991.

28. Oberdorfer, *Tet*, 246.

29. Dallek, *Flawed Giant*, 515.

30. *Report of the National Advisory Commission on Civil Disorders* (New York: Bantam, 1968), 1.

31. *Report of the National Advisory Commission on Civil Disorders*, 9; Dallek, *Flawed Giant*, 516; Witcover, *85 Days*, 53.

32. "Man of the Year: Lyndon B. Johnson, the Paradox of Power," *Time*, January 5, 1968; James Reston, "Washington: The Paradox of America," *New York Times*, March 6, 1968.

33. This theme is explored in Doris Kearns Goodwin's biography of Johnson, *Lyndon Johnson and the American Dream*.

34. Max Frankel, "Johnson Confers with Eisenhower; Briefs Him on War," *New York Times*, February 19, 1968.

Chapter 6

1. "President Widens Margin in Poll: Gallup Finds McCarthy and Kennedy Further Behind," *New York Times*, February 4, 1968; "Paradox of Power," *Time*, January 5, 1968; Lewis Gould, "Never a Deep Partisan," in *The Johnson Years*, vol. 3, *LBJ at*

Home and Abroad, ed. Robert A. Divine (Lawrence: University Press of Kansas, 1994), 21–52.

2. Gerry Studds Oral History, McCarthy Oral History Project, 12; Hoeh, *1968, McCarthy, New Hampshire*, 124–25.

3. Herzog, *McCarthy for President*, 88; "Unforeseen Eugene," *Time*, March 22, 1968; Richard Goodwin Oral History, 5, 8.

4. Herzog, *McCarthy for President*, 79, 83, 87; Hoeh, *1968, McCarthy, New Hampshire*, 154–55, 242; Sandbrook, *Eugene McCarthy*, 174–75; Chester, Hodgson, and Page, *American Melodrama*, 88–89; "Unforeseen Eugene," *Time*, March 22, 1968.

5. See Theodore H. White, *The Making of the President 1968* (New York: Harper Collins, 2010); also Chester, Hodgson, and Page, *American Melodrama*, 76; Chafe, *Never Stop Running*, 279; "A Statesman Who . . .," *New York Times*, December 4, 1967; Gerry Studds Oral History, 24; "Reminiscences of Gary Hart," 13–14.

6. Stellato, *Not in Our Name*, 145–46; McCarthy, *Frontiers in American Democracy*, 61.

7. Eugene McCarthy, "Why I'm Battling LBJ," *Look*, February 6, 1968; Hoeh, *1968, McCarthy, New Hampshire*, 244 (see photo inserts); also see Hoeh, *1968, McCarthy, New Hampshire*, 234–38, on efforts to get the antiwar group SANE and others to coordinate their activities with the McCarthy campaign, and also 271.

8. "Unforeseen Eugene," *Time*, March 22, 1968; "McCarthy Talks about Kennedy and the Issues," *US News and World Report*, April 1, 1968.

9. Richard Goodwin Oral History, 9–10; Chester, Hodgson, and Page, *American Melodrama*, 96; "McCarthy Style: Rhetoric Lesson," *Wall Street Journal*, July 15, 1968.

10. Rising, *Clean for Gene*, 67; Ben Stavis, *We Were the Campaign* (Boston: Beacon, 1969), 17.

11. Rising, *Clean for Gene*, 100; White, *Making of the President*, 101; also see Richard Stout's *People* on the Clean for Gene phenomenon.

12. Jeremy Larner, *Nobody Knows: Reflections on the McCarthy Campaign of 1968* (New York: Macmillan, 1970), 38; "1968 and the Johnson Presidency," April 30, 1998, Newseum panel discussion, http://www.c-span.org/video/?105040-1/1968-johnson-presidency; "All Is Changed, Changed Utterly...by Army of Students," *Boston Globe*, March 10, 1968.

13. Walter Lafeber, *A Deadly Bet: LBJ, Vietnam, and the 1968 Election* (Lanham, MD: Rowan & Littlefield, 2005), 40; Stavis, *We Were the Campaign*, 10, 27–28.

14. Herzog, *McCarthy for President*, 90.

15. John B. Henry II, "February, 1968," *Foreign Policy*, Autumn 1971, 23, 32.

16. Clark M. Clifford, "A Vietnam Reappraisal: The Personal History of One Man's View and How It Evolved," *Foreign Affairs*, July 1969; the work of the Clifford task force is covered in Clifford and Holbrooke, *Counsel to the President*, 492–96.

17. "Westmoreland Requests 206,000 More Men, Stirring Debate in Administration," *New York Times*, March 10, 1968; also see Clifford and Holbrooke, *Counsel to the President*, 500.

18. John Roche Oral History, LBJ Library, 60.

19. Philip E. Converse, Warren E. Miller, Jerrold G. Rusk, and Arthur C. Wolfe, "Continuity and Change in American Politics: Parties and Issues in the 1968 Election," *American Political Science Review* 63 (December 1969): 1083–1105.

20. Larner, *Nobody Knows*, 41; also see Richard Goodwin Oral History.

21. "Kennedy Is Ready to Run; Says Vote for McCarthy Discloses Split in Party," *New York Times*, March 14, 1968; Boomhower, *Robert F. Kennedy*, 28; Eisele, *Almost to the Presidency*, 300.

22. Fred Dutton Oral History, Robert F. Kennedy Oral History Program, JFK Library, 38; Witcover, *85 Days*, 60; Thomas, *Robert Kennedy*, 359; Newfield, *RFK*, 239.

23. Witcover, *85 Days*, 60; "RFK Cites Party Unity as Reason not to Run," *Washington Post*, March 11, 1968; Schlesinger Papers, 1968 Campaign (States A–C), folder 1 for Lewis letter; William vanden Heuvel and Milton Gwirtzman, *On His Own: Robert F. Kennedy, 1964–1968* (Garden City, NY: Doubleday, 1970), 304; Thomas M. C. Johnston Oral History, Robert F. Kennedy Oral History Program, JFK Library, 20; George McGovern, *Grassroots* (New York: Random House, 1977), 112; also see George McGovern Oral History, Robert F. Kennedy Oral History Program, JFK Library, July 16, 1970.

24. Shesol, *Mutual Contempt*, 418–19; Schlesinger, *Robert Kennedy*, 914–16; Clifford and Holbrooke, *Counsel to the President*, 503; also see Witcover, *85 Days*, 70–71.

25. Herzog, *McCarthy for President*, 105; McCarthy, *Year of the People*, 89.

26. "McCarthy Aims Jab at Kennedy," *Associated Press*, March 19, 1968; Schlesinger, *Robert Kennedy*, 918–19; Abigail McCarthy, *Private Faces/Public Places* (Garden City, NY: Doubleday, 1972).

27. Schlesinger, *Robert Kennedy*, 919–20.

28. "Politics: The New Context of 1968," *Time*, March 22, 1968; Newfield, *RFK*, 227; Shesol, *Mutual Contempt*, 422.

29. "Kennedy's Statement and Excerpts from News Conference," *New York Times*, March 17, 1968.

30. "Tart, Tough and Telegenic," *Time*, March 22, 1968; Witcover, *85 Days*, 87.

31. Schlesinger, *Robert Kennedy*, 922; "Who Will It Be in November," *US News & World Report*, April 15, 1968; senatorial quotes from Schlesinger Papers, box 491, LBJ, folders 6–7.

32. "Senator Kennedy Farewell," *New York Post*, March 26, 1968.

33. Shesol, *Mutual Contempt*, 425; Guthman, *RFK*, 236; James Tolan Oral History, RFK Oral History Project, JFK Library, June 26, 1969, 6.

34. Clarke, *Last Campaign*, 59; also see Thomas, *Robert Kennedy*, 364; Witcover, *85 Days*, 88.

35. Newfield, *RFK*, 230; "Democrats: The Rivals," *Newsweek*, April 8, 1968.

36. Guthman, *RFK*, 328; Newfield, *RFK*, 234–35; Schlesinger, *Robert Kennedy*, 929.

37. Scammon and Wattenberg, *Real Majority*, 19; Witcover, *85 Days*, 84–85.

38. White, *Making of the President*, 202–3.

39. Fred Dutton Oral History, 49; Witcover, *85 Days*, 147.

40. Robert F. Kennedy, "Remarks at the University of Kansas, March 18, 1968," online at http://www.jfklibrary.org/Research/Research-Aids/Ready-Reference/RFK-Speeches/ Remarks-of-Robert-F-Kennedy-at-the-University-of-Kansas-March-18-1968.aspx.

41. Ibid.

42. Johnson, *Vantage Point*, 538; Shesol, *Mutual Contempt*, 429; "Under Way with LBJ," *Newsweek*, April 1, 1968.

43. Townsend Hoopes, "The Fight for the President's Mind—And the Men Who Won It," *Atlantic*, October 1, 1969; "Excerpts from Speech by President," *New York Times*, March 19, 1968.

44. Arthur Krim Oral History, Addendum to Interview III, LBJ Library, March 18, 1994, 11; Townsend Hoopes, "The Fight for the President's Mind—And the Men Who Won It," *Atlantic*, October 1, 1969.

45. Memorandum: "Peace with Honor in Vietnam," box 491, folder 6–7, LBJ, Schlesinger Papers; "Under Way with LBJ," *Newsweek*, April 1, 1968; Krim Oral History, 11.

46. Lawrence F. O'Brien Oral History 20, LBJ Library, April 23, 1987; Lawrence F. O'Brien Oral History 21, LBJ Library, June 18, 1987; Watson and Markman, *Chief of Staff*, 276–77; Dallek, *Flawed Giant*, 529; "Democrats: Rivals," *Newsweek*, April 8, 1968, 36; O'Brien Oral History 21; also see Lawrence O'Brien, *No Final Victories* (Garden City, NY: Doubleday, 1974), 215–21.

47. Dallek, *Flawed Giant*, 529; "Man of the Year: Lyndon B. Johnson, the Paradox of Power," *Time*, January 5, 1968; Goodwin, *Lyndon Johnson*, 340–41, 343.

48. Clifford and Holbrooke, *Counsel to the President*, 511–19; David S. Patterson, ed., *Foreign Relations of the United States, 1964–1968*, vol. 6, *Vietnam, January–August 1968* (Washington, DC: Government Printing Office, 2002), Document 158, Summary of Notes, March 26, 1968.

49. James Jones Oral History, Association for Diplomatic Studies and Training Foreign Affairs Oral History Project, September 10, 2002, 31, online at http://www.adst .org/OH%20TOCs/Jones,%20James%20R.toc.pdf; Watson and Markman, *Chief of Staff*, 268; Krim Oral History, 6; Arthur Krim Oral History: Addendum to Interview III, March 18, 1984, offers a comprehensive take on the evolution of LBJ's views on withdrawal.

50. Goodwin, *Lyndon Johnson*, 251, 344.

Chapter 7

1. "President Lyndon B. Johnson's Address to the Nation Announcing Steps to Limit the War in Vietnam and Reporting His Decision Not to Seek Reelection," March 31, 1968, online at *The American Presidency Project*, http://www.presidency.ucsb.edu/ws/?pid=28 772.

2. Tom Wicker, "Lyndon Johnson Is 10 Feet Tall," *New York Times Magazine*, May 23, 1965; "Why He Did It—What Now," *Newsweek*, April 15, 1968; Dallek, *Flawed Giant*, 528–29; Johnson, *Vantage Point*, 425–26, 435; Horace Busby, *The Thirty-First of March: An Intimate Portrait of Lyndon Johnson's Final Days in Office* (New York: Farrar, Straus & Giroux, 2005), 205.

3. "The Renunciation," *Time*, April 12, 1968; Sandbrook, *Eugene McCarthy*, 187.

4. Roper Center for Public Opinion Research, University of Connecticut, Harris Survey, April 1968; "The Renunciation," *Time*, April 12, 1968; Stout, *People*, 32.

5. Woods, *Architect of Ambition*, 837; "President's Visit Here for Cooke's Installation Is Marked by a Series of Surprises," *New York Times*, April 5, 1968.

6. "President Lyndon B. Johnson's Address to the Nation Announcing Steps to Limit the War in Vietnam and Reporting His Decision Not to Seek Reelection," March 31, 1968.

7. *Report of the Select Committee on Assassinations of the U.S. House of Representatives: Findings in the Assassination of Dr. Martin Luther King, Jr.*, 289–94, http://www .archives.gov/research/jfk/select-committee-report/part-2a.html#king.

8. Donald Janson, "Negroes Crowd Jails in Chicago," *New York Times*, April 9, 1968.

9. Dana Lanier Shaffer, "The 1968 Washington Riots in History and Memory," *Washington History*, Fall/Winter 2003/2004.

10. "Gun Problem: The Citizens Arm as Congress Looks the Other Way," *New York Times*, April 21, 1968; "Army to Increase Riot Duty Troops: Adding 10,000 in View of Disorders Following Dr. King's Assassination," *New York Times*, April 24, 1968. On Polling see Hazel Erskine, "The Polls: Speed of Racial Integration," *Public Opinion Quarterly* 32, no. 3 (Autumn 1968): 513–24.

11. Paul Gorman Oral History, McCarthy Oral History Project.

12. Warren Weaver, Jr., "65% at Convention to Back Johnson, Survey Indicates," *New York Times*, March 24, 1968, provides an excellent overview of the confusing delegate choosing process.

13. "Anchors Aweigh," *Time*, October 20, 1967.

14. "McCarthy and Kennedy: Philosopher vs. Evangelist," *Washington Post*, May 26, 1968.

15. Tolan Oral History, June 26, 1969, 45.

16. Clarke, *Last Campaign*, 95; Boomhower, *Robert F. Kennedy*, 65; "Statement on the Death of Martin Luther King, Jr.," April 4, 1968, John F. Kennedy Presidential Library and Museum, http://www.jfklibrary.org/Asset-Viewer/H0SE-5I0kUyRrXm WyQRsIw.aspx.

17. "Statement on the Death of Martin Luther King, Jr.," April 4, 1968, John F. Kennedy Presidential Library and Museum.

18. John Lewis, with Michael D'Orso, *Walking with the Wind: A Memoir of the Movement* (New York: Simon & Schuster, 1998), 393.

19. Halberstam, *Unfinished Odyssey*, 83.

20. "Remarks of Senator Robert F. Kennedy to the Cleveland City Club," Cleveland, Ohio, April 5, 1968, Senate Papers 1964–1968, Books, case files, correspondence, speeches, press releases, RFKSEN, JFK Presidential Library and Museum.

21. Ibid.

22. Newfield, *RFK*, 250.

23. Thomas, *Robert Kennedy*, 371; Halberstam, *Unfinished Odyssey*, 128; Witcover, *85 Days*, 194, makes a similar point.

24. Richard Harwood, "Kennedy's Words Miss Crowd Mood," *Washington Post*, April 20, 1968.

25. "Kennedy: Meet the Conservative," *New York Times*, April 28, 1968; "Kennedy Courts the Conservatives," *Christian Science Monitor*, April 26, 1968; also see Gerard F. Doherty Oral History, RFK Oral History Collection, JFK Library.

26. Thomas, *Robert Kennedy*, 370; Jeff Greenfield Oral History, RFK Oral History Collection, JFK Library, January 5, 1970, 53; also see "1968 Presidential Primary Campaign (RFK: Campaign Journal)," Box 82, John Bartlow Martin Papers, Library of Congress, 11–18; Dutton Oral History, 51; Johnson, *Vantage Point*, 549.

27. Thomas, *Robert Kennedy*, 316; Robert Kennedy Conference.

28. Stephen E. Ambrose, *Nixon*, vol. 2, *The Triumph of a Politician, 1962–1972* (New York: Simon & Schuster, 1989), 156; Democratic National Committee, "Political News Summary (PNS)," May 27, 1968, Personal Political Correspondence, Press Releases, Humphrey Papers; "It Is Much Better to Win," *Newsweek*, May 19, 1968.

29. Schlesinger, *Robert Kennedy*, 961.

30. Speech at University California, Davis, May 28, 1968, Eugene J. McCarthy Papers, University of Minnesota, Special Collections and Rare Books (henceforth EJM Papers), box 74,; Speech to Businessman's Lunch, Miami Florida—Address to Tiger Bay Club, February 9, 1968, EJM Papers, box 74.

31. Martin Luther King, Jr., on *Face the Nation*, CBS, April 16, 1967, available on YouTube, https://www.youtube.com/watch?v=G0FlXe9zomQ.

32. George McGovern, "Address Accepting the Presidential Nomination at the Democratic National Convention in Miami Beach, Florida," July 14, 1972, online at *The American Presidency Project*, http://www.presidency.ucsb.edu/ws/index.php?pid=25967.

33. McCarthy, speech at the University of California, Davis.

34. See Larner, *Nobody Knows*.

35. See Robert F. Kennedy, *To Seek a Newer World* (New York: Bantam, 1968), 162–219. Kennedy is critical of the war and recognizes his own role in the conflict's evolutions, but continues to adhere to the basic tenets of the domino theory and US Cold War policy.

36. Speech at Whitewater State University, EJM Papers, box 73, March 31, 1968; also Speech, February 6, 1968, Concord, New Hampshire, EJM Papers, box 73.

37. Address by Senator Eugene J. McCarthy, Cow Palace, San Francisco, May 22, 1968, EJM Papers, box 74; also see "McCarthy Gibes at Both Rivals," *New York Times*, May 23, 1968.

38. Sandbrook, *Eugene McCarthy*, 195, and Chester, Hodgson, and Page, *American Melodrama*, 167; "McCarthy and Kennedy: Philosopher vs. Evangelist," *Washington Post*, May 26, 1968.

39. Gorman Oral History, 30; "Two from Minnesota," *New Republic*, June 8, 1968; Sandbrook, *Eugene McCarthy*, 195–96, and Chester, Hodgson, and Page, *Melodrama*, 167; Richard Harwood, "Humphrey's a Lesser Politician," *Los Angeles Times*, April 26, 1968.

40. O'Brien Oral History 23, 10; Stout, *People*, 219.

41. Stout, *People*, 216; Jeremy Larner, "Nobody Knows ... Reflections on the McCarthy Campaign, Part 1," *Harper's*, April 1969, 71; Eisele, *Almost to the Presidency*, 310; Stout, *People*, 216; "Negroes Are Cool to McCarthy as He Opens Indiana Campaign," *New York Times*, April 19, 1968.

42. Larner, "Nobody Knows," 68; Seymour Hersh Oral History, part 1, McCarthy Oral History Project, 24; Stavis, *We Were the Campaign*, 137; Robert Miraldi, *Seymour Hersh: Scoop Artist* (Lincoln, NE: Potomac: 2013), 112–15.

43. Vanden Heuvel and Gwirtzman, *On His Own*, 373; Victor Navasky, "The Haunting of Robert Kennedy," *New York Times,* June 2, 1968; The Roper Center for Public Opinion Research, University of Connecticut Harris Survey, May 1968.

44. Ronald Steel, *In Love with Night: The American Romance with Robert Kennedy* (New York: Simon & Schuster, 2000), 173, and Thomas, *Robert Kennedy*, 376; Milton S.

Gwirtzman, April 4, 1972, Robert F. Kennedy Oral History Project of the John F. Kennedy Library, 151; "Kennedy's Indiana Victory Proves His Appeal Defuses Backlash Voting," *Washington Post*, May 9, 1968; "Kennedy's Camp Voices Optimism," *New York Times*, May 7, 1968; Brian Dooley, *Robert Kennedy: The Final Years* (New York: St. Martin's, 1996), 125; Jefferson Cowie, *Stayin' Alive: The 1970s and the Last Days of the Working Class* (New York: New Press, 2010), 77.

45. Cowie, *Stayin' Alive*, 81; vanden Heuvel and Gwirtzman, *On His Own*, 348–49; Dooley, *Robert Kennedy*, 126; Rhodes Cook, *US Presidential Primary Elections, 1968–1996* (Washington DC: CQ Press, 2007), 233–35; Gwirtzman Papers, JFK Library, box 4, folder "Drafts: Unidentified Fragments, #2"; Louis Harris, "Part Way with RFK: The Price He Paid," *Newsweek*, May 20, 1968.

46. Thomas, *Robert Kennedy*, 376; see also "Harris Poll Results," *Washington Post*, May 6, 1968, on Kennedy's declining poll numbers; Steel, *In Love with Night*, 173; Gwirtzman Oral History, 152; Harris, "Part Way with RFK."

47. "Indiana: A Test for Bobby Kennedy," *New York Times*, May 5, 1968; "Funds Cited by McCarthy," *Baltimore Sun*, April 27, 1968; Chester, Hodgson, and Page, *American Melodrama*, 166–67.

48. Thomas, *Robert Kennedy*, 377; Witcover, *85 Days*, 202; Peter Edelman, August 19, 1969, RFK Oral History Collection, JFK Library, no. 3, 353; Chester, Hodgson, and Page, *American Melodrama*, 299; John Bartlow Martin, "Campaign Journal (RFK)."

49. Stout, *People*, 252.

50. Gwirtzman Paper, box 5, folder "Memoranda, 4/68–8/69", "Possible 'Non-Crowd' Campaign Activities…"; see Dutton Oral History; Jean Stein, *American Journey* (New York: Harcourt Brace Jovanovich, 1970), 272; also see Larner, *Nobody Knows*, 99–102, on the Kennedy/McCarthy zoo meeting.

51. Vanden Heuvel and Gwirtzman, *On His Own*, 322; Newfield, *RFK*, 191; Peter Edelman Oral History, 47–50.

52. Tom Shea, "Bobby Kennedy, Taylor Branch and What Happened to Pat Sylvester?" MassLive.com, June 5, 2011, http://www.masslive.com/tomshea/index.ssf/2011/06/tom_shea_taylor_branch_recalls.html; Witcover, *85 Days*, 181.

53. Arthur Herzog Oral History, McCarthy Oral History Project, 1; Joel Berger Oral History, McCarthy Oral History Project, 1.

54. Allard Lowenstein Oral History, McCarthy Oral History Project, 19–23; "All Is Changed, Changed Utterly … by Army of Students," *Boston Globe*, March 10, 1968.

55. Herzog Oral History, 143; Lowenstein Oral History, 34; Richard Harwood, "Kennedy Still McCarthy's Prime Target," *Washington Post*, May 19, 1968, offers a good take on McCarthy's views about RFK.

56. Stout, *People*, 208; Larner, "Nobody Knows," 65; Stein, *American Journey*, 304.

57. Frank Mankiewicz Oral History, December 16, 1969, JFK Library, 48.

58. Roper Center for Public Opinion Research, University of Connecticut Harris Survey, May 1968, and Harris Survey, November 1967; Roper Center for Public Opinion Research, University of Connecticut, Gallup Poll, May 1968; "Humphrey Seen Gaining if McCarthy Drops Out," *Indianapolis Star*, April 25, 1968.

59. Halberstam, *Unfinished Odyssey*, 183; vanden Heuvel and Gwirtzman, *On His Own*, 369.

60. "Kennedy's Oregon Defeat Gives Party Fence-Riders to Humphrey," *Washington Post*, May 30, 1968.
61. Stout, *People*, 265.
62. Stout, *People*, 268–70; also see Goodwin Oral History, 182–211; Chester, Hodgson, and Page, *American Melodrama*, 328; JFK Library, Steve Smith Papers, box 1, Pacific Polls, May 16–19, 1968 poll.
63. JFK Library, Steve Smith Papers, box 1, Pacific Polls, April 28–May 2 and May 16–19; Chester, Hodgson, and Page, *American Melodrama*, 335; vanden Heuvel and Gwirtzman, *On His Own*, 373; also see "Kennedy Taking Campaign Risks," *New York Times*, June 2, 1968; Thomas, *Robert Kennedy*, 385; Stein, *American Journey*, 299.
64. "Kennedy Assails McCarthy Tactics," and "McCarthy Renews Kennedy Attack," *New York Times*, June 1, 1968.
65. "Excerpts from the Kennedy-McCarthy Televised Discussion of Campaign Issues," *New York Times*, June 2, 1968.
66. Ibid.; Steve Smith Oral History, February 24, 1970, RFK Oral History Collection, JFK Library, 27; Newfield, *RFK*, 281.
67. "Kennedy Sees 'Desperation' in McCarthy Talk," *Los Angeles Times*, June 4, 1968; Schlesinger, *Robert Kennedy*, 979. Kennedy claimed that he intended to refer to Marin County but couldn't remember the proper pronunciation, so instead he named the first county that came to mind.
68. "Excerpts from the Kennedy-McCarthy Televised Discussion of Campaign Issues," *New York Times*, June 2, 1968.
69. Debate polls from Stout, *People*, 273, and Larner, "Nobody Knows," 78. Debate coverage overall from Larner, "Nobody Knows"; Stout, *People*, 272–73; Witcover, *85 Days*, 241–45; and Chester, Hodgson, and Page, *American Melodrama*, 339–49.
70. Gwirtzman Oral History, no. 5, 183.
71. "Transcript of Kennedy Primary Victory Speech," *New York Times*, June 5, 1968; "One of RFK's Final Interviews, ABC News, June 5, 1968," YouTube, https://www.youtube.com/watch?v=NaB34CNjWJw.
72. "Bobby's Last, Longest Day," *Newsweek*, June 17, 1968; Thomas, *Robert Kennedy*, 391; Clarke, *Last Campaign*, 273–75.
73. Califano, *Triumph and Tragedy*, 299; "Bobby's Last, Longest Day," *Newsweek*, June 17, 1968.

Chapter 8

1. Humphrey, *Education of a Public Man*, 358.
2. Solberg, *Hubert Humphrey*, 322; Eisele, *Almost to the Presidency*, 323.
3. Solberg, *Hubert Humphrey*, 322.
4. Humphrey, *Education of a Public Man*, 355–56.
5. Solberg, *Hubert Humphrey*, 322; Hubert H. Humphrey Oral History, March 30, 1970, RFK Oral History Collection, JFK Library, 38; Humphrey, *Education of a Public Man*, 360; Connell Oral History, 36.
6. Chester, Hodgson, and Page, *American Melodrama*, 144.
7. "Democrats: Humphrey Renewed," *Time*, April 19, 1968; Solberg, *Hubert Humphrey*, 324, Chester, Hodgson, and Page, *American Melodrama*, 144; Eisele, *Almost to the Presidency*, 326.

8. Hughes Interview; Humphrey, *Education of a Public Man*, 374; "Businessman to Raise $4 Million War Chest for HHH Candidacy," *Washington Post*, April 24, 1968; Eisele, *Almost to the Presidency*, 327; "How He Plans to Get the Boss's Job," *Life*, May 3, 1968.

9. "Humphrey Almost Says 'I'm In'" *Boston Globe*, April 5, 1968; "Democrats: Humphrey Renewed," *Time*, April 19, 1968; Chester, Hodgson, and Page, *American Melodrama*, 144.

10. Eisele, *Almost to the Presidency*, 328 "How He Plans to Get the Boss's Job," *Life*, May 3, 1968; Eisele, *Almost to the Presidency*, 328; Max Frankel, "Humphrey Believed Changed by Sense of Success in Campaign," *New York Times*, May 28, 1968.

11. "The Happy Man Who..." *Newsweek*, May 6, 1968; Hubert Humphrey, "Declaration of Candidacy for Presidential Nomination," April 27, 1968, available online at http://www.4president.org/speeches/hhh1968announcement.htm.

12. Clarke, *Last Campaign*, 203; Humphrey, *Education of a Public Man*, 370; English, *Divided They Stand*, 216.

13. "Political News Summary (PNS)," Democratic National Committee, May 22, 1968; "HHH Hits Own Party Candidates," *Hartford Courant*, May 22, 1968; PNS, May 25, 1968.

14. Eisele, *Almost to the Presidency*, 330; "The Once and Future Humphrey," *Time*, May 10, 1968.

15. Eisele, *Almost to the Presidency*, 330–31; Walter Mondale Oral History, RFK Oral History Collection, JFK Library, 18; Schlesinger Papers, box 492, folder: 1968 Campaign States (O-R); vanden Heuvel and Gwirtzman, *On His Own*, 362–63; also see O'Donnell Oral History.

16. English, *Divided They Stand*, 216; George Gallup, "HHH Top Choice for County Chairmen," *Boston Globe*, June 22, 1968.

17. Van Dyk, *Heroes, Hacks and Fools*, 70.

18. McCarthy, *Up 'Til Now*, 197–98.

19. O'Brien Oral History, 23, 4; Goodwin Oral History, 33.

20. Newfield, *RFK*, 81; vanden Heuvel and Gwirtzman, *On His Own*, 355.

21. Chester, Hodgson, and Page, *American Melodrama*, 338; vanden Heuvel and Gwirtzman, *On His Own*, 357; "Robert Kennedy's Chances: What a Survey Shows," *US News and World Report*, June 3, 1968; "The Once and Future Humphrey," *Time*, May 3, 1968.

22. JFK Library, RFK Papers, 1968 Presidential Campaign: Black Books, Background Materials, box 1, folder: General Memo, Esther Newberg; "65% at Convention to Back Johnson, Survey Indicates," *New York Times*, March 24, 1968.

23. "Robert Kennedy's Chances: What a Survey Shows," *US News and World Report*, June 3, 1968; see Garry Wills, "Waiting for Bobby," *New York Review of Books*, February 10, 2000.

24. Eisele, *Almost to the Presidency*, 332; Hubert H. Humphrey Oral History, JFK Library, 41–42.

25. "Candidates Halt Drives; Voice Shock and Sympathy," *New York Times*, June 6, 1968.

26. Eisele, *Almost to the Presidency*, 321; Stout, *People*, 282–83; Sandbrook, *Eugene McCarthy*, 206.

27. "Democrats: The Quiet Party," *Newsweek*, June 24, 1968.

28. Sandbrook, *Eugene McCarthy*, 206; Eisele, *Almost to the Presidency*, 338; Abigail McCarthy, *Private Faces/Public Places* (Garden City, NY: Doubleday, 1972), 407; Norman Mailer, *Some Honorable Men* (New York: Little, Brown, 1976), 179.

29. Eisele, *Almost to the Presidency*, 342; Stout, *People*, 304–7.

30. White, *Making of the President 1968*, 313.

31. "The Agony of Gene McCarthy," *Los Angeles Times*, June 9, 1968.

32. Larner, *Nobody Knows*, 122; see Roper Center, Gallup and Harris polls, July–August 1968.

33. Stout, *People*, 288, 312; Thomas Finney Oral History, McCarthy Oral History Project, 11.

34. Gloria Steinem, "Trying to Love Eugene," *New York*, August 5, 1968; Tom Wicker, "Kennedy Without Tears," in *Smiling through the Apocalypse: Esquire's History of the Sixties*, comp. Harold Hayes (New York: McCall, 1970), 33.

35. Eisele, *Almost to the Presidency*, 340–41.

36. EJM Papers, box 75; "Jefferson-Jackson Dinner, Oklahoma City," June 28, 1968; "Humphrey Corrals 37 of Oklahoma's 41 Votes," *Los Angeles Times*, June 30, 1968.

37. "Kennedy Youth Say McCarthy Is Indifferent," *Los Angeles Times*, July 4, 1968.

38. Jerome Grossman Oral History, McCarthy Oral History Project, 4; author interview with Thomas Hughes.

39. Finney Oral History, 15; Grossman Oral History, 4.

40. "Eugene McCarthy: A Blend of Humility, Arrogance and Humor," *New York Times*, August 29, 1968; author interview with Paul Gorman; "My Dog Can Beat Kennedy's," *Christian Science Monitor*, April 30, 1968.

41. Stout, *People*, 293–98, is authoritative on the efforts of Humphrey supporters to increase their delegate counts; see also "Politics USA: A Testing Time," *Newsweek*, July 1, 1968; Solberg, *Hubert Humphrey*, 342.

42. "Politics USA: A Testing Time," *Newsweek*, July 1, 1968; "We'll All Get Together after the Nomination," *New Republic*, July 13, 1968; "Humphrey Hits Tactics of McCarthy Backers," *Los Angeles Times*, July 7, 1968.

43. "Apprehensions Showing on HHH," *Washington Post*, August 22, 1968; "Calling All Delegates," *New Republic*, July 27, 1968.

44. Victor Navasky, "Report on the Candidate Named Humphrey," *New York Times*, August 25, 1968; Solberg, *Hubert Humphrey*, 343; "Democrats: Waiting for an Alternative," *Time*, July 12, 1968; "Nation: Hubert's Problems and Gene's Progress," *Time*, June 28, 1968; Chester, Hodgson, and Page, *American Melodrama*, 416; "Convention of the Lemmings," *Time*, August 20, 1968; Richard Harwood, "Humphrey's Burden: Vice President Tries But Can't Shed Image as the President's Boy," *Wall Street Journal*, July 31, 1968; "Humphrey's Campaign Had Its Roughest Day," *Los Angeles Times*, July 3, 1968.

45. Victor Navasky, "Report on the Candidate Named Humphrey," *New York Times*, August 25, 1968; "Democrats: The Nonconsensus," *Time*, July 5, 1968; "Democrats: Waiting for an Alternative," *Time*, July 12, 1968; Chester, Hodgson, and Page, *American Melodrama*, 417.

46. "Humphrey's Slips Are Showing," *Los Angeles Times*, July 11, 1968.

47. "President Lyndon B. Johnson's Address to the Nation Announcing Steps to Limit the War in Vietnam and Reporting His Decision Not to Seek Reelection," March 31, 1968, *Public Papers of the Presidents of the United States: Lyndon B. Johnson, 1968–69*, vol. 1 (Washington, DC: Government Printing Office, 1970), 469–76; Herring, *America's Longest War*, 207–11; Herring, *LBJ and Vietnam*, 167–68; Dallek, *Flawed Giant*, 536–38.

48. Larry Berman, *No Peace, No Honor: Nixon, Kissinger, and Betrayal in Vietnam* (New York: Free Press, 2001); Herring, *America's Longest War*, 207–11; Herring, *LBJ and Vietnam*, 168–71; Dallek, *Flawed Giant*, 536.

49. Dallek, *Flawed Giant*, 571; George E. Reedy Oral History Interview 27, December 13, 1990, LBJ Library; Recording of Telephone Conversation Between Johnson and Nixon, August 8, 1968, 4:09 PM, tape F6807.02, PNO 21 available online at http://www.lbjlib.utexas.edu/johnson/archives.hom/Dictabelt.hom/highlights/janapril1968/nixonD1202-15/13309.mp3; Recording of Telephone Conversation Between Johnson and Richard Hughes, tape WH6807.02, citation 13222.

50. Dallek, *Flawed Giant*, 571–72; Califano, *Triumph and Tragedy*, 320.

51. Watson and Markman, *Chief of Staff*, 297–99.

52. Recording of Telephone Conversation between Johnson and Marvin Watson, August 26, 1968, tape WH6808.02; James Reston, Jr., *The Lone Star: The Life of John Connally* (New York: Harper & Row, 1989), 353, 359; "Connally Scores Doves on Vietnam," *New York Times*, August 23, 1968.

53. Dallek, *Flawed Giant*, 572; O'Brien Oral History 23, 25; Humphrey, *Education of a Public Man*, 390.

54. Van Dyk, *Heroes, Hacks and Fools*, 74; and Solberg, *Hubert Humphrey*, 348; Chalmers Roberts, "Humphrey Advisors Complete Draft on Vietnam War Policy," *Washington Post*, July 29, 1968; Solberg, *Hubert Humphrey*, 348; Dallek, *Flawed Giant*, 571.

55. Van Dyk, *Heroes, Hacks and Fools*, 374; Solberg, *Hubert Humphrey*, 349–50.

56. Solberg, *Hubert Humphrey*, 351; Recording of Telephone Conversation Between Johnson and Humphrey, August 18, 1968, tape WH6808.01, citation 13307.

57. Solberg, *Hubert Humphrey*, 352; Humphrey, *Education of a Public Man*, 388.

58. Humphrey, *Education of a Public Man*, 388.

59. Solberg, *Hubert Humphrey*, 353; "Telephone Conversation between President Johnson and the President's Counsel (Murphy)," in *Foreign Relations of the United States, 1964–1968*, vol. 6, *Vietnam, January–August 1968*, ed. David S. Patterson (Washington, DC: Government Printing Office, 2002), Document 339; also see Charles Murphy Oral History, LBJ Library, May 29, 1969: David Ginsburg; Oral History Project, Historical Society of the District of Columbia Circuit, April 8, April 22, July 15, and October 7, 1998, http://www.dcchs.org/DavidGinsburg/DavidGinsburg_Complete.pdf.

60. Humphrey, *Education of a Public Man*, 389; Eisele, *Almost to the Presidency*, 338.

61. Humphrey, *Education of a Public Man*, 389–90.

Chapter 9

1. Press conference coverage based on Jules Witcover, *The Resurrection of Richard Nixon* (New York: G. P. Putnam's Sons, 1970), 15–24; on Nixon's false sincerity see Garry Wills, *Nixon Agonistes: The Crisis of the Self-Made Man* (Boston: Houghton

Mifflin, 1970), 415; Perlstein, *Nixonland*, 57; Ambrose, *Nixon*, 668–71; "California Loser Angry at Press," *Washington Post*, November 8, 1962; Richard Nixon, *RN: The Memoirs of Richard Nixon* (New York: Simon & Schuster, 1978), 244–46.

2. As quoted in David Greenberg, *Nixon's Shadow: The History of an Image* (New York: W. W. Norton, 2003), xvii.

3. Mailer, *Some Honorable Men*, 134; "Richard Nixon's Farewell: A Tragic Story," *New York Times*, November 8, 1962.

4. "California: Career End," *Time*, November 16, 1962; "The Gubernatorials," *New York Times*, November 8, 1962.

5. Perlstein, *Nixonland*, 61; Nixon, *RN*, 246; Earl Mazo and Stephen Hess, *Nixon: A Political Portrait* (New York: Harper & Row, 1968), 293; see also, "TV Controversy," *New York Times*, November 15, 1962, and "Nixon Aide Says TV Program Twisted 'Life of Great American,'" *New York Times*, November 13, 1962; Patrick J. Buchanan, *The Greatest Comeback: How Richard Nixon Rose from Defeat to Create the New Majority*, Kindle ed. (New York: Crown, 2014), 13–14; Nixon, *RN*, 246.

6. Stephen Hess and David Broder, *The Republican Establishment: The Present and Future of the G.O.P.* (New York: Harper & Row, 1967), 163.

7. Fawn McKay Brodie, *Richard Nixon: The Shaping of His Character* (New York: W. W. Norton, 1981), 479; Nixon, *RN*, 249, 256–58.

8. Witcover, *Resurrection*, 64; Rick Perlstein, *Before the Storm* (New York: Nation Books, 2001), 298.

9. See Stephen E. Ambrose, "Coping with Catastrophe, 1964," in *Nixon*, vol. 2, *The Triumph of a Politician, 1962–1972*, 38–51.

10. Hess and Broder, *Republican Establishment*, 169; also see Perlstein, *Before the Storm*, chapter 17; Ambrose, *Nixon*, 51.

11. Perlstein, *Before the Storm*, chapter 17.

12. Ambrose, *Nixon*, 51; David Stokes, "The Forgotten Lesson of 1964," *Townhall*, October 10, 2010, http://townhall.com/columnists/davidstokes/2010/10/10/the_forgotten_lesson_of_1964/page/full.

13. "Goldwater's 1964 Acceptance Speech," *Washington Post* website, http://www.washingtonpost.com/wp-srv/politics/daily/may98/goldwaterspeech.htm.

14. Nixon, *RN*, 260.

15. Witcover, *Resurrection*, 101; and Nixon, *RN*, 26; James Reston, "What Goldwater Lost," *New York Times*, November 4, 1964; Robert Donovan, "The Future of the Republican Party: GOP Must Return to Old Ground," *Los Angeles Times*, November 22, 1964; Godfrey Hodgson, *The World Turned Right Side Up: A History of the Conservative Ascendancy in America* (Boston: Houghton Mifflin, 1996), 107; "In There Fighting," *Time*, November 13, 1964.

16. Kruse, *White Flight*, 44; also see Lisa McGirr, *Suburban Warriors: The Origins of the New American Right* (Princeton, NJ: Princeton University Press, 2001).

17. "A Spoilsport Too," *New York Times*, November 6, 1964; "Nixon Recommends Move to the Center—Rejects Rightist Extremism," *New York Times*, November 11, 1964.

18. "Retort Is Strong," *New York Times*, November 6, 1964.

19. "Nixon Recommends Move to the Center—Rejects Rightist Extremism," *New York Times*, November 11, 1964; Nixon, *RN*, 264; "Richard Nixon's Model Campaign,"

New York Times, May 10, 2012; author interview with Patrick J. Buchanan; also see Buchanan, *Greatest Comeback*, 21, 32–33.

20. Buchanan, *Greatest Comeback*, 34, 39–40.

21. Ambrose, *Nixon*, vol. 2, 86.

22. David Broder, "Election of 1968," *History of American Presidential Elections, 1789–1969*, ed. Arthur Schlesinger, Jr. (New York: Chelsea House, 1971), 3726; Hess and Broder, *Republican Establishment*, 180; Buchanan, *Greatest Comeback*, 72–73.

23. Hess and Broder, *Republican Establishment*, 180–81; Ambrose, *Nixon*, 89; Nick Thimmesch, *The Condition of Republicanism* (New York: W. W. Norton, 1968), 140.

24. Ambrose, *Nixon*, vol. 2, 59–60.

25. "Nixon and GOP Comeback," *Newsweek*, October 10, 1966; Richard Nixon Library, Wilderness Years Collection, Series IV: 1966 Campaign—Reference Files, box 2, folder 2, Congressional Wins, "Recapitulation."

26. "Nixon and GOP Comeback," *Newsweek*, October 10, 1966; "Nixon on the Stump," *New York Times*, October 2, 1966; "Nixon's Gamble," *Wall Street Journal*, November 1, 1966; also see Ambrose, *Nixon*, 85–88.

27. "Campaign 1966 Collection: Inventory," Campaign 1966 Reference Files, Richard Nixon Library, PPS 136, Box 3, Detail Schedule.

28. "Nixon on the Stump," *New York Times*, October 2, 1966; "Nixon and GOP Comeback," *Newsweek*, October 10, 1966.

29. Andrew L. Johns, *Vietnam's Second Front: Domestic Politics, The Republican Party, and the War* (Lexington: University Press of Kentucky, 2010), 82; Nixon, "Why Not Negotiate in Vietnam," *Reader's Digest*, December 1965; also see Ambrose, *Nixon*, 61, 68, 77, 91.

30. "Campaign 1966 Collection: Inventory," Campaign 1966 Reference Files Richard Nixon Library; also discussed in Ambrose, *Nixon*; Buchanan, *Greatest Comeback*, 52–56; also see Perlstein, *Nixonland*, 137.

31. Dallek, *Flawed Giant*, 383–84.

32. Rick Perlstein, *Richard Nixon: Speeches, Writings, Documents* (Princeton, NJ: Princeton University Press, 2008), 119; "Republican Party: Back from the Brink," *Time*, November 18, 1966.

33. "Transcript of the President's News Conference on Foreign and Domestic Matters," *New York Times*, November 5, 1966.

34. "Republican Party: Back from the Brink," *Time*, November 18, 1966; Witcover, *Resurrection*, 165; Hess and Broder, *Republican Establishment*, 197; Perlstein, *Nixonland*, 162.

35. Califano, *Triumph and Tragedy*, 291; also see Ambrose, *Nixon*, vol. 2, 97.

36. Perlstein, *Nixonland*, 161; author interview with Buchanan; "An Off-Year Election with Difference," *Life*, December 4, 1966.

37. "Nixon Predicts G.O.P Will Gain 40 House Seats in 1966 Election," *New York Times*, September 27, 1965; also see Nixon Letter to UPI, November 2, 1966: Wilderness Years Collection, Series IV: 1966 Campaign—Reference Files, box 2, folder 1, Election Predictions for UPI; Perlstein, *Nixonland*, 161; Loudon Wainwright, "A Spell of Hickory Weather," *Life*, August 26, 1966; author interview with Buchanan.

38. "Republican Party: Back from the Brink," *Time*, November 18, 1966.

39. "Issues and Answers, Sunday, November 6, 1966," Richard Nixon Library, Wilderness Years Collection, series iv, box 10–12: Appearance File by Rose Mary Woods (PPS 138); author interview with Buchanan.

Chapter 10

1. Perlstein, *Nixonland*, 173; "Nixon and GOP Comeback," *Newsweek*, October 10, 1966; Clark Mollenhoff, *George Romney: A Mormon in Politics* (New York: Meredith, 1968), 5; Stewart Alsop, "It's Like Running against God," *Saturday Evening Post*, October 22, 1966, 20.
2. Thimmesch, *Condition of Republicanism*, 118; "George H. W. Bush Endorsed Romney? Big Surprise, They're Cut From the Same Cloth," *Daily Beast*, March 30, 2012; T. George Harris, *Romney's Way: A Man and an Idea*, Kindle ed. (New Orleans: Garrett County, 2012), 232; Roper Center for Public Opinion Research, University of Connecticut, Harris Survey, November 1966, Gallup Poll (AIPO), November 1966.
3. Ambrose, *Nixon*, vol. 2, 105; "Politics: The Temper of the Times," *Time*, April 14, 1967; author interview with Buchanan.
4. Chris Bachelder, "Crashing the Party: The Ill-Fated 1968 Presidential Campaign of Governor George Romney," *Michigan Historical Review* 33 (Fall 2007): 131–62.
5. Mollenhoff, *George Romney*, 175–82, 189; Thimmesch, *Condition of Republicanism*, 134.
6. Harris, *Romney's Way*, 221; Mollenhoff, *George Romney*, 214; Wills, *Nixon Agonistes*, 203; Harris, *Romney's Way*, 236.
7. "Text of Romney's Letter to Goldwater after Defeat of Presidential Nominee in '64," *New York Times*, November 29, 1966; Bachelder, "Crashing the Party"; Kabaservice, *Rule and Ruin*, 130.
8. Witcover, *Resurrection*, 197; "Romney Invades South in Attack on Wallace," *Los Angeles Times*, April 30, 1967; "Republican Governor's Association," June 26, 1967, box 45, folder: Romney and Associates, Romney Papers, Bentley Historical Library, University of Michigan.
9. "Troubles with the Press?—Romney Rolls His Own!" *Los Angeles Times*, January 10, 1968; Jack Germond, *Fat Man in the Middle Seat* (New York: Random House, 1999), 71.
10. Witcover, *Resurrection*, 188; author interview with Jonathan Moore; "White House Pleased: Romney Thanked by White House," *New York Times*, April 8, 1967; "Excerpts of Address by Romney on Vietnam," *New York Times*, April 8, 1967.
11. Jack Bohrer lecture at New York Public Library, September 13, 2012; "The Brainwashed Candidate," *Time*, September 15, 1967; George Romney, interview by Lou Gordon, *Hot Seat*, WKBD, August 31, 1967, online at the Bentley Historical Library, University of Michigan, http://ummedia10.rs.itd.umich.edu/flash/bentley/bhlflash.html?dep=bentley&file=852178_5/852178_5-208.flv.
12. White, *Making of the President 1968*, 68.
13. "The Brainwashed Candidate," *Time*, September 15, 1967.
14. "A Lift for LBJ?" *Wall Street Journal*, June 12, 1967; "Nixon Plans to Meet Reagan," July 17, 1967, *Washington Post*; George Gallup, "Nixon Maintains Party Lead as Romney Support Declines," *Washington Post*, July 11, 1968; Roper Center for Public Opinion

Research, University of Connecticut, Gallup Poll, September 1967; George Gallup, "Nixon First Choice of GOP County Chairmen for '68," *Washington Post*, April 16, 1967.

15. "Slumming It," *Newsweek*, September 11, 1967.
16. "The Big Show," *Newsweek*, January 8, 1968.
17. "Romney on the Trail: Day Not to Remember," *Washington Post*, February 17, 1968; "The New Rules of Play," *Time*, March 8, 1968.
18. White, *Making of the President*, 70; "The New Rules of Play," *Time*; Witcover, *Resurrection*, 51.
19. "Nixon Declares Viet Involvement Is in U.S. Interest," *Los Angeles Times*, December 31, 1967.
20. Richard Nixon, "What Happened to America?" *Reader's Digest*, October 1967.
21. Ambrose, *Nixon*, vol. 2, 133.
22. Ambrose, *Nixon*, vol. 2, 134–35; "The Temper of the Times," *Time*, April 14, 1967.

Chapter 11
1. "Transcript of Rockefeller's Statement and Excerpts from the News Conference," *New York Times*, March 22, 1968.
2. White, *Making of the President, 1968*, 261–62. Alton Marshall Oral History, November 11, 1979, NAR Family Archives, Record Group III, 4Q.2; Morrow Interview, box 26, folder 2, 17.
3. "Ronald Reagan: Rising Star in the West," *Newsweek*, May 22, 1967.
4. "Rockefeller Has Had Real Comeback Push," *Milwaukee Journal*, June 18, 1958; Thimmesch, *Condition of Republicanism*, 96; and Michael S. Kramer and Sam Roberts, *"I Never Wanted to Be Vice President of Anything!": An Investigative Biography of Nelson Rockefeller* (New York: Basic Books, 1976), 201–10, on governor's race; Cary Reich, *The Life of Nelson A. Rockefeller: Worlds to Conquer* (New York: Doubleday, 1996, 767); Joseph Alsop, "Rockefeller, Harriman Eat Blintzes, Pizza in NY Race," *Toledo Blade*, October 13, 1958.
5. Perlstein, *Before the Storm*, 209.
6. Richard Norton Smith, *On His Own Terms: A Life of Nelson Rockefeller* (New York: Random House, 2014), 316; see James Desmond, *Nelson Rockefeller: A Political Biography* (New York: Mcmillan, 1964), 212–38, which looks at Rockefeller's 1959 "campaign" for the presidential nomination.
7. Theodore H. White, *The Making of the President, 1960* (New York: Atheneum, 1964), 72–77; also see David Reinhard, *The Republican Right since 1945* (Lexington: University Press of Kentucky, 1983), 176.
8. "Rockefeller Open to Draft by Party," *New York Times*, May 26, 1960; Desmond, *Nelson Rockefeller*, 240–42, also 245, on announcement and regret, and 257–58, on foreign policy.
9. White, *Making of the President 1960*, 184; Kramer and Roberts, *I Never Wanted*, 227; Mazo and Hess, *Nixon*, 220–22; Lewis Gould, *Grand Old Party* (New York: Random House, 2003), 343–44; Smith, *On His Own Terms*, 340–41; Desmond, *Nelson Rockefeller*, 256–59; "Debate in the GOP," *New York Times*, June 12, 1960.
10. Mazo and Hess, *Nixon*, 226–27; Gould, *Grand Old Party*, 344–45; Smith, *On His Own Terms*, 343–44.

11. Interview with Emmet Hughes, April 11 and 18, 1980, NAR Family Archives, Record Group III, 4Q.2, NAR Associates & Family Members, box 1, folder 11, 3; "George Hinman Interview, October 10, 1979," Rockefeller Family Archives, NAR R64 III 4, Q2, 8, 10.

12. Perlstein, *Before the Storm*, 162, 193. "Rockefeller Far Ahead for 1964 Nomination, Woos Conservatives," *Wall Street Journal*, December 10, 1962; Smith, *On His Own Terms*, 394–95, on outreach to conservatives.

13. Perlstein, *Before the Storm*, 195; Smith, *On His Own Terms*, 407.

14. Thimmesch, *Condition of Republicanism*, 30–31; Perlstein, *Before the Storm*, 197.

15. Reinhard, *Republican Right*, 177; Perlstein, *Before the Storm*, 225.

16. Smith, *On His Own Terms*, 439–45.

17. Robert Hartmann, *Palace Politics: An Inside Account of the Ford Years* (New York: McGraw-Hill, 1980), 408; Nelson Rockefeller, "Remarks on Extremism at the 1964 Republican National Convention," July 14, 1964, available online at http://www.rockarch.org/inownwords/nar1964text.php; "Goldwater Backers Defeat Scranton on His Anti-Bircher and Civil Rights Plank," *New York Times*, July 15, 1964; Smith, *On His Own Terms*, xxxi.

18. "Republicans: The New Rules of Play," *Time*, March 8, 1968; Richard Reeves, "Rocky (Is, Is Not, May Be) Running," *New York Times*, November 26, 1967.

19. "Republicans: The New Rules of Play," *Time*; "Politics: Long Hot Winter," *Time*, January 12, 1968; Wills, *Nixon Agonistes*, 206.

20. "Republicans: The New Rules of Play," *Time*, March 8, 1968; Witcover, *Resurrection*, 252; Chester, Hodgson, and Page, *American Melodrama*, 218.

21. English, *Divided They Stand*, 200; Chester, Hodgson, and Page, *American Melodrama*, 221.

22. Witcover, *Resurrection*, 264.

23. Ibid.; author interview with Pat Buchanan; Smith, *On His Own Terms*, 515–16.

24. Perlstein, *Before the Storm*, 244; English, *Divided They Stand*, 197; Smith, *On His Own Terms*, 514–16; Witcover, *Resurrection*, 264–65; "Why Did Rockefeller Pull Back? Lack of Appetite for Battle Is Found a Key Factor," *New York Times*, March 26, 1968.

25. "Transcript of Rockefeller's Statement and Excerpts from the News Conference," *New York Times*, March 22, 1968; "Rockefeller Not to Run, but Would Accept Draft," *New York Times*, March 22, 1968; Author interview with Pat Buchanan; Buchanan, *Greatest Comeback*, 221–227; also see Drew Pearson and Jack Anderson, "Rumors Quoted against Rockefeller," *Washington Post*, March 26, 1968; "Rockefeller's Refusal Shocks Agnew," *Washington Post*, March 22, 1968; Chester, Hodgson, and Page, *American Melodrama*, 223.

26. "Rocky: 'Majority of Party's Leaders Want . . . Nixon,'" *Washington Post*, March 22, 1968; Tom Wicker, "Rockefeller's Decision," *New York Times*, March 22, 1968; Witcover, *Resurrection*, 266–67.

27. "Rocky Joins Race and Vows Fight 'to the Last Vote,'" *Washington Post*, May 1, 1968; "A Political Puzzler," *New York Times*, March 22, 1968.

28. Roper Center for Public Opinion Research, University of Connecticut, Harris Survey, March 1968; Witcover, *Resurrection*, 292.

29. Emmett Hughes Oral History, NAR Archives, 6; "Summary Memorandum on Substantive Policy, Meeting of May 30, 1968," NAR Archives, Personal, record group 4, J3 Politics—Reubhausen Papers, NAR Political Themes, box 4, folder 42.
30. NAR, Personal Record III, 4JS, Reubhausen Files, box 1, folder 3.
31. NAR Papers, JI Politics, NYC Office, record group 4, box 65, folder 706; also Marsha Eileen Barrett, "Nelson Rockefeller, Racial Politics, and the Undoing of Moderate Republicanism," PhD diss., Rutgers University, 2014, 7–10; "Rockefeller Begins Race for White House, But Nixon Nomination Is Nearly Locked Up," *Wall Street Journal*, May 1, 1968; "Excerpts From Address by Rockefeller," *New York Times*, April 19, 1968; NAR Papers, JI Politics, NYC Office, record group 4, box 65, folder 706; "Disappointed," *Washington Post*, April 19, 1968.
32. "Rockefeller Assails Economic Failures," *Washington Post*, May 22, 1968; "Rockefeller Charges 'Grave' Failures to President," *New York Times*, May 22, 1968; Family Archives, 4 NAR Personal, J1-Politics, National Campaigns 68-Speeches, box 28, folder 259.
33. Chester, Hodgson, and Page, *American Melodrama*, 389; "Rocky Takes on Kennedy, Nixon in a Rough Speech," *Washington Post*, May 25, 1968.
34. "Rockefeller Links His Goals to Those of Kennedy," *New York Times*, June 12, 1968; Joseph Persico, *Imperial Rockefeller: A Biography of Nelson Rockefeller* (New York: Simon & Schuster, 1982), 75; also see "Rockefeller Moves to Capture Kennedy Backers in New Drive," *Baltimore Sun*, June 11, 1968; Smith, *On His Own Terms*, 532.
35. "Excerpts from Address by Rockefeller," *New York*, April 19, 1968; "Address of Governor Nelson A. Rockefeller at Hirsch High School, Chicago, Illinois, July 17, 1968," NAR, Personal, J3-Politics, Reubhausen Papers, box 4, folder 41; "Rockefeller Scores Talks by Kennedy," *New York Times*, May 24, 1968; Witcover, *Resurrection*, 319.
36. PNS, May 28, 1968; "Rocky Lessens GOP Opposition in the South," *Washington Post*, May 23, 1968; "Rockefeller Is Running Too Fast for His Own Party," *Los Angeles Times*, July 2, 1968; Harry S. Dent, *The Prodigal South Returns to Power* (New York: Wiley & Sons, 1978), 79.
37. "A Time for Choosing," October 27, 1964, available online at http://www.reagan.utexas.edu/archives/reference/timechoosing.html.
38. PNS, June 1, 1968.
39. James G. Driscoll, *Elections 1968* (Silver Spring, MD: National Observer, 1968), 51; "Ronald Reagan: Rising Star in the West," *Newsweek*, May 22, 1967; "Reagan Says Democrats Weighing Super-States," *Richmond Times-Dispatch*, July 21, 1968; "Reagan Compares Hecklers to Nazis," *New York Times*, July 28, 1968.
40. "Ronald Reagan: Rising Star in the West," *Newsweek*, May 22, 1967; see the chapter "Pragmatist" in Lou Cannon, *Governor Reagan: His Rise to Power* (New York: Public Affairs, 2003), 185–203.
41. Matthew Dallek, *The Right Moment: Ronald Reagan's First Victory and the Decisive Turning Point in American Politics* (New York: Free Press, 2000), 195.
42. M. Dallek, *Right Moment*, 187–88; Warren Weaver, Jr., "Four Hearties on the Good Ship G.O.P.," *New York Times Magazine*, November 27, 1966.
43. Cannon, *Governor Reagan*, 271; "Reagan, Scoring Courts, Links Shooting to Permissive Attitude," *New York Times*, June 6, 1968.

44. M. Dallek, *Right Moment*, 186–99; "Reagan Calls for Full War Effort If Talks Collapse," *Los Angeles Times*, May 12, 1968.

45. "Ronald Reagan: Rising Star in the West," *Newsweek*, May 22, 1967; Weaver, "Four Hearties"; and M. Dallek, *Right Moment*, 195; Chester, Hodgson, and Page, *American Melodrama*, 195; Hess and Broder, *Republican Establishment*, 273; also see Driscoll, *Elections 1968*, which provides insight into Reagan's appeal on the campaign trail.

46. Cannon, *Governor Reagan*, 258; Chester, Hodgson, and Page, *American Melodrama*, 204.

47. Cannon, *Governor Reagan*, 258–62; "Reagan's Attack on Today's Rebels," *San Francisco Chronicle*, July 5, 1968; "Humphrey-RFK Possible Demo Team—Reagan," *New Orleans Times Picayune*, May 20, 1968; "Reagan Sees US Problems Rooted in Permissiveness," *Evening Star* (Washington, DC), June 14, 1968; Driscoll, *Elections 1968*, 58.

48. "Reagan Sees US Problems Rooted in Permissiveness," *Evening Star* (Washington, DC), June 14, 1968; "Reagan Asks Warning to Reds at Paris Talks," *Christian Science Monitor*, June 20, 1968.

49. "Statements of Nelson Rockefeller, June 11, 1968," NAR Personal, Series J.3 Political Reubhausen Files, Current Events 1968, box 2, folder 3.

50. Cannon, *Governor Reagan*, 261–62; Ambrose, *Nixon*, vol. 2, 155, Witcover, *Resurrection*, 294, 304.

Chapter 12

1. "T.R.B from Washington: Wallace," *New Republic*, November 9, 1968; Walter Pincus, "'Computerized Defense' Is Criticized by Wallace," *Washington Post*, October 25, 1968; Sara Davidson, "Street Clashes Greet Wallace at N.Y. Rally," *Boston Globe*, October 25, 1968; "Clashes," *Newsday*, October 25, 1968; Homer Bigart, "3,000 Police Ring Garden as Wallace Stages a Rally," *New York Times*, October 25, 1968.

2. Philip Crass, *The Wallace Factor* (New York: Mason/Charter, 1976), 1.

3. Robert Mayer, "For God, Country and Wallace," *Newsday*, October 25, 1968.

4. Bob Greene, "19,000 at Garden Hail Wallace," *Newsday*, October 25, 1968; Patrick O'Donovan, "Wallace Makes It in Madison Sq," *London Observer*, October 27, 1968; Robert Healy, "George Wallace Makes Believers," *Boston Globe*, October 25, 1968; "3,000 Police Ring Garden as Wallace Stages a Rally," *New York Times*, October 25, 1968; Arthur Schlesinger, ed., *History of US Political Parties*, vol. 4, *1945–1972: The Politics of Change* (New York: Chelsea House, 1973), 3491–97; George C. Wallace, "Speech at Madison Square Garden," *American History Online*, Facts On File, http://www.fofweb.com/activelink2.asp?ItemID=WE52&iPin=E14523&SingleRecord=True.

5. "T.R.B from Washington: Wallace," *New Republic*, November 9, 1968; Joe Flaherty, "The Legions of Fear Huddle Against the Night," *Village Voice*, October 31, 1968.

6. Dan T. Carter, *The Politics of Rage: George Wallace, the Origins of the New Conservatism, and the Transformation of American Politics* (New York: Simon & Schuster, 1995), 12.

7. Tom Wicker, "George Wallace: A Gross and Simple Heart," *Harper's Magazine*, April 1967.

8. Schlesinger, *History of US Political Parties*, 3430; Seymour Martin Lipset and Earl Raab, *The Politics of Unreason: Right-Wing Extremism in America* (Chicago: University

of Chicago Press, 1978), 341; "Red Neck New York: Is This Wallace Country?" *New York*, October 7, 1968.

9. Jefferson Cowie, *Stayin' Alive: The 1970s and the Last Days of the Working Class* (New York: New Press, 2010), 5; Stephan Lesher, *George Wallace: American Populist* (Cambridge, MA: Perseus, 1994), 408.

10. "George Wallace: Settin' the Woods on Fire," *The American Experience*, PBS, April 23–24, 2000, available on YouTube, https://www.youtube.com/watch?v=wLkCY0f73iE; Wayne Greenhaw, *Fighting the Devil in Dixie: How Civil Rights Activists Took on the Ku Klux Klan in Alabama* (Chicago: Lawrence Hill, 2011); Marshall Frady, *Wallace: The Classic Portrait of Alabama Governor George Wallace* (New York: Random House, 1996), 127; Carter, *Politics of Rage*, 90–93, 96.

11. George Wallace Inaugural Address, January 14, 1963, available online at the Alabama Department of Archives and History, http://digital.archives.alabama.gov/cdm/singleitem/collection/voices/id/2952/rec/5; George Wallace, "School House Door Speech," June 11, 1963, , available online at the Alabama Department of Archives and History http://www.archives.alabama.gov/govs_list/schooldoor.html.

12. As quoted in Lloyd Earl Rohler, *George Wallace: Conservative Populist* (Westport, CT: Praeger, 2004), 18, and Carter, *Politics of Rage*, 156; George C. Wallace, *Stand Up for America* (Garden City, NY: Doubleday, 1976), 83; Frady, *Wallace*, 175

13. Wallace, *Stand Up for America*, 89; also explored in Michael Rogin, "Wallace and the Middle Class: The White Backlash in Wisconsin," *Public Opinion Quarterly* 30 (1966):1; Carter, *Politics of Rage*, 206.

14. Joseph Lowndes, *From the New Deal to the New Right: Race and the Southern Origins of Modern Conservatism* (New Haven, CT: Yale University Press, 2008), 88; Carter, *Politics of Rage*, 207; also see Dan Carter's interview with Seymore Trammell, January 11, 1988, manuscript, Archives and Rare Book Library, Emory University, 22–23.

15. Carter, *Politics of Rage*, 207.

16. Wallace, *Stand Up for America*, 91; "George Wallace: Settin' the Woods on Fire," *The American Experience*, PBS, April 23–24, 2000, available on YouTube, https://www.youtube.com/watch?v=wLkCY0f73iE.

17. Frady, *Wallace*, 181; Rogin, "Wallace and the Middle Class."

18. William Bradford Huie, "Humanity's Case Against George Wallace," *Genesis Magazine*, March 1976; Rohler, *George Wallace*, 37; Matthew E. Welsh, "Civil Rights and the Primary Election of 1964 in Indiana: The Wallace Challenge," *Indiana Magazine of History* 75, no. 1 (March 1979): 1–27.

19. Lesher, *George Wallace*, 300; Carter, *Politics of Rage*, 215; "Maryland's Vote Held Anti-Negro," *New York Times*, May 21, 1964.

20. Edsall and Edsall, *Chain Reaction*, 40; Rohler, *George Wallace*, 37.

21. Greenhaw, *Fighting the Devil in Dixie*, 158; George Wallace, "Speech at Southern Fairgrounds in Atlanta, July 4th, 1964," Alabama Department of Archives and History, Montgomery, Alabama; Carter, *Politics of Rage*, 216–17.

22. Schlesinger, *History of US Political Parties*, 3433; Wills, *Nixon Agonistes*, 35.

23. "Brewster Victor, Wallace Has 43% in Maryland Vote," *New York Times*, May 19, 1964.

24. "Alabama Police Use Gas and Clubs to Rout Negroes," *New York Times*, March 7, 1968; Lesher, *George Wallace*, 333.

25. "President Johnson's Special Message to Congress: The American Promise," March 15, 1965, *Public Papers of the Presidents of the United States: Lyndon B. Johnson, 1965* (Washington, DC: Government Printing Office, 1966), 281–87, available online, http://www.lbjlibrary.org/lyndon-baines-johnson/speeches-films/president-johnsons-special-message-to-the-congress-the-american-promise/; "George Wallace: Settin' the Woods on Fire," *The American Experience*, PBS, April 23–24, 2000, available on YouTube, https://www.youtube.com/watch?v=wLkCY0f73iE.

26. Lesher, *George Wallace*, 348; Carter, *Politics of Rage*, 264–66.

27. Carter, *Politics of Rage*, 266.

28. James Jackson Kilpatrick, "What Makes Wallace Run?" *National Review*, April 18, 1967; Carter, *Politics of Rage*, 281.

29. Jeff Frederick, *Stand up for Alabama: Governor George Wallace* (Tuscaloosa: University of Alabama Press, 2007), 66, 91; Lesher, *George Wallace*, 361–64; Carter, *Politics of Rage*, 282–83.

30. Samuel Lubell, "Reprisal Mars Alabama Vote," *Spokane Daily Chronicle*, May 9, 1966.

31. Wicker, "George Wallace"; Kilpatrick, "What Makes Wallace Run," 6.

32. Carter, *Politics of Rage*, 307; McGirr, *Suburban Warriors*, 211.

33. Carter, *Politics of Rage*, 310–13, 342; George Wallace: Settin' the Woods on Fire," *The American Experience*, PBS, April 23–24, 2000, available on YouTube, https://www.youtube.com/watch?v=wLkCY0f73iE; Lesher, *George Wallace*, 398–400.

34. White, *Making of the President*, 409.

35. Wicker, "George Wallace"; Cowie, *Stayin' Alive*, 5; Matusow, *Unraveling of America*, 424; Wallace, "Speech at Madison Square Garden"; Rohler, *George Wallace*, 153; Robert Mason, *Richard Nixon and the Quest for a New Majority* (Chapel Hill: University of North Carolina Press, 2004), 24; Rohler, *George Wallace*, 158; Lipset and Raab, *Politics of Unreason*, 350.

36. Lipset and Raab, *Politics of Unreason*, 346; Schlesinger, *History of US Political Parties*, 3447.

37. "George Wallace Tells His Plans," *US News and World Report*, June 17, 1968; Michael Kazin, The Populist Persuasion: An American History (New York: Basic Books, 1995), 237; Lipset and Raab, *Politics of Unreason*, 348; Converse et al., "Continuity and Change," 1100–1102; Garry Wills, as quoted in Jody Carlson, *George C. Wallace and the Politics of Powerlessness* (New Brunswick, NJ: Transaction, 1981), 14.

38. Pete Hamill "Wallace," *Ramparts*, October 26, 1968; Max Frankel, "Wallace in the North: Friends and 'Anarchist' Critics Cheer and Scream," *New York Times*, July 26, 1968; Schlesinger, *History of US Political Parties*, 3492; PNS, June 14, 1968; Jules Witcover, "Wallace's Potential for Mischief," *The Progressive*, July 1968.

39. Lafeber, *Deadly Bet*, 145; Dan T. Carter, *From George Wallace to Newt Gingrich: Race in the Conservative Counterrevolution, 1963–1994* (Baton Rouge: Louisiana State University Press, 1996), 16; Rohler, *George Wallace*, 156, 159.

40. Carter, *Politics of Rage*, 343; Trammell, Oral History, Carter Papers, Emory University, 22–23.

41. Carter, *Politics of Rage*, 338–40; transcript of Elena Verobovic interview with Ed Ewing and Skyler Baker, November 10, 1988, Dan Carter Papers, Emory University,

box 9, folder 28; Tom Turnipseed speech to the 17th Annual Meeting of Project Equality of Wisconsin, October 16, 1986, Carter Papers, box 9, folder 94; Richard Cohen, "A Walk With the Wallace Campaign," January 24, 1969, Carter Papers, box 6, folder 66, 24–25.

42. Carter, *Politics of Rage*, 337–42; Lesher, *George Wallace*, 409–10; Trammell Oral History, January 11, 1988, 19–22.

43. Chester, Hodgson, and Page, *American Melodrama*, 293; Frady, "Gary Indiana"; Joseph Alsop, "Wallace's Aim—Apartheid," *Boston Globe*, February 16, 1968.

44. As quoted in Kazin, *Populist Persuasion*, 240; see also "Wallace's Army: The Coalition of Frustration," *Time*, October 18, 1968; "George Wallace: The Angry Man's Candidate," *Saturday Evening Post*, June 15, 1968.

45. "George Wallace: The Angry Man's Candidate," *Saturday Evening Post*, June 15, 1968.

46. Lesher, *George Wallace*, 405; "Fist Fight Erupts at Wallace Speech," *Associated Press*, July 3, 1968; Max Frankel, "Wallace in the North: Friends and 'Anarchist' Critics Cheer and Scream," *New York Times*, July 26, 1968.

47. "Wallace Backers Show Gain in Poll," *New York Times*, July 14, 1968; Warren Weaver, "Wallace Gains Disturb Governors of Both Parties," *New York Times*, July 23, 1968.

Chapter 13

1. Witcover, *Resurrection*, 324; "The Scene of the Strip," *Time*, August 9, 1968; Mailer, *Some Honorable Men*, 110; Chester, Hodgson, and Page, *American Melodrama*, 430.

2. Wills, *Nixon Agonistes*, 234, "A Chance to Lead," *Time*, August 16, 1968.

3. "Those Much-Wooed Delegates," *Time*, August 2, 1968.

4. Chester, Hodgson, and Page, *American Melodrama*, 393; Persico, *Imperial Rockefeller*, 79; Witcover, *Resurrection*, 329.

5. Witcover, *Resurrection*, 289; Chester, Hodgson, and Page, *American Melodrama*, 393; "A Nibbling Process," *Time*, August 2, 1968; "Two Top Pollsters Say Rockefeller Gains 'Open Lead,'" *New York Times*, August 2, 1968.

6. "Reagan Bears Down to Dent Nixon's Strength in South," *Milwaukee Journal*, July 25, 1968; "Alton G. Marshall, 86, Nelson Rockefeller's Top Aide, Is Dead," *New York Times*, January 26, 2008; "The Reminiscences of Alton Marshall," Oral History Collection of Columbia University, 235; Chester, Hodgson, and Page, *American Melodrama*, 435.

7. Witcover, *Resurrection*, 326–27; Excerpts of Statement by Governor Ronald Reagan, Republican National Convention, Platform Committee Hearing, July 31, 1968, 1, 3–4, Rockefeller Archive Center, Graham Molitor Collection, IV, 3A, 18, box 24, folder 618.

8. Witcover, *Resurrection*, 326; "Team of Reagan-Lindsay Sparks Convention Doings," *Milwaukee Sentinel*, August 1, 1968; also see "Glamour Boys of Left, Right Liven Session," *Washington Post*, August 1, 1968. This topic is covered exhaustively in Geoffrey Kabaservice's *Rule and Ruin*.

9. "Republican Party Platform of 1968," August 5, 1968, online at *The American Presidency Project*, http://www.presidency.ucsb.edu/ws/index.php?pid=25841#axzz1eBtHRXxk; for discussion of the growing policy impact of liberal Republicans see Nicol C. Rae, *The Decline and Fall of the Liberal Republicans* (New York: Oxford University Press, 1989), 80–84. See also "A Chance to Lead," *Time*, August 16, 1968.

10. R. W. Apple, Jr., "Rockefeller Clings to Hope of Winning Nomination," *New York Times*, August 5, 1968; Theodore Braun Oral History, NAR Archives, 44.

11. Wills, *Nixon Agonistes*, 242; English, *Divided They Stand*, 283; Mailer, *Some Honorable Men*, 132; Wills, *Nixon Agonistes*, 216–17.

12. Wills, *Nixon Agonistes*, 258; Witcover, *Resurrection*, 339; "Eisenhower Backs Nixon, Praising His 'Experience,'" *New York Times*, July 19, 1968; Jules Witcover, *White Knight: The Rise of Spiro Agnew* (New York, Random House, 1972), 201–2.

13. Hinman Oral History, NAR Archives, 7; Chester, Hodgson, and Page, *American Melodrama*, 466; "Pragmatism, Republican Style," *Deseret News*, "Evans and Novak: Inside Report," August 8, 1968.

14. Chester, Hodgson, and Page, *American Melodrama*, 450, Witcover, *Resurrection*, 339; Cannon, *Governor Reagan*, 268; "Reagan Officially in Race," *New York Times*, August 5, 1968; Ronald Reagan, *An American Life* (New York: Simon & Schuster, 1990, 177–78).

15. Author interview with Pat Buchanan; Nixon, *RN*, 304; Wills, *Nixon Agonistes*, 247; Chester, Hodgson, and Page, *American Melodrama*, 459; Dent, *Prodigal South*, 96–97.

16. Carter, *Politics of Rage*, 329; also see Dent, *Prodigal South*, chapter 5, "Victory in 1968."

17. Witcover, *Resurrection*, 344; Chester, Hodgson, and Page, *American Melodrama*, 462–63.

18. Ambrose, *Nixon*, 147–54; also Johns, *Vietnam's Second Front*, 219.

19. Carter, *Politics of Rage*, 330; Chester, Hodgson, and Page, *American Melodrama*, 465.

20. "Anchors Aweigh," *Time*, October 20, 1967.

21. Tom Wicker, "Nixon Is Nominated on First Ballot," *New York Times*, August 9, 1968; Mailer, *Some Honorable Men*, 158; "Nixon Is Nominated on First Ballot," *New York Times*, August 9, 1968.

22. Witcover, *Resurrection*, 347; Nixon, *RN*, 311; "Reagan Says 'There's Nothing I Could Have Done Differently,'" *Associated Press*, August 8, 1968; "Reagan Cheerful Despite Setback," *New York Times*, August 9, 1968; Cannon, *Governor Reagan*, 270; Reagan, *American Life*, 177–78.

23. Persico, *Imperial Rockefeller*, 80–81.

24. Wills, *Nixon Agonistes*, 285; "The Unlikely no. 2," *Time*, August 16, 1968; Richard Reeves, "Is That Really Nelson Rockefeller Crawling to Richard Nixon?" *New York*, October 18, 1971.

25. Wills, *Nixon Agonistes*, 277–79.

26. Wills, *Nixon Agonistes*, 277–80; Jules Witcover, *Very Strange Bedfellows: The Short and Unhappy Marriage of Richard Nixon and Spiro Agnew*, Kindle ed. (New York: Public Affairs, 2007), pg. 11; Wills, *Nixon Agonistes*, 280–81; Chester, Hodgson, and Page, *American Melodrama*, 491; "The Candidate from Maryland: Spiro Theodore Agnew," *New York Times*, August 9, 1968.

27. Wills, *Nixon Agonistes*, 283; Witcover, *Very Strange Bedfellows*, pg. 11–12; Gloria Steinem, "Is Spiro Agnew Really W. C. Fields?" *New York*, December 15, 1969; Jacki Lyden, "Maryland Town Recalls Racial Unrest in 1967," *All Things Considered*, July 29, 2007, available online at http://www.npr.org/templates/story/story.php?storyId=12420016.

28. "The Unlikely no. 2," *Time*, August 6, 1968; "No, Governor," *Baltimore Sun*, April 12, 1968; Negroes Quit Conference with Governor," *Baltimore Sun*, April 12, 1968.

29. "The Candidate from Maryland: Spiro Theodore Agnew," *New York Times*, August 9, 1968; Witcover, *White Knight*, 214.

30. "Reagan Cheerful Despite Setback," *New York Times*, August 9, 1968; Witcover, *White Knight*, 230.

31. Nixon, *RN*, 312; Chester Hodgson, and Page, *American Melodrama*, 493.

32. See Joe McGinnis, *The Selling of the President, 1968* (New York: Pocket Books, 1970).

33. Chester, Hodgson, and Page, *American Melodrama*, 497; Richard Nixon, "Address Accepting the Presidential Nomination at the Republican National Convention in Miami Beach, Florida," August 8, 1968, online at *The American Presidency Project*, http://www.presidency.ucsb.edu/ws/?pid=25968.

34. Richard Nixon, "Address Accepting the Presidential Nomination at the Republican National Convention in Miami Beach, Florida," August 8, 1968.

35. Ibid.

36. "Now the Republic," *Time*, August 16, 1968.

37. Richard Nixon, "Address Accepting the Presidential Nomination at the Republican National Convention in Miami Beach, Florida," August 8, 1968.

Chapter 14

1. "The Battle of Chicago," *Newsweek*, September 9, 1968.

2. Robert Caro, interviewed on *The Colbert Report*, Comedy Central, May 6, 2013, available online at http://thecolbertreport.cc.com/videos/wm2xsq/robert-caro; Marshall Frady, "The Big Guy," *New York Review of Books*, November 2002.

3. "A Party Divided," *Wall Street Journal*, August 29, 1968.

4. "Humphrey First-Ballot Win Looks Certain, Though Mayor Daley Defers Endorsement," *Wall Street Journal*, August 26, 1968.

5. White, *Making of the President*, 328; Solberg, *Hubert Humphrey*, 357; George Gallup, "Nixon Leads Both Democratic Rivals in First Test since GOP Convention," *Washington Post*, August 21, 1968.

6. "Teddy Kennedy's Decision," *Newsweek*, August 5, 1968.

7. Reston, *Lone Star*, 359-61.

8. Herzog, *McCarthy for President*, 265; Solberg, *Hubert Humphrey*, 360; Jimmy Breslin, "Police Riot," *New York*, September 16, 1968.

9. Chester, Hodgson, and Page, *American Melodrama*, 548; "Democrats Had Kafka as Stage Manager," *Washington Post*, August 25, 1968.

10. "Democrats Had Kafka as Stage Manager," *Washington Post*, August 25, 1968; Mailer, *Some Honorable Men*, 194.

11. Jules Witcover, *The Year the Dream Died: Revisiting 1968 in America* (New York: Warner, 1997), 319; Chester, Hodgson, and Page, *American Melodrama*, 559.

12. White, *Making of the President*, 311; McGovern, *Grassroots*, 123.

13. Mailer, *Some Honorable Men*, 199-208; Eisele, *Almost to the Presidency*, 352-53.

14. Stout, *People*, 345; Herzog, *McCarthy for President*, 268; Witcover, *Year the Dream Died*, 330; Chester, Hodgson, and Page, *American Melodrama*, 572-75, offers an authoritative take on this meeting.

15. "Humphrey Picks Up Vital Dixie Support as Movement Builds to Draft Kennedy," *Wall Street Journal*, August 28, 1968; Stout, *People*, 270; Edward M. Kennedy, *True Compass: A Memoir* (New York: Twelve, 2009), 272.

16. Herzog, *McCarthy for President*, 267; Stout, *People*, 353–54.

17. Lawrence O'Brien Personal Papers, series 4, 1968 Presidential Campaigns, box 167, "Voter Opinion on Campaign Issues, August 1968"; Solberg, *Hubert Humphrey*, 361–62.

18. Mike Royko, *Boss: Richard J. Daley of Chicago* (New York: New American Library, 1971), 167; "Man Who Runs Chicago: Richard Joseph Daley," *New York Times*, August 26, 1968; Adam Cohen and Elizabeth Taylor, *American Pharaoh: Mayor Richard J. Daley—His Battle for Chicago and the Nation* (New York: Hachette, 2001).

19. White, *Making of the President*, 309; "This Is Chicago, and He Doesn't Dig Anything Else," *Life*, September 6, 1968; Royko, *Boss*, 177.

20. Frank Kusch, *Battleground Chicago: The Police and the 1968 Democratic National Convention* (Westport, CT: Praeger, 2004); Flamm, *Law and Order*, 155; David Farber, *Chicago '68* (Chicago: University of Chicago Press, 1988), 145; Royko, *Boss*, 165.

21. Cohen and Taylor, *American Pharaoh*, 457–58; Royko, *Boss*, 170–73; Chester, Hodgson, and Page, *American Melodrama*, 518; Marty Jezer, *Abbie Hoffman: American Rebel* (New Brunswick, NJ: Rutgers University Press, 1992).

22. Eisele, *Almost to the Presidency*, 348; "This Is Chicago, and He Doesn't Dig Anything Else," *Life*, September 6, 1968; Royko, *Boss*, 178; Jezer, *Abbie Hoffman*, 150–51.

23. Arthur Miller, "The Battle of Chicago: From the Delegates' Side," *New York Times Magazine*, September 15, 1968; Chester, Hodgson, and Page, *American Melodrama*, 581.

24. "TV Networks Angered by Curb on Newsmen Covering Convention," *Wall Street Journal*, August 27, 1968; Museum of Television and Radio Archive, CBS Convention coverage; Mailer, *Some Honorable Men*, 197, 251.

25. Kusch, *Battleground Chicago*, 24; Lewis L. Gould, *1968: The Election That Changed America* (Chicago: Ivan R. Dee, 1993), 126; David Farber, *The Age of Great Dreams: America in the 1960s* (New York: Hill & Wang, 1994), 221; Farber, *Chicago '68*, 70, 78–79; Flamm, *Law and Order*, 156.

26. Mailer, *Some Honorable Men*, 213; Todd Gitlin, *The Sixties: Years of Hope, Days of Rage* (Toronto: Bantam, 1987), 322; Jezer, *Abbie Hoffman*, 125.

27. Farber, *Chicago '68*, 165.

28. Farber, *Chicago '68*, 178; John Schulz, *No One Was Killed* (Chicago: Big Table, 1969), 87.

29. Daniel Walker, *Rights in Conflict; Convention Week in Chicago, August 25–29, 1968* (New York: Dutton, 1968), 4 (henceforth Walker Report); Cohen and Taylor, *American Pharaoh*, 472.

30. Farber, *Chicago '68*, 183; Farber, *Age of Great Dreams*, 223; Jezer, *Abbie Hoffman*, 126, 151–52.

31. Farber, *Chicago '68*, 182; Walker Report, 5, 7–8; Cohen and Taylor, *American Pharaoh*, 473–74; Godfrey Hodgson, *America in Our Time* (Garden City, NY: Doubleday, 1976), 372.

32. Democrats Set to Nominate Humphrey; Pro-Johnson Vietnam Plank Adopted," *New York Times*, August 29, 1968; *American Experience: Chicago 1968*, PBS, 1996, pt. 3, http://www.youtube.com/watch?v=LB8gkkbf_Zk.
33. Eisele, *Almost to the Presidency*, 356–57.
34. Farber, *Chicago '68*, 195; "Vietnam Planks," *New Republic*, September 21, 1968.
35. "Chicago 1968," *The American Experience*, PBS, November 13, 1995, pt. 3, available on YouTube at http://www.youtube.com/watch?v=LB8gkkbf_Zk; see also Chester, Hodgson, and Page, *American Melodrama*, 581.
36. Walker Report, 220–25; also see Farber, *Chicago '68*, 196; Tom Hayden, *Rebel: A Personal History of the 1960s* (Los Angeles: Red Hen Publishing, 2003), 294.
37. White, *Making of the President*, 347–49.
38. Ibid.; "Police Battle Demonstrators in Streets," *New York Times*, August 29, 1968; Farber, *Chicago '68*, 200–201.
39. Walker Report, 256–57.
40. Farber, *Chicago '68*, 201; Stout, *People*, 363; Eisele, *Almost to the Presidency*, 362; Witcover, *Year the Dream Died*, 336–37; Museum of Television and Radio Archive, CBS Convention coverage; O'Brien Oral History 23.
41. Farber, *Age of Great Dreams*, 223; Museum of Television and Radio archive, CBS Convention coverage.
42. Witcover, *Year the Dream Died*, 336; Farber, *Chicago '68*, 249; Cohen and Taylor, *American Pharaoh*, 478.
43. "A Party Divided," *Wall Street Journal*, August 29, 1968.
44. "Chicago 1968," *American Experience*, http://www.youtube.com/watch?v=GaqVaugcIf0; E. Berman, *Hubert*, 189; Solberg, *Hubert Humphrey*, 365.
45. Hubert H. Humphrey, "A New Day for America": Address Accepting the Presidential Nomination at the Democratic National Convention in Chicago," August 29, 1968, online at *The American Presidency Project*, http://www.presidency.ucsb.edu/ws/?pid=25964.
46. Ibid.; Humphrey, *Education of a Public Man?* 394.

Chapter 15

1. Alexis de Tocqueville, *Democracy in America* (New York: Vintage Books, 1945), 140–41.
2. "Campaign '68: Nixon, Humphrey and Wallace," *Atlantic Monthly*, November 1968; Roscoe Drummond, "Both Nixon and Humphrey Are Waging Empty Campaigns," *Los Angeles Times*, October 26, 1968.
3. Lesher, *George Wallace*, 408.
4. James Reston, "The Party and the Police," *New York Times*, August 29, 1968; Kusch, *Battleground Chicago*, 116; LBO Personal Papers, series 4, 1968, box 167, folder "Voter Opinion on Campaign Issues."
5. Ira Kapenstein Personal Papers, JFK Library, box 10, "Memorandum from Larry O'Brien to the Vice President, August 12, 1968"; LBO Papers, series 4, box 173, folder: Memos From L. F. O'Brien, August 21–28, 1968, "Critique of Freeman Outline, August 24, 1968"; O'Brien Oral History, Interview 24, 4; also see Orville Freeman

Oral History, February 14, 1969, LBJ Library, 38–39, available online at http://
transition.lbjlibrary.org/files/original/e702ad2e34e6a386637511c61e21786b.pdf.

6. Eisele, *Almost to the Presidency*, 369; Lyndon B. Johnson, "Remarks in New Orleans
before the 50th Annual National Convention of the American Legion," September
10, 1968, online at *The American Presidency Project*, http://www.presidency.ucsb
.edu/ws/index.php?pid=29107&st=&st1=; "Vietnam Heats Up as a Campaign
Issue," *New York Times*, September 15, 1968.

7. Humphrey, *Education of a Public Man*, 298; see PNS from September and October,
1968.

8. Humphrey, *Education of a Public Man*, 397–99; Eisele, *Almost to the Presidency*, 370–
72; Frank Cormier, *Associated Press*, September 19, 1969, via PNS, September 19,
1968; "Ted All Out for Humphrey," *UPI (Arizona Republic)*, September 20, 1968;
"Demonstrators Jar Humphrey; Listen to Dissent, Nixon Says," *Des Moines Register*,
September 20, 1968; also see Tom Wicker, "In the Nation: Evil on Washington
Street," *New York Times*, September 22, 1968; John Ehrlichman, *Witness to Power*
(New York: Simon & Schuster, 1982), 50.

9. Connell Oral History, 40–41; PNS, September 12, 1968; PNS, September 12,
1968; "Lurching Off to a Shaky Start," *Time*, September 20, 1968; PNS, September
19, 1968; Memo from Bill Gavin to Len Garment, box 76, SMCF, Garment, Len
1968 Political Campaign File, topical file box 10 of 2, Copies of Memoranda; LBO
Papers, box 165, folder, Florida, September 30; John Barlow Martin Papers, Library
of Congress, box 85, "Memorandum on the Hubert Humphrey Campaign," 32;
NBC Evening News, September 19, 1968, available for purchase through the
Vanderbilt Television News Archive, http://tvnews.vanderbilt.edu/program.pl?
ID=441961.

10. PNS, September 12, 1968; "Humphrey Faces Dilemma on Vietnam," *Washington
Post*, September 21, 1968; PNS, September, 24, 1968; LBO Papers, series 4, 1968
Presidential Campaigns, box 172, folder "Humphrey Campaign Memos, "Re:
Campaign Strategy. Napolitan to O'Brien, September 14, 1968"; LBO Papers, box
172, folder "Humphrey Campaign Memos," September 14th Issues Meeting, Office
of Secretary Freeman; PNS, September 17, 1968; Bob Considine, "HHH Is the
Most Booediful Candidate," *Playground Daily News*, September 23, 1968.

11. PNS, September 19, 1968, "Campaign '68: A Look at How the States Will Probably
Vote," *UPI*, September 22, 1968, via PNS, September 22, 1968; "Nixon Holds Wide
Lead, Wallace at New High," *Washington Post*, September 29, 1968; PNS, September
24, 1968; LBO Papers, series 4, box 173, folder "Memos from L. F. O'Brien, 1–15
August 1968," "Response to Secretary Freeman's Request for Guidance about the
Fall Campaign Organization," August 15, 1968; "The Wallace Siren," *Washington
Post*, September 21, 1968; "HHH Has 2 Passions in Campaign," *UPI (Dixon Evening
Telegraph)*, September 28, 1968.

12. Eisele, *Almost to the Presidency*, 374–75; "The Hecklers: Humphrey's Big Problem,"
New York Times, September 30, 1968; "HHH, Top Aides in Huddle," *UPI (The
Argus)*, September 30, 1968.

13. Chester, Hodgson, and Page, *American Melodrama*, 650; Humphrey, *Education of a
Public Man*, 400.

14. Eisele, *Almost to the Presidency*, 376–77; O'Brien Oral History 24, 12–13; LBO Papers, box 172, folder, Memo to L. F. O'Brien.

15. Humphrey, *Education of a Public Man*, 403; Johnson Library, Recordings and Transcripts, Recording of Telephone Conversation between Johnson and Humphrey, September 30, 1968, 7:30 PM, tape F6810.01, PNO 4.

16. Hubert Humphrey, "Speech in Salt Lake City," September 30, 1968, Hubert H. Humphrey Papers, Minnesota Historical Society.

17. Johnson Library, Recordings and Transcripts, Recording of Telephone Conversation between Johnson and Dirksen, October 1, 1968, 10:31 AM, tape F6810.01, PNO 7, available online at https://history.state.gov/historicaldocuments/frus1964-68v07/d42; LBO Papers, series 4, 1968, box 163, folder, Campaign Policy Meeting Minutes, September 23–27, 1968, "Minutes from September 27, 1968" and Campaign Policy Meeting Minutes, 2–11 October 1968, "Minutes from October 5, 1968"; LBO Papers, box 172, "A Campaign Strategy, September 17, 1968," 5.

18. "Humphrey Vows Halt in Bombing if Hanoi Reacts," *New York Times*, October 1, 1968; Joseph Kraft, "Televised Speech on Vietnam Gets Humphrey Off the Ground," *Washington Post*, October 3, 1968.

19. Johnson, *Vantage Point*, 548; also see Dallek, *Fallen Giant*, 579–80; "Humphrey Didn't Impair Talks, Harriman Says," *Washington Post*, October 3, 1968.

20. "Choose If You Can," *New Republic*, October 19, 1968; "The Scandals of '68," *The Nation*, October 14, 1968; "As We See It," *The Nation*, October 28, 1968; Converse et al., "Continuity and Change."

21. Connell Oral History, 46; Humphrey, *Education of a Public Man*, 403.

22. Martin Papers, "Campaign Journal," 33; "Humphrey Vows to Set 'a Fire' Under Nixon," *Los Angeles Times*, October 3, 1968; "Wallace Wins over Humphrey in Auto Union Poll, 49% to 39%," *New York Times*, October 6, 1968; "Union Members Revolt Against Democrat Chiefs: Union Members Revolt, Plan to Back Wallace," *Los Angeles Times*, September 26, 1968; "Union Chiefs Worried by Wallace Strength," *Beaver County Times*, September 30, 1968; "Union Men Switch to Wallace," *Evans and Novak*, October 3, 1968.

23. "Some Forward Motion for H.H.H," *Time*, October 11, 1968; "Humphrey Blasts Aims, Methods of Wallace," *Los Angeles Times*, October 2, 1968; also see "Humphrey's New Confidence: He May Have Found an Issue," *Los Angeles Times*, October 6, 1968, and "Wallace the Apostle of Hate and Racism, Humphrey Says," PNS, October 2, 1968; Carter, *Politics of Rage*, 359.

24. Matusow, *Unraveling of America*, 433; "Study Finds Nixon Winning 34 States to 7 for Wallace," *New York Times*, October 6, 1968.

25. Trammell interview, 2 "He's No Conservative," *St. Petersburg Times*, September 11, 1968; Carter, *Politics of Rage*, 355–56.

26. Carter, *Politics of Rage*, 356.

27. "Bomber on the Stump," *Time*, October 18, 1968; Warren Kozak, LeMay: The Life and Wars of General Curtis LeMay (New York: Regnery, 2009), 341.

28. "Excerpts from the Comments by Wallace and LeMay on the War and Segregation," *New York Times*, October 4, 1968.

29. Ibid.

30. Chester, Hodgson, and Page, *American Melodrama*, 697–700; Carter, *Politics of Rage*, 359; "Excerpts from the Comments by Wallace and LeMay on the War and Segregation," *New York Times*, October 4, 1968; Ed Ewing Interview, Dan Carter Papers.

31. "Excerpts from the Comments by Wallace and LeMay on the War and Segregation," *New York Times*, October 4, 1968.

32. "LeMay Remarks 'Shock' Humphrey," *New York Times*, October 4, 1968; "Politics: Nixon, Abandoning Silence on Wallace, Attacks Him and LeMay as Hawks," *New York Times*, October 4, 1968.

33. "The Wallace Sickness," *New York Times*, September 22, 1968; "Wallace's H-Bomb," *New York Times*, October 4, 1968.

34. Carter, *Politics of Rage*, 360; "Politics: LeMay Blames 'Traitors' in U.S. for China's Entrance into Korean War," *New York Times*, October 16, 1968; "LeMay Supports Legal Abortions," *New York Times*, October 24, 1968.

35. David Broder, "Election of 1968," in Schlesinger, *History of American Presidential Elections*, 3746; Cowie, *Stayin' Alive*, 83.

36. PNS, October 13, 1968; PNS, October 18, 1968; *NBC Evening News*, October 18, 1968, available for purchase through the Vanderbilt Television News Archive, http://tvnews.vanderbilt.edu/program.pl?ID=440266; *NBC Evening News*, October 9, 1968, available for purchase through the Vanderbilt Television News Archive, http://tvnews.vanderbilt.edu/program.pl?ID=440580.

37. Nixon Presidential Returned Materials Collection: White House Central Files (WHCF), box 85: SMOF- Garment, Len 1968 Political Campaign File—File Cabinet box 19 of 29, File Cabinet: Kevin Phillips, Memo to Len Garment from Kevin Phillips Re: "Wallace, HHH and the need for an RN Second Offensive."

Chapter 16

1. Flamm, *Law and Order*, 176.

2. "Subject on but not limited to: Campaigning General Approach, and Agenda," Richard Nixon Presidential Library, WHSF Collection, box 33, folder 13; "Memo to RN from John Sears," box 81: SMOF–Garment, Len 1968 Political Campaign File—topical file box 15 of 29, Strategy.

3. "Subject on but not limited to: Campaigning General Approach, and Agenda," Nixon Library; also see Nixon Library, Speech File (PPS 208) "Q&A TV Program. Campaign issues. Cleveland, OH," September 13, 1968, 97:1; Katherine Hall Jamieson, *Eloquence in the Electronic Age: The Transformation of Presidential Speechmaking* (New York: Oxford University Press, 1990), 267.

4. "Republicans: The Politics of Safety," *Time*, September 13, 1968.

5. These commercials are available online at the Museum of the Moving Image website *The Living Room Candidate: Presidential Campaign Commercials 1952–2012*, http://www.livingroomcandidate.org/commercials/1968.

6. "Unite," online at *The Living Room Candidate: Presidential Campaign Commercials 1952–2012*, http://www.livingroomcandidate.org/commercials/1968/unite.

7. "Memo from Buchanan to Bob (Haldeman?) Re: the uses of television," Richard Nixon Presidential Library, WHSF Collection, box 35, folder 19; "The Operatic Life of Richard Nixon," *Atlantic*, January 9, 2013, PNS, September 12, 1968.

8. PNS, October 25, 1968.

9. PNS, September 14, 1968; LBO Papers, series 4, Presidential Campaign Files, box 163, Campaign Policy Committee Memos, October 2–11, 1968, "Campaign Policy Minutes, October 2, 1968"; *NBC Evening News*, October 22, 1968, available for purchase through the Vanderbilt Television News Archive, http://tvnews.vanderbilt .edu/program.pl?ID=440338.

10. "Richard Nixon WBTV (CBS) Interview," Richard Nixon Library, Speech File (PPS 208), 96:26, September 11, 1968; Broder, "Election of 1968," 3741–42.

11. Richard Nixon Presidential Library, White House Special Files Collection, box 35, folder 19, September 24, 1968, "Memo from Shakespeare to Haldeman."

12. LBO Personal Papers, series 4, 1968, box 167, folder, "Voter Opinion on Campaign Issues"; "Political Race Moves West," *US News and World Report*, May 27, 1968.

13. "The Overshadowing Issue," *Time*, August 2, 1968; "The Fear Campaign," *Time*, October 4, 1968; LBO Personal Papers, series 4, 1968, box 163, folder "Campaign Policy Meeting Minutes, 23–27 September 1968," Minutes from September 27, 1968; Flamm, *Law and Order*, 173; "Campaign rally. Monument Circle. Indianapolis, Ind.," Richard Nixon Library, Speech File (PPS 208), September 12, 1968, 96:28; Speech File (PPS 208) September 29, 1968; "Order and justice under law. Radio address. Enlargement on crime message," 99:4; PNS, September 20, 1968.

14. "Order and justice under law. Radio address. Enlargement on crime message," 99:4; PNS, September 20, 1968, and October 27, 1968; John Osborne, "Nixon Out West," *New Republic*, September 28, 1968.

15. "Memo from Buchanan to RN, Breakdown of the Gallup Poll," Richard Nixon Presidential Library, White House Special Files Collection, folder list, box 33, folder 13, July 13, 1968.

16. Louis Harris, "Attitudes on Race Affecting Election," *Iowa City Press-Citizen*, September 16, 1968; PNS, September 16, 1968, and September 28, 1968; "Wallace Vote Wasted, Nixon Tells Dixie," UPI (*The Argus*), September 28, 1968.

17. "Humphrey Maps Program to 'Halt Riots, Protect Liberty,'" *Associated Press* (*Des Moines Register*), September 17, 1968; Flamm, *Law and Order*, 169; "Sep. 13, 1968. Statement on crime and HHH's position," 97:2; Nixon Library, Speech Files, PPS 208.

18. An excellent example of Nixon's conflation of crime, riots, and political protest: "Order and justice under law. Radio address. Enlargement on crime message," September 29, 1968, Richard Nixon Library, Speech File (PPS 208), 99:4; Flamm, *Law and Order*, 169; Memo from Kirkpatrick to Secretary Freeman, September 27, 1968, LBO Personal Papers, series 4, 1968, box 163, folder, "Campaign Policy Meeting Minutes, 23–27 September 1968"; Jeremy D. Mayer, "Nixon Rides the Backlash to Victory: Racial Politics in the 1968 Presidential Campaign," *The Historian*, December 2002, 360.

19. Lawrence O'Brien Personal Papers, series 4, 1968 Presidential Campaigns, box 167, "Voter Opinion on Campaign Issues, August 1968."

20. White, *Making of the President*, 419–20; "Facts without Figures," *Washington Post*, October 26, 1968; "Humphrey Urges Higher Pensions," *New York Times*, September 26, 1968; White, *Making of the President*, 419–20; Tom Wicker, "In the Nation: Once More, with Feeling," *New York Times*, October 17, 1968; PNS, October 18, 1968.

21. Wicker, "In the Nation"; "Nixon Advisors against Debates," *Kingsport Times*, September 18, 1968; PNS, September 17, 1968; White, *Making of the President*, 417.

22. Broder, "Election of 1968," 3746; Witcover, *Resurrection*, 424–25; PNS, October 22, 1968; Buchanan, *Greatest Comeback*, 354–355.

23. Chester, Hodgson, and Page, *American Melodrama*, 722–23.

24. "Laughter," Citizens for Humphrey-Muskie, 1968, online at *The Living Room Candidate: Presidential Campaign Commercials 1952–2012*, http://www.livingroomcandidate .org/commercials/1968/laughter; O'Brien Oral History, Interview 25, 14.

25. Witcover, *Very Strange Bedfellows*, 38–39; PNS, September 12, 1968; "Agnew Regrets Linking Veep with Communism," UPI, September 13, 1968; "Agnew Firing Verbal Blasts," *Associated Press (Odessa American)*, September 11, 1968.

26. Witcover, *Very Strange Bedfellows*, 47.

27. Ibid. 43–44; PNS, September 24, 1968; PNS, September 28, 1968.

28. Witcover, *Very Strange Bedfellows*, 46; Nixon, *Memoirs*, 320.

29. "Muskie Bids Heckler Share Platform," *New York Times*, September 26, 1968; PNS, September 26, 1968; Williams S. White, "Whatever the Outcome May Be, Ed Muskie Is Bound to Win," *Washington Post*, October 14, 1968; PNS, October 7, 1968.

30. "Muskie Urges Pennsylvanians to Reject 'Apostles of Division,'" *New York Times*, September 25, 1968; PNS, October 11, 1968; PNS, October 14, 1968; O'Brien Oral History, Interview 25, 1.

31. Lewis Gould, "Never a Deep Partisan: Lyndon Johnson and the Democratic Party, 1963–1969," in *The Johnson Years*, vol. 3, *LBJ at Home and Abroad*, ed. Robert Divine (Lawrence: University Press of Kansas, 1994), 45; Ira Kapenstein Papers, box 10, folder "1968 Presidential Campaign Manual."

32. Clifford and Holbrooke, *Counsel to the President*, 571.

33. L. Berman, *No Peace, No Honor*, 24.

34. See David S. Patterson, ed., *Foreign Relations of the United States, 1964–1968*, vol. 14, *Soviet Union* (Washington, DC: Government Printing Office, 2001), documents 296 and 299; Anatoly Dobrynin, *In Confidence: Moscow's Ambassador to American's Six Cold War Presidents, 1962–1986* (New York: Random House, 1997), 174–76.

35. Presidential Recording Program, Miller Center, Johnson Tapes Transcripts, Wednesday, October 16, 1968, 11:41 AM–11:57 AM; WH6810-04-13547-13548; available online at http://millercenter.org/presidentialrecordings/lbj-wh6810.04-13547; Clifford and Holbrooke, *Counsel to the President*, 577 and 581; Lyndon B. Johnson, "The President's Address to the Nation Upon Announcing His Decision to Halt the Bombing of North Vietnam," October 31, 1968, online at *The American Presidency Project*, http://www .presidency.ucsb.edu/ws/?pid=29218.

36. Nixon, *Memoirs*, 327.

37. Ken Hughes, *Chasing Shadows: The Nixon Tapes, the Chennault Affair, and the Origins of Watergate*, Kindle ed. (Charlottesville: University of Virginia Press, 2014), 7.

38. Hughes, *Chasing Shadows*, 7–8; Anna Chennault, *The Education of Anna* (New York: Times Books, 1980), 174–75.

39. Christopher Hitchens, *The Trial of Henry Kissinger* (London: Verso, 2003), 13; also see Nixon, *Memoirs*, 323; William P. Bundy, *Tangled Web: The Making*

of Foreign Policy in the Nixon Presidency (New York: Farrar, Straus & Giroux, 1988), 42.

40. White, *Making of the President*, 445.

41. "Transcript of Telephone Conversation Among President Johnson, Vice President Humphrey, Richard Nixon, and George Wallace," in *Foreign Relations of the United States, 1964–1968*, vol. 7, *Vietnam, September 1968–January 1969*, ed. Edward C. Keefer (Washington, DC: Government Printing Office, 2003), document 166; also see "Lyndon Johnson and James Rowe on 1 November 1968," Conversation WH6811-01-13704, in *Presidential Recordings of Lyndon B. Johnson Digital Edition*, ed. David G. Coleman, Kent B. Germany, Ken Hughes, Guian A. McKee, and Marc J. Selverstone (Charlottesville: University of Virginia Press, 2010–), available online at http://prde.upress.virginia.edu/conversations/4006122.

42. "Notes of Meeting," October 29, 1968, in Keefer, ed., *Foreign Relations*, document 140; "Information Memorandum from the President's Special Assistant (Rostow) to President Johnson," October 29, 1968, in Keefer, ed., *Foreign Relations*, document 145.

43. Clifford and Holbrooke, *Counsel to the President*, 582; L. Berman, *No Peace, No Honor*, 34; Chennault, *Education of Anna*, 174–75; Anthony Summers, *The Arrogance of Power: The Secret World of Richard Nixon* (New York: Penguin, 2001), 300; Bundy, *Tangled Web*, 41; "Transcript of Tom Charles Huston recorded interview by Tim Naftali," April 30, 2008, Richard Nixon Oral History Project of the Richard Nixon Presidential Library and Museum

44. Johnson, *Vantage Point*, 549; Clifford and Holbrooke, *Counsel to the President*, 583; Keefer, ed., *Foreign Relations*, document 181.

45. Solberg, *Hubert Humphrey*, 397; telephone conversation between President Johnson and James Rowe, November 1, 1968, 1:58 PM.

46. Hughes, *Chasing Shadows*, 46–49; "Nixon Willing to Go to Saigon or Paris," *New York Times*, November 4, 1968.

47. O'Brien, Oral History, Interview 26, 8; Connell Oral History, 47; Witcover, *Resurrection*; Solberg, *Hubert Humphrey*, 401; Bundy, *Tangled Web*, 43; "Memorandum on the Hubert Humphrey Campaign," Library of Congress, Martin Papers, 111.

48. Humphrey, *Education of a Public Man*, 406; Lyndon B. Johnson: "Remarks at the Astrodome in Houston at a Democratic Party Rally," November 3, 1968, online at *The American Presidency Project*, http://www.presidency.ucsb.edu/ws/?pid=29221.

49. Nixon, *Memoirs*, 330; Summers, *The Arrogance of Power*, 301; also see Raymond K. Price, Jr., recorded interview by Timothy J. Naftali, Paul Musgrave, and David Greenberg, April 4, 2007, the Richard Nixon Oral History Project of the Richard Nixon Presidential Library and Museum.

Chapter 17

1. White, *Making of the President*, 458; Nixon, *Memoirs*, 331–33; *The American Presidency Project*, Election 1968, http://www.presidency.ucsb.edu/showelection .php?year=1968; Eisele, *Almost to the Presidency*, 392.

2. American National Election Study (ANES), 1968, University of Michigan, Survey Research Center. 3rd ICPSR ed. Ann Arbor, MI: Inter-university Consortium for Political and Social Research 1999; Scammon and Wattenberg, *Real Majority*, 102–3.

3. Scammon and Wattenberg, *Real Majority*, 342; *The American Presidency Project*, Election 1964, http://www.presidency.ucsb.edu/showelection.php?year=1964; *The American Presidency Project*, Election 1968, http://www.presidency.ucsb.edu/showelection.php?year=1968; Converse et al., "Continuity and Change," 1084.

4. Lynn Vavreck, *The Message Matters: The Economy and Presidential Campaigns*, Kindle ed. (Princeton, NJ: Princeton University Press, 2009), 105; Richard Boyd, "Popular Control of Public Policy: A Normal Vote Analysis of the 1968 Election," *American Political Science Review* 66 (1972): 429–49.

5. "Republican Runs Ahead in Gallup Poll, 43–31, A Slight Decline," *New York Times*, September 15, 1968; *The American Presidency Project*, Election 1968, http://www.presidency.ucsb.edu/showelection.php?year=1968; Converse et al., "Continuity and Change," 1085.

6. Gallup Poll no. 1968-0771: Elections/Vietnam; November 9–14, 1968; Converse, Verba, and Rosenberg, *Vietnam and the Silent Majority*, 50–51.

7. Converse et al., "Continuity and Change," 1088.

8. ANES, 1964; Converse et al., "Continuity and Change," 1086.

9. As quoted in "The Liberal-Conservative Debate of the 1960s," in *Debating the 1960s: Liberal, Conservative and Radical Perspectives*, ed. Michael Flamm and David Stiegerwald (Lanham, MD: Rowman & Littlefield, 2008), 130.

10. Converse et al., "Continuity and Change," 1085.

11. Scammon and Wattenberg, *Real Majority*, 176; Andrea Louise Campbell, "Parties, Electoral Participation, and Shifting Voting Blocs," in *The Transformation of American Politics: Activist Government and the Rise of Conservatism*, ed. Paul Pierson and Theda Skocpol, Kindle ed., Princeton Studies in American Politics (Princeton, NJ: Princeton University Press, 2007), 96.

12. Frederick Siegel, *Troubled Journey: From Pearl Harbor to Ronald Reagan* (New York: Hill & Wang, 1984), 204; Rick Perlstein, "The Myths of McGovern," *Democracy*, Winter 2008, 109; Boyd, "Popular Control of Public Policy," 432, 435; Scammon and Wattenberg, *Real Majority*, 97–100; Edsall and Edsall, *Chain Reaction*, 76; Ehrlichman, *Witness to Power*, 222.

13. Kevin Phillips, *The Emerging Republican Majority* (New Rochelle, NY: Arlington House, 1969), 473.

14. ANES, 1964–1972; "Trust in Government," Gallup: http://www.gallup.com/poll/5392/trust-government.aspx; Kabaservice, *Rule and Ruin*, 342.

15. *The American Presidency Project*, Election 1968, http://www.presidency.ucsb.edu/showelection.php?year=1968; Boyd, "Popular Control of Public Policy," 435; J. Michael Ross, Reeve D. Vanneman, and Thomas F. Pettigrew, "Patterns of Support for George Wallace: Implications For Racial Change," *Journal of Social Issues*, 32, no. 2 (1976): 86; also see Lipset and Raab's analysis of Wallace factor in *The Politics of Unreason* and Scammon and Wattenberg, *Real Majority*, 97–100 and 397.

16. Converse et al., "Continuity and Change," 1100; Lipset and Raab, *Politics of Unreason*, 402.

17. Pierson and Skocpol, *Transformation of American Politics*, 23; Mason, *Richard Nixon and the Quest*, 80; William C. Berman, *America's Right Turn: From Nixon to Clinton*

(Baltimore: Johns Hopkins University Press, 1998), 12; Dionne, *Why Americans Hate Politics*, 197, 202; also see Kim Phillips-Fein, *Invisible Hands: The Businessmen's Crusade against the New Deal* (New York: W. W. Norton, 2010), chapter 7.

18. Greenberg, *Nixon's Shadow*, 31; Pierson and Skocpol, *Transformation of American Politics*, 111.

19. James Reichley, *Conservatives in an Age of Change: The Nixon and Ford Administrations* (Washington, DC: Brookings Institution, 1981), 232; Siegel, *Troubled Journey*, 255; Nixon, *Memoirs*, 761–72; Mason, *Richard Nixon and the Quest*, 53–54.

20. "Address to the Nation on the War in Vietnam," November 3, 1969, available online at *The American Presidency Project*, http://www.presidency.ucsb.edu/ws/?pid=2303; Spiro Agnew, "The Dangers of Constant Carnival," October 30, 1969, available online at http://wps.prenhall.com/wps/media/objects/108/111235/ch29_a4_d2.pdf; Kabaservice, *Rule and Ruin*, 267; Gitlin, *The Sixties*, 415; Edsall and Edsall, *Chain Reaction*, 85; Lipset and Raab, *Politics of Unreason*, 42; Mason, *Richard Nixon and the Quest*, 108.

21. Rowland Evans, Jr., and Robert D. Novak, *Nixon in the White House: The Frustration of Power* (New York: Random House, 1971), 345; Mason, *Richard Nixon and the Quest*, 92, 101, 103; Kabaservice, *Rule and Ruin*, 313; Richard Reeves, "Is That Really Nelson Rockefeller Crawling to Richard Nixon?" *New York*, October 18, 1971.

22. Cowie, *Stayin' Alive*, 227.

23. Bruce Miroff, *The Liberals' Moment: The McGovern Insurgency and the Identity Crisis of the Democratic Party* (Lawrence: University Press of Kansas, 2007); George McGovern, "The Lessons of 1968," *Harper's*, January 1970.

24. Nixon, *Memoirs*, 491; Miroff, *Liberals' Moment*, 42.

25. Siegel, *Troubled Journey*, 246; Roper Center for Public Opinion Research, University of Connecticut, Gallup Poll, October 1971, Gallup Poll, August 1971, Gallup/Newsweek Poll, February 1972; also see Carter, *Politics of Rage*, 418, 425, 432, 436; "Busing Ban Wins by Large Margin," *New York Times*, March 15, 1972.

26. Lesher, *George Wallace*, 481, 485.

27. Solberg, *Hubert Humphrey*, 430; Seymour M. Hersh, "The Scene of the Crime," *New Yorker*, March 30, 2015; "Interview with Governor George Wallace, Montgomery, Alabama, July 15, 1974, conducted by Jack Bass and Walter De Vries," Southern Historical Collection, CB#3926, Wilson Library, the University of North Carolina at Chapel Hill, 9, available online at http://dc.lib.unc.edu/utils/getfile/collection/sohp/id/8706/filename/8748.pdf.

28. Cowie, *Stayin' Alive*, 105; Penn Kimble, "The New Politics and Democrats," *Commentary*, December 1972; Siegel, *Troubled Journey*, 248.

29. Miroff, *Liberals' Moment*, 127, 128, 130; Roper Center for Public Opinion Research, University of Connecticut, Nixon Poll, October 1972, Harris Survey, October 1972, Time/Yankelovich Voter Study Wave 4, October 1972, Time/Yankelovich Voter Study Wave 1, July 1972; Kimble, "New Politics and Democrats."

30. Mason, *Richard Nixon and the Quest*, 122; Berman, *America's Right Turn*, 16; Miroff, *Liberals' Moment*, 257.

31. Perlstein, *Before the Storm*, 745; Hodgson, *America in Our Time*, 427; Cowie, *Stayin' Alive*, 122.

Chapter 18

1. Hodgson, *America in Our Time*, 17.
2. Miroff, *Liberals' Moment*, 257; Jimmy Carter Acceptance Speech, July 15, 1976, http://www.4president.org/speeches/carter1976acceptance.htm.
3. Jimmy Carter, "Address to the Nation on Energy and National Goals: 'The Malaise Speech,'" July 15, 1979, online at *The American Presidency Project*. http://www.presidency.ucsb.edu/ws/?pid=32596; Cowie, *Stayin' Alive*, 225, 283; Siegel, *Troubled Journey*, 266–67.
4. See Danny Hayes, "Candidate Qualities through a Partisan Lens: A Theory of Trait Ownership," *American Journal of Political Science* 49, no. 4 (October 2005): 908–23; John R. Petrocik, William L. Benoit, and Glenn J. Hansen, "Issue Ownership and Presidential Campaigning, 1952–2000," *Political Science Quarterly* 118, no. 4 (Winter 2003): 599–626.
5. Mark A. Smith, "Economic Insecurity, Party Reputations, and the Republican Ascendance," in Pierson and Skocpol, *Transformation of American Politics*, 138–39; Edsall and Edsall, *Chain Reaction*, 105.
6. Pierson and Skocpol, *Transformation of American Politics*, 149–50.
7. "'Welfare Queen' Becomes Issue in Reagan Campaign," *New York Times*, February 15, 1976; also see Edsall and Edsall, *Chain Reaction*, 198–214; Paul Frymer and John David Skrentny, "Coalition-Building and the Politics of Electoral Capture during the Nixon Administration: African Americans, Labor, Latinos," *Studies in American Political Development* 12 (Spring 1998): 131–61.
8. William J. Clinton, "Address Accepting the Presidential Nomination at the Democratic National Convention in New York," July 16, 1992, online at *The American Presidency Project*, http://www.presidency.ucsb.edu/ws/?pid=25958; "Sister Souljah Moment," June 13, 1992, available on the C-Span website, http://www.c-span.org/video/?c4460582/sister-souljah-moment.
9. Petrocik, Benoit, and Hansen, "Issue Ownership and Presidential Campaigning," 609, 611; also see David F. Damore, "The Dynamic of Issue Ownership in Presidential Campaigns," *Political Research Quarterly* 57, no. 3 (September 2004): 395–96.
10. Petrocik, Benoit, and Hansen, "Issue Ownership and Presidential Campaigning," 610; James E. Campbell, "Why Bush Won the Presidential Election of 2004: Incumbency, Ideology, Terrorism, and Turnout," *Political Science Quarterly* 120, no. 2 (2005): 219–41.
11. Edsall and Edsall, *Chain Reaction*, 175–76; Danny Hayes, "Candidate Qualities Through a Partisan Lens: A Theory of Trait Ownership," *American Journal of Political Science* 49, no. 4 (October 2005): 908–23.
12. "Democrats Are in an Odd Position on Iraq," *Wall Street Journal*, April 7, 2004.
13. "Republican Candidates Debate in Sioux City, Iowa," December 15, 2011," online at *The American Presidency Project*, http://www.presidency.ucsb.edu/ws/index.php?pid=97978.
14. Barack Obama, "Remarks on Health Care Reform," September 10, 2009, online at *The American Presidency Project*, http://www.presidency.ucsb.edu/ws/?pid=8660.

15. See David Frum, *Dead Right* (New York: Basic Books, 1994), 32–46; Hacker and Pierson, *Winner-Take-All Politics*, 188; Stephen Hayward, "Modernizing Conservatism," *Breakthrough Journal*, November 14, 2011.
16. Rieder, "The Rise of the 'Silent Majority,'" in Fraser and Gerstle, *Rise and Fall*, 242.
17. Suzanne Mettler, *The Submerged State: How Invisible Government Policies Undermine American Democracy* (Chicago: University of Chicago Press, 2011), 200–201; Kevin Drum, "Why Screwing Unions Screws the Entire Middle Class," *Mother Jones*, March/ April 2011; Hacker and Pierson, *Winner-Take-All Politics*, 184; also see Julian Zelizer, "Rethinking the History of American Conservatism," in *Governing America: The Revival of Political History* (Princeton, NJ: Princeton University Press, 2012), 68–89.
18. House Committee on the Budget, "The Path to Prosperity: Restoring America's Promise," available online at http://budget.house.gov/uploadedfiles/pathtopro sperityfy2012.pdf.

BIBLIOGRAPHIC ESSAY

The greatest challenge in writing a book about the 1960s and, in particular, the 1968 e-lection, is that there are more books on the subject—and the individuals who ran for president that year—than any one person could possibly consult. So in lieu of providing a laundry list of bibliographic sources that I consulted, I've compiled instead some thoughts on the historical materials that were most useful in writing this book and might be of further interest to readers and researchers. This essay covers much of, but certainly not all, the source material that I consulted for the book.

The Essentials

There are two major histories of the 1968 presidential election, *American Melodrama*, by Lewis Chester, Godfrey Hodgson, and Bruce Page, and Teddy White's *The Making of the President, 1968*. While both suffer, in some measure, for being first drafts of history, they are indispensable texts, particularly *American Melodrama*, which is simply one of the best presidential campaign histories ever written.

An academic article in the *American Political Science Review* written by Philip Converse, Warren Miller, Jerrold Rusk, and Arthur Wolfe and titled "Continuity and Change in American Politics" provided me with some of the best postelection analysis of the race. The online poll database hosted by the Roper Center at the University of Connecticut was also a vital source of detailed public opinion data from the era, as are the quadrennial American National Election Studies housed by the University of Michigan. During the '68 campaign, the Democratic National Committee produced a daily "Political News Summary" of events around the campaign housed in the Humphrey archives at the Minnesota Historical Society. To whoever made the decision to compile this daily summary—and save it for posterity—I offer a thousand thank-yous.

I relied heavily on the archives of the *New York Times*, the *Washington Post*, the *Wall Street Journal*, *Time*, and *Newsweek*, as well as countless other newspapers. Reading the fantastic daily dispatches from an extraordinary group of political reporters and analysts made for one of the great joys of researching this book. These journalists included Richard Harwood, David Broder, R. W. Apple, Warren Weaver, Max Frankel, Scotty Reston, Richard Reeves, Elizabeth Drew, Mary McGrory, Michael Janeway, Stewart Alsop, Wallace Frady, Richard Stout, Tom Wicker, John Osborne, Nick Thimmesch, and many others.

Jules Witcover wrote five books that address the key themes and actors of 1968—*85 Days* covers Robert F. Kennedy's presidential campaign; *The Resurrection of Richard*

Nixon focuses on Richard Nixon's wilderness years and the '68 race; *White Knight* looks at the rise of Spiro Agnew; *Very Strange Bedfellows* deals with the relationship between Nixon and Vice President Spiro Agnew; and *The Year the Dream Died* looks back, with the benefit of hindsight, on the events of 1968, political and otherwise. No one can write competently on this era without consulting Witcover's prodigious output, and I am indebted to him for being such a good reporter and prolific writer.

On the broader era of the 1960s, several books are worthy of mention. First and foremost is a work oriented around US public opinion, Lloyd Free and Hadley Cantril's *The Political Beliefs of Americans*. Richard Scammon and Ben Wattenberg's *The Real Majority* was a deeply influential book in the Nixon White House, and for good reason. Like Free and Cantril's book, it captures the diverse and at times incoherent views of the American people in the late 1960s.

In addition, I relied on *The Age of Great Dreams* by David Farber and his edited book titled simply *The Sixties*; G. Calvin Mackenzie and Robert Weisbrot, *The Liberal Hour*; Irwin Unger, *The Best of Intentions*; *America Divided*, edited by Maurice Isserman and Michael Kazin; Richard Goodwin's autobiography, *Remembering America*; Allen Matusow's *The Unraveling of America*; Mary Brennan, *Turning Right in the Sixties*; and two books by Godfrey Hodgson, *The World Turned Right Side Up: A History of the Conservative Ascendancy in America* and *America in Our Times*. Hodgson, who is a coauthor of *American Melodrama*, is one of the most perceptive and insightful analysts of postwar America. There was also E. J. Dionne's underrated *Why Americans Hate Politics* and David Steigerwald's *The Sixties and the End of Modern America*. *The Rise and Fall of the New Deal Order, 1930–1980*, edited by Steve Fraser and Gary Gerstle, is a great collection of smart essays on the era. *Esquire* magazine's *Smiling through the Apocalypse: Esquire's History of the Sixties* is a book little cited in the text here, but it greatly informed my thinking.

I'm only slightly exaggerating when I say that the best analyst, at the time, of the political cross-currents so evident in 1968 is... Norman Mailer. His book *Some Honorable Men*, which contains his major essays on the Chicago and Miami Beach conventions, is a priceless document.

Backlash

Thomas Sugrue's *The Origins of the Urban Crisis* shaped much of my thinking about the white backlash of the 1960s. Close behind was Michael Flamm's *Law and Order* and Thomas Edsall and Mary D. Edsall's *Chain Reaction*. Other essential reading included Jonathan Rieder's *Canarsie*, Kevin Kruse's *White Flight*, Lisa McGirr's *Suburban Warriors: The Origins of the New American Right*, and the aforementioned Matusow, Hodgson, and Fraser and Gerstle books.

Lyndon Johnson

There is no more complicated historical figure in this book than Lyndon Johnson. While I never found a definitive biography of LBJ, several texts were useful in helping me better comprehend this deeply inscrutable man. Robert Dallek's *Flawed Giant* comprehensively covers the basic trajectory of Johnson's presidency. Randall Woods's *LBJ: Architect of Ambition* fills a similar niche, as does Irving Bernstein's *Guns or Butter*. Robert Caro has yet to publish his tome on the Johnson presidency, but I consulted his prodigious biographies of Johnson, in particular, *Master of the Senate*. The two books that were most useful in helping me get a handle on Johnson's unique psychology were Doris Kearns Goodwin, *Lyndon Johnson and the American Dream*, and, surprisingly, a small, long forgotten book by Hugh Sidey called *A Very Personal Presidency*. I've read or skimmed most of the biographies of LBJ's confidants. The three that stand out are Joseph Califano's *The Triumph and Tragedy of Lyndon Johnson*, Clark Clifford's *Counsel to the President*, and Harry McPherson's *A Political Education*. While I read many of the oral histories at the LBJ Library (many of which are now housed by the Miller Center at the University of Virginia), the ones from Arthur Krim, John Roche, and Larry O'Brien provided the greatest insights on Johnson. The Miller Center also hosts the database of Johnson's White House phone conversations, which for the history geek and Johnson obsessive provides hours of procrastination.

Vietnam

I probably consulted as many books and primary documents on Vietnam as I did any other subject in this book. Several books stand out: William Conrad Gibbons's history of the conflict, *The U.S. Government and the Vietnam War*, particularly volumes 3 and 4, are as comprehensive a description of US policy during the war as any that exist. Robert Mann's *Grand Delusion* is a great source; so too are George Herring's *LBJ and Vietnam* and *America's Longest War*. Finally, there is Fred Logevall's *Choosing War*. This is, in my opinion, the best analysis of US decision-making—and particularly that of Johnson— on Vietnam that has ever been written. Perhaps above all, many of the primary documents from that era are available at the website of the State Department. These are crucial documents—and that so many are digitized makes the process of conducting research that much easier.

A few other important sources include Larry Berman's *Lyndon Johnson's War*; Robert McNamara's memoir on Vietnam, *In Retrospect*; Stanley Karnow's one-volume history, *Vietnam*, David Halberstam's *Best and the Brightest*, Clifford's aforementioned bio; Neil Sheehan's *Bright Shining Lie*, which may be the single best book on the US war; and, of course, the *Pentagon Papers*. There is also Townsend Hoopes's October 1969 article in the *Atlantic*, "The Fight for the President's Mind—And the Men Who Won It," which expertly covers Vietnam and the tail end of Johnson's presidency. For the section on the Tet Offensive, Don Oberdorfer's book *Tet!* was my go-to book on the political impact of the attack.

The Democrats

For a short-lived campaign that won only a handful of presidential primaries, there have been an inordinate number of books written about Eugene McCarthy's 1968 presidential campaign. For the purposes of my research, the two best were Richard Stout's *People* and Albert Eisele's *Almost to the Presidency*. The former was a vital resource for the basic facts of the campaign; the latter, which is a dual biography of McCarthy and Humphrey, offers great insights into the man himself. Same goes for Dominic Sandbrook's *Eugene McCarthy: The Rise and Fall of Postwar Liberalism*, though admittedly my impressions of McCarthy differ rather dramatically from those of Sandbrook. Also of great use was Arthur Herzog's *McCarthy for President* and David Charles Hoeh's tome on the New

Hampshire campaign, *1968, McCarthy, New Hampshire*. Two other books written by campaign veterans, Jeremy Larner's *Nobody Knows* and Ben Stavis's *We Were the Campaign*, offer contrasting views on the McCarthy campaign—the former is a more cynical take; the latter covers the nuts and bolts of what went on behind the scenes among the McCarthy volunteers. The Anderson Library at the University of Minnesota has a voluminous collection of oral histories from the campaign. Those of Thomas Finney, Richard Goodwin, Gerry Studds, Paul Gorman, and Jerome Grossman stand out.

Hubert Humphrey

For Hubert Humphrey, there is thankfully a great single-volume biography of the man by Carl Solberg, *Hubert Humphrey*. That, along with Eisele's book and Humphrey's own memoir, *The Education of a Public Man*, was my primary source material on the former vice president.

While I consulted many of the early biographies on Humphrey, Edger Berman's personal take on Humphrey, *Hubert: The Triumph and the Tragedy of the Hubert I Knew*, offers an unusually intimate and sympathetic portrayal of the former vice president. *Drugstore Liberal* by Robert Sherrill and Harry W. Ernst is the opposite—a harsh and unforgiving portrayal of Humphrey from two liberal journalists. One doesn't have to fully share Sherrill and Ernst's unsympathetic perspective to recognize that the book's judgments have more than a grain of truth to them.

Ted Van Dyk's *Heroes, Hacks, and Fools* helps to fill in some of the gaps on the '68 campaign, as does William Connell's oral history at the LBJ Library. Of even greater importance was campaign manager Larry O'Brien's lengthy oral history, which is located at the LBJ Library. His personal papers at the JFK Library, along with those of his assistant, Ira Kapenstein, provides the most useful primary material on the fall campaign. My interview with Humphrey's old friend Thomas Hughes helped me better understand the former vice president, and he was kind enough to share an unpublished manuscript that he'd written on Humphrey.

Robert F. Kennedy

An amazing amount of material has been written about Robert F. Kennedy's forty-three years, including Arthur Schlesinger's magisterial tome on RFK, *Robert Kennedy and His Times*. However, I found Evan Thomas's biography to be the most balanced and candid look at Kennedy's life. I have similar praise for Jeff Shesol's *Mutual Contempt*, which better than any book in the RFK canon covers the fascinating interpersonal dynamics of the LBJ–RFK rivalry.

For the '68 campaign itself, Witcover's *85 Days* is comprehensive, insightful, workman-like reporting. I was also rather partial to William vanden Heuvel and Milton Gwirtzman's *On His Own*, which like Thomas's book offers an unvarnished and honest appraisal of the candidate—particularly the truth behind Kennedy's supposed black-blue coalition in Indiana. Jack Newfield's *RFK*, David Halberstam's *The Unfinished Odyssey of Robert Kennedy*, and Thurston Clarke's more recent *The Last Campaign* are great secondary sources, but all are undermined, in some way, by their overly rosy view of the man. Conversely, Ronald Steel's *In Love with Night* suffers for the opposite reason—the author's clear antipathy toward his subject and the hagiography around him.

However, the best source of material came from the candidate himself (in the form of his speeches, most of which are available at the JFK Library or in *RFK: Collected Speeches*, edited by Edwin Guthman) and also the oral histories of his staffers. I relied heavily on the recollections of Kenny O'Donnell, Pierre Salinger, Frank Mankiewicz, Fred Dutton, Ted Sorensen, Peter Edelman, Milton Gwirtzman, Thomas Johnston, Adam Walinsky, and Gerard Doherty and John Bartlow Martin's "Campaign Journal" of the Kennedy (and later Humphrey) campaign.

Many of these are available online at the JFK Library website.

Republicans

A number of excellent books from the 1960s were essential in helping me understand the cross-currents affecting the Republican Party as it emerged from the disaster of 1964. Stephen Hess and David Broder's *The Republican Establishment: The Present and Future of the G.O.P* is among the best, as is *Condition of Republicanism* by Nick Thimmesch. More recent histories include David Reinhard's *The Republican Right since 1945*; Lewis Gould's *Grand Old Party*; the *Decline and Fall of the Liberal Republicans* by Nicol C. Rae; Geoffrey Kabaservice's fascinating look at the decline of moderate Republicanism, *Rule and Ruin*; and Rick Perlstein's excellent *Before the Storm*. Andrew Johns, *Vietnam's Second Front*, focused on the impact of Vietnam on Republican politics, and Harry Dent's *The Prodigal South Returns to Power* provides an interesting, personal view of the GOP and the South.

Nixon

One could practically spend a lifetime reading all the books written about Richard Nixon. For my purposes, Witcover's *The Resurrection of Richard Nixon* and Garry Wills's *Nixon Agonistes* are great on '68, as is, ironically, Nixon's own memoir, *RN*, which provides a unique perspective on the political thought process that the candidate brought to the campaign. Pat Buchanan's *The Greatest Comeback* is chock-full of anecdotes and stories—many of which I heard in interview with Buchanan before he wrote the book. The Nixon archives in Yorba Linda are a treasure trove of material, particularly extremely candid memos from Buchanan, Kevin Phillips, Len Garment, John Sears, Frank Shakespeare, and others on the race.

I also relied on Rick Perlstein's *Nixonland*, David Greenberg's *Nixon's Shadow*, and Earl Mazo and Stephen Hess's great pre-1968 *Nixon: A Political Portrait*, Stephen Ambrose's *Nixon*, as well as Fawn Brodie's *Richard Nixon: The Shaping of His Character* and Herbert Parmet's *Richard Nixon and His America*. For the Nixon presidency, two books, beyond those cited here, were of great help: Robert Mason's *Richard Nixon and the Quest for a New Majority* and *Nixon in the White House* by the reporting team of Rowland Evans, Jr., and Robert D. Novak.

Romney

On George Romney, the two best secondary sources were Clark Mollenhoff's *George Romney: A Mormon in Politics* and T. George Harris's *Romney's Way*. Kabaservice's aforementioned book is great on Romney, as is Chris Bachelder's article from the *Michigan Historical Review*, "Crashing the Party: The Ill-Fated 1968 Presidential Campaign of

Governor George Romney." Jonathon Moore, who was a foreign policy aide to Romney, provided me with some behind-the-scenes perspective on the campaign. I also relied on Romney's papers, which are housed at the University of Michigan's Bentley Historical Library.

Nelson Rockefeller and Ronald Reagan

When I began writing this book there was no comprehensive biography of Nelson Rockefeller in the 1960s. The best book on the man was Cary Reich's *The Life of Nelson A. Rockefeller: Worlds to Conquer*, which follows Rocky's life up until his victory in the New York governor's race in 1958. Tragically, Reich passed away before he could write a second volume. I received an advance copy of Richard Norton Smith's *On His Own Terms*, which appeared in 2014 and helped fill in some of the gaps in my initial research. Other books I consulted included Michael Kramer and Sam Roberts's *"I Never Wanted to Be Vice President of Anything!"* and James Desmond's mid-1960s book *Nelson Rockefeller: A Political Biography*. But again, the best material on Rockefeller came from his personal archives, the oral histories of Emmet Hughes, George Hinman, and Ted Braun, among others, and the campaign memos and documents from his ill-fated '68 run. I am especially indebted to Marsha Barrett, who did her doctoral work on Rockefeller. Her dissertation served as an invaluable source of information and insight for me. For the research on Ronald Reagan I relied almost exclusively on secondary-source material. Two books stand out: Lou Cannon's biography *Governor Reagan* and Matt Dallek's *The Right Moment*.

George Wallace

There are two great books on George Wallace. One is the personal portrayal of Wallace in Marshall Frady's *Wallace*, and the other is one of the finest political biographies I've read, Dan Carter's *The Politics of Rage*. While both approach the subject in different ways—one as a more traditional biography, the other as a New Journalism–style essay, they present a surprising unified picture of the man and his particular political appeal.

These two do not stand alone in the Wallace canon. Stephan Lesher's *George Wallace: American Populist* is an excellent source on the man, from a journalist who covered him directly. Wallace Greenhaw's *Fighting the Devil in Dixie* provides wonderful material on Wallace in Alabama, as does Jeff Frederick's *Stand up for Alabama*. The University of North Carolina at Chapel Hill's Documenting the American South collection has several oral histories of those close to Wallace. While I don't cite them in the text, I learned as much from reading those who worked with Wallace closely in Alabama as I did from practically any other research material. In addition, I also relied on Dan Carter's notes and interviews, including those with Seymore Trammell and Ed Ewing, which are housed at Emory University in Atlanta.

Seymour Martin Lipset and Earl Raab's *The Politics of Unreason: Right-Wing Extremism in America* contains some of the best analysis of Wallace's impact on national politics. Michael Rogin's "Wallace and the Middle Class: The White Backlash in Wisconsin," in *Public Opinion Quarterly*, and Matthew Welsh's "Civil Rights and the Primary Election of 1964 in Indiana: The Wallace Challenge," in the *Indiana Magazine of History*, do an excellent job of explaining Wallace's success in the '64 presidential primaries.

In addition, Marshall Frady's chapter on the American Independent Party in Arthur Schlesinger's edited volume *History of US Political Parties* is the best overview of that short-lived political party. Jody Carlson's *George C. Wallace and the Politics of Powerlessness* and Lloyd Earl Rohler's *George Wallace: Conservative Populist* are recommended for their focus on Wallace's use of rhetoric, and Richard Cohen's "A Walk with the Wallace Campaign" provides unusual insight into the workings (or lack thereof) of the Wallace '68 campaign. Cohen's article can be found among Dan Carter's papers at Emory. There is also an excellent documentary that is part of the *American Experience* series called *George Wallace: Settin' the Woods on Fire*, with firsthand accounts from some of Wallace's closest advisors.

Conventions

For the two chapters on the Democratic and Republican conventions in 1968, many of the books already mentioned provided a wealth of material: Witcover et al., Garry Wills's *Nixon Agonistes*, *American Melodrama*, Teddy White's history of '68, Harry Dent's memoir, Solberg on Humphrey, Eisele on McCarthy and Humphrey, Larry O'Brien's oral histories, and perhaps above all Mailer's two long essays on Miami Beach and Chicago. Of course, there is also the fantastic daily reporting done by journalists from the *New York Times*, the *Washington Post*, *Time*, *Newsweek*, and many other media outlets.

For the chapter on the violence in Chicago, several books stand out. The best is David Farber's *Chicago '68*, which captures in great detail the mindset and logistical planning of the protesters. There is also Marty Jezer's biography of Abbie Hoffman, *American Rebel*. Mike Royko's *Boss* and *American Pharaoh* by Adam Cohen and Elizabeth Taylor offer a view from the other side. I also relied on Frank Kusch's *Battleground Chicago*, John Schulz's *No One Was Killed*, and the Walker Report, a federal study looking at the police riot that took place in Chicago the week of the DNC.

General Election

The chapter on the general election relied on virtually all the aforementioned books, periodicals, newspapers, and magazines. The DNC's Political News Summaries were instrumental in my research, as were the Paley Center at the Museum of Television and Radio video archive and Vanderbilt University's Television News Archive, an online collection of nightly news broadcasts—a resource that thankfully begins in the late summer of 1968. Beyond the material cited in the text, Ken Hughes's recent book on the Chennault affair, *Chasing Shadows*, brings together some of the best research done on this episode. Also useful in regard to Chennault is William Bundy's *Tangled Web*, Clark Clifford's memoir, and an oral history from Tom Charles Huston housed at the Nixon Library and available online.

After

I could not have written this chapter without the raw polling data from the ANES survey of voters and the analysis of Converse and Miller as well as Lipset and Rabb on Wallace. There were several other academic studies that I utilized, including Richard Boyd, "Popular Control of Public Policy: A Normal Vote Analysis of the 1968 Presidential Election," in the *American Political Science Review*, and J. Michael Ross, Reeve D. Vanneman, and

Thomas F. Pettigrew, "Patterns of Support for George Wallace: Implications for Racial Change," in the *Journal of Social Issues*.

The Transformation of American Politics: Activist Government and the Rise of Conservatism, a collection of scholarly essays compiled by Paul Pierson and Theda Skocpol, became my virtual bible for writing on the aftermath of 1968. Of nearly equal importance was the Edsalls' *Chain Reaction*, Scammon and Wattenberg's *Real Majority*, Frederick Siegel's *Troubled Journey*, William C. Berman's *America's Right Turn*, *Invisible Hands* by Kim Phillips-Fein, James Reichley, *Conservatives in an Age of Change*, Todd Gitlin's *The Sixties*, Bruce Miroff's wonderful book on the McGovern campaign called *The Liberals' Moment*, Jefferson Cowie's great *Stayin' Alive: The 1970s and the Last Days of the Working Class*, Hodgson's *The World Turned Right Side Up* and *America in Our Time*, Julian Zelizer's *Governing America: The Revival of Political History*, Suzanne Mettler's *Submerged State*, Stephen Skowronek's *The Politics Presidents Make*, and Douglas Brinkley's *Unfinished Presidency: Jimmy Carter's Journey Beyond the White House*. In addition, I was influenced by several magazine and academic articles, including James Reichley, "Elm Street's New White House Power," in *Fortune*; James Fallows, "The Passionless Presidency," in the *Atlantic*; Paul Frymer and John David Skrentny, "Coalition Building and the Politics of Electoral Capture during the Nixon Administration: African-American, Labor Latinos," in *Studies in American Political Development*; David F. Damore, "The Dynamic of Issue Ownership in Presidential Campaigns," in *Political Research Quarterly*; Danny Hayes, "Candidate Qualities through a Partisan Lens: A Theory of Trait Ownership," in the *American Journal of Political Science*; and John R. Petrocik, William L. Benoit, and Glenn J. Hansen's "Issue Ownership and Presidential Campaigning, 1952–2000," in *Political Science Quarterly*.

INDEX